Prospect Research: A Primer for Growing Nonprofits

Cecilia Hogan

with contributions by David Lamb

JONES AND BARTLETT PUBLISHERS
Sudbury, Massachusetts
BOSTON   TORONTO   LONDON   SINGAPORE

World Headquarters
Jones and Bartlett Publishers
40 Tall Pine Drive
Sudbury, MA 01776
978-443-5000
info@jbpub.com
www.jbpub.com

Jones and Bartlett Publishers Canada
2406 Nikanna Road
Mississauga, ON L5C 2W6
CANADA

Jones and Bartlett Publishers International
Barb House, Barb Mews
London W6 7PA
UK

Library of Congress Cataloging-in-Publication Data

Hogan Cecilia.
   Prospect research : a primer for growing nonprofits / Cecilia Hogan.
     p. cm.
   Includes bibliographical references and index.
   ISBN 0-7637-2580-3
    1. Fund raising. 2. Nonprofit organizations--Finance. I. Title.

HG177.H64 2003
658.15'224--dc21

2003047437

Production Credits:
Production Manager: Amy Rose
Associate Production Editor: Karen C. Ferreira
Associate Editor: Theresa DiDonato
Production Assistant: Jenny McIsaac
Director of Marketing: Alisha Weisman
Manufacturing and Inventory Coordinator: Amy Bacus
Cover Design: Anne Spencer
Interior Design: Anne Spencer
Composition: Studio Montage
Printing and Binding: Malloy Incorporated
Cover Printing: Malloy Incorporated

Printed in the United States of America
07 06 05   10 9 8 7 6 5 4 3

Preface

". . . A collaborative effort among a cross-section of sectors will be critical to train and truly cultivate the next generation of philanthropists."
—Carol L. Cone, interviewed about the 2000 Cone/Roper Raising
Charitable Children Survey, Nonprofitxpress.com, November 29, 2000.

Let's face it. Philanthropy is burgeoning. It is a time of growth for donors as well as nonprofits. According to *The Chronicle of Philanthropy*'s annual "Philanthropy 400" survey (November 1, 2001, p. 35), donations to nonprofits grew 13 percent for the second year in a row, second only to the 1998 pace of 16 percent, and well above the annual 3.4 percent inflation rate. The number of grant-making foundations doubled between 1984 and 1999 ("Foundation Trends," *The Chronicle of Philanthropy*, from Foundation Center figures, July 26, 2001). The cultural phenomenon of philanthropy grows and, behind the scenes, the science of fund raising continues to be refined. And, while the techniques for cultivating and stewarding donors are discussed at fund-raising conferences, the greatest advances in fund-raising methods may be occurring in the field of prospect research. It is here, in the research office, that new ways of segmenting databases, mining for information, and identifying and qualifying prospective donors using a wealth of new electronic resources are tested and evaluated.

So, where are the directions? How can a new researcher, the leaders at a young nonprofit, or even an established researcher or fund raiser needing a fresh approach get on this fast-moving train? And where will it take us? At this writing, there is no college course that leads to a career in prospect research. There is no sanctioning body to turn to, no certification program, no established course of study to qualify someone to be a prospect researcher. But researchers are an inventive lot. With few resources available, they design their own learning opportunities. Researchers meet in small and large gatherings. They invite the leaders in their field and from similar (or not so similar) fields to share their knowledge. They form research groups locally and regionally. They established an international prospect research association that has a primary mission to provide education to researchers. And researchers now serve as the roots, branches, and leaves of that organization by volunteering, speaking at seminars and conferences, and joining one another in sharing their talents and skills.

Missing is a selection of books about prospect research. While our development colleagues can fill their shelves with books about philanthropy and fund raising, researchers have only a few tomes for their own shelves. They are an interesting, if small, collection. But they are characterized by their age, focus, and lonely number. A close examination shows books written many years ago, before the explosion of information that the Internet brought to the profession. Other titles are compendiums and one or two newer Internet manuals that, as such, do not cover prospect research from start to finish. These books have been important resources for prospect researchers, but they have been woefully alone on that shelf.

Prospect researchers are, for the most part, self-taught or taught by others in the profession. We have met researchers who came to this line of work from teaching, banking, lawyering, politics, libraries, and newspapers. The message is clear: You do not start out as a prospect researcher—at least, not very often. Your evolution as a researcher—as ours continues to be— is a work in progress. But researchers bring a few key talents to the job. They have strong observation and analytical skills. They can keep a goal in sight. They are efficient. They are good writers, an important asset since they are, for the most part, storytellers. They are agile, ready to adapt to a changing profession filled to the brim with changing resources. They like math. They pay attention to details. They love to read. They are consensus-builders. Most of all, they are leaders at their nonprofits. They often lead the entire development team to new thinking about prospective donors.

Many of us have spent our research careers passionate about prospect research. We have had the good fortune to expend our research time in the midst of grand missions. The nonprofits we have worked for ask us to identify and qualify major financial support for the next generation of leaders, for great art, for science, for preservation and innovation, and for the well-being of all. These are only a few of the fund-raising missions profiting from prospect research. There are many causes calling for prospect researchers, all with important work to be done. We are witnesses to incredible moments of philanthropy, many whose trail began when we "introduced" a fund raiser to a prospective donor. Our work has led to deep and profound changes at our own nonprofits and in our communities and, on a larger scale for the national and international nonprofits, in our global community.

We researchers are people of high ambition. We dream big, entertaining grand schemes and plans—sort of the "let's put on a show" folks of development. Maybe that comes from the "magic" part of our work. When you are the key to a humming research component, you will hear people say, "She can find anything." There is not really any magic, just plenty of hard work and skill, but we are often dealt with as if magic is in our domain. Research leads every fund-raising effort by segmenting the donor pool and identifying major gift possibilities. No matter how often you try to qualify those accolades, your protests will fall into a vacuum. That is bound to go to a person's head. The reality is closer to something truly great: She can find new prospective donors who can give five- and six- and seven- and eight-figure gifts to this nonprofit. Now, that is magic.

So, what are the goals of this book? We want to do more than provide a book to fill space on that nearly empty research bookshelf in your office. This book is all about prospect research, not a few chapters about research in a book about fund raising. There is plenty about fund raising here, of course, but it is set in the context of research. There are not entire chapters about gift processing, data entry, or any of the other pieces of the fund raising equation to which prospect research is sometimes wedded. These pieces are briefly covered, and are always covered in the context of prospect research.

Our intention is to create a handbook for prospect researchers. We also want this book to be a tool for our colleagues working at nonprofits who have not made the leap to funding prospect research yet. We hope this book can be your guide to adding a research component to your development plan. We will explain how research works. We will bring the tools. We will assemble the directions for researching prospective donors, creating a research library, and establishing a research office. We will lay out the plaster and lathe you will need to construct a research office at your nonprofit—forms and formats, processes and procedures. You will be the architect and the builder. We will give you the framework to learn about prospect research or to establish that research office. We hope to serve as your one-stop hardware store for all that you need to custom-build the research component—or your research skills—for your organization.

If you are a researcher in an established nonprofit, this book will give you a chance to review the concepts that drive your team's fund-raising effort. You can renew your research skills, evaluate another approach or two, and check your nonprofit's research process to see how it is working. Although we have geared this work to beginners and young nonprofits, we hope that you will find a few things you either did not know or forgot. We are certain that you will be glad to have a central place where many of the concepts and processes you have been using are now housed. And we hope that you will find a few passages about research worth sharing with your fund-raising team. After all, education is the most direct route to understanding, right?

There is work for you to do. We are believers in the "teach them to fish" approach, so we will be sending you to Web sites and directing you to contact information providers yourself. You are, after all, a researcher. When it comes to Web sites, be prepared for a fluctuating environment. Some Web sites simply cease to exist. Some of them, once gratis, begin to charge a fee for their premium content. You are bound to find that, by the time you read this, some of the Web sites we list here are charging a small or even a significant fee and that others are gone. At this writing, we believe that it will not be difficult to find substitutes for the Web sites that seemed promising on our lists and are now unavailable or too expensive. By the time you finish this book you will know how to join a network of researchers who can help you learn about the latest Web sites to use.

Those of you who have been prospect researchers for a time will find a few things missing from this book. Two things had an effect on the content. First of all, we wrote a book about prospect research, not about the entire process of fund raising. There are things associated with the other divisions of fund raising that we did not cover in this book. Second, we had a page limit set by the publisher. We simply had to draw some lines about what we could include and what will have to wait for another book. Our aim, to create an A-to-Z book about how to be a prospect researcher, was a challenging one. With starry-eyed ambition, we hope that you will dog-ear your copy of this book by turning to it over and over again. We hope that you will let us know where we made mistakes and what should be included in the next edition.

One of the most difficult things to relinquish was a wish to write a prospect research book that was global in every way. But here we are, wrestling with page limits and scope again. While concepts of fund raising and research may be generally universal, there are nuances for these activities in each part of the globe that belong in another book. There are many resources for international research now that we have the Internet bringing to our desktops information from every country. But we could not eliminate U.S.-based resources to make room to include an adequate collection of international resources. You will find a brief start on international research in the "Suggested Reading" section of this book and by visiting the international section of *Internet Prospector*, an electronic resource we reference. One day there will be enough interest for a U.S.-based researcher to write an entire book about this fascinating and fast-growing subject.

Language Difficulties

When we began our careers as researchers, we were surprised by fund-raising terminology. The first time you encounter them, words like "moves management" and "prospect" and "suspect" do not seem to reflect the respectful relationship the fund-raising team has with donors. Time among the team helps a new researcher realize that, just like any industry, fund raising has a lingo. Abbreviated terms, usually down-to-business terms, help everyone focus on the goals. Do we like all of these terms? No. Do we think that we could change an entire industry by suggesting new terms in this book? No. We also knew that we would do new researchers and fund raisers a disservice by excluding these terms from the language we share here since this is the language currently in use. Instead, we have made careful explanation of the longhand for these terms.

There are a few language difficulties that are simpler to resolve. It is cumbersome to read "he/she" and "him/her," so we alternated between the genders in our writing. We wish to be inclusive about all types of nonprofits and their supporters, so we call your database of affiliated people "constituents" instead of "alumni," "patients," or "subscribers."

There are other language issues that represent more complex problems. In our line of work, some researchers are in the throes of a struggle. Researchers have not always been valued appropriately and, for some researchers, this antiquated approach to the role of researchers persists. Unfortunately, the nearest yardstick for the value placed on researchers is the same one used to value fund raisers. Using this yardstick has researchers coming up short at some nonprofits. In efforts to improve the image of researchers, some in our profession now call themselves and their research colleagues "fund raisers." Because this becomes confusing, they call the major gifts officers "front-line fund raisers" and the researchers "backstage fund raisers." Once again, that trouble with language. This may presage an evolution of terms, although we think not, if only because it is so cumbersome (and because we do not wish to be stuck backstage for the entire fund-raising performance).

We are so proud to be prospect researchers that we call ourselves—and you—by that very title throughout this book. We call the folks who meet with donors and ask for gifts by three names: fund raisers, major gifts officers, and development officers. Are researchers fund raisers? Of course we are. Everyone in the fund-raising effort—the gift processors, the phonathon crew, data entry folks—are fund raisers. In *Planned Giving Simplified: The Gift, the Giver, and the Gift Planner* (John Wiley & Sons, New York, 1999, p. xxv), Robert F. Sharpe, Sr., refers to the people who ask for the gifts as "fund gatherers." As a planned giving expert, Mr. Sharpe sees the long, long process major gift giving can be. He points out that the fund raiser who walks in the door with the check is just one of the people who facilitated the philanthropy that unfolded. As you can see, we do not really need to quibble over who is a fund raiser and who is not.

Whatever you call us, we have the grand fortune of being a part of the act of giving. The measure of a major gift is taken on many scales—how large it is, how transforming it is for the recipients, how broadly it changes the community of givers who witness it. Another measure, one we prefer to use, is how deeply affected the giver is by the giving. It is our aim as researchers to keep opening opportunities for donors to feel that powerful measure.

About the Author

Cecilia Hogan has been the development researcher for the University of Puget Sound in Tacoma, Washington, for more than 10 years. She attended The George Washington University and earned a bachelor's degree from University of Waterloo in Ontario, Canada. She is the international editor for *Internet Prospector,* a volunteer-driven electronic newsletter and Web site reviewing Internet resources for development researchers. With David Lamb, Cecilia developed the pioneer electronic course, "Prospect Research on the Internet," for Council for Advancement and Support of Education (CASE) Online Education Network in the 1990s. She has made many presentations about prospect research to both regional and national groups. Cecilia is a former president of the Northwest chapter of the Association of Professional Researchers for Advancement (APRA) and served on the APRA International Board of Directors from 1999–2002. In the latter position she managed APRA's professional journal, *APRA Connections.*

Acknowledgments

"The request hit us in the face like a bucket of cold water.
It was a major decision for us."
—Philanthropist and retired Microsoft executive Scott Oki, about the first time he and his wife,
Laurie, were asked for $1 million from a nonprofit organization, *Town & Country*, June 2000, p. 166.

It seems naïve to say that writing a book, no matter what the topic, is harder than one anticipates. In a book about writing called *Bird by Bird,* author Anne Lamott tells the charming story for which the book is named (Anchor Books, 1994, p. 19). Her school-aged brother sat at the kitchen table, stalled and frustrated as he tried to complete a paper about birds that was due the next day. Their father calmly told the near-tears boy just to write the paper "bird by bird." How clear and wise this direction is when trying to write about (or do) prospect research. Bird by bird. It became my mantra for completing this project.

Being able to write this book is, "bird by bird," an outgrowth of the strong role I have had at my nonprofit, the University of Puget Sound in Tacoma, Washington. The University's fund-raising team educated me, embraced my ideas, and encouraged my efforts as a prospect researcher. In that, my fund raisers have no equal. From the day I began working at the university, this team has wanted a researcher who sits with the development officers at the strategy table, not one who just delivers bits of information. I have been honored to have the chance to nurture the partnership they celebrate.

I want to mention specifically two members of the fund-raising team at the University of Puget Sound. Everything about planned giving in Chapter 11 comes from the education Steve McGlone, the Director of Planned Giving, gave me. He is the champion of planned gifts, a generous mentor, and a true partner to a researcher. The ideas for mining for planned giving prospects outlined in Chapter 11 are methods designed by Steve that he and I have carried out.

Beth Herman, the Associate Vice President for Development at the University of Puget Sound, brought all the fund-raising tools a nonprofit could need with her when she arrived. I began there a short time before her as someone brand new to research, so Beth has been my educator about fund raising. In fact, it is impossible to separate what Beth taught me from what I know—I am certain that they are the same thing. Many of the fund-raising concepts you will learn about in this book are ones I learned from Beth. Beth loves to teach and is very good at it, to the great joy of the Council for Advancement and Support of Education (CASE), where Beth has generously shared her teaching. Beth's straightforward approach includes her belief in prospect research. She places great value in the unbreakable team that fund raisers and researchers build. Those beliefs, and the actions that follow on those beliefs, have placed me in the enviable position of only knowing a nonprofit world where my work as a researcher is not only valued but also relished and championed.

I offer a special thanks to the researchers who shared their prospect research forms and other materials. Hillary Wonderlick, Bozena Popovic, Sarah Choi, Karen Alpert, Mary Feeney, Christian Lillis, Frankie Tatum, Becky Van Zante, Bill Czyzyk, Allan Friedman, and Joan Berg happily shared profile forms, research request forms, contact report forms, and more. Their contributions give you, the reader, a range of samples for the forms you will design (or redesign) for your nonprofit. Chris Mildner allowed me to create one of my charts from a good idea she had years ago at the very nonprofit where I now work. And the Association of Professional Researchers for Advancement (APRA) shared their hallmark "Statement of Ethics" with me. All of these contributors give us another reminder of the generosity of researchers.

Speaking of APRA, there is nothing that approaches the educational opportunities offered through its conferences, its publications, and the meetings carried out by its chapters. The network of support and information that APRA members create and sustain is irreplaceable. My first APRA conference sent me back to my nonprofit full of new ideas and so did my last conference. Much of my research education grew from those years of attending conferences and reading *APRA Connections* articles and the subsequent "experiments in prospect research" they encouraged.

I am grateful that David Lamb invited me to this party. After he wrote the introduction to *The Grantseeker's Handbook of Essential Internet Sites* (2000-2001 edition), David was asked by Aspen Publishers what he thought about writing a prospect research book. He telephoned me to see if I was interested in the project. David and I met during my first year in prospect research at a local meeting of the Washington State research group (now an APRA chapter known as APRA-NW). Soon after, David was creating opportunities for us to collaborate. One of the first partnerships David suggested—several years ago—was that we compare fee-based electronic resources with free resources available on the Web and make a conference presentation out of it. At least he did not suggest that we invent electricity or anything. Our next collaborations included local and national speaking engagements and the pioneer Council for Advancement and Support of Education (CASE) online course for prospect researchers, and now this. I am delighted that he considered me for this important project. David and I created the outline for this book together. He wrote about prospect tracking and contributed his insights and ideas to the electronic screening, research math, and other sections of the book.

Jones and Bartlett Publishers, the company that acquired Aspen Publishers' fund-raising section in 2002, moved quickly to put this prospect research book into production. They assigned a crack team to copy edit, design, and produce the book. Right along with me, researchers long in this profession will be delighted and grateful for the deliberateness of the wonderful people at Jones and Bartlett Publishers.

Two skilled writers and long-time researchers threw themselves into this project when asked. Pam "P.J." Smith of Sacred Heart University and Pam Patton of Drake University were the book's alpha readers—the first readers and wisest counsel. Our long relationship began when we "met" electronically as volunteer editors for *Internet Prospector,* a monthly newsletter and Internet site reviewing Web sites useful for prospect researchers. *Internet Prospector* editors are located across the United States and, for more than seven years, we have produced a monthly newsletter without ever having met one another. *Internet Prospector* has received attention and praise from nonprofits and important information providers in philanthropy, and we have been proud to be a part of this amazing project. Pam, P.J., and I have actually met several times now. For *Prospect Research: A Primer for Growing Nonprofits,* P.J. and Pam separated the breeches from the breaches, untangled the mixed metaphors, caught the missing pieces, and left smiles and cheers in the spots where the writing hit them just right. Their support, encouragement, and talent with words cannot be measured. The hours they happily gave to this project deepened our relationship with one another forever. That was an unanticipated gift that is now mine.

A funny thing happened on the way to completing this book. As I was writing the last chapters, my sister Kathy Hogan added prospect research to her duties at the Museum of Glass in Tacoma. The museum was under construction when Kathy joined our family of prospect researchers. A journalist by trade, Kathy needed instruction in how to be a prospect researcher, and she needed it fast. What better way to dive into her new responsibilities (and turn a favor for her sister) than to test-drive the manuscript for the book as a new researcher. If we did this right, she learned a few things about fund raising and prospect research along the way. I appreciate the attention she gave to this during a demanding time in her life.

My sister Marion Hogan offered me her insights about organizing this project as well as ideas about how to construct the chapters to make them easier for readers. She cheered me during the rough parts, suggesting ways to push through to the next goals. My first conversations about this project were with Marion as we approached Boston for a presentation I was to give to New England Development Research Association (NEDRA) members. Marion matched my enthusiasm about this project then and all along the way.

My son Anthony Pantley, the young man who taught me airport codes (this will mean more to you later), brought his clear vision and undeniable common sense to this project. He reminds me every step of the way to look at the best in any situation. He is a visionary when it comes to cutting to the core of a matter.

Finally, my husband Tony Pantley should have his name on the cover of this book. He listened to every single word, each one read aloud to him. And then, after the next edit, he listened again. I am certain that he could be a prospect researcher now, if you could get him to give up his love for gardening and come in from the outside. He understands the work we researchers do, as many others do not, after hearing tens of thousands of words on the topic. Driving home together after work each day, he will respond to my stories with insights he did not have before. But even more important than the time and interest he gave to listening, he relentlessly prodded me into the "writing room" again and again. He cooked for me, chided me, and pushed me to tell him my plan. He is the great supporter every spouse dreams of when a project of this size and scope comes along. I humbly accept the gift he gave me—the gift of himself.

As you begin each chapter of this book, you will see that I love quotations. In fact, I collect them. I have included a few from my collection in *Prospect Research: A Primer for Growing Nonprofits*. At work, I include a quotation about philanthropy or wealth at the end of each issue of an electronic newsletter I send my fund-raising team each week. I find the quotations in the reading materials that are a part of my weekly tasks as a researcher. I like quotations because I like good writing, and I like being in a perpetual state of inspiration. I will end this, the last thing I am writing for this book, with the quote that has been tacked onto my writing desk during this entire project. It served as my grounding wire:

"Do all things with a sense of propriety."
—Peter Santucci, Washington CEO, February 2001, p. 5.

Cecilia Hogan

Table of Contents

The History, Evolution, and Mission of Prospect Research

"Philanthropy is a hard thing to define . . . . And it's not a popular subject. No one wants to talk about it."
—Stamp advocate Milton Murray on why it took the U.S. Postal Service 18 years to approve a stamp honoring philanthropy (issued in 1998); *The Chronicle of Philanthropy,* January 15, 1998, p. 33.

A tattered news clipping has served as our benchmark (*The Chronicle of Philanthropy,* June 26,1990, p.1). David had been a researcher for barely a year when he saw this article. It set prospect research in a context that rang true then and rings true today.

The article profiles Aryeh Nesher, a minor legend in his role as fund raiser for the United Jewish Appeal. The article is full of gems of fund-raising wisdom, such as "People don't like to be sold. Don't sell them. People like to buy things. Help them buy . . . . People like to give gifts. Help them to give." It's a donor-centered philosophy of fund raising.

Nesher puts a lot of stock in prospect research. "The whole art of fund raising is in what you do before you go in," he says. "I'm crazy for knowing as much as I can before I go in, knowing that, in the encounter, half of it isn't worth a penny."

He tells a story about visiting a potential donor who did not have a tradition of giving to the United Jewish Appeal. When Mr. Nesher asked for $100,000 the man said he had to speak to his wife before he could make a commitment to give that amount. Nesher glanced at the preparation materials he held in his hands, and he noticed that the information reported that the man divorced 10 years ago. Nesher said to the man, "I'm fascinated by what you say. I've never heard that someone who hasn't spoken to his wife for 10 years only talks to her about his gift to the Jews."

Talk about chutzpah—Nesher admits that this approach was risky. The chance that he would alienate this potential donor was great. Fortunately, Nesher had read the man correctly. The donor made the gift and said, "You know, Nesher, you've helped me a lot. I've used this lie for many years to avoid doing my share. You've helped me get rid of the lie."

This is the gospel of fund raising according to Nesher: Fund raising is about helping people do what is most important to them. It is about connecting with a person's deepest values and providing them with a way to do something good. The negative stereotypes of fund raisers who pry money out of the hands of stingy donors have nothing to do with the central tenet of Nesher's philosophy. This philosophy guides not only the fund raiser who visits and cultivates donors, but the prospect researchers as well. As researchers we must always keep the donors' interests in mind. We are not just catalogers of donor information. We are caretakers. Our pursuit of donor information is in the service of the donor, not just for the sake of the hunt. Nesher tells us that the researcher's role is crucial to fund raising. Ninety percent of "what you do before you go in" is prospect research.

Know Where You Came from to Get Where You Want to Go: A Bit of History

You might be inclined to skip this part of the book—unless you are a researcher, that is. Researchers are fascinated by history. The essence of research is divining the history of wealth, affiliation, and philanthropy on a person-by-person basis. Unfortunately, the history of prospect research is elusive. It is surprising that, for a group of people who tend to save too much, few records documenting the emergence of prospect research were kept. What little information there was has never been gathered into one place. Regardless, we can have some fun looking at the probable origins of this essential piece of the fund-raising process. Along the way, we will learn more about the reason for prospect research and how it fits into the development process.

Which came first—the philanthropist or the researcher who initially identified the philanthropist? It is not difficult to surmise that people were philanthropic long before development teams—including researchers—were offering them opportunities to give. We discovered this when we taught the pioneer Council for Advancement and Support of Education (CASE) Internet course on prospect research in 1998. The CASE people gave us a nearly perfect virtual classroom of students for that inaugural class. Participants from across the United States, Canada, England, and Scotland registered for the course. The international current flowing through the class had benefits hard to list. One benefit of this global classroom was that it powered a broader discussion and a deeper understanding of the universal mission of philanthropy. Remember, we were working in an electronic environment. We did not have faces to attach to each participant. The composite researcher who emerged was a fund-raising professional with an expansive and clearly directed vision. Meeting this "virtual" researcher lifted our own viewpoint of prospect research.

The most telling moment came in the first few days of the five-week course. Initially, each class member and instructor introduced herself and wrote about her organization, length of service, and the scope of the development task at her institution. One by one, we each described small and large development teams, pending and ongoing capital campaigns, new research opportunities, and older components needing a fresh approach.

How old is philanthropy and how young is prospect research? Here is one answer. Lizzie Robinson, hailing from Scotland, had signed up for that first online research class. Lizzie introduced herself as the first prospect researcher hired by Scotland's 450-year-old University of Edinburgh. Can you imagine that? The University of Edinburgh did not need a prospect researcher for 450 years! Lizzie patiently explained that it was an exaggeration to make that conclusion from her fresh hiring, that there had been people—but not researchers—who did a bit of research over the years. Lizzie said that now Edinburgh (and, really, the rest of the philanthropic universe) had entered an era when two important events converge: There is greater competition for philanthropic dollars, and there is more new, harder to identify wealth than ever before. *All nonprofits—even old, established institutions that have been well supported for hundreds of years—need a researcher now.*

Lizzie's story tells us that deliberate, professional prospect research entered the fund-raising timeline about 15 minutes ago. In fact, the history of prospect research goes hand-in-hand with the growth and sophistication of the development process. Cultivating prospective donors began—and still begins—with glad-handing, known philanthropists. If we look at Any Nonprofit in Main Town, USA, we know that, for a time, Any Nonprofit turns to those people who are known for their generosity throughout the town or throughout that philanthropic cause. Identifying prospective major gift donors was as easy as turning to the boards of directors, looking in the front row at a symphony performance, joining the chamber of commerce, or attending the welcoming reception for the new college president. But after those donors have been spotted and solicited, where would development go next? And as more and more nonprofits, each with a worthy mission, vie for these same "easily spotted" donors, where does the next philanthropic dollar come from for each institution? That is a large piece of the mission of an effective prospect research operation: to uncover potential donors unknown to development.

So, where precisely was prospect research born? Before it walked into the fund-raising process, arms loaded with information, where was research? Corporate culture holds a model for both development and the research propelling it. Individuals with a dream and not much experience running a business often begin nonprofits. So, in seeking a model for operating a successful enterprise, young nonprofits turn to the corporate world. The manner in which companies keep track of their customers and the process they establish for communicating with those clients on a regular basis are transformed into the backbone of the nonprofit's approach to donors. It seems natural that the next step in this copycat method is applying the formula for how new "customers" are added to the family. Our sales-driven culture has fine-tuned the art of cultivation and closing the deal. Is nonprofit development's approach to closing a gift similar? Yes. Even the language of the gift-getting process mimics that used by commerce: cultivation, tracking, solicitation, and stewardship. In *You're Too Kind: A Brief History of Flattery* (Simon & Schuster, 2000, p. 41), Richard Stengel reports that "reciprocal altruism is . . . a kind of calculated favor, an action or gesture performed for an expected return." Might this describe some approaches to philanthropy— and even development? Donors give for many reasons, with a few of the primary ones centering on the good feelings and the legacy they will generate with their gift. Development teams are adept at touting not only those experiences but also those *opportunities*. This partnership in feeling and doing good has the added benefit of promoting a much greater good. Fund raisers know that, and they share that wonderful gift, the opportunity for a life filled with greater purpose and meaning, with prospective donors.

The Evolution of Prospect Research, Part One

So, we could never identify the first prospect researcher or pinpoint the first institution to fund a research component. We can more readily identify the growth of prospect research in America through a series of events that parallel that growth. Many large nonprofits, primarily large universities, can date their research function to the early 1970s. This coincides with the arrival of the first desktop computers in offices and the first primitive electronic databases used to hold and manage donor information. It also coincides with the increasing competition for resources among nonprofits and the increasing sophistication of fund raising in general.

As the electronic era dawned, fund raisers equipped with computers could do something they could not do before. They could efficiently create lists of donors by nearly any characteristic they cared to code. But fund raisers are not interested in divining list parameters. They simply want names of individuals they might visit. The right individuals, the ones with major gift potential. Did you hear that sound? The door opened and prospect research walked in.

The people first identified to perform prospect research tasks were often already working in development. They were clerks, secretaries, institutional librarians, and even development officers. Sometimes they were constituents or the spouses of other fund-raising employees. In this story, the research professional evolved out of a position with no true prospect research skills. This person was assumed to be someone who enjoyed poking around in reference books, someone with good math skills, connections in the community, and a persistent attitude when it came to finding information. Since there were no training opportunities for researchers among development's professional groups, an initial set of research skills grew out of the tasks at hand.

By the late 1970s, researchers were looking for advice, peers who were prospect researchers, and training opportunities. Intrepid leaders in every tribe appear at this point in any story to take the tribe over the next developmental hurdle. Researchers began meeting informally, most notably in Minnesota. A sense of comradery, a shared experience, even among competing nonprofits, might have encouraged these researchers to continue meeting. By 1981, researchers in Minnesota formed a statewide professional organization and, within a short time, established bylaws, elected officers, and made plans to meet on a regular basis. By the mid-1980s, the Minnesota researchers registered their congenial group as a nonprofit organization. At nearly the same time, New England researchers also established a professional group.

In early 1988, the Minnesotans transformed their group into a national organization for development researchers. With a slightly different name, this was the infant form of the Association of Professional Researchers for Advancement (APRA). State chapters followed quickly in a half-dozen states, with Indiana holding the distinction of being the first official chapter. Groups began meeting across the country, with some becoming affiliated chapters then and some meeting for a number of years before affiliating with the national group. Some groups, like the New England Development Research Association (NEDRA), remained independent.

APRA emerged as the international representation of researchers and, at this writing, APRA has 28 affiliated chapters, representing more than 30 states, and individual members in 49 states. APRA also has members in Canada, France, England, Scotland, Ireland, and Spain, as well as a few other countries. A detailed account of APRA's history can be found at the APRA Web site at **http://www.aprahome.org/**. There you will learn about the first meetings researchers held and the meetings they are having now. You may be surprised to see that many of the same topics that occupy you now were holding the attention of researchers 20 years ago.

This brief history of research tells us a few memorable things. First of all, the message is clear: Organized, deliberate prospect research is a young enterprise. Second, the concept of researchers sharing their experiences and their skills with one another is equally youthful. And third, you are not alone. There are many opportunities for you to connect with your peers in similar organizations or with similar philanthropic agendas. All you have to do is pick up the phone or begin an email message. You will find details about who to write or call in the appendix section of this book.

The Evolution of Prospect Research, Part Two

Should we say, "From these small beginnings . . ." to describe what happened next? No. Instead imagine a cacophony of sound, a rush of activity, and a burst of sophistication.

The technological clock was racing ahead, and all of development, on the coat tails of research, raced ahead with it. The race would have been more haphazard and frantic if it were not for the organizational skills inherent in good research. From nonprofit offices where slips of paper held the names of prospective donors, fund raising began to lurch into the present and future with the purchase of the first computers and their best friends, electronic databases and search tools. The most logical computer code-writing model might be applied to what happened next in fund raising. Process became the theme: How could a nonprofit identify, cultivate, solicit, close, and steward a prospective donor and *track* all of this activity? And who would manage that information and even augment it? Well, research of course.

To be accurate, the tasks often began with clerks and data processors. Too quickly to even measure, the new tasks were beyond the parameters of a typical data-crunching job. And the crunching was growing exponentially, so it became more and more difficult to simply tag the newly discovered research tasks onto the chore lists of the processors and clerks. This would be the point in the story when the primeval fish flops up on the bank and uses its fins to walk. The people who fell into research, on the strength of the mission at hand, the new set of tools available, and the unique talents and interests of the individuals present to witness it all, nudged the new profession of prospect research into existence. Mind you, this was a knock-you-down nudge.

A new sun rose the next day. You have already heard about it—the dawn of the Information Age met these new, young researchers and their development teams when they turned on their computers. Information in nearly every form you could imagine flooded fund raising. Histories began to be captured, kept, and treasured. Collections of lore and anecdotes from those scraps of paper were formalized when they were turned into megabytes. Information brick upon information brick, a new mansion was being built at the frontrunner institutions. It was the mansion of information—read "donor"—management. The tools to collect, segment, merge, and dissect information quickly followed. Tools tailor-made for fund raising joined the mix. Information-holding and information-gathering tools gave fund raisers— via researchers—a new set of possibilities for gifts from existing donors and donors-to-be.

In less than 25 years, the options available to development teams exploded. Fund raisers with researchers as partners were now able to review comprehensive donor pools by geographic region, by gift history, by affiliation, or by nearly any element that could be coded. As the reach of development grew, the dependence on research to bring an element of familiarity through *meaningful* information also grew. Distant and unknown donors could now be (relatively) known before the development staff left the office to meet those donors. Augmenting paper directories, fee-based electronic tools offered adept researchers the opportunity to search and sift through oceans of information.

A perfect world, right? Actually, the work of research has just begun. A power surge in the direction of research occurred when the Internet was set on nonprofit desks. The pile of information now became a Rockies-size mountain range. How to manage information, how to collect the right information and, through analysis, turn it into *knowledge*, becomes the next chapter in the story of prospect research. It is being written in these times we live in by you and prospect researchers just like you.

You see? You live in times that give you the chance to build a prospecting process at your institution, regardless of the size of your endowment or the scope of your annual gift campaign. These times have given you the imperative to do so, for the health of your organization, since the gift you do not identify and cultivate might escape you now.

The Mission of Prospect Research

Prospect research identifies, analyzes, and recommends avenues of financial support so that the fund-raising goals of a nonprofit organization can be realized. This seems simple and direct. It is not as simple as it seems.

Where is the next philanthropic dollar for your institution lying right now? The mission of prospect research is clear. Prospect research's mission is to use the first philanthropic dollar raised to efficiently identify the next. The essence of the mission is simple—efficient dedication to uncovering the possibility of the largest gifts an institution can realize. The math formula is that one dollar spent on research reaps many, many more dollars in gifts.

The Chronicle of Philanthropy (August 10, 2000, p. 12) analyzed charitable giving by Americans who used itemized tax returns in 1998. Itemizing taxpayers earning $200,000 or more annually reported about three and one-half percent of their incomes going to charity. In "Who's Got the Bucks" (*Forbes,* July 5, 1999, p. 88), Peter Brimelow writes that only one percent of households in America has a net worth over $2.7 million. *The Economist* (May 30, 1998, p. 15) reports that "By one count, eight in ten Americans earning more than $1 million a year leave nothing to charity in their wills." The consistent feature of these statistics about wealth and philanthropy is the small numbers involved. The greatest wealth is held by a small number of people. Although philanthropic, those in the top income groups significantly limit their giving. Too many who are not philanthropic in life maintain that tradition in death. Their last chance to leave a philanthropic mark is missed.

One fund-raising adage is that most nonprofits raise about 90 percent of their major gifts each year from less than 10 percent of their constituency. For fund-raising goals to be met, donors in the top income groups must be cultivated. The way donors congregate in the fund raiser's view of things is illustrated with a donor pyramid (see Figure 1-1). Prospect research focuses on the top level of the pyramid, the spot in the donor hierarchy where the wealthiest sit. This part of the donor hierarchy is where the 10 percent of the

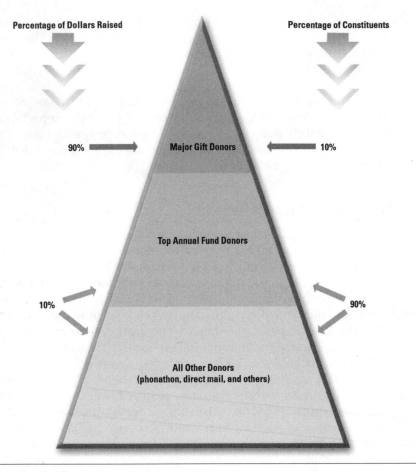

FIGURE 1-1 The Donor Pyramid.
Most donors (in number) are giving below the top annual fund level defined by your organization. Major gift donors, the smallest group in number, give the largest amount in total dollars.

Source: Authors

people who give 90 percent of the gifts reside. It is the location of the highest and best opportunities for large philanthropic gifts. Research has a relationship with the other layers of the pyramid, but only in this sense: In its purest and most directed form, research might identify prospective donors in those layers and determine when they will be elevated to the top of the pyramid in terms of the attention they might receive from fund raisers. Beyond that imperative, there is little for research to do with the other levels of the hierarchy.

Why concentrate on the top of the pyramid? Are there not many more donors—and maybe the potential for more support—in the middle or bottom tiers? The keynote of prospect research, beginning at its very mission, is efficiency. Remember the math formula? Where can the most money be raised with directed effort? That is where the most effective money spent to raise money goes. The return from mail and telephone fund-raising campaigns often hovers around 10 percent or so of the total raised by sophisticated development organizations. Younger nonprofits, those not yet *deliberately* raising money from major gift donors, rely on more support from the middle part of the pyramid. But the first large gifts they receive demonstrate even to the youngest nonprofit that identifying new support among the small groups who have the ability to make large gifts is the most efficient and effective way to approach the science of fund raising.

The Science of Fund Raising?

Yes, in the broadest tradition of science, fund raising is built upon a set of theories, tested outcomes, and sets of methodology. Like most professional practices, the act of raising money to support a nonprofit's cause has evolved into an established process that enhances the likelihood of success. Research has a role in each stage (see Figure 1-2). The process is time- and talent-consuming. The more efficient the effort is, especially when it is consistently directed at the people likely to make a major gift, the better the nonprofit's resources are used. And a nonprofit's resources, whether they involve money, time, or people, probably began as a donation. That beginning speaks to the ethic of responsible stewardship driven by the origin and intent of the gift itself. By studying Figure 1-2, you can see that placing a donor who cannot give a major gift in the path of the intensive fund-raising effort staged by development wastes the resources of your nonprofit.

Other Destinations

We have outlined the mission of prospect research. The aim for research seems true and straight: Find the opportunities for significant financial support. Analyze the information gathered and recommend the next step. Prospect research at its best will identify, qualify, and further define major gift donors (see Exhibit 1-1). When an organization loses this clear-sighted aim, the research function can become anything but so accurately directed. It is surprising how often the mission gets clouded by both researchers and by those who research serves. The information management business is rife with roadblocks, detours, and washouts. It is often difficult for a researcher to keep the goal in sight and equally difficult for other members of the development team to help research stay on track. By looking at some of the detours—detours researchers construct and those built by other members of the development team—the mission of prospect research becomes even clearer. By looking at some of the detours, we can focus on a vision of how to stay on track.

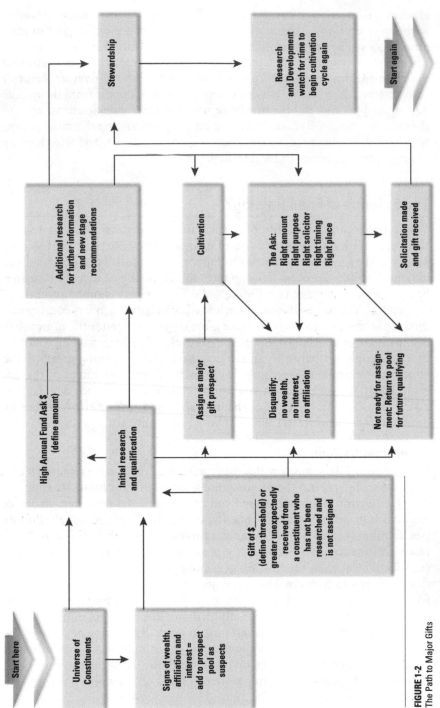

FIGURE 1-2
The Path to Major Gifts

Source: Authors, inspired by a chart by Chris Mildner.

Exhibit 1-1	Prospect Research: Identify, Qualify, and Define

Identify: Find prospective major gift donors.

Qualify: Research affiliation, giving, financial capacity, and life events that impact giving.

Define: Profile the prospective donor for cultivation assignment.

Qualify: Review initial contact report for second-stage research opportunities.

Define: Recommend cultivation strategies.

Qualify: Analyze financial capacity.

Define: Recommend the amount of the gift to be requested.

Define: Assist in timing the solicitation by reviewing pertinent financial developments.

Define: Brainstorm who the right solicitor is by reviewing the pool of peer donors and volunteers.

Identify: After the gift closes, track the donor through stewardship.

Identify: Recommend the next cultivation based on new financial or life events.

Source: Authors

(Don't) Take the Road Less Traveled

What interesting things we researchers can find! One researcher tells about discovering the kennel club trials at which a prospective donor was showing cocker spaniels. Another uncovered statistics about a prospective donor's prize bull. The vacation photos a prospective donor posted on the Internet were fun to see. Are any of these finds useful to identifying and qualifying prospects? Sometimes they are, but often they are only minimally or anecdotally useful. Much of this information, if important, would come out during the cultivation stage with far less effort. Sometimes researchers are so excited to find *anything* that they lose their way. A researcher can travel down the road of inconsequential information for hours. This less traveled road is overgrown and dense for a reason—there is not much on it useful to gift getting. Focus. Remember the goal. Keep your aim true.

Around and Around in Circles

Raise your hand if you have ever begun a project, dug deeper and deeper into the information wormhole, and then looked at the clock on the wall only to realize that more than half the day had passed. Where were you? That constituent you began researching hours ago is still an open question. You are no closer to the answers than you were when you started. What should you do? Stop. Take a breath. Step away from this project. Reevaluate your approach. Measure the value and the potential return for your involvement in this task. There is another route to the information that is not in your directories and electronic sources. Sometimes the answer you seek is simply not there. There is another prospective donor waiting for you to discover him. A good researcher develops a sense about the limits to this work. No need to worry: That sense of the limits will come along, holding hands with experience and intuition.

Lost in the Woods, Never Alone (Because the Wolves are Baying)

The amount of information available to researchers is now as thick and dense as the darkest Pacific Northwest forest. Branch after branch of interlocking and tangential data astound even seasoned researchers. Researchers recognize the kind of information that identifies capacity and helps qualify a gift range. They discipline themselves to evaluate quickly other information and to leave behind that which does not contribute to the mission. The best skill a researcher develops is the ability to *prioritize* and *evaluate* information.

In a time when information is available from many sources in many formats, researchers must rank the reliability as well as the thoroughness of the sources. They must choose where to get information and how many times it is necessary to get the same information. Although the best skill a researcher has is to evaluate information, the next best skill is to realize when a question is answered. As hard as this is to believe, there is often so much information now that it is no longer possible to get *all* of the information. No one even wants it. And they are waiting outside the door for information about other prospective donors. There is no time to spend mired in spaniels or the fifth newspaper article repeating how much money a constituent made selling a company. Information, the right information that has been efficiently gathered, is transformed into *knowledge* through analysis and application to the mission. That is the paramount task of research.

On the Brink of Failure

Most of us in development come from backgrounds very different from those of the constituents we research. We may even find it hard to believe that those very people are going to the same concerts, art galleries, and schools that we attend. We may find it hard to believe that the very wealthy could be in our donor pool. This might be why we sometimes fail to see them there. It may be why we often work as if they will not be there.

Each organization establishes the threshold for what will be called a major gift by examining its donor pool, mission, geographic location, and its own philanthropic history. Many researchers set their sights on this major gift point, at the precise level of giving identified as a major gift. They find themselves trying to "stretch" a prospective donor up to fit that gift threshold. Instead of raising their sights to what we can think of as the "really big gift" level, they spend their work time mired in researching potential donors who really fit better into the mid-level of the pyramid. Every minute of research is spent working on the brink of failure, working at the edge of dipping below the major gift threshold. Some development officers operate this way, too. They begin talking about pursuing gifts that are well below the major gift definition.

Working at the very edge of the major gift definition is working on the brink of failure. There are, in fact, large gift-makers in your donor pool. They are among nearly every organization's constituency, or they are nearby, looking for philanthropic opportunities like the one your organization offers. It is difficult to see them when you spend your time looking in the middle tier of the pyramid instead of the top tier. We know that you may sometimes find yourself there. We urge you to climb back up to the top of the tier and concentrate your energies there.

Driving Directions

What was that mission again? Researchers who clearly remember their purpose are destined to enrich their organization's donor lists. All the while we are completing research assignments, looking for new prospects, or simply managing the chores that keep a research operation efficient and effective, we do so with the mission in mind. Does your nonprofit need you to be tracking job changes for people who are not in high-return positions? Although your nonprofit might like to know about all those people and their new jobs, you will not be serving the mission when you spend time—and resources—on that task. Since the scope of the research task is already so large, researchers must establish boundaries around an information-gathering process that precisely serves the major gift mandate.

Research is not alone in muddying the trail to major gift donors. The rest of the development team can mistake research for a broader function on that team. The other people in the organization get the false impression that research's involvement with the database, gift records, and central files means that the researcher should manage all those functions, too. Without adequate staffing, attending to these other functions will impede the true mission of research. Some of this, particularly in very small nonprofits, is unavoidable, particularly when the research function is young. By studying a few of these detours, researchers can be prepared to find their way back to the mission.

Generic Research

There are many different kinds of research. Scientific, institutional, statistical, and market research are branches of this field that each yield far different results. They also require different skills than the ones used by development researchers. How often you will be asked to do research that fits better into one of these other branches of the field will vary from nonprofit to nonprofit. How well you perfect your ability to gracefully help the asker to remember your true mission is a matter for another book.

Lists, Lists, and More Lists

There simply are not enough ways to parse a donor pool. Did we sort this group by geographic area yet? Did we rank them by gift range? Did we prioritize them based on past giving? Did we rebuild the list with those most affiliated to our nonprofit near the top? In the meantime, who is doing the organization's research? Who is finding new donors? Research has a close relationship with the database in terms of extracting information and segmenting groups for a deeper examination of philanthropic potential. But getting trapped in the list-making vortex will leave a researcher with little time for actual research.

Hey, Researcher, is There Anything Else You Can Do for Me?

As we discussed earlier in this chapter, many research roles grew out of gift recording, data processing, or clerk positions. The problem is that, at some institutions, the new research job never finished growing. Researchers are asked to take on additional responsibilities at these institutions. Sometimes these duties involve information-processing chores or updating data. Sometimes they involve maintaining or overseeing central filing systems. While researchers spend time on those tasks, little research is done. And these valuable tasks do not receive the attention and dedication they require. Development teams begin to fidget about flawed information in the database, a lack of prospects, and gift processing errors.

Within any team, the art of negotiation and an unwavering belief in the value of each member will help a team remember its mission when the demands of the moment have clouded it. The service that prospect research offers the team is essential and irreplaceable. It is development's gift to the nonprofit to keep that aim true and straight.

The Limitations of Research

Have you seen those ads offering to let you get all the secrets of your friends, neighbors, lovers, business partners, or just about anyone who has reason to trust you? Just send in $19.95 for the Internet Spy Kit, and all will be revealed. We must admit that, as fantastical and intrusive as these ads are, they leave us a little amazed. We certainly cannot uncover private facts, and we are professional prospect researchers.

The truth is, these pitches are 100 percent pure, high-grade snake oil. They cannot uncover private information any more than we can. The people behind the ads are taking advantage of the public's perceptions about the loss of privacy in today's information-rich society. And they imply, since the walls of privacy are falling down, why not take advantage of that?

Those walls have weakened a little, but they have not come crashing down just yet. What the snake oil salespeople actually tap into are information resources very similar to some of the ones you would find in a prospect researcher's library. And as we mentioned, those tools will not pry open any locks that are intended to stay locked.

Here are some of the things that are usually unavailable to prospect researchers and would-be Internet spies:

- Bank balances
- Unpublished salaries of private individuals
- Specifics about a person's complete stock or asset portfolio

- A full listing of liabilities
- Sealed public records (i.e. sealed divorce documents)
- Unlisted telephone numbers
- Unpublished donations

Information that researchers (and anyone who wants to) have a reasonably good chance of finding includes:

- Stock and options holdings of public company officers and directors in that company
- Compensation of the top officers (usually the top four to six) in public companies
- Unsealed or open public records, such as property assessments, liens, divorces, probates, vital records, and business licenses (the availability of these documents varies widely from state to state, county to county, city to city)
- Published donations
- Business information in directories and in documents published by a company
- News about constituents who have attracted the attention of reporters working for newspapers, journals, and magazines
- Miscellaneous bits of data, depending on who the constituents are and how they are plugged into the business, philanthropic, and social spheres of influence.

Defining a Major Gift

So, research focuses on identifying prospective donors who can make a major gift to an organization. What is a major gift? The definitions of a major gift are nearly as varied as the types of nonprofit organizations. At one large university, for example, a major gift is defined as a gift of $250,000 or more. Okay, swallow hard and keep reading because it gets easier from here. At the small nonprofit down the street from you, a major gift might be $10,000. At many institutions, a major gift is further qualified by the option to pay the gift over a number of years. So, a $25,000 major gift is often a $5,000 annual gift over five consecutive years. You may be concluding that the person who can give $5,000 a year is somewhat different than the one who can give $25,000 in one gift. You are right. The bottom line is that each institution defines what a major gift is, usually based on its own history of gift getting and the general propensity of its constituency to give (see Exhibit 1-2). Do institutions raise the bar for what a major gift is? Yes, they do. Young organizations may create a definition of a major gift based upon "seed" gifts received during startup. As the nonprofit grows, the concept of a major gift grows, too.

Exhibit 1-2   **What is a Major Gift at Your Institution?**

To set the amount for a major gift at your organization:
1. *Review* daily gifts. What gifts appear to be sizable "out of pocket" gifts?
2. *Study* history. What gifts are already noted in your nonprofit's history as major gifts?
3. *Analyze* the capacity of your current greatest supporters and their giving histories.
4. *Research* the major gifts given to similar organizations in your area or in other areas with similar characteristics.
5. *Establish* a major gift mark and review it at the end of a year or two. Was this the right estimate for your organization?

Source: Authors

Regardless of the dollar number defining a major gift, this definition forms the starting point for research at your organization. Prospective donors who can give at the major gift level are the domain of prospect research (see Exhibit 1-3). Other donors to your organization—Tiers 2 and 3 of the pyramid—can be managed by other divisions in your fund-raising effort. Tier 3 forms the pool of donors for the direct mail and phonathon efforts. Tier 2 may be the next group who moves into major gift consideration. They can be "tested" through a program of personal solicitations by volunteers who will ask them for your organization's top annual fund gift.

Exhibit 1-3   **It's the Gift that Counts**

There are many ways that donors give to nonprofits. Some donors give time instead of money or goods. In major gift research, we are primarily interested in gifts of money, gifts that can be converted to money, or gifts of goods (which may or may not be converted to money). Here are a few of the words you will hear associated with gifts:

Annual fund gift: A gift to the unrestricted fund that supports the expense of running a nonprofit. Gifts in this group are solicited each year.

Major gift: A gift greater than that given annually; a gift of a size determined by a nonprofit and given with a significant effort on the part of the donor; a large gift that often comes from assets instead of income.

Outright gift: A gift of real or personal property given to the nonprofit for its immediate use. The donor has no connection to the gift after it is given.

Deferred gift: A gift for which a nonprofit waits; a planned gift such as a remainder trust or annuity, a bequest.

Pledge: A gift promised. The pledge may be short term (until the check arrives) or a longer term, even a number of years.

Gift-in-kind: A gift of something other than money, usually an object (books or equipment, for example) or an expense incurred in service to the nonprofit by the donor (airfare to come to a board meeting, for example).

Restricted gift: A gift that must be applied to a specific use. For example, gifts to scholarships or special funds or departments are restricted gifts.
Unrestricted gift: A gift that the nonprofit may use in the way it determines to be the best use.
Matching gift: A gift made by a foundation or corporation in the name of an affiliate after the affiliate makes a gift. The "match" may be expressed by the ratio at which the institutional giver gives in relation to the affiliate's giving. For example, the match may be 1:1, that is, for each single dollar given by the affiliate, the institutional giver gives a single dollar. Match ratios vary.
Anonymous gift: A gift given on the condition that the donor is never revealed. This type of gift requires strict security in gift processing, record keeping, and other procedures, even among development staff members, in order to live up to the agreement for anonymity made with the donor.
Named gift: A gift large enough to give the donor the option to attach his or someone else's name. The name may be placed on a room, a building, an architectural feature, a scholarship, a performance, an exhibition, a preserve, or a special fund, for example.

Source: Authors

The bottom line for research—the brink of failure—will be measured at that major gift precipice. That is the area roped off for research. Your universe is the donors who appear to be capable of making a major gift (the definition of a major gift and *anything greater than that*).

Two by Two (or What are We All Doing in this Boat Anyway?)

Although we have struggled mightily to be focused on research, there is good reason to view research as mixed up in the rest of the process on the fund-raising team. The entire fund-raising process is deeply co-dependent (in a healthy sort of way), with each component relying on the other members of the development family (see Figure 1-3). Let's take a look at how research is intertwined in a relatively sophisticated fund-raising team.

Data Processing: The name and address information as well as information about family relationships, marriages and deaths, and other donor data form the entire basis of the organization's fund-raising operation. From a researcher's viewpoint, this is the most critical element in the effort. Researchers cannot find donors if they have not been entered into the database correctly. They cannot identify those most likely to give major gifts if names or addresses are incorrect or outdated. Constituent records must be updated accurately and promptly. A fund raiser we know once urged an audience of researchers to develop righteous circles. What is a righteous circle? It is a group of people who share a vision and who stand ready to support one another in making that vision a reality. Each person working on the development team has a

FIGURE 1-3 The Fund-Raising Family

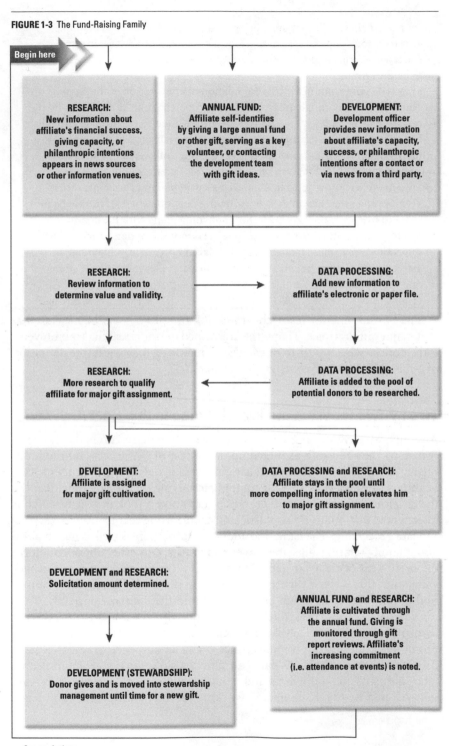

Source: Authors

role in supporting one another and the mission. This same fund raiser told us that data processing is not just updating an address. It is the first stage in cultivating a donor.

Gift Processing: Every nonprofit has an obligation to accurately record gifts received. Donor records with reliable gift totals and well-maintained links to foundations, corporations, and matching gifts are the next critical point for research. Not only do those accurate records serve as a point of cultivation for the donors, they are a gateway to identifying the next major gift donors. Gift processing also provides research with daily or weekly gift reports to review for outstanding gifts. The gift processors are the other members of the righteous circle researchers cultivate.

Annual Fund: This division of the fund-raising effort concentrates exclusively on getting gifts of any size from donors on a yearly basis. This division uses mail and telephone campaigns as well as volunteers who will make personal solicitations to meet annual fund goals. For research, the donors who give to the annual fund today may be the major gift prospects of tomorrow. The annual fund is giving donors an opportunity to practice their philanthropy on a regular basis. Additionally, donating is a way of affiliating with an organization, another way to be connected. The annual fund gardeners are, in fact, "growing" philanthropists. In sophisticated fund-raising operations, young up-and-comers are given a priority position in the annual fund pool. This might involve asking them for gifts at the highest level of annual fund giving, just below the major gift level, each time they are contacted. A large out-of-pocket gift from a telephone or a mail solicitation is a signal to research that this donor may have even greater potential. Many researchers consider the annual fund solicitation or "ask" to be a sort of proving ground for potential major gift donors.

The Major Gifts Development Team: If you were asked to name your closest relatives, whom would you name? Your parents or spouse? Your siblings or children? Your very best friend? At work, a researcher's closest relatives are on the development team. The major gifts development officers, or fund raisers, are charged with contacting prospective major gift donors, building a close relationship for the organization and the donor through a planned cultivation, and then asking the donor to provide financial support to the organization. Finding prospective donors is wedded to needing someone to cultivate them for a gift. It is impossible (and maddening) to try to track the progress of each prospective donor identified alone. A fundamental faith in the partnership research has with development is imperative. The flash points in any marriage—respect, trust, and faith—are often used to describe the nurtured or floundering relationship between research and development. Like all good relationships, there is an ebb and flow in the intensity between research and development. And like all good relationships, research and development rely on the strength and commitment of both partners to succeed. The fund raisers are holding hands with the researchers in the righteous circle we are building.

A Research Roadmap to Major Gifts

We have looked at research's role in the history of fund raising. We have outlined the mission of prospect research, folding in a few concepts and definitions along the way. Now let's place research in the journey a nonprofit takes to reach its full stature in a community, a position of service and value.

It is rare to hear about a nonprofit that adds a research component at startup. Usually the fund-raising imperative, the mission, is engineering the train, and the founders cannot imagine a need for research. Will donors not be standing in line to give to this worthy cause? This euphoria lasts for awhile, perhaps a few years, during the years in the basement of a church, the back of a storeroom, or in a rented building. The turning point is often when the organization faces underfunded programs or imminent building construction. When a nonprofit needs to erect a building or finance a program upon which people have begun to rely, suddenly there are not enough prospective donors. Where can a nonprofit find more donors? Well, research is at its best identifying new prospective donors. The gifts being given in the geographical or topical community are readily tracked through research. The names of the wealthiest constituents in a donor pool float to the top when the pool is segmented and analyzed by a trained researcher.

But a young nonprofit might still resist an investment in research. The math formula, although profoundly simple, is elusive. Remember: Spending one dollar on research nets a return of many, many dollars in major gift opportunities. Some researchers will tell you that they return the cost of their position to their nonprofit each year when they find one or two major gift donors. But since young nonprofits often look first to their own founders and to foundations for support, research can be delayed another year or two. Foundations clearly spell out their giving priorities and even indicate the range of gifts they typically give. They set a schedule for applicants and will often coach a development team through gift-getting. But this is "the terrible toos" for both the nonprofit and the foundation—too many needs, too few foundations, too little opportunity for continued support. Foundation support represents about 10 to 20 percent of total gifts raised annually at mature nonprofits. The percentage may be greater in small, new nonprofits, but it is doomed to drop off. Foundations, by their very nature, spread the wealth. They rarely continue to support a single organization at a level that sustains the organization. Many foundations encourage nonprofits to view their gifts as launching points. Some prominent foundations make gifts contingent on the nonprofit raising a similar (or even greater) amount from its constituents.

The nonprofit showing strength and resilience continues to spread its fund-raising wings. It will begin to look to individuals for support. Trustee selection skills are fine-tuned as the imperative shifts from the initial dream to the roll-up-your-sleeves programming. Trustees who share the vision and who are philanthropic are sought. Trustees who can demonstrate both intellectual or spiritual leadership and philanthropic leadership are pursued. Research can identify these individuals. As the nonprofit's reliance on foundation gifts wanes and the importance of support from individual donors rises, initiating a research component becomes mandatory. Our worlds have grown vast and complex. Only research can uncover the hierarchy of wealth in our donor communities today.

Many nonprofits experience a period of rapid growth as the development team, including research, is established and flourishes in its tasks and goals. There is a rush to implement programs, build buildings, hire staff. It is at this point that many nonprofits plan their first formal fund-raising campaign. Experienced development teams will tell you that a campaign is nearly half over by the time it "goes public." The success of a campaign is virtually ensured by the planning and strategy work done years before the campaign kick-off reception. The core of that work involves database screenings, peer screenings, months and even years of identifying prospects and building the donor pool through research, long before the first campaign gift is processed.

As the institution grows, its need for support grows, too. New programs, a broader mission, demand for its services and a greater sophistication as it ages combine to present new challenges. New programs mean a whole new group of potential donors from whom those programs will draw attention. The sheer increase in the size of the mission means that the donor pool will have to grow deeper. New campaigns and selective fund-raising efforts will follow. Just as this nonprofit reaches the strongest point in its history, the economic times will change, the need for its services will shift, and a new agenda will have to emerge. The organization's charter supporters will age and even die. They will leave their mark, their legacy, in the gifts they planned to survive them through trusts and bequests. Their potential as legacy donors was often identified through research.

And now we are back home again. New prospective donors will have to be identified. The community in which this nonprofit lives has grown. There is new young wealth in town, looking for causes to support. This strong nonprofit is providing an integral service to its community. It will be difficult for anyone to remember when this nonprofit was young or how the community got along without it. The lives of those served by it are changed, as are the lives of those who have been offered the chance to support its mission. And what helped facilitate this transformation of people and community? Hand in hand, prospect research and development did.

Fitting Prospect Research into Your Organization

You are excited about prospect research now, right? If you are a new researcher who is reading this from a large, established nonprofit, you now know the importance of your mission. If you are reading this from a small nonprofit that is just beginning a research unit, the good fortune of establishing that unit is yours. If you are reading this book because you are thinking about adding research to your nonprofit, you are on the right track. Ask yourself—and your organization's leaders and board members—the following questions:

1. Is there funding to support a research function? Adequate funding includes salary and benefits for the researcher(s), money for training, and a budget from which to buy resources. This formula assumes that your organization has already made a commitment to an electronic donor database to manage and track prospective donors.

2. Is there a support system for research in place? Are there staff members who will process data and gifts, write grants, and steward donors? Hiring a lone researcher does not mean that you get an individual who can do all those jobs, too. If your nonprofit plans to use a researcher this way, little research will get done.

3. Is your board comfortable with the concept of prospect research? Young boards filled with people who believe in your nonprofit but who are unfamiliar with philanthropy may be inexperienced with the art of identifying, cultivating, and soliciting major gift donors. Those board members can be educated. Are they ready?

4. Is the leadership of your organization prepared to support and nurture research? Nonprofit administrators are usually fund raisers, too. If your nonprofit has been busy with other startup tasks, can your leadership switch to fund raising now? Are there people in place who can cultivate major gift donors and ask them for sizable gifts? Once the prospect research unit is identifying and qualifying major gift possibilities, you will be surprised how quickly the stack of prospective donors will pile up. Someone must be ready to ask those constituents for gifts. If they are not, everyone on the team will become disillusioned.

5. Is your nonprofit ready to receive, manage, and honor large gifts? If it is not, the first gifts received may be among the last.

Your answers to these questions will form an assessment of your organization's need for research. Your answers will also be good indicators of your nonprofit's readiness to make a commitment to prospect research and its readiness for a successful major gifts program. If your organization is ready, a new era of support is about to begin.

A Good Time for Ethics

"It's not about me!"
—Personal mission statement of Rich Blair, president of Western Paging; *Washington CEO,*
October 1998, letters, p. 3.

"If I can find it, doesn't that mean it's publicly available information?"

"Shouldn't I do whatever my supervisors tell me to do?"

"The development team ought to know this—it's juicy!"

"If I tell them who I am when I telephone for information, it might get back to the donor."

"But they told me that it is alright to collect this information."

"I have to get *some* information, don't I?"

"It's okay to look at this guy's performance review—one of the company's employees gave it to me."

"I am not the boss around here—why should I have to propose the privacy policies?"

Our times are full of ethical battles. Story after story tells the tale of leaders betraying the trust given them, money misused, relationships abused, and the uninformed exploited. Every profession faces the mandate to establish a set of standards, an ethical way of operating that closely follows—or goes beyond—the intrinsic values of the culture. The questions and statements at the start of this chapter represent a few of the struggles of prospect research. Information that is private can sometimes be murky with regard to what is publicly available. The rush of our electronic times makes information available that was once private, only to have it disappear from availability a moment or two later. Those unfamiliar with what is available think that everything is obtainable and, worse, that they must have it all. The rare insecure fund raiser wants more and more information in order to go into a

23

donor meeting "armed." A stockpile of information becomes a substitute for the confidence it takes for a fund raiser to uncover much of the same information through conversation. In this section we will examine the reason for ethical considerations in our profession and why prospect researchers stand at the center of this struggle. We will begin by examining the role researchers have as information gatherers and analyzers as well as the emergence of information as a touchstone of development. These topics will lead us to our discussion of ethics and privacy and the policies you will develop, review, or update.

Why a Struggle? The Modern Times of Gatherers and Storers

Research has a strange role on the development team. As gatherers and analyzers of information, researchers are often labeled as the people in the fund-raising office who know everything. Quite a seat to sit in, right? Well, you do not want that throne and, in fact, you must convince your development team that you do not actually know *everything*. You will only accept a reputation of knowing as much as you can about major gift acquisition and wealth identification. To development officers, that may seem like the same as knowing everything. It is hard to shake the know-it-all reputation. Members of your development team will ask that you, the information maven, find out who won the 1965 World Series, how many hospitals there are in Paris, and other questions seemingly far removed from prospect research.

Between locating the capital of Madagascar or who invented balloons, the researcher, by default, becomes not only the gatherer but also the curator of information. In a museum or art gallery, a curator is responsible for overseeing a collection. The curator often becomes the collection's guardian or, at the very least, its best advocate. The curator is charged with designing the process for handling, sharing, and storing the collection. This is a good description of prospect research's role in the management of information in the fund-raising environment. In this data-driven era, collecting information effectively approaches an art. What precisely is important to know? More accurately, what is important to know to facilitate the acquisition of major gifts? Let's examine these issues on our way to developing an ethical approach to information gathering, management, and dissemination.

The Gallery of Giving: Curating Fund-Raising Stories

Curators are deeply attached to history. The history of art, culture, and science are housed and pampered in museums and galleries. The treatment of collections and how those treasures are shared with the museum's constituency is the very lifeblood of a museum. Development has a similar mandate. The information gathered by research forms a biographical sketch of a donor's relationship with a nonprofit. In fact, the information about intentions, gifts, beneficiaries, and recognition becomes each donor's philanthropic history. The philanthropic mark left by donors through their gifts is the development researcher's universe. It is precisely what research collects, analyzes, and maintains.

Surprising things happen along the way to gathering and maintaining this collection. Research, almost accidentally, assembles the even broader history of the entire organization. The fund-raising history of a nonprofit closely reflects the evolution of its place in a community. The funding and construction of buildings, the growth of the endowment, the support for new and innovative programs—each of these milestones is recorded and saved by research. In fact, research almost incidentally assembles a history of the entire nonprofit community in which this particular fund-raising effort resides. Gifts to other institutions, the founding of symphonies, food banks, and schools, and the role key people played in these projects in their growing communities—all of these events are recorded in the information prospect researchers gather.

The greatest wealth for any organization—for-profit or nonprofit organizations—is in the wealth of information available and the wise way in which that information is converted to knowledge and applied to a worthwhile process. "Information is more important than steel," the general manager of a pipe production company declared in Forbes in 1999 (*Forbes,* May 17, 1999, p. 322). In the corporate world, information is money. Information applied to the marketing plan, product development, and other aspects of business can mean the difference in which company gets a contract, which startup secures financial backing, and when a corporation enjoys exponential growth.

It is the same in the fund-raising community. Information leads to support. A casual networking approach to fund raising that only involves who knows who no longer serves most nonprofits. Our communities are too big and too full of strangers. Our population is mobile and fluid. Wealth is mobile and fluid, too. The old stereotypes that spelled out for whom and when wealth emerges fell like dominoes throughout the 1980s and 1990s. There is no longer a handy roadmap to the wealthy in our communities. Not long ago, one grand dame told us, "I simply don't know who has the money in town anymore. It's all changed. The concert halls and theatres are full of young people with money who are not related to anyone!"

Cultivation, Corporate-Style

To maximize the opportunity to succeed, corporate and government leaders formally prepare for each business encounter. Whether the potential dealmaker is going to buy 10,000 yo-yos or sign a peace treaty, the art of cultivation involves learning enough about a prospective partner so the pending deal, not the players' differences, becomes the central focus of the encounter. Many cultures now take this advance preparation as a point of respect. It is efficient and thoughtful, cutting out time that would be wasted bumbling through proposals that are inappropriate or misdirected. It lets the parties involved know that they value one another, that they clearly put each other at an elevated point in the hierarchy of business encounters.

When prospect research is a part of the major gift formula, development has this same option. Development professionals can use their time most effectively because the information tools in the ready hands of corporations are now part of fund-raising research. But what information is useful in identifying, defining, and closing major gifts? In an era in our planet's history when nearly any type of information might become available, what should research collect? Gathering any and all information, we have already learned, does not reflect the mandate for efficiency inherent in the mission of prospect research. Our discussion now moves beyond issues of efficiency.

What Prospect Research is *Not*

Gathering information for corporate agendas reaches into realms unfamiliar to fund-raising professionals, including prospect researchers. Corporate researchers profile not only prospective clients but also competitors. Some corporate research involves a sort of intrigue that would never be a part of fund-raising research. Company secrets, new product details, marketing plans—all of these elements that are vulnerable to theft may fall into the corporate research arena. In the 1990s, prospect researchers flirted with the similarities between their research and the corporate research known as competitive intelligence. It turns out, though, that competitive intelligence professionals spend their time concentrating on incidences of *competition*—collecting and analyzing information about competitors—while prospect researchers spend their time concentrating on opportunities for *cultivation* within their own organization. The distinction here is, once again, a relationship originating in contention or in common interest. The starting point, *the mission,* for research is bound to have an impact on the work.

Another information-gathering profession sometimes tossed into prospect research's extended family is private detective or investigative work. Nowadays, "researchers"—more aptly, agents—in this line of work are involved in electronic "stakeouts" for information instead of the old-fashioned surveillance that involved sitting in a car with hours-old coffee, binoculars, and a camera. In fact, these investigators serve commercial clients too, uncovering corporate espionage, contract breaches, theft rings, and more.

Sleuths, spies, and snoops. Hearing what prospect researchers do, people outside of fund raising will sometimes use these words to describe our work. Even colleagues in fund raising will occasionally mistake the work of prospect researchers for that aligned with detectives, competitive intelligence researchers, or spies. In fact, what do these other information-gathering professions have in common with prospect research? *Close to nothing.* Prospect researchers are no more similar to detectives and spies than they are to genome researchers. In fact, equating prospect research to detective work is a disservice to our profession. There are several key differences. In prospect research:

1. The information sought is not related to criminal activity. It is not based on broken commitments, intrigue, or disrupted relationships.
2. The position of the entities involved is not adversarial. If a prospective donor were alienated from the nonprofit, he would be unlikely to give a major gift. In most cases, it would be a waste of development's resources to concentrate on a disaffected constituent.
3. The stereotype is that some investigative research involves subterfuge. No element of prospect research involves hiding one's identity or purpose or collecting information that is not readily available to anyone. The cornerstone of the information collected by prospect researchers is public knowledge.
4. Investigators might access police records, credit reports, and other proprietary information. Prospect researchers do not use these databases. Prospect researchers have a deep respect for the donors they research and therefore they do not access information that is private or generally inaccessible to the public.
5. The stereotype is that investigators might use information channels not available to the general public to complete assignments. The stereotype is that detectives build "insider" contacts and gain access to information that is not available through regular channels by this method. Prospect research uses only resources available to anyone and collects data that can be obtained through regular channels. All of the resources used by prospect research are available to the public or are bits of information freely offered to the nonprofit by its constituency. The "insiders" prospect researchers cultivate are generally librarians, other researchers, and "grand old dames"—volunteers who can pave the way to information.

Miss Marple, Columbo, Dalgliesh—that is not prospect research. Sorry, no shabby trench coats, break-ins, or wire taps in this profession. Instead of days full of intrigue, dodging angry clients or investigative targets, prospect researchers spend their hours building stories of great financial success and the people changing the present and the future of entire communities through their generosity. A development officer we know once said that she saw her job as helping people shape their philanthropic futures. Research points her toward the people interested in doing just that.

Researcher, Know Thyself

As you can see by this discussion, you will set the tone for the quality of the relationship your institution has with its donors by the ethical standards you develop about information gathering and analysis. Even the way you collect information will set the tone for your colleagues and your research department. Your honest and forthright approach to information gathering and to updating donor records is one of the first places you set the standard.

It is an onerous responsibility, but yours nonetheless. If you are willing to collect inappropriate information or to be deceptive on your way to that information, you will color the view the entire development team has of the potential donor—and the view they have of you. You will also put your organization at risk. Your organization will be at risk of losing donors, losing its good reputation, and losing its own good self-esteem. It may even be at risk of court action. Most of all, you will interfere with the possibility of grand philanthropic gestures.

Do not worry, you are not alone in facing these seemingly oppressive responsibilities. Researchers have struggled with these issues since they began collecting information, and experienced researchers have formed policies and procedures for the ethical gathering, keeping, and disposing of information. Several organizations working together have composed a "Donor Bill of Rights" that includes standards for information handling. You can see a copy of the "Donor Bill of Rights" at **http://www.case.org/about/donor.cfm.** The Association of Professional Researchers for Advancement (APRA) "Statement of Ethics" was developed for all prospect researchers, information collectors, and managers of nonprofit institutions. APRA's membership application includes a signatory agreement to the ethics statement. You can find APRA's "Statement of Ethics" in the appendix section of this book. Other researchers have developed and shared their ethics or policy statements. Some of these are accessible through the researchers' electronic discussion group, PRSPCT-L. Directions for joining PRSPCT-L, where you will find these documents, are also in the appendix section. You can adopt these guidelines and procedures as your institution's policies. You can also adapt these models and add other restrictions that are appropriate to the specific fund-raising mission of your institution.

By now you realize that your own value system will play a key role in the quality of the research you do. It will be important for you to explore your feelings on the issues we are discussing and to develop not only opinions but also a formal position on these topics. You will be challenged many times during the course of your work as a researcher. You will be challenged by the availability of inappropriate or invasive information. You will be challenged by your development colleagues' desire for more information. You will be challenged by the mandate to find new prospects and to qualify the capacity of known prospects. You may even be challenged by an erosion of security, access, and information disposal policies. It will be up to you to construct responses to these challenges and to maintain a clear idea of what is right to do and what is not.

In baseball, a player faces a similar job with each at-bat. The batter must not let a pitched ball get over home plate without trying to send it back out to the playing field, thus staying in the game until the right pitch comes. Home plate is a fort and fans urge the batter, "Protect the plate!" The batter keeps his team in the game by swinging the bat over and over again, catching a piece of any ball grazing the strike zone. When it comes to your organization's fund-raising tradition, you the researcher are incited to "protect the plate." If you are pitched an ethically close call, you will get that bat off your shoulder and swing. The worst you will do is foul it off. By protecting your nonprofit with the standards you help your team create, nothing will get past home plate, an honorable legacy of philanthropy for your donors.

What's Left to Collect?

By this point you are probably wondering if there is any information left to collect and what precisely it might be. Take heart because there is still plenty of information that is public, constituent-generated, and accessible. Let's outline the key types of information that form the framework for an ethical approach to prospect research.

1. Private Information

Free societies throughout the world value privacy. As soon as a government moves away from a democratic model, leaders seem to place less value on privacy. A state of paranoia or invasive control of the citizenry begins to preclude an individual's ability to maintain privacy about certain things. In this way, privacy becomes a barometer of the state of a democracy. Do the citizens continue to have the right to keep to themselves? Do they choose their own religion, friends, and political persuasions without interference from the government? In the United States, certain issues about privacy are protected in the Bill of Rights and the amendments to the Constitution. For example, these include limitations to a police search of one's property and the general right to expect no government interference while pursuing a reasonable lifestyle. Privacy breaches continue to appear on court dockets for resolution, therefore, issues of privacy must be considered dynamic, changing and adapting to the changes in our culture.

At the same time, we live in an era where people are giving up their privacy in record numbers. News stories report voyeuristic or narcissistic incidences nearly every day. Some individuals willingly fling their privacy aside when they mount cameras in their homes to track their own movements and post them on their Internet sites. By the millions, people are constructing Internet sites to share their hobbies, family dynamics, jobs, and more with anyone who finds the Web address. We hand our credit cards, telephone numbers, and Social Security numbers over to purveyors without breaking stride. We fill out postcard surveys that ask what magazines we read, where we shop, how many people live with us, how they are related, and what our household income is. What does this mean to prospect research? Does it mean that we are in an information free-for-all? Does it forecast a fast-approaching time when prospect researchers will be able to collect anything they are inclined to uncover? No. This is what it means: Researchers must be ever more diligent about the kind of information they collect. What is available does not set the standard for what we ought to retrieve. Researchers have to continually clarify the information boundaries, pressing to focus on the information that facilitates major gift cultivation, that is respectful of the potential donor, and that recognizes the information-gathering partnership between research and development. Researchers must have a clear sense of what is private information, unavailable or unimportant to them or to their development colleagues (see Exhibit 2-1).

Exhibit 2-1   **What is Private Information?**

Private information, information unavailable to researchers includes:

- Salaries of people who work for privately-held companies
- Stock holdings in privately-held companies
- Stock holdings of anyone but the top five officers, directors, or those holding 5 percent or more of the stock of a publicly-held company
- Income tax records for individuals or private companies
- Drivers license records
- Trust agreements
- Medical and psychiatric records
- The names of donors of anonymous gifts
- Academic records such as grades or disciplinary actions
- Police records
- Sealed court records
- Credit reports on individuals

Source: Authors

Although we live in an age where people willingly give up their privacy and corporations and governments ask for pieces of information traditionally viewed as private, invasions of privacy are alarming people nonetheless. The sense of alarm has been heightened by a significant change in the availability of information in recent years: Electronic access has put a great deal of information within the reach of anyone with a computer and a modem. New ways of collecting information, particularly from Internet users—electronic product registrations which include income and other personal information, software that tracks which Web pages were visited, profiling at the individual level based on electronic purchases, even hacking—raise red flags for privacy advocates and for people who have never given privacy much thought.

This sense of alarm hastens a broader and urgent discussion of privacy issues. It launches a reexamination about what information has traditionally been available within organizations and to the public. For example, in 2000, legislators began to review precisely what information from hospital admission records is available to other departments within a hospital. Hospital fund raisers have relied on contact information from patient registrations to build solicitation lists since an organization's best supporters are usually found among those that have used its services. This issue and others, such as access to college admission records, will continue to be evaluated as privacy in our fast-moving, electronic society becomes an even larger issue. The issues surrounding electronic tracking and profiling of Web users is virtually unexplored. Its impact on our culture is unassessed. It looms as perhaps the largest issue in the privacy debate in the years to come.

2. Public Information, Part One

The flipside of privacy in U.S. society—and soon, across the globe—is a standard of openness regarding certain kinds of information. This openness is called *transparency*—the concept that a company or individual postures itself so that you can see *through* or *into* it. A government term, "*sunshine laws,*" alludes to letting "the sun shine in" on certain information by making that information available for collecting or comparison. Once again, to guard against power winding up in the hands of a few, government has enacted safeguards. The goal is to protect those who would be affected by improper tax collecting, illegal investments, or other business matters. The regulations primarily involve registrations, taxes, and profit-making where public investors are involved (see Exhibit 2-2).

Exhibit 2-2 **What is Public Information? Government-Mandated "Sunshine" and More**

- Real estate assessments for residential and commercial properties
- Contributions to political campaigns
- Salaries of elected officials
- Salaries, by classification, of government and military workers
- Salaries of the top five officers of publicly-held companies
- Stock holdings of the top five officers, the directors, and other insiders (those holding 5 percent or more of the company) of publicly-held companies
- Basic state registration information for corporations and foundations
- Basic state registration information for individuals in certain professions
- Purchase price of publicly-held companies or of privately-held companies purchased by publicly-held companies
- Tax filings for charitable foundations
- Certain court records (wills, divorce decrees)

Source: Authors

For example, real estate assessments are made public so that taxpayers are protected from unfair tax burdens on a particular neighborhood or section of town. Foundations are required to file public reports about the distribution of their assets to charities, since law mandates that they give away a certain percentage of those assets. Public companies, supported by the funds of thousands or millions of investors in the form of stock purchases, are required by law to reveal the way they use that investment. They do this by publishing financial information in a variety of U.S. Securities and Exchange Commission (SEC) documents. The information shared with the public in these documents includes the return on the investment, the expenses met and paid, and the compensation given to chief officers and directors. Much of the information described here is available through federal or local government sources. Sometimes the information is aggregated by information sellers and provided to the public in paper directories, CD-ROMS, and through online sources.

Requiring these information sets to be accessible to the public provides a web of protection for all citizens. Incidentally, this information forms the core of data gathered by prospect research. This public information is ethical and reasonable to gather. This information is readily available to the public. From this information, researchers make conclusions or predictions about financial capacity and gift-making ability.

3. Public Information, Part Two

There are other types of information available through public sources. Stories touting the accomplishments of individuals, companies, and foundations form the subject of press releases and news articles. These may be stories about mergers, awards, new leadership, large philanthropic gifts, or new programs. They may include information about the number of employees, gross sales, and the founders of private companies. Other information made public includes milestone events such as births, marriages, and deaths. Life stories of prominent and financially successful people are captured and shared through news stories, magazine articles, and books. Often these stories contain both the successes and the tragedies that make up every life. Many times they offer insight into what motivates a person and what his goals are for the legacy he intends to leave.

The information from these resources, freely shared or the result of a life lived in the public eye, forms the second information set critical to the prospect researcher's work (see Exhibit 2-3). These life stories, milestone events, and other biographical portraits are intrinsic to the benefit research provides to the fund-raising process. The stories often outline critical elements in qualifying prospective donors or in timing the gift request. A researcher develops an "eye" for the worthwhile stories. Not all of the stories printed are accurate or even factual. Many of the stories deal in a level of minutia that has no intrinsic value for fund raising. Many stories do not contribute to the relationships your organization is building with its constituents. Some stories are exploitive or even slanderous. It is up to you to determine each of these things, holding respect for the constituent and for your organization as the gauge for the decisions you make.

Exhibit 2-3	Public Information: Other Sources

- Birth, marriage, and death announcements
- Press releases
- News stories
- Magazine and journal stories
- Books
- Internet databases of professional groups and other lists
- Donor rolls from other nonprofit organizations
- Director and trustee lists from other nonprofit and for-profit organizations
- Company and individual Web sites
- Biographical sketches posted in directories
- Company contact, performance, and leadership information published by information aggregators

Source: Authors

4. Constituent-Generated Information

Constituents and others share information about themselves with development officers. Constituents are their own best storytellers. They tell development officers about their interests, their intentions, and their ability to support causes. Development departments gather this information during visits and telephone calls. It is then recorded in reports that development officers write and send to the nonprofit's centralized files. The report, called a contact report, includes the date of contact, the place of contact, those present, and a narrative relating the important information that the constituent shared with the fund raiser. Usually the information is about the constituent herself, but sometimes the constituent also shares information about family, friends, and other affiliated people who might be interested in the fund-raising cause that is the purpose of the visit.

Other information the constituent generates includes his philanthropic history and precisely how he affiliates with the organization. The constituent may have shared family news for publication in the organization's constituent newsletter or completed a survey that included questions about philanthropic interests, involvement in other nonprofit or for-profit organizations, and demographic information such as household income range. Correspondence with development or other staff members may outline the depth of the constituent's sense of affiliation and his interest in the mission of the organization (see Exhibit 2-4).

Exhibit 2-4	Constituent-Generated Information

- Affiliation information (registration, ticket purchase, membership data)
- Survey responses
- Charitable donation history with your organization
- Correspondence
- Summaries of contact with staff

Source: Authors

Why would a constituent share these pieces of her life story with an institution? Prospective donors know why a fund raiser is visiting from the very start. They share their stories because they are willing to be cultivated, to share the success in which your nonprofit may have played a small role. They share their stories because they are stories worth telling and hearing, stories that often have a place in local, regional, or national histories. But even as development officers listen to these stories, they sort through the chapters and verses to strip away the parts that are not relevant to the fund-raising process. Those parts of the story stay where they were spoken and do not return to the office with the fund raiser. The other parts of the story, the parts that relate to the fund-raising process, come back to the office to appear in the contact report and cultivation plan written by the development officer. When you examine the ethics guidelines of other organizations, you will see that they usually include a process for rewriting contact reports or other filed papers that include inappropriate information. While we expect the very best from our colleagues, a systematic review of what is going to file is a safeguard for your ethics policies and your organization.

Those stories, now a part of the donor's philanthropic history you are curating, are usually housed in the nonprofit's electronic database. Depending on the type of non-profit organization, there may be other pieces of information housed in the constituent's electronic record that are not in the interest or domain of prospect research. These pieces of information may include academic grades and performance, disciplinary actions, medical or psychiatric records, and other personal data. What separates these pieces from the others? You have been developing a clear concept of this. You will by now hold a value about what should be in your constituent files and what should not be. The information that has no intrinsic value in identifying gift capacity or in securing a major gift is of no interest to research. When was the last time that your college grades had an impact on anything? Do you think years-old difficulties in a marriage should concern anyone other than the couple involved? Should the records of your visits to a doctor to treat your chronic foot infection be available to the public? *Prospect research does not support access to this level of information and therefore, were it even available, researchers would not seek it.* There are laws governing the distribution of data that would contain this information. As we discussed earlier, some of these regulations are being examined now that information is more readily available to everyone. Prospect research celebrates the discussions of privacy issues since they serve to further clarify our own ideas. Our primary goal is a respectful approach to a prospective donor, not gathering any and all information. Prospect research encourages the uncovering and resolution of evolving privacy issues.

Confidentiality: All of the information *except constituent-generated information* is from public sources. Because constituent-generated information was given expressly to your organization, you must protect the confidential nature of this information. What parts of constituent-generated information will you share? With whom? When? Nonprofits publish annual reports listing donors. Does that not amount to sharing constituent-generated information? In fact, the gifts are listed in ranges so the precise amount given, whether the gift was one of stock or property, and other particulars about the gift, are not shared with the public. These details are, in fact, the type of information that ends up in another private document—your donor's tax return. Remember, too, that all donors have the option to ask for anonymity regarding their giving. We cannot recall an incident of a nonprofit declining a gift because the donor did not wish the gift to be touted.

Publicly funded institutions or those affiliated with publicly funded organizations face extra cautions, but ones that private institutions must monitor. Privacy issues may bring legislative attention to donor records as the public's concern increases. Legislation that opens records to the public may at some point reach to the donor records of organizations that receive public funds. The confidentiality and ethics policies a nonprofit drafts should be reviewed by the organization's attorney before they are enacted.

Other personal information constituents share with development may include, for example, the names and ages of their children and grandchildren, their employment status, and the location of their vacation homes. They may not wish this information to be shared with other institutions or with the press or public. It is up to you to establish a method for maintaining the confidential nature of this information. Since it is difficult to track who wanted what held in confidence when your constituency numbers in the thousands, the best course is to keep all of this information in confidence. All staff members must be instructed on how to handle this information.

Volunteers: Many institutions rely on volunteers, usually major gift donors themselves, to assist with the cultivation of prospective donors. Volunteers serve nonprofits in many capacities (see Exhibit 2-5). They are intrinsic to the success of sophisticated fund-raising operations. First of all, volunteers are philanthropists. They are philanthropists in that they have given nonprofits large gifts. But their volunteering is also their philanthropy. They willingly give something precious many of us no longer have to give—time. Volunteers are so devoted to the mission of a nonprofit that they give their money *and* their time to promote and support that mission. And the effects that volunteers have on an institution are staggering. Volunteers help development reach many more donors. They help development reach the right donors, their peers who can give major gifts. They are one of the central reasons that complex fund-raising efforts continue year after year. They are the very best example of the benefits of philanthropy. Volunteers radiate the emotional and spiritual wealth garnered from a generous approach to life. By this virtue, volunteers are points of leverage when prospective donors are asked to support an institution. In fact, many fund raisers ask themselves, "To whom can this prospective donor not say no?" It is a reliable approach to emphasize the importance of the pending gift. It is a clarifying point for the prospective donor. Cold feet and donor remorse (like buyer remorse) can melt away when the philanthropic experience of a good volunteer is in the mix.

Exhibit 2-5   **Major Gifts Program Volunteers**

- Give at a major gift level
- Identify other prospective donors
- Screen lists of peers for prospective donors
- Sign fund-raising letters
- Telephone prospective donors
- Introduce prospective donors to fund raisers
- Attend cultivation meetings with prospective donors
- Suggest the solicitation amount for a major gift
- Complete the solicitation ("the Ask") for a major gift

Source: Authors

What constituent-generated information should be shared with volunteers? Each institution forms a policy about this based primarily on the depth of their use of volunteers. Are the volunteers functioning almost like employees? Are they "insiders," exposed to a level of decision-making and planning that elevates their vision of the entire process? Or are they only stepping into the fund-raising process to make a few telephone calls or lend their good name to a campaign letter? The complexity of information shared is linked to this evaluation. Regardless, the policies about confidentiality and privacy that your organization adopts and to which its employees are committed must be shared with volunteers. Volunteers must agree to those same standards to keep their "insider" status.

What's Next? You Become the Barometer

Okay, you have examined your own value system. You have thought about the boundaries of public and private information, including the not so black and white areas of news stories and constituent-provided data. You have read the policies and procedures created by other prospect researchers. You have read the "Donor Bill of Rights" and the APRA "Statement of Ethics." You have considered your institution's actual and potential use of volunteers. Now it is time to gather this information into a comprehensive document that will establish your organization's policies and procedures about information gathering, distribution, storage, and disposal. This document will then be shared with the entire development staff. It will be the standard of operation for your department. From the research perspective, the following are the areas you will cover in that document.

Gathering Information

Accuracy, Part One: As a researcher's skill at gathering information grows, she becomes more adept at determining the accuracy and relevance of information. Each researcher develops a favorite set of resources based on feedback from others in the profession, on the specific needs of the organization, and on how often what is sought is found in those resources. Are your donors primarily located in your own community? You will rely on different resources than researchers who work for multinational organizations. Regardless of where the information you seek lies, it is important to determine the reliability of the resources you are using. Is the information in agreement with that found in other resources? Does the information provider have a reliable reputation?

Privacy: What information will you not collect? You are getting a handy guide to the answer to that question here. As you develop your policies and procedures, you may wish to spell that out. This chapter and the resources in the appendix section give you a good outline for this part of your document.

Accuracy, Part Two: In addition to outlining what is available and appropriate to retrieve from public information sources, this is your opportunity to discuss precisely what research can conclude from the information gathered. It would be a good time to examine the expectations of your organization in regard to a few issues involving wealth evaluation. In some cases, you will be bringing salary, bonus, stock holdings, and real estate assessment information into the discussion. How can these numbers be added and multiplied to tell development officers what size gift to ask of a prospective donor? Can we foretell the precise capacity of a prospective donor by these numbers? Can researchers determine net worth? Researchers, of course, know that they cannot. Fund raisers, of course, wish that researchers would and could. When researchers try to assess capacity by pulling and pushing the numbers retrieved, they are practicing the art of research and not the science. It is simply not true to say that a prospective donor has a net worth of $1 million or $1 billion when you do not know and cannot discover the other side of the constituent's financial picture, his debts. We will discuss this in detail in chapter 5. In the meantime, keep in mind that how you manipulate numbers is an issue of ethics. How you communicate those numbers to development officers becomes an issue of ethics.

Respect: In addition to information that is written in commercial publications or available from government sources, the development team will have access to another type of information. The source for much of the information in this category is encounters with constituents. As we discussed, some information shared by constituents is reliable and valuable to the cultivation process. Another class of information could be called hearsay, rumor, and innuendo. During visits with constituents or others, development officers will sometimes be burdened with stories that do not advance the cause of philanthropy. They will be regaled with stories of family intrigues, faults and flaws, jealousies, and even more serious trespasses. The greatest danger in repeating, or worse, recording these stories, is that they are usually from the perspective of only some the people in the drama and, by that circumstance, inaccurate. They are sometimes slanderous. They often have value only in affording the storytellers the chance to unburden themselves. The ethics document your organization adopts must include guidelines about these types of stories.

Storing Information

After deciding what you will collect, you—the curator—will need a safe place to store it. The integrity of the information will be preserved when someone has control over access. Who accesses the information, where they may take it, how it is returned, what may be copied—all of these issues must be governed by policy. Information storage policies must cover both paper and electronic information. Although it is easy to see and track the location of paper, it is difficult to trace the trail electronic information takes after it leaves your domain. At the same time, it is easier to share information electronically—it happens by tapping a key or two on your computer keyboard. That information you send can move from where you sent it to places beyond the recipient you targeted and even beyond your institution.

Being mindful of the greater vulnerability of electronic information, your organization must decide what information can be shared in this manner. Those receiving electronic information must be trained in storage issues. The integrity of your organization's entire electronic system will be a factor in your decisions. Is the organization protected from electronic intrusion? What steps are in place for monitoring and preventing information fissures?

What goes into a constituent's paper or electronic file? (See Exhibit 2-6.) Most of this is determined by the policies you establish about what you will collect. Since others in your organization, including volunteers, will generate material that goes to file, a monitoring procedure will be necessary. Who will review new material periodically to make sure that it conforms to the established policies? How will new staff members and volunteers be trained regarding these policies? What will occur when the policy is broken? Your organization must establish policies regarding each of these circumstances.

Exhibit 2-6	What Goes in a Donor's File?

- Correspondence
- News stories
- SEC information
- Portions of donor rolls from other organizations
- Gift records
- Biographical data
- Contact reports

Source: Authors

Confidential Information on the Loose: Privacy Horror Stories

Organizations that fail to develop ethics and confidentiality policies are vulnerable to disastrous accidents and even dangerous failures that are not accidents. Horror stories whose star is confidential information discovered in the wrong place quickly reach folklore status among researchers. Stories about violations of confidentiality and mishandling of private information strike fear in researchers' hearts because researchers know that these mishaps were, for the most part, avoidable. The damage done to an organization whose donor files appear in the newspaper or on the five o'clock news is immeasurable. Stories we have heard include:

- Files that disappear from the central file repository and surface in the apartment of the development officer who quit and moved away months ago
- Files that disappear and never surface (this one is worse than reappearing files)
- A new employee who was reported to be talking loudly in the institution's cafeteria on a lunch break about the wealth of specific donors
- Information about a donor sent to the wrong volunteer, to a constituent who has a name similar to that of the volunteer
- Confidential information sent electronically to the wrong email address
- Confidential information sent electronically and left in the "Attachments" folder when the computer is passed on to workers in another department or organization
- Donor records discarded in the paper recycling box that was then taken to the local daycare to be used as scrap paper
- The overturned trash truck that spills confidential academic and donor records from the local college
- Hospital records found in cardboard boxes, awaiting trash pickup, by the side of a rural road
- Laptop computers stolen (and the donor information stored on the hard drives stolen along with them).

How can you save your institution from a fate like those described? It is simple. Encourage the leadership to establish information storage procedures and policies that will prevent these disasters. To do so, your organization will:

1. Lock files that contain donor records or lock the room the files are in. If locking the files is not feasible, an overseer can monitor access to the files.
2. Train all personnel, including volunteers and student or temporary helpers, in information handling, storing, and disposal procedures.
3. Establish procedures for erasing confidential information from discarded computers.
4. Provide a location for appropriate information disposal.
5. Form a check-in and check-out procedure for paper files. Establish who will monitor adherence to the policy by spot-checking the files.
6. Establish an exit procedure for departing employees where they surrender their passwords; passwords are changed; and where all the files checked out to those employees are returned.
7. Create a document that will outline all of these procedures. Have all employees, volunteers, and student helpers who have access to confidential information read and sign this document.
8. Make each individual's access to information or their employment dependent on adherence to the ethics policies.

Distributing Information

Who will have access to the information you gather? Will everyone have the same access? What form will the information take when it is distributed? The development team, the heads of your organization, key volunteers, and the donor are among those who will have access to some or all of the information you collect and store.

You may establish a hierarchy of confidentiality about information. First of all, confidential or limited-access documents must be so marked. Many organizations include a document header such as "Confidential: For Development use only—please shred these materials."

Distribution to volunteers: Just like development officers, volunteer fund raisers need to be prepared to meet with donors so that each meeting is effective and meaningful. If your organization's structure includes volunteers whose duties are similar to those of staff members, it will be important to outline what information will be available to them. It is common for volunteers to receive less information than the nonprofit's employees receive. Since volunteers are actually the peers of the donors they solicit, the donor's detailed giving record and other financial information might be withheld from the volunteer. Research and the development staff have used that information to qualify the constituent with major gift potential and to determine the precise gift to pursue. Since this work has already been completed when the volunteer solicitor enters the process, there may be no reason to share that level of information with the volunteer.

Sharing information with volunteers prompts discussion of another aspect of the ethics policy you are developing. Most major gift donors realize that they are being formally tracked and cultivated by the development team. If they have served as volunteers, they have seen a summary of information about the prospective donors they are asked to cultivate and solicit. At some point, a donor may ask your organization to share his own file with him. You will be well prepared to do this, since you have only filed things that are public information, factual, and useful in cultivating the donor and securing a major gift. The file you have compiled, in fact, has become a philanthropic biography, a celebration of your donor's financial success and generous approach to life. Each donor who requests access to their own file should be granted that access. Your position on donor access to his own file must be a part of your ethics policies.

Disposal

What will you do with donor documents that you no longer need? This portion of your policies will be easy to write. You'll need a two-word sentence: "Shred everything." Shred any record that includes financial information. Shred all records that include donors' names, addresses, and telephone numbers. Can you remember each and every donor who has shared an unlisted telephone number with your development staff? No, so shred them all. Shred records that include the names of family members and their birth dates. Did you get that information from the donor, in information that was meant only for your institution? You cannot remember? Shred it.

There are companies that will leave a secure bin at your location and then pick up the material to be shredded and disposed of properly. If this is not an option, portable shredders in many price ranges are available from office supply stores. Each staff member should be instructed to keep a separate trash receptacle nearby so that "to be shredded" documents head to the shredder and not to recycling or the garbage bins.

The Home Stretch

If you are the first researcher at a young nonprofit, you are in luck. You get to be the person who establishes the ethics code for your organization before any bad habits become a tradition. If you are a new researcher at an old institution that has managed to stay in business without an ethics code, you may face significant obstacles as you bring ethics issues forward. You will do yourself and the donors you research a disservice if you shy from this task. You will also do your organization a disservice, since it will continue to sit in a dangerously vulnerable position.

Make time now to create your institution's ethics code. If your nonprofit has an established code, your fresh eyes can evaluate how effective it is and whether it is actually being used. It may fail to address advances in information distribution and disposal as well as staff training issues that go hand-in-hand with those technological advancements. Randomly pull donor files and use our simple ethics checklist to evaluate the content of those files (see Exhibit 2-7).

Exhibit 2-7	Ethics Checklist

- Is it public?
- Is it accurate?
- Is it respectful?
- Is it important to donor cultivation?
- Is it important to securing the gift?

Source: Authors

You may discover that the research department is actually the designated monitor of these policies. It does not add much to your responsibilities, since reading materials about prospects is among your regular duties. If you are the monitor of old files, have a broad-point pen at hand to blacken inappropriate information you find in files. Ask development officers to rewrite contact reports, omitting the offensive sentences. Remove from file old papers that pre-date the organization's policies and that contain private, invasive, or gossipy information. It is a tough job, one for which you did not intend to sign on. As the curator of the information you and others have gathered and stored, it is an unavoidable task that essentially becomes your organization's annual physical. You may find that, as your organization realizes the value of a healthy information system, the service you provide to the cause of ethics will be valued, too. One thing about ethics, though—it does not matter if anyone else values them since they have their own intrinsic value. There is no clearer way to state it than to say that they simply make you feel good.

You will use your best negotiating and peace-making skills to create and enforce the ethics policy at your institution. It would be unfair to let you think that monitoring ethics policies will not involve confrontation. It is too often human nature to choose the expedient path, and some of the people with whom you work may have built their fund-raising plans on expediency. It will surprise you to discover how often your colleagues simply have not considered the security and privacy issues about which you are now knowledgeable. The good health of your organization, the quality of your job, and the celebratory nature of the philanthropic experiences you are working to facilitate for donors depend on the job you do to establish and maintain a code of ethics at your organization. As a curator of your organization's philanthropic success stories, your collection of information will hold the polish of a set of precious stones.

Ethics Exercise: What Would You Do?

It is difficult to anticipate all the circumstances that might arise for you as a researcher. This exercise will help you test your response to simple and complex dilemmas that you may encounter as a prospect researcher. Read each statement and record your responses to them.

1. Unable to locate any information at all about a prospective donor, Mary decides to get a credit report. She has noticed an Internet site that claims it will provide credit reports, drivers' licenses, and Social Security numbers for anyone. She cannot believe her luck in finding this site. She decides that it must be okay to get this information or it would not be available.

2. Jim is reviewing a donor file that goes back 60 years. As he digs deeper into the file, he discovers a copy of the donor's freshman-year performance. There is a letter in file outlining a prank in which the donor, a fraternity, and the school mascot, a donkey, were involved in 1948. The letter threatens expulsion. Jim thinks this may be just the leverage development needed with this donor.

3. Jenny telephones the prospective donor's company to find out what the constituent's job title is. When the receptionist asks who is calling, Jenny stutters and says, "I'm from the furniture store. He has applied for a loan to buy a new dining room set." Jenny does not realize that the receptionist has the Caller ID feature on her telephone.

4. Sue leaves her desk to freshen her coffee in the employee break room. Jack and Dan are there when she arrives. She hears Jack telling Dan about a donor's bout with alcohol. He and Dan are laughing about a recent incident another constituent reported. Jack finishes by saying how much fun he had writing this story in his contact report. Sue shrugs and thinks that Dan is a big boy and can make his own choices.

5. Rick hears an odd noise as he approaches the central file room. When he enters, he notices a stranger quickly closing a filing cabinet and heading to the door. As usual, the keys to the file room and the cabinets are lying next to the copy machine. Rick stops the stranger and says, "Excuse me, I don't believe we've met . . . ."

6. There are paper-recycling bins next to the copy machine at Nancy's museum. One day, Nancy is copying news stories. A copy comes out of the machine too light to read well. As Nancy places the flawed copy in the recycling bin, she notices that the paper on top of the bin's pile is a list of donors who are paying to bring a special exhibition to the gallery. The copy is light but not too light to read. Donors' names, addresses, and the precise amount given can be clearly read.

7. Karen, a former colleague, telephones Marta, the researcher at an Eastside hospital. They share news about colleagues and how Karen

likes her new boss at the hospital across town. In the course of the conversation, Karen asks if that donor from Nebraska ever gave that big gift everyone was working to secure. "How much was it? Did he wind up giving stock or cash outright?" Karen asks.

8. Steve gets an email from his supervisor telling him to cancel the shredding contract with the disposal company. Steve's boss has decided that it is overkill to pay for this service because trash is trash, and it all goes to the garbage dump. Who would care about a bunch of numbers from their little hospice organization anyway?

9. Jeff's boss is excited when he enters Jeff's office one morning. "You will be thrilled with what I got for you," he says. "I was meeting with a donor and he gave me a copy of the exact salary records of the attorneys at his firm. You'll want to get working on profiles of these people right away!"

10. Margaret insists that Greg, the researcher, can tell the development staff the net worth of all of their assigned prospects. She tells everyone that the researcher at her old job did it all the time and was rarely wrong. When pressed, she concedes that there was not a way to test the reliability of the information. She does not relent though, and repeats her expectation of research to anyone who will listen.

Answers: Well, you will not be surprised to discover that there is no answer key for this exercise. How you handle each situation (barring a response to the last one like "hit Margaret over the head with a hammer") will be dependent on your own style of problem solving. If you meet one of these situations—we should write *when* you meet one—you may choose to write an email, request a meeting with those involved, or change the course of the matter with humor. You may circulate the ethics policies you created that everyone read and signed. Regardless of your style, you will do something. That is what matters the most.

CHAPTER 3

Who are the Prospects? Definitions, Process, and Tools

"I'm only giving up nine months' earnings. It's not that big a deal."
— Ted Turner, about his gift of $1 billion to the United Nations, *The Sunday Telegraph* (London), September 21, 1997, p. 37. (Turner's net worth of $2.2 billion grew to $3.2 billion in the following nine months due to a surge in the value of his Time Warner stock.)

A Research Term by Any Other Name

When Cecilia's son was training to be a baggage handler for a regional airline, she learned about AOA, hazwopper, and marshalling planes. Thinking she had landed on another planet with no ready translation tools, she dived into the manual provided by the airline to identify the "English" versions of these industry-based terms. After we (every parent reading this knows the "we" of whom we speak) learned the airport codes for cities in five states and two countries, Cecilia was convinced that there was little sense to be made out of this insider language. Sure, she understood SEA for the Seattle-Tacoma airport and EUG for Eugene, Oregon. But YEG for Edmonton, Alberta, Canada? SJD for Los Cabos, Mexico? The reality is that every profession has its own "secret language," industry slang, or insider talk. The field of development, including research, does not escape this odd affliction. Industry slang serves as a convenient and efficient ramp to access more complex concepts. It often acts as an out-loud shorthand. Insider talk even helps build comradery within a group by elevating its members to positions "in the know." But terms and their use in the secret language can be misconstrued by the broader population. If you heard that a hazwopper was boarding your plane, you would squirm in your seat until you saw the person with the dustpan and broom heading to clean up the overhead bin spill in row 15.

Exhibit 3-1	Prospect

Prospect: A person, foundation, or corporation able to make a major gift; a prospective donor.

Source: Authors

The term prospect is used in fund raising to identify a person, foundation, or corporation with the potential to make a major gift to a nonprofit organization (see Exhibit 3-1). The term might have begun as "prospective donor" and shrunk to its shortest form through regular use. Or it might have evolved from sales terminology. Regardless, it is an apt word to describe the high status afforded potential donors in the development formula. "What are your prospects?" your mother asked when you told her about a grand job for which you had applied. Miners in the United States' old West prospected for riches and sometimes found them. Interestingly, the mining metaphor for undiscovered wealth has been embraced by development research as a perfect fit.

But some within our profession anticipate that those outside of development, especially donors, will squirm at the term "prospect." It sounds targeted. It sounds, well, mercenary. Let's be honest—it is targeted. And, in the sense that the concept defines a relationship driven by the intention for financial outcome, it is mercenary. Let's get comfortable with that idea by examining a few ideas about philanthropy and fund raising.

Work or Play?

Philanthropy—and fund raising, in particular—suffers from the "is it a business or a game?" dichotomy familiar to professional baseball. Each year when major league baseball players ask for more money or owners beg for new stadiums, the United States and Canada are thrown into a debate about the origins and intent of "the game." Is baseball a sport, played for the pleasure and enjoyment of the participants and fans? Is major league baseball a grown-up version of the sandlot game played by children? Or is baseball a business, with the same goals of making money, sharing profits, and growing financially (through price increases and product expansion) that every business has? The debate rages on year after year and, in the meantime, hundreds of millions of dollars pass among the players, team owners, major and minor league cities, the broadcast media, advertising firms, and logo licensing entities.

Philanthropy has a box seat in the same park. From a Dickensian scenario of a top-hatted gentleman offering a coin to a ragged child under a street lamp, philanthropy has grown into a wide world of financial support for opportunities to cure disease, house the homeless, feed the hungry, care for the elderly, educate the masses, and enhance lives through art, music, and theatre. What began as a very small donation to one child on a single corner multiplied into trillions of dollars in support for millions of people around the planet—and even beyond when we include causes that support advances in space exploration. Is there any other instance where we would entrust the identification, maintenance, and growth of that much in resources to a casual enterprise? No. Of course, philanthropy is a business and, as such, it works best when there is a structure in place that nourishes and supports its growth.

Does this take away from the irreplaceable moment when an individual slips a $50 bill into the hand of a food drive volunteer? Does it overshadow the moment when, after a lifetime of saving, a donor funds a scholarship for young people with few chances and plenty of hurdles? No, it doesn't. It simply enhances the opportunities for those moments of philanthropy and many others to occur.

Insider terms like development, prospect, and cultivation reflect the framework of a formula for getting to the gift-giving. And professional formulas for action often raise the standard of behavior in any endeavor. They create a pathway to reach goals, an accepted course to travel to an end. They can elevate the entire process to a higher standard of action. And a point of elevation in a process is something to celebrate.

What (and Who) is a Prospect?

Now that we have settled on the idea that we will examine the insider language of prospect research throughout this book, let's talk about prospects. Here a hierarchy of definitions begins. Prospect . . . major gift . . . cultivation period . . . one term tumbles into the next. Let's begin.

We said that a prospect is a person, foundation, or corporation able to make a major gift to your institution. A prospect is further defined by the amount of time, the *cultivation period,* that it will take for the nonprofit to get a commitment for the major gift. That prescribed cultivation period is determined by your organization. Just as the *size* of major gifts varies from institution to institution, the *time* a prospect spends in cultivation varies. Sophisticated development operations label about 18 to 24 months as the cultivation and solicitation period—the time from assignment of the prospect to receipt of the gift commitment. This must be considered a framework, not a formula. Plenty of gifts arrive in a shorter period of cultivation and some gifts take much more time to reach fruition. Although prospects can be people, foundations, and corporations, in this discussion we will concentrate our attention on people as prospects. In the next chapter, we will cover foundations and corporations as prospects.

So far, so good. Prospects are donors-to-be who can make major gifts in a timely manner. How will we decide who has the *capacity* to make a major gift? Welcome. You are now crossing the threshold into the research workshop.

Capacity reads like a noun but most prospect researchers would tell you that it is an adjective. Capacity is a collection of attributes, of financial and personal characteristics, that sketch out what only can be described as a grainy silhouette for most prospects. In a later chapter we will discuss how you will convince the development staff that this silhouette is enough to initiate contact with the prospect. In the meantime, we will scrutinize the silhouette in this chapter.

Gateways to Major Gifts

The financial characteristics that point to capacity congregate in varying, even weighted, clusters. They involve easy-to-identify features like salary and stock options for the publicly employed and more subtle markers like lifestyle or hobbies for these and other constituents. Drawn together, these financial characteristics form a structure upon which the course of cultivation unfolds. On the way to a major gift, a researcher draws a more and more detailed financial portrait of the prospect. Each portrait takes the prospect (and the researcher) through a series of gateways that lead to the grand finish, a treasured moment of philanthropy. There are five gateways that we will now visit. They are:

1. Qualifying the Prospect
2. First Contact
3. Cultivating, Tracking, and Strategizing
4. Recommending the Ask
5. Stewardship Tracking (and Here We Go Again)

Gateway One: Qualifying the Prospect

Three ingredients make up the formula for qualifying a prospect: affiliation, capacity, and interest.

Affiliation

Before you consider someone to be a prospect, you must establish through research that the "potential prospect" (many research offices use the term "suspect" here) has a link to your organization or has a reasonable likelihood of forming such a link (see Exhibit 3-2). The potential prospect will be a person who has participated in your institution's programs, responded to a request for support in the past, served your organization as a volunteer, or is related to or friendly with someone connected to your organization (see Exhibit 3-3). Of course there are other ways to measure affiliation, but these are the primary ones. Like other characteristics, affiliation is weighted. Each nonprofit must create a hierarchy of affiliates from "most closely related" to "least related." This hierarchy then becomes a point of balance for research and development to use to weigh time and resources to be spent. Other factors will combine with affiliation to shift the scale, but the affiliation hierarchy essentially remains the first important section of the gateway to pass through in qualifying potential major gift donors.

Exhibit 3-2　　**Suspect**

Suspect: A person or other entity (foundation or corporation) not yet researched but demonstrating preliminary indicators of wealth. These indicators might be an unexpected gift or a news story about a job promotion or windfall, for example.

Source: Authors

Exhibit 3-3	**Affiliate**

Affiliate: A person or entity with an existing relationship of significance with a nonprofit organization.

Source: Authors

Schools consider their best affiliates to be their alumni. Faculty, staff, and parents and grandparents of alumni, and other supporters of the school are also affiliates. They are in line after alumni (see Exhibit 3-4). A theatre company may consider season subscribers to be their best affiliates. But anyone who attends a performance or two might be considered an affiliate. Hospitals may consider people who have used their facility to be their closest affiliates. The family members of patients might follow next, with doctors and their families, community members involved with the hospital and community leaders following closely. The boards of trustees for each of these types of organizations are usually constructed from these pools of best affiliates. Trustees, of course, become an institution's very best affiliates since they serve as the closest insiders and biggest supporters of the nonprofit.

Exhibit 3-4	**Ranking Affiliates by Attachment Proximity**

Affiliates to a college ranked in order of proximity (closest to most distant):

- Trustees
- Alumni who graduated and are current donors
- Alumni who attended but did not graduate but who are current donors
- Friends (board members, faculty, staff, other non-alumni) who are current donors
- Alumni who graduated who are not donors
- Parents of current students who are or are not donors
- Parents of former students who are current donors
- Alumni who attended but did not graduate and are not donors
- All other non-donors

Source: Authors

Prominent or wealthy people in a community are often considered affiliates before they actually attend an event or sign up for a class. Many nonprofits anticipate that those individuals will use their services and so add them to their prospect lists. It is assumed that wealthy but unaffiliated people will enter the local hospital, attend plays and art exhibition openings, and look for opportunities locally to express their philanthropic spirit. Each nonprofit would like those prominent people to learn about its mission, hoping that it will match their own philanthropic dreams. This is a reasonable goal, but each development team must carefully calculate the time and effort to be spent on this sort of "long-shot" cultivating. Remember our research mantra: to use the first philanthropic dollar to efficiently identify and secure the next dollars. We are stewards of the funds already donated, a nest-building spot in the philanthropic chain. It is our mission to multiply the resources through wise investment. Our resources are time and energy. They need to be spent in a way that maximizes the likelihood of the greatest return.

Good research involves *strategy*. As every winning baseball coach will tell you, play your best hitters first. Look first for prospects among those most closely affiliated with your organization. Unaffiliated people are more difficult to place in the research lineup, and it is more difficult to predict their support. The super-wealthy, not affiliated with your nonprofit, are often the source of stratosphere-level gifts to the nonprofits with which they affiliate. Can you imagine how many prospect lists at nonprofits around the world included Microsoft founder Bill Gates' name in the last five or ten years? Those billionaire donors may not be affiliated with your nonprofit today, but they should not be ignored. Nonetheless, it is important to measure the point where efforts to affiliate the unaffiliated have failed and to move on. And it is particularly important to not spend your fund-raising energies (and dollars) in places where your best affiliates are *not*.

Capacity

Initial identification of a new prospect calls for a general assessment of financial capacity (see Exhibit 3-5). When many of us first became researchers, we interpreted our task in this regard quite simply: Is this person wealthy? If you were raised near a city where residents with great wealth were easy to identify, you probably developed a concept about wealth. Big homes, news stories of elaborate parties, fund raisers for exclusive schools and political causes— those are a few of the signs of wealth in an urban community. As you grew up, wealth probably became an even more clearly defined concept. Particularly in the last quarter of the twentieth century, our society moved into an era where wealth became a facet of a person's life to applaud and publicize. Magazines with the mission to track the rich and famous emerged. Established publications added annual wealth rankings. What did this do to your personal concept of wealth? It is important for you as a researcher—and as one of the key sources for a definition of wealth at your nonprofit—to examine your own ideas about wealth.

Exhibit 3-5	Capacity

Capacity: The financial measure of a prospect's ability to give a major gift.

Source: Authors

Wealth is a relative concept based on the size and location of your nonprofit, the scope of its mission, and the definition you establish for a major gift. Large nonprofits with national or international missions include the wealthiest people on the planet among their prospects. Small nonprofits define wealth on a different scale. One of our friends became a major gift prospect for a very small homeless program in her community. How? She was not a person we would identify as wealthy. But for this young nonprofit with a close-to-home agenda, her larger-than-average annual gift and her expressed intention about including this nonprofit in her estate plans made her a major gift prospect.

Do initial indicators predict that this person could make a major gift to my organization? The question is that simple. It is not the researcher's imperative to uncover all the details about the prospect's capacity at this stage. Other questions will rush to the forefront, but they must not stop you from your initial, qualifying research. Where does your organization fall in the prospect's priorities? Does the prospect have other financial obligations that preclude a gift? What precisely is this prospect capable of doing for your organization financially? Some of these questions may be answered during initial research. Some of the answers may even cause a prospect to be moved higher in the cultivation priority list. Some of the answers may cause a prospect to be dropped from consideration. But additional research to find the answers to these and other questions will not be done until later stages. Many facets of wealth and capacity are fluid. Many aspects of a prospect's wealth are not visible in the domain of fund raising. Further, at this stage, it is not the researcher's imperative alone to determine the likelihood of the gift being made during the prescribed cultivation period. There are too many factors that figure into this determination outside the realm of research. The prospect's feelings about the nonprofit, her philanthropic character, the emerging goals of the institution, and how these might appear to the prospect—these are only a few of the factors that will change the prospect's placement in the priority list as a relationship with the prospect evolves. Much of this is out of the realm of research, and the task for research at this stage is simple and clear: Is the prospect likely to be able to make a major gift?

Signs of Wealth
One of the measures of achievement in our society is financial success. *Forbes* and *Fortune* publish lists of who is wealthiest each year. Publications in other parts of the world (*Asia Week, The Financial Times,* Australia's *Business Review Weekly*) publish similar lists. *Town & Country* and other monthlies report on the social events and vacation spots of the very wealthy. *People* magazine brought reporting on the famous and often rich to waiting and living rooms with their first issue in 1974. Television shows profile the wealthy and the accoutrements of wealth. The very same attributes that our culture uses to measure wealth are the yardsticks of prospect research. They include real estate, salary, business ownership, family legacy, collections, hobbies, philanthropic experience, and more. These are a prospect's financial attributes that will indicate capacity. We will examine these benchmarks of wealth in a moment.

Interest
This part of the preliminary prospect-identifying triad is the most difficult to pinpoint and, because of this, it most aptly demonstrates the development-research partnership. Interest refers to the idea that we can identify what the essence of the prospective donor's philanthropic leanings are, what her passions might be. Sometimes this is easy to do. Former President Jimmy Carter's interest in housing for the homeless has become well-known throughout the

world. Christopher Reeves's interest in spinal cord injury research has become an anchor for fund raising for that cause. But the philanthropic interests of the donors in your neighborhood (or in your database) are probably more difficult to identify. This marks an early stage in the partnership you will forge with the development team. A fund raiser talking to a potential donor, and the role research plays in that stage, form the next gateway.

Gateway Two: First Contact

The most efficient way for your organization to identify the philanthropic interests of your prospects is to simply ask them. It is often in that first contact that the donor will reveal his interests: "I'm so happy you called. That last concert I attended was fabulous. You'd like to come over and update me about the symphony's growth plans? Of course! How does Thursday afternoon look for you?"

Development officers are the best "first screen" after research identifies and qualifies a prospect. Development officers, through one phone call or visit, will answer many of these questions: Does the prospect regard his affiliation with your nonprofit as a top philanthropic priority? If not, could such a feeling be seeded through development's efforts to bring the prospect closer to the institution? Does the prospect indeed appear to have the capacity to make a major gift in the prescribed amount of time? Did the prospect indicate that there are unforeseen and unpredictable financial commitments that preclude gift-giving in the time period? Does the prospect regard your nonprofit's mission to be closely aligned with his own philanthropic ideals? Getting the answers to these questions is the goal of the first contact a development officer makes with a new prospect.

After research moves the constituent through the first gateway by qualifying him as a prospect, a development officer will be charged with contacting the prospect to assess interest in the nonprofit and to begin cultivation. The prospect will be assigned to the development officer who will then manage the course of the cultivation. Sometimes this process is very simple, since a small nonprofit may have only a few development officers. For some nonprofits, the development officer and the researcher are the same person. Whatever the particulars about the composition of your nonprofit's team, this first contact with the prospect opens the gate to gathering more information for the silhouette research is drawing.

A development officer visits a new prospect and then returns to the office full of information. The development officer has verified several things in the first contact. She now knows if the prospect is interested in being involved with the organization's fund raisers. She may also be able to verify or refute the general conclusion that the prospect is capable of making a major gift. Every experienced fund raiser returns to the office with a raft of new information and a rack of questions for research.

Trained development officers are skilled relationship-builders and, to the benefit of research, adept interviewers. We in research even think of them as "field researchers," a team of data-collectors who go directly to the prospect to gather information and who can fine-tune the team's approach to cultivation and gift-getting when this additional information is analyzed and applied to the mix by research.

Development officers return to the office with information about a prospect's interests, obligations, and goals. The very best development officers relish donor stories—stories of philanthropy, of hopes and dreams about giving. Skilled fund raisers can facilitate the realization of those dreams for prospects. Fund raisers are at their best when they help prospects reflect on their philanthropic histories and their goals as donors. One of the best development officers we know asks prospects, "What is your dream for this project?" Her direct and respectful approach sparks prospects to revel in their secret hopes for legacy gifts, for making an impact on programs, for establishing a philanthropic example in their own families.

The fund raiser who is fresh from a prospect meeting, full of new information and new questions, then completes the next step in the development of this prospect: She writes a *contact report* and sends it to the prospect's file (see Exhibit 3-6). The fund raiser captures the most important information gathered through the encounter (face-to-face visit, telephone call, or email correspondence) with the prospect. The prospect's story begins to unfold. Whether the fund raiser will continue cultivating this prospect may even be at issue at this point. All information pertinent to cultivation will be included in the contact report. You will recall from our discussion in chapter 2 that some things the fund raiser learns will not be included in the contact report. Gossip, innuendo, slanderous material, and anything that does not advance the goal of securing a major gift will not be recorded in the contact report.

Exhibit 3-6	Contact Report

Contact Report: A written summary of the important facts garnered through a planned encounter with a prospect. Particular attention is paid to information about capacity, affiliation, interests, and timing for asking for a gift. See the appendix section of this book for sample contact report forms.

Source: Authors

After initial contact, research will have more information from which to develop a portrait of a prospect. With signs that this prospect has the resources to give at the major gift level, it is time for the researcher to compile all the information gathered through both initial research and the development officer's first contact. At this or an earlier stage, the information may be assembled into a comprehensive document called a prospect *profile*. What does a profile include? Profiles are usually in outline form and contain contact information, affiliation, education, personal demographics (birth date, marital status, family composition), employment history, philanthropic history, board memberships, and a summary of financial attributes. Profiles will also contain a "comments" or "news" section, where a researcher will assemble the life events that bring a prospect to development's attention. A "contact history" section will give a researcher the opportunity to describe the history of the prospect's relationship with the nonprofit (see Exhibit 3-7).

Exhibit 3-7	Profile

Profile: A capsulized portrait of a prospective donor. It may include:

- Full name and date of birth
- How the prospect affiliates with the institution
- Home and work contact information
- Job title
- Work history
- Family information (spouse, life partner, parents, children, other family members affiliated with the institution)
- Directorships, boards, volunteer positions
- Awards
- Financial information such as salary and other compensation, stock holdings, private company sales and other asset data
- Real estate holdings and their assessed values
- History of contact with the nonprofit
- Giving history
- Gifts to other nonprofits
- The latest news about the prospect or the prospect's company

See the appendix section for sample profile formats.

Source: Authors

Capacity Analysis

Until this point, research served almost exclusively as an information-gathering service. But things are about to change dramatically. More financial information has been added to the mix so it is now time to separate the monetary pieces and then reassemble them to form a financial portrait of the prospect. This is rarely as simple as reporting a few six- or seven- or eight-digit numbers. Now, with the information returned by the fund raiser, the researcher can look for additional asset data. The prospect owns three companies, not just the one mentioned in that recent news story? The prospect sits on the boards of four other companies? She was an early investor in that company that went public last spring? How did that turn out? The new information forms additional links in the chain of data that will create a financial portrait. Research will now be able to move beyond the type of information that simply qualifies a major gift prospect for attention from development. Research will now move the process into the realm of making conclusions about capacity and recommending the size of the gift for which the prospect will be asked. This is called rating the prospect (see Exhibit 3-8).

Exhibit 3-8 **Rating a Prospect**

Rating a Prospect: Making a recommendation based on an analysis of financial and other factors about the range of gift possible from a prospect.

Source: Authors

Rating a Prospect

Although rating prospects is a complex exercise, you completed your first rating when you named the constituent as a major gift prospect. At that moment, the prospect was rated as capable of making a gift *at least* as large as your defined major gift. Now, with additional financial information, including the prospect's giving history with other organizations, you will be able to elevate the prospect from that qualifying line. Researchers and development officers have created a cache of formulas that help them focus on a presumed gift capacity for a prospect. Once again, we encounter delineations. In addition to outright financial capacity, the amount of the gift for which the prospect will be asked is further qualified by the prospect's closeness to the institution, by her age, by her experience with philanthropy, by what volunteers have told you about the prospect, and by other factors. We will discuss these facets of analyzing capacity in detail in chapter 5.

Gateway Three: Cultivating, Tracking, and Strategizing

The prospect has passed first contact. She is willing to be involved with development; there are signs of wealth and capacity, and no roadblocks to securing a major gift have surfaced during this initial period. The third gateway for the team begins. The development officer's relationship with the prospect will now be ongoing, on a course for a staff member or volunteer to ask the prospect for a gift within 18 to 24 months or less. The development officer is designing ways to engage the prospect and to enhance the prospect's link to the organization. This is the art of cultivation (see Exhibit 3-9). This highly valued patron, alumna, volunteer, or other affiliate is given opportunities to be exposed to the inner workings of the nonprofit, to sit in a decision-making position about the nonprofit's present and future, and to bring her wealth of experience and insight to the organization. All of these experiences will bring the prospect's wisdom to the nonprofit and will, in turn, bring the prospect into a close alignment with the nonprofit and its needs.

Exhibit 3-9 **Cultivation**

Cultivation: The set of planned encounters through which a fund raiser brings a prospect nearer to readiness for making a major philanthropic gift within the prescribed time period.

Source: Authors

What is research's role at this stage? Research can be instrumental to the course cultivation takes now. Information gathered by research will point to the types of leadership roles the prospect has held with other organizations. The kinds of events and activities the prospect is likely to attend or for which the prospect might volunteer will be reflected in the data research collects and outlines in the prospect profile. The latest news about the prospect's financial successes may alter the pace of the cultivation or the timing of asking for the gift. During cultivation, research monitors the information stream for further developments that will alter the course of the fund raiser's progress.

Tracking Life (and Financial) Events

As we have outlined, once research has identified a prospective donor, several events occur. In both small and large organizations, the researcher shares the pertinent facts about affiliation and capacity with the development officer in charge of assigning prospects. The prospect is then assigned to a development officer. To whom the prospect is assigned may be based on the prospect's capacity, geographic location, the way the prospective donor affiliates, or a number of other factors. The assignment may happen by a brief report handed to a development officer by his supervisor. It may happen at a prospect management meeting led by the director of development or by the researcher. Regardless of how the assignment is made, cultivation officially begins.

During the cultivation period, research attempts to track the prospect's life events that might affect making a gift. Additions to the family, job changes, significant changes in income or financial well-being, and other events are reported to the development officer assigned. Of course, it is likely that the development officer may hear about many of these events before research sees them in news stories or press releases since the development officer is maintaining consistent contact with the prospect. Whoever gets the news first, development officer or researcher, the news is often a prelude to additional research.

The cultivation status of a prospect may change during this period. Life events can speed up the process, for example. Taking a company public or approaching the age of retirement may prompt a fund raiser to move toward asking for a gift quickly. It would be in the best interest of both the institution and the prospect to understand the benefits of certain types of gifts at these life stages. Evolving tax laws may draw a prospect's attention to philanthropic opportunities. Some potential donors are first identified as having major gift capacity when they are, in fact, already deeply cultivated. Fully engaged in the institution's goals and mission, many donors introduce themselves as major gift prospects to development through a significant annual fund gift, by a query about helping to fund an event or project, or when planning life estates and bequests.

A program officer for a donor-advised foundation serving young, wealthy individuals spoke at a research meeting we attended. She told us about an interesting phenomenon. The young wealthies in this group participate in choosing the fund's recipients by serving on a committee that reviews applications for funding from local nonprofits. After reading dozens of applications, the committee chooses a handful of nonprofits that will receive support. But the philanthropic activity does not end there. The young committee members learn so much about the other contenders for gifts that they often find themselves attracted to those causes, too. They then donate directly, as "already cultivated" individuals, to those organizations not chosen for the pooled funds. This is the sort of unexpected gift that delights a nonprofit and calls for more research on a newly identified prospect entering the cultivation timeline at a markedly later stage. This story illustrates what, in a less formal way, is happening to most nonprofits every single day. Inadvertently, nonprofits are educating potential prospects unknown to them about the nonprofit's mission and goals. When identified, these prospects may enter the cultivation timeline ready to give.

During the cultivation process, research continues to sit at the decision-making table. Organizations with advanced development functions have regular *major gifts strategy meetings* (see Exhibit 3-10). At these meetings, development officers may "case" one or more of their prospects, updating the group on the progress of the cultivation and asking for advice regarding roadblocks to the gift. Research is often asked, "How can we engage this prospect?" Persistent development officers do not give up when prospects are difficult to reach or distracted by other life events. The presence of philanthropy in a donor's life often takes a back seat to things making louder and larger demands on the donor's time and energy. This does not make philanthropy any less important. Fund raisers can help prospects remember that philanthropy affords great benefits to many aspects of life. Research is at hand to inspire and inform the development team about what has been a good connection for the prospect in the past. Research remembers and records that the prospect is particularly attached to post-modern art, to programs connecting the elderly to young people, to efforts to bring literature to non-readers. Each of these pieces of information opens another door to how the prospect might engage with your institution.

Exhibit 3-10	Major Gifts Strategy Meeting

Major Gifts Strategy Meeting: A meeting held on a regular basis where development officers and researchers review a few prospects and offer advice for moving the cultivation efforts forward. Other agenda items may include assigning new prospects, reviewing lists of gifts to be closed, and other actions related to keeping the fund-raising process dynamic.

Source: Authors

Gateway Four: Recommending the Ask

The prospect is now fully cultivated, feeling as knowledgeable and close to the mission and needs of the nonprofit as possible. We approach the most critical gateway, determining the size of the gift for which the prospect will be asked and the events around the Ask. You will notice that we are now referring to the size of the gift and the event of asking for it with two words, *the Ask* (see Exhibit 3-11). Once again, this is insider shorthand for the precise amount of the gift which will be requested from a prospect and the moment in time when the prospect is actually solicited for that gift.

Exhibit 3-11	The Ask

The Ask: Refers to the amount of money for which the prospect will be asked and to the moment when development requests the gift from the prospect. The Ask distinguishes itself from the prospect's rating by being the precise amount to be requested from the prospect.

Source: Authors

We will discuss how you will evaluate gift capacity and recommend the Ask in detail in chapter 5. In the meantime, let's glance at what we will look at closely later. There are some adages in fund raising related to the amount of the Ask:

- Do not leave money on the table. (In other words, do not ask for less than the donor is willing or able to give.)
- If the prospect says a ready "yes," you probably asked for too little.
- If you ask for too much, you will scare the donor away from any gift.
- If you ask for the wrong amount (it could be either too high or too low), you will insult the prospective donor.
- There are different major gifts in a person's life, depending on their age, stage of wealth, and other factors.

What these adages have in common is that they frame anxiety about determining the right amount for the Ask. Development officers with successful gift-closing experiences in their pasts will tell you that often the prospect leads the team to the amount of the gift during the cultivation process. When a prospect talks about wishing that an operating room could be named for her mother, she probably has an idea about what that naming opportunity involves, dollar-wise. But, more often, development needs the help research can provide to determine the amount of the Ask. Which elements of this equation will help in forecasting the right amount for each prospect? Here are a few of the factors.

The Prospect's Age

Traditionally, development has anticipated that the people with the resources to make major gifts—just like the rest of us—reach a point in life when they have more disposable income, more resources other than income into which they can tap, fewer pulls on their financial resources, and less insecurity about the hazards of sharing some of their good fortune. Prospects usually reach the optimal giving age at the same time they reach the peak of their earning power and at a time in their lives when their children need less financial support. Exceptions to the age benchmark are growing along with the growth of new, young wealth. The young wealthy can transform stock options and the sale of companies into major gifts in short order. They can do so at a younger age than their parents could. But most fund raisers and researchers hold close to the adage that people give large gifts to philanthropy from assets, not income. Being asset-rich often comes with age.

Affiliation (Again)

We see this one rear its head again. Let's fine-tune affiliation so that it now means this: just exactly how close does the prospect feel to your organization? Where does your cause rank in the prospect's hierarchy of philanthropic priorities? The answers to these questions emerge out of the development and research partnership. Research can sometimes discover the prospect's charitable giving to other organizations. This can be critical information. It can hint at the prospect's experience as a philanthropist, and it can shout what the prospect cares about. Development can ask the prospect where your organization stands in her giving plans. Together, the development-research team can evaluate affiliation in the Ask equation. How close (or far) a prospect is to your organization emotionally may elevate (or decrease) the size of the Ask. Being closely affiliated can turn into being highly motivated to give.

Giving History

One of the first stops on the research trail is always the prospect's giving history with your own organization. To paraphrase Jimi Hendrix, is your prospect experienced? Has your prospect had practice supporting your organization, increasing the size of his gifts with the increases in his financial well-being? Has the prospect already given gifts that would rank as major gifts or near-major gifts? What have the prospect's donations said about what he thinks of your organization?

Passion

This, of course, is the most important element in research and development's conclusions about the Ask. Passion might be the wild card. How much does this project mean to the prospect? Is the prospect likely to stretch financially to make this project happen? Has the prospect picked a cause that reaches deep into his heart? It is surprising how often passion can alter the amount of the gift.

With research analyzing the prospect's financial resources, age, giving history to this and other nonprofits, and with development learning the prospect's feelings toward this nonprofit and what lights a fire in the prospect's heart, we have created an unbeatable duo. This team is ready to focus on the right Ask. Is that all there is to asking? No. But we can share an easy formula from the development side of the hall with you. It is called the Four and a Half Rights, and we understand that it was developed by Karen E. Osborne, principal of The Osborne Group. They are:

1. Amount
2. Purpose
3. Solicitor
4. Timing
4½. Place and other details of the solicitation

Research plays a part in four of the Four and a Half Rights. Researchers do not worry too much about the half-Right, the location of the solicitation (although a few will tell us about being asked to identify the best restaurants in a locale). We have discussed the first Right, the right amount. The second Right, the right purpose, often emerges in research's work. What part of the nonprofit's mission intrigues the prospect? One prospect has had a life-long interest in deep-sea exploration, scuba diving, and underwater photography. It is an easy match to educate this prospect about your organization's environmental initiatives. Fund raisers are often hunting for a way to engage a prospect in the early stages of cultivation. Research can assemble a picture of the causes to which the prospect has connected philanthropically. That information will help development place the right purpose for this prospect in the forefront.

The third Right presents research with one of the more intriguing parts of our work. Who is the right person to ask the prospect for the gift? Linking people between company and nonprofit boards, building a network of information about who knows whom, who is whose peer, who cannot, as we said earlier, say no to whom, are some of the adventurous aspects of research. Remember the worksheet teachers gave you in grade school? Match the names of birds in column one with the colors in column two, the worksheet directed. Now imagine those same columns, but instead of matching birds and colors you are matching executives with company names. Why? Because *they have something in common.* The crossed lines between the columns begin to look like telephone line strung by crows. Your prospect's connections to his business and philanthropic peers become a key to the third Right.

Research helps determine the right time for the Ask, the fourth Right, by being sensitive to spikes in the prospect's financial well-being or dramatic changes in the prospect's needs due to age or other time-dependent factors. Did the prospect just enter an option phase of her employment? Did the prospect's company go public this year? Is the company being sold and are all the investors cashing out? Is the prospect retiring soon? All of these life events can alter the timing of gift-making opportunities.

Who sits at the grown-up's table? Researchers sometimes complain that they are not a part of decisions made after the initial identification of prospects.

Development departments that approach fund raising this way cheat themselves. They have short-circuited the path to finding the answers to the Four and a Half Rights. They leave one of the most knowledgeable members of their team back at the water cooler while they rack their brains for the amount and timing of an Ask. They waste their organization's resources by leaving research's best work undone.

This is the point in the prospect portrait-making when the most comprehensive package of information and analysis is readied. All the pieces are pulled into place. The research and development team brings their nonprofit to its most fully empowered fund-raising point, the place where philanthropy happens. Make room for the giving to begin.

Gateway Five: Stewardship Tracking (and Here We Go Again)

And then, just like that, the prospect has been asked for the gift and has given it. After the celebration, development moves this prospect through the stewardship gate. The fund raiser assigned makes a plan to keep the prospect attached to the organization through news mailings and annual fund Asks. The stewardship manager will remind the prospect periodically about the value of the gift given and will include the prospect in events and celebrations. Except for letters updating the prospect about the use of their donation and invitations to events, the work of the development team is finished, right? Actually, research moves through this gateway in a slightly different way.

Research will continue to monitor news about the prospect, watching for significant financial or life changes that will signal the time to move the prospect back into the cultivation cycle. Researchers learn how to recognize which gift the prospect just gave and what gift might be next—and when. The first major gift, often one just at the threshold mark for a major gift at your institution, might occur when the prospect is relatively young. Several years later, the prospect may make a larger gift, one attached to recognizing a family member or to creating a new program at your institution. As the prospect retires or enters the last part of his life, he may make what development calls a "transformational" gift. This is a gift—a bequest or an outright gift—so large that it may have the power to change the way your nonprofit works. It also transforms the prospect—it changes the prospect's standing in the community and fundamentally changes the prospect's own concept of self. It is a gift that large, with that much power.

This brief outline of the kinds of gifts (based on size) that a philanthropist might give to a single institution over a lifetime illustrates the importance of research's scouting during stewardship. An active fund-raising program does not wait for the prospect to "wake up" from the stewardship slumber. Instead, research can alert the development team about the right time to introduce the prospect once again to the institution's needs and dreams. They just may match the prospect's dreams and financial capabilities.

Signs of Wealth: How Will We Tell the Trees from the Forest?

Our potential donor (suspect) pool has so many names, so many affiliated people (see Exhibit 3-12). How will we notice the wealthiest ones, the ones with capacity, in the dense forest of affiliates? Although many institutions begin fund raising by focusing on foundations and corporations next door, we begin with a study of individual wealth. Now you know why. Individuals form the largest group of major gift donors to healthy, established nonprofits.

Exhibit 3-12   The Pool

The Pool: A holding place for the names of affiliates who may be major gift prospects. The pool consists of:

- Affiliates for whom little or no research has been completed but who have demonstrated a hint of major gift capacity by:
  - — giving an annual fund or uncultivated gift at a level higher than the typical gift to an institution, or
  - — appearing in a news story regarding business success, real estate holdings, inheritance, or other wealth-related events, or
  - — emerging through information shared by other affiliates (when asked to rank their peers by major gift capacity), or
  - — emerging through a commercial database screening as possible prospects
- Affiliates who were researched and assigned, but who subsequently did not turn out to be major gift prospects at this point in their lives
- Affiliates who, in the distant future, may be expected to become major gift prospects, such as the young adult children of wealthy affiliates.

The pool is an electronic holding pen, an electronic marker on each constituent record that allows research to compile lists of possible prospects for future research and to replenish the assignment lists of the development officers.

Source: Authors

Gifts to nonprofit institutions come from individuals. The true face of philanthropy actually has a face. People give from their own pockets, of course. They create cross-generational giving through foundations. They initiate corporate giving plans to support and improve the community in which their companies prosper. People, even years later when the founders are gone, continue the legacy begun through corporate giving plans.

So, giving begins and ends with individuals. Research does, too. Here is another fund-raising adage: Healthy nonprofits beyond their startup years generally receive about 80 percent of their gifts from individuals. Knowing this, wise researchers spend the greater part of their time researching the wealth and giving capacity of individuals closely affiliated with their nonprofit.

We will now explore how researchers identify wealth and where they look for signs of wealth.

Back to School: Studying Wealth

You may be surprised to learn that wealth is situationally defined. The wealth of the world's kings is not the same as the wealth of your town's tire barons. Both the kings and the barons may nonetheless be wealthy and, in any researcher's realm, the tire baron may be the more likely prospect. When our work as professional researchers asked us to step outside of our own experience with wealth, the school bell rang. Time for class, the bell pealed— classes in wealth. The perception of wealth that each of us has developed is inadequate for our work as researchers. Regardless of your background, prospect research tells you this: You ain't seen nothin' yet. The media-driven concept of wealth (often neatly paired with fame) is limited by the era in which we grew up, the size of our town, and even by the financial resources we have observed among our families and friends. None of these images will be enough for what we meet in our jobs as prospect researchers. Our line of work obligates us to stretch beyond those limits of our past and develop an understanding of wealth that is larger than our own experience, a concept of wealth that finds its bearings on a global compass. That new concept will exercise our eyes so that we move beyond *seeing* to *vision*. It will include not only the various sizes of wealth but also many types of wealth. With our new vision, we will be able to *see* the tire baron and the king. We will see the wealth on another continent as well as the wealth right under our noses. We will recognize wealth whether it takes the form of real estate, stock, horses, art, inheritance, or prudent investments made by someone usually classified as anything but wealthy.

Prospect researchers study wealth. They become knowledgeable about the characteristics of wealth in their communities. If the philanthropic mission they support is broader than their local communities, they become knowledgeable about the nature of wealth on that larger scale, whether it is regional, national, or international. Prospect researchers specialize in nearly every aspect of getting, keeping, transforming, and—most importantly— recognizing wealth. The education that researchers create for themselves will surprise you. Researchers, of course, seek out formal training opportunities and some of those are even in fields of study outside traditional prospect research channels. They take business classes, attend genealogical society meetings, visit technology fairs. But a large part of their education is in their own hands or with the one-on-one help of other researchers. You see, part of the education occurs as an adjunct to the actual work the researcher does.

A researcher who must report on a prospect's pop art collection becomes a near-expert on researching art collections. The researcher may even uncover values for that particular art by exploring sales of similar collections and then taking a plunge to suggest a value range for the prospect's collection. At the end of this project, the researcher knows where to look, what resources produced reliable information, and even where artists and art collectors are to be found in printed directories. If another nonprofit needed research on art collectors at that moment, there would not be a better researcher to show them how to do it.

In their work, researchers find prospects who "collect" other things like ranch land, race horses, vacation homes, jewels, cars, shopping centers, companies, stock options—nearly anything. With each project, a researcher becomes almost an authority on that type of wealth. Ask Northern California researchers about the value of San Francisco real estate. Quiz Gold Coast researchers about boats. Let Texas, Oklahoma, and Colorado researchers expound on the value of great expanses of land, oil wells, and cattle. Each researcher will excitedly share the niche resources and the sometimes convoluted method they developed to reach conclusions about these points of wealth. In essence, they have added another skill to their set.

We can generalize the avenues of wealth that researchers explore as earned wealth, inherited wealth, and windfall wealth. The road signs researchers watch for along these routes to wealth are both clear and obscure. Let's examine each route and their signs.

Earned Wealth: Public Company Employees

The top officers, directors, and others who hold 5 percent or more of the stock of public companies in the United States are obligated under law to disclose the financial interest they hold in the public company (see Exhibit 3-13). If the individual you are researching is a top officer (one of the top five or so), a large investor (someone who holds 5 percent or more of the company stock), a decision maker, or a director of a public company, you will be able to find salary, stock holdings, retirement compensation plans, and separation agreements in the company's annual proxy statement. Remember that there is a qualification: Only the salaries of top officers are available in public documents. Salaries (and stock holdings) of individuals who are not the top officers of public companies are not available.

Exhibit 3-13   **Public Company**

Public Company: In the United States, a public company is a company in which many unrelated people have invested. These individuals become stockholders in the company by virtue of their investment. In return, the company is obligated to report its financial well-being, its leadership and their remuneration and financial interest in the company, and other economic details to the stockholders each year. This reporting is accomplished through various U.S. Securities and Exchange Commission documents, including the annual report and the proxy statement.

Source: Authors

The Securities and Exchange Commission (SEC) is the regulating body in the United States for public company disclosures. What precisely is available regarding individual public company employees or affiliates in SEC documents? In addition to the information listed here, brief biographies of the top officers and directors, including job history and college affiliation, may be a part of the proxy statement. Other information about each individual's financial relationship with the company will be outlined in detail.

Each nonprofit's researcher has a farmhand's day of work to do when they begin setting public company affiliates into the prospect track. What level of compensation (salary and bonus) will be enough to generate a major gift to your institution? What exactly do the stock option and stock holding figures mean in terms of wealth? As a prospect researcher, you will set the thresholds for this analysis. By learning to read and interpret proxy statements, you will develop prospecting expectations about what constitutes someone with major donor potential for your own institution. The range of combinations of salary, bonus, stock option prices, and stock holdings is endless, but the framework you establish for what makes a major gift prospect will emerge from this analysis. Stock holdings and stock options are important indicators of wealth or potential wealth. They are also giving mediums. Remember that we said big gifts often come from assets, not income. Stock is an asset. Prospects give stock as a charitable gift. They may consider the timing of their gift based on the current or anticipated value of their stock or the expiration of their options. Researchers help development officers set the Ask amount and the timing of the Ask by gathering and analyzing information about both stock holdings and options.

In chapter 5 the pieces will come together. When we go into the details of gleaning financial information about your prospect from the company's proxy statement, we will add essential terminology specific to this public company employee research. You will hone your math skills and acquire the tools to establish a general profile of the type of public company affiliate who will be able to make a major gift to your nonprofit.

Earned Wealth: Private Company Owners and Chief Officers

Another way that individuals accumulate wealth is by founding or leading successful private companies (see Exhibit 3-14). Often these companies are family affairs, with husbands and wives and adult children operating the company. Private companies are the backbone of a nation's commerce: They provide food, shelter, transportation, goods, and services—necessities and luxuries—the essential and extraneous elements of our lives. They come in all sizes, from small one-person shops down the street to multinational corporations with tens of thousands of employees. They all have something in common: Their roots are in the hard work and vision of their founders. Many times, understanding those origins points the way to the possibilities for philanthropy.

Exhibit 3-14	Private Company

Private Company: A company in which the chief investors are the company founders or those who are close and well-known to the company founders. In return for their investment, these individuals may be given private stock, a voice in the direction of the company, or other financial benefits. A private company is under no obligation to make a public report of the compensation it makes to its chief officers, directors, or investors.

Source: Authors

The financial benefits of employment with or ownership in a private company are different from those with a public company, and the two should not be paralleled. Some analysts in our profession hope that comparing, for example, the salaries of public company officials with those in similar jobs in private companies will hint at the compensation those in private companies enjoy. Years ago, a financial analyst speaking at a seminar told a group of researchers that comparing private and public compensation is a grave error because those involved in private companies are receiving *considerably larger remuneration packages* than their public company counterparts. That surprises you, right? It reminds us that preconceived notions are not well suited to prospect research.

So, what can a prospect's association with a private company tell a researcher? What precisely is available to researchers? No salary or other compensation information will be available. No stock holding or stock price information will be retrievable. A few details about the company and its officers will be available, like the year the company was founded, its gross sales, the number of people it employs, and the names of top officers. These demographics can be found in electronic and paper business reference directories. More detailed information about the company's performance may also be retrievable, usually for a fee. These characteristics of the company, when taken together, allow a researcher to develop an opinion about the philanthropic potential of the private company owner. There are no reliable formulas that parse these characteristics into an answer about gift capacity though.

Generally, a researcher may only be able to point a development officer in the direction of prospects with healthy companies or to steer a development officer away from prospects with companies suffering economic downturns. When this information is combined with other information—the prospect's experience with philanthropy and the depth of the prospect's connection to your institution—it may lead to major gift support for your organization.

There are a few other opportunities to collect information that might augment conclusions about private companies, and these may be found in news stories or company press releases. Researchers look for press releases and news stories that report:

- Company expansion
- Layoffs or cutbacks
- Plant or branch closures
- Mergers (the purchase, acquisition, or sale of companies)
- Leadership changes
- Turmoil in performance or product reliability
- Company or chief officer awards or recognition
- An initial public offering by the company ("going public")
- Philanthropic gifts made by the company
- Programs or initiatives created by the company that support the community

Each of these events will be noteworthy. Some of these developments will be an opportunity to gather additional financial information. For example, the sale of a private company to another private company rarely includes the sale price. But the sale of a private company to a public company means that the sale price will be available in the public company's annual report. The cash sale of a generations-old company may mean that your prospect has realized a windfall.

Research about prospects with private company affiliations relies on the strong partnership between researchers and fund raisers. Development officers may, through conversations, uncover information about the financial strength of the prospect's company. The information gathered through their visits will be a compass for finding the next bit of valuable information. A prospect may appear to be retired from active involvement in his company, for example, when a fund raiser returns from a visit with the news that the prospect retained ownership of the company's real estate and leases it to the new operators. These are the details thorough researchers seek and explore.

Earned Wealth: Other Paychecks, Owners, and Operators

Other working people have an opportunity to accumulate great wealth, of course. There are too many lines of work to list, but you know many of them already. They include professional athletes, entertainers, doctors, financial advisors, private investors, stockbrokers, bankers, lawyers, venture capitalists, real estate investors, and others. Some of the professions listed here involve self-employment (private company owners). Many doctors and lawyers, for example, own and run the businesses that are their practices.

What do the members of this diverse group have in common? Most of them see themselves as working people, and many do not think of themselves as wealthy until late in their careers. Most of them worry about their future performance and whether the opportunities available to them at one point in their careers will be available later. Because of this, they may be overly protective about their financial future. Many people in this group are having their first experience with significant wealth. Many have no experience with philanthropy.

Earned Wealth (Okay, Sometimes Windfall Wealth): Real Estate

Often the potential prospect you are researching does not work for a public company and does not own or work for a private company. The prospect-to-be may be retired, a great saver and investor, or have another route to wealth. When there is little information to find about salary, stock holdings, company ownership, or other significant indicators of wealth or giving capacity, real estate holdings may offer a clue.

Assessed values for land and buildings across the United States are held as public information. The information is usually available through county or township assessor offices, and many assessors now provide online access to their records. There are also assessment information providers who assemble this information for real estate sellers, appraisers, bankers, and others who use the data in their work. The search tools for these resources vary by provider. Some allow users to search for property holdings by an individual's name; others allow for searching by property address only. Some reports include the last sale price for the property, details about the improvements at the site, and an ownership history. Generally, the information aggregators who charge a fee provide the easiest searching and the most information. Directions to find a few real estate information providers are in the appendix section of this book.

What does the value that an assessor places on a property tell a researcher? Many researchers would answer, "Not much." In fact, the first thing this information may—or may not—indicate is the prospect's lifestyle. Does this part of the prospect's lifestyle—his primary residence's assessed value—reflect the level of wealth usually found among the very wealthy? The prospect's financial well-being might be reflected in the number and type of properties she holds. It may be in the length of time the property has been held (asset rich). The value of real estate research is simply that assessments can offer a hint at wealth or even financial capacity for gift-giving.

Wealth built from real estate investments is an even larger factor when buying, developing, and selling properties is your prospect's business. Prospects who own or develop shopping centers, apartment complexes, office buildings, subdivisions, and other commercial properties build wealth not only on the value of the properties but also on the income generated by those properties as they are developed or held.

We began this section implying that real estate might represent windfall wealth. Real estate windfalls came during the exponential growth in land and building values in some areas of the United States during the last half of the twentieth century. People who bought their homes for tens of thousands of dollars in the 1950s and 1960s discovered that they owned homes worth hundreds of thousands of dollars at the turn of the twenty-first century. As values grew, housing in some parts of the country became unaffordable to all but the wealthy. Researchers who know the locations of this growth know where to look for new prospects.

The rate at which assessors value property and the relationship of assessed value to market value varies from state to state and county to county. There are many cautions about adding real estate values to the financial mix. In chapter 5, we will outline the meaning of assessed values for real estate and how you, the researcher, may want to add it to your analysis of wealth and capacity.

Inherited Wealth: Old Money

Researchers who advance beyond the overt signs of wealth will stumble— the first time is always a happy stumble— upon another kind of wealth: old wealth. By old wealth we mean inherited wealth, the kind of wealth that is garnered in one generation, invested and expanded, and passed on to subsequent generations. The wealth often grows during the long time it is held and often it grows significantly. Along the way, many families establish systems for managing the wealth, distributing it among family members, and sharing it philanthropically.

Inherited wealth is hard to identify if you are not studying wealth. Most of us know that the names of the big buildings and stores in large cities and the names of many companies are actually family names. We have read stories of Martha's Vineyard, Pebble Beach, and Aspen. We have seen the inheritors noted on rich lists or read the wedding or funeral stories in newspapers and magazines. But, after we get beyond the person who died or married, who is actually related to whom? That is the tough part. There are inheritors in your community or within your database. Tracing your prospect's wealth back to earlier generations is a difficult task. To do so, some researchers, particularly those living in the enclaves where the inheritors live, collect family trees. They track who married whom and what names rest on the branches of each family tree. They are self-made experts on genealogy. If you have a constituency that includes inherited wealth, you will find that volunteers, history books, and biographical resources that profile individuals and families will be your best route to generation-to-generation information.

There are signs of inherited wealth that you will begin to notice as your study of wealth advances. Did your prospect's parent spend a lifetime as the chairman of a company? Does someone in your prospect's family sit on the board of the local bank? Are sports facilities, museum buildings, or concert halls named for your prospect's family? Is your prospect giving to your organization through a foundation bearing a family name? These and other signs of long-held wealth will begin to appear to you as you exercise your skills at wealth identification.

New Wealth (Known to Many as Windfall Wealth)

The 1990s saw a surge in individual wealth that might only be paralleled by the wealth that was created when the infrastructure of the United States was built in the mid- to late-1800s. In a way, a new kind of infrastructure has been under construction in the latter part of the 1900s. Just like the railroad tracks and telephone lines laid all those years ago, the United States has now laid the backbone for electronic information to travel. Great wealth was born out of this movement. It often fell upon those who, previously, had little experience with wealth. This new wealth created a ripple effect, so wealth in other areas of commerce also grew. The electronic wealth created booms in real estate development, banking and investing, consumer goods and services, and other areas. We are classifying this group as the windfall wealthies only because the wealth they met was sudden, larger than anyone anticipated, and came to them at a much younger age than wealth often does for the workers and owners we described earlier. It sounds a bit like the gold rush in the American West in the 1800s, does it not?

Researchers discovered that many of the tried and true adages about prospects flew out the window when the young wealthies blew in. Valuing potential prospects by factors like age, life stage, or philanthropic history, for example, was defied by young wealthies who are knowledgeable and savvy major gift donors in unprecedented numbers. The young wealthies did not always spend their money in the ways their parents did. Ideas about status shifted when this generation donned their crowns as wealthy (and philanthropic) leaders.

The Last Round-up

Who else is a prospect? Dr. Thomas Stanley and William Danko peeled the lid off of this question for many wealth watchers with their 1996 book, *The Millionaire Next Door: The Surprising Secrets of America's Wealthy* (Marietta, GA: Longstreet Press). Their research outlines a sort of wealth that is usually overlooked in the high technology era. The millionaires they interviewed and wrote about are the business owners in their own (and your) community. They are diligent savers, economizers, and steady, hard-working wealth gatherers. In some cases, the development officers know the millionaires next door to your nonprofit. Most nonprofits are not overlooking the gravel pit operator, the real estate developer, or the convenience store owner. But many of these individuals remain unknown to your nonprofit until you find them.

Who is a prospect? You know now that anyone with the capacity to give a major gift may be a prospect. But there are many other factors besides capacity alone that add up to who is the *best* prospect. Prospects cut a wide swath across many professions, age groups, backgrounds, and experience with philanthropy. In the coming chapters, you will learn how to qualify prospects by evaluating capacity. You will also learn how to direct your research efforts among the many prospects in your database so that you may find those who are the best prospects for the fund-raising initiatives of your organization.

Exercise: Who is Your Nonprofit's Typical Donor?

Is there a typical donor to your institution? Explore this concept by answering the following questions. There are no right answers, but this exercise will help you uncover your next major gift prospects.

1. Who are the big donors to your nonprofit? Name 10 to 15.
2. What do they have in common? What personal, professional, or financial traits do they share?
3. Who are the founders and cornerstone-builders in your organization? Name 10 to 15.
4. What does this group have in common with the big donors you outlined?
5. What group or individuals—not yet giving at a major gift level—share the traits and characteristics you outlined in the first four questions?

Now you are naming your next major gift prospects.

Institutional Prospects: Corporations, Foundations, and Government Funding

"In networking with other foundations, we've found a lot of them say, 'What am I going to do with all this money?' Some of these people have got these millions, even billions, and it's a chore."

—Ike Leighty, *The Chronicle of Philanthropy,* May 18, 2000, p. 9.

Meet the Other Prospects: Part Two

Take a deep breath. Now exhale. The tough part of learning the basics of prospect identification and qualification is over. Individual prospects constitute the difficult research task. The other prospects—foundations, corporations, and government funding—are easy work for researchers by any measure of comparison. You have a few things to learn, a bit of language and some boundaries, but the work we do next will have you feeling strong and capable as a new researcher. Believe us. Have we steered you wrong yet?

You will remember what we said about the prospects that are not people. Ideally, they will form about 20 percent of your donor pool. The split between corporation and foundation giving is weighted toward foundations, according to the statistics gathered by *Giving USA* (see Figure 4-1). While individuals lead total annual giving to charities in the United States, foundations and corporations represent about 17.3 percent of the total in *Giving USA's* figures. Let's round this to 20 percent—that is the figure most nonprofits target for the support they hope to garner from foundations and corporations. Although 20 percent does not seem like a lot when you are searching for the other 80 percent to support your organization, 20 percent of your support is too much to neglect or leave to chance. So, as you develop your prowess as a researcher of individuals, you will keep your institutional prospecting skills sharpened. You will effectively add institutional prospects to your donor lineup.

Let's begin with a roll call. Who is on the information quest with you when it comes to institutional prospects?

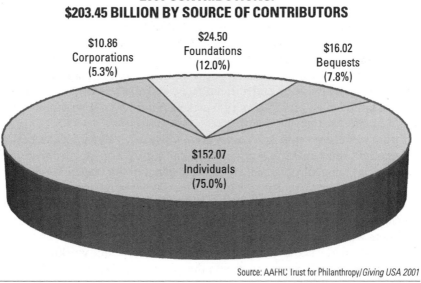

2000 CONTRIBUTIONS:
$203.45 BILLION BY SOURCE OF CONTRIBUTORS

$10.86
Corporations
(5.3%)

$24.50
Foundations
(12.0%)

$16.02
Bequests
(7.8%)

$152.07
Individuals
(75.0%)

Source: AAFRC Trust for Philanthropy/*Giving USA 2001*

FIGURE 4-1
2000 Contributions by Source of Contribution

Grant Writer + Researcher = Love at First Site

As your organization's researcher, it may be a part of your duties to introduce foundation and corporation prospects into the fund-raising mix. If your organization has a grant writer, consider yourself lucky because that grant writer will take a great deal of institutional prospecting off your shoulders. Grant writers are the closest kin to researchers on the development team. When it comes to uncovering foundation guidelines and learning what charities corporations support, they are, by default, able researchers. Because they usually visit prospects, too, they build relationships with corporate and foundation giving agents and return to your organization with a wealth of information. Like you, they maintain a network of peers who are good advisors and information providers. The grant writer peer network has traditionally nurtured an admirably vigorous flow of information. In addition to alerting one another to changes in funding opportunities, grant writers will help one another understand the limitations of particular foundations and what pitfalls to avoid. Grant writers generously share their professional experiences, sometimes even acting as grant-getting mentors. They are, like researchers, storytellers. And they know "the love you take is equal to the love you make," as John Lennon and Paul McCartney put it. In other words, sharing their knowledge and experience does not diminish their own organization's chances for support. Foundations and corporations use their guidelines to clearly spell out where their grants will go. A nonprofit's formula becomes having a compelling cause and the ability to communicate it well in writing, with a bit of who knows whom thrown in for good measure. That mix of skill and luck seems to diminish the threat of competition between nonprofits to get that institutional support. Regardless of the reasons for the permeable barriers, grant writers remain a friendly lot who seem comfortable showing their treasure map to gifts with others. These qualities—general research skills, a reliable network of information and guidance, and a generous spirit—make a grant writer a researcher's best friend on the development team.

Grant writers are easy to identify, even when they carry job titles that do not include the words "grant" or "writer." Director of corporate and foundation giving, institutional giving manager, funding manager—these are examples of what a grant writer might be called at your organization. You will not have any trouble recognizing them. They are the members of your development team who hardly ever ask you for anything. They are the team members who have something for you.

But in the perfect co-dependent world that is the average workplace, what does your grant writer need from you that she is not asking for? What need can you anticipate before your development soul mate even knows she needs it? This is the easy part. There are several things you will be doing as a researcher that benefit your grant writer. You are tracking the news in a way that your grant writer is not. You are likely to be the first to uncover news that a foundation has changed its guidelines to include nonprofits like yours. You may be the one who discovers that a nonprofit similar to yours received support from a corporation your organization has yet to approach. Grant writers are not researching individuals, so you may be the one who finds that a constituent established a foundation or started a company that has a corporate giving division. While your grant writer is busy writing, you are busy researching. Your institutional research opens another door for you to identify possibilities for major gifts for your organization. Your grant writer—and your entire development team—will see this and know that it is good.

In the Beginning . . . Your Nonprofit's, That Is

Foundations are aptly named. For both the donor and the recipients, these philanthropic entities often serve as a base upon which small and great changes are built. Corporate giving works in a similar way. Companies want their communities to have the cultural amenities and social services that enrich the lives of the employees. Institutional donors have long histories of giving to nearly all the nonprofit causes you can imagine. They give "seed money" or startup funds. They fund the construction of buildings, found new programs and initiatives, and underwrite forums and conferences. They fund visiting artists and bring exhibitions and performers to town with their support. Institutional givers happily roam into every corner of a noprofit's house of needs to leave money and other forms of support there.

Foundations are donation-making, cause-supporting entities with a structure in place to make decisions and to keep their own financial resources viable so that they may continue to give. Why do foundations even exist? People establish foundations. Alone or in concert with family members or business colleagues, individuals decide how much to give and who will receive it. They decide how the legacy they create will continue. Foundations are a tax-protected place to put the money a donor intends to give to charity. They are like a philanthropic bank. Money goes in and money comes out, with all banking done by distinct depositors and withdrawers. Only this "banking" is done by nonprofits following steps that have been strictly outlined by the foundation's directors. Nonprofits hoping to make a "withdrawal" must examine several characteristics of the foundation before making overtures. We will closely examine these characteristics next, but first let's talk about a few general features of foundations.

Foundations have rules to meet to keep their tax status. By law, a foundation is required to give a percentage of its assets, or corpus, to charity. The rest of the assets will be invested year after year to insure that the foundation's mission continues to be financed. Some foundation donors only place what they will expend in the foundation's realm. Some foundations give more than the legal minimum, although most give away close to the amount required by law.

What is the required percentage? At this writing, it is 5 percent of net assets. Philanthropy circles ring with talk that the percentage should grow larger. Can you imagine the impact such an increase would have? Even a one-half percentage increase in the required amount would drop millions more dollars into nonprofit organizations' budgets. You can follow developments on this topic by keeping in close touch with foundation and corporation philanthropy news. Any change will affect your nonprofit.

You will recall, we said most nonprofits receive about 20 percent of their support from corporations and foundations. Actually, small, young nonprofits often depend upon foundations and corporations for a greater percentage of the support they need. This is common in the beginning of the life of a nonprofit, usually because they have yet to identify and cultivate the individual prospects who will support them. As they begin to solicit individual prospects, the percentage of gifts they receive from those constituents will assume a larger percentage of the total raised. By the time a young organization has matured into a stable, healthy nonprofit, the percentage of support from institutional donors will pencil out closer to the *Giving USA* statistics.

Genus and Phylum

Remember, in high school, when you learned the way scientists organize plants and animals? The system serves to categorize the world's occupants for us. It outlines relationships and clear distinctions. We think fund raisers could use a grant maker's phylum and genus. What would we put in the institutional givers' phyla? Five philanthropic entities will fill our phyla:

1. Private foundations—nonprofit giving entities formed by individuals or families to serve as the primary vehicle for charitable giving. The money placed in the foundation has income benefits for the donors.
2. Community foundations—nonprofit giving entities that amalgamate the giving of groups of usually unrelated donors.
3. Company foundations—nonprofit giving entities established and administered by for-profit businesses or their agents.
4. Corporate giving programs—the arm of a company that oversees the money and other resources allocated for philanthropy.
5. Government giving programs—the giving administered by local, state, and federal government, from community-based arts and social services programs to national departments that oversee government branches managing the distribution of huge contributions to nonprofits.

Private Foundations

Let's begin our study of our institutional donor phyla with private foundations. In this section, we will also explore the reporting requirements that apply to the other institutional donors in this system.

Private foundations are as varied as the individuals who establish them. They range from small funds with no staff, no office, and no administrative overhead to mega-operations that, in size, scope and influence, rival the largest private company.

The Foundation Center, a leading foundation information provider, defines a foundation as "a nongovernmental, nonprofit organization with its own funds (usually from a single source, either an individual, family, or corporation) and program managed by its own trustees and directors that was established to maintain or aid educational, social, charitable, religious, or other activities serving the common welfare, primarily by making grants to other nonprofit organizations" (*The Foundation Center Directory*, 2000).

Organizations that solicit funds from the public—like United Way, for example—are excluded from the Foundation Center's definition. Foundations with a mission to support and endow one cause—the foundation that is the fund-raising branch of a hospital or public university, for example—are also excluded from this definition. In this chapter, we are also excluding operating foundations, a type of foundation created to support a single cause or mission and which can accept contributions from the public as well as the primary support it receives from those who established it. The foundation that supports the Ronald McDonald Houses is an example of an operating foundation.

Gentle Researcher, Start Your Engine

You, Researcher, will pay attention to these characteristics of foundations:

- Who established the foundation
- When the foundation was established
- The foundation's assets (recent year and a year or two earlier)
- Expenditures (recent year and a year or two earlier)
- Current giving guidelines
- Limitations in giving
- How to apply for money
- Which organizations won gifts in the previous few years
- Amount of those gifts (average grant size and the range in the sizes of gifts)
- Planned use of those gifts
- Board members and primary staff
- Recent news about the foundation

The value of paying attention to many of these characteristics is already apparent to you. You are remembering what you learned in chapter 3. You will parallel your research of institutional givers with what you learned about researching individual prospects. You were interested in how your individual prospects gained their wealth; now you will be interested in how each foundation arrived at its position in philanthropy. You will want to know who established the foundation, who is on the board, and who administers the foundation. That close review may uncover someone among the foundation ranks who affiliates with your organization. The age of the foundation will interest you because it will tell you a little bit about the level of experience in philanthropy your fund raisers will encounter as they cultivate this prospect.

You will measure the giving potential of the foundation with two pieces of information—the size of its assets and the size of the gifts it typically gives. This will begin to build a framework for placing each foundation you research into a gift range. To narrow these ranges and begin to approach an Ask amount, you will weigh the asset and gift history information with how close your organization is to the foundation and its key people. The closer your nonprofit is to the foundation—in the form of the affiliation hierarchies we outlined in chapter 3—the more likely your organization is to receive one of the largest gifts the foundation typically gives. Your nonprofit may, in some cases, receive a gift even larger than any gift the foundation has ever given, if your relationship facilitates that sort of uncommon support.

As we said, some foundations give away all of their assets each year. The foundation acts as a "pass-through" for the amount the foundation donor wants to give annually to charities. It is worthwhile to look at how much a foundation gave away in the current year and a few earlier years. The giving history of the foundation and whether it maintains a corpus year after year or acts as a pass-through, will point you toward several important signs.

In what dollar range are the grants? This will be the first thing you notice about the foundation's giving history. As you gather the foundation's history of giving and analyze it, a size range for the grants made will emerge. Does the foundation typically give grants of $5,000 or grants of $500,000? You will have no trouble seeing that some foundations give only small gifts. You may be surprised to learn that some foundations give only large gifts. Which gift size fits your nonprofit's programs and mission?

Which nonprofits won support? While you are assembling the giving history of a foundation, you will instinctively begin to look for the names of your peer institutions. Or, broadly, what do the nonprofits that won grants from this foundation have in common with your nonprofit? If you work for a social service agency and you discover that all the grant recipients are art institutions, you will be able to conclude that pursuing this foundation's support is not a good idea. Remember your mission: to identify the most likely major gift prospects, not the unlikely or improbable. But you must also keep in mind that, if your organization has a close relationship with the person who created or manages the foundation, another doorway to winning grants may open through your research.

What projects won support? Once you conclude that the nonprofits that won support are similar to your nonprofit, you will study what projects they proposed. What projects attracted the foundation? Some foundations are all over the philanthropic map in their giving. They support such a variety of projects that you will find it difficult to find commonality. Other foundations are deliberate and consistent about what they fund. Their mission is so clearly defined that the programs they support are near copies of one another.

You see that we are examining information about the foundation from two distinct perspectives. We are looking at what the foundation says about itself. We are also looking at what the foundation actually does. These two elements often match. Sometimes they do not. You will make important conclusions about this as you gather information. If the foundation breaks its own giving rules, is it likely that your organization might fit in a way not spelled out? Once again, your nonprofit's relationship to the people involved with the foundation is likely to change the path your research—and your development team—takes.

On the Trail of Foundation Information
The larger part of the information you will seek about foundations is so easy to find that you will make terrible conclusions about researching individuals. After all the hard work of researching individuals, you will find that foundation research spoils researchers. The hard work you did uncovering the hidden wealth of individuals or in researching people who do not think of themselves as philanthropic will find no parallel in foundation research. Why is foundation

research relatively easy? It is simple: Foundations are in the business of giving away money. The personality of nearly all foundations is to be direct and clear about what they support, at what level they offer support, and how to get the foundation's attention so that it can give your nonprofit the support it seeks. Even the foundations that tell you they do not support your type of nonprofit and do not take letters of application or telephone calls of inquiry are being direct and clear. A few hours of researching foundations gives most intrepid researchers a close-up view of the meaning of "a walk in the park." You will look for foundation information in several places: U.S. tax forms, annual reports and guidelines, the Internet, books, CD-ROMS and electronic databases, news sources, and by going directly to other grantees and to the foundation itself.

Federal Tax Forms
Because U.S. foundations receive tax breaks and are required to distribute a specific portion of their assets, they are regulated by the Internal Revenue Service (IRS). Foundations must report the money they receive, the amount they give away, what is spent on administrative costs, who the foundation's leadership is, what organizations received support from the foundation in the previous (tax) year, and how much each organization received. Foundations report these details to the IRS on a Form 990-PF. The 990-PF for each foundation is available to the public. Researchers used to acquire 990-PFs by writing to the IRS in their region, sending the costs of copying the 990-PF, and then waiting weeks to receive a copy of the document. A few information providers, offering a quicker turn-around, sold copies of 990-PFs. Now 990-PFs are available on the Internet (see Exhibit 4-1).

Exhibit 4-1 **990-PFs on the Internet**

Organizations posting 990-PFs on the Internet scan the actual 990-PFs. To read 990-PFs on the Internet, you must have the program, Adobe Acrobat Reader (http://www.adobe.com), on your computer. If you do not find the 990-PF for the foundation you are researching at one of the following Web sites, try another site. One site may even have a more recent year's filing than another site, so it is worthwhile to check more than one resource.
- GuideStar - http://www.guidestar.org
- GrantSmart - http://www.grantsmart.org (go to the Search section)
- The Foundation Center - http://www.fdncenter.org

Source: Authors

Annual Reports and Guidelines
Foundations are required by law to provide information about their giving to members of the public who request the information. For large foundations, this often means mailing glossy brochures and polished annual reports to

inquirers. For small foundations with few or no staff members, meeting the reporting requirements has traditionally meant sending inquirers a brief letter and a copy of the foundation's 990-PF. The movement to post 990-PFs on the Internet was developed to improve the public's access to foundation information. The U.S. government ruled that, as an alternative to mailing information, posting 990-PFs on the Internet meets the IRS reporting requirements. This ruling became an opportunity for small foundations to easily meet reporting requirements, which formerly involved staff time and mailing expenses that could reach beyond their resources.

Among those foundations publishing paper versions of annual reports and giving guidelines, there is a range of products available to researchers. Some foundations have quarterly mailings that update those interested about developments in the foundation's giving. Others publish an annual report and update giving guidelines each year. Some foundations update their published materials on a two-year cycle. Researchers can get a foundation's printed materials by asking for them. But remember this: Every contact with a foundation—including the ones made by you, the researcher—may become moments of cultivation. It is wise to first research whether your organization is in the realm of possibility for support from the foundation. That way, you save yourself the trouble of reviewing the materials and you save the foundation the expense of paying to print and mail them. Thus, you live by your mission to use your nonprofit's dollars efficiently.

The Internet

The Internet has been a lifesaver for both large- and small-budget foundations (see Exhibit 4-2). Many foundations now maintain Web sites. A foundation's Web site is the best place to learn about the foundation's latest giving, the types of organizations and programs it supports, the way to apply for support from the foundation, and any limitations on giving that rule the foundation's operation. In addition to Web sites designed and maintained by single foundations or their agents, there are Web sites that amalgamate information about many foundations. Some of the organizations doing this were in the business of providing information about foundations before the rise of the Internet. Others began providing foundation information when the Internet grew into a reliable information conveyer. A few U.S. Secretary of State Web sites have posted databases that include grant-making foundations. Some college libraries, community groups, nonprofits, and individual prospect researchers have posted information about and links to foundation Web sites on their own Web sites. In other words, there is a sea of information about foundations on the Internet. Researchers who once fished all day without a bite now cast a wide net and then sort out what information is useful and what to toss back.

Exhibit 4-2   Internet Search Tips for Researching Institutional Givers

- Join listservs where members discuss foundations. A listserv is an electronic community communicating via email messages about something they all have in common.
- The Web sites returned when you search for information about a foundation often lead to other collections of foundation links. Visit those sites or bookmark them for later visits.
- To decide which sites to visit, study the "root" of the Web site name to see if it reveals any clues. The root is the part of the Web address between the "www" and the ".org" or other ending. Root names that are libraries, foundation tracking organizations, community groups, or research pages may lead to good links to other foundations. A visit to a Web site with an address like http://www.grantgivers.org or http://www.library.foundations.org will be worth the time you spend.
- Try to guess at the institutional giver's name. You will be happily surprised to discover how often the giver's Web address is as simple as "www.giver'snamehere.org" or "www.giver'snamehere.com"

Source: Authors

The Internet has, in fact, created a new set of information problems when it comes to foundation giving. Uneven access to information plagues small nonprofits and worries foundations and other institutional givers. The Internet gives foundations instant access to an audience of nonprofits. Sounds good, right? It can be. But it requires a new kind of diligence on the part of foundations and nonprofits. That instant access is only to an audience of wired nonprofits. Small nonprofits lagging in joining the "Information Age" are out of the running in this race. The Internet allows a foundation to change the course of its behavior in the time it takes to rewrite a Web page. The option to file applications online pares down the process and can be an equalizer for writing skills and funding purpose. Whether small nonprofits have access to these resources in the same way that larger institutions do remains an important concern. A hard wire to the Internet and a fast computer become essential grant-getting tools in this scenario. If your organization is one of those late to the electronic information party, you must do what you can to advocate for joining. One of the ways you may begin is by researching funders who provide equipment and other electronic resources—software, setup, and training—to small nonprofits.

Books, CD-ROMs, and Electronic Databases
Government documents, the foundation's own publications—where else will we look for information about foundations? Remember those solid objects that sit on shelves, the ones we called "books?" They continue to be a part of the world of prospect research. Sometimes foundation directories are made

of paper and sometimes the information contained in them has been transformed into an electronic form like CD-ROMs or fee-based databases accessed through special software or the Internet. The electronic versions are easier to search, of course. But generally all of these versions contain the same sort of information—a way to look at foundations by name, by state, by the type of support they give, by their directors, and by other factors. There are advantages to choosing the electronic versions of these directories. The electronic versions allow easy searches by more factors than those provided by the books, such as by grant size or by grant recipients. They are also updated more often than the paper directories.

The Secretary of State office in your area may produce directories of foundations registered in your state. Associations that organize, counsel, or support grant makers or grant writers often produce paper or electronic directories listing foundations. It will be important for you to learn about all the options for gathering information about institutional givers in your area or the area in which your prospects are based.

What's the News?

As you can see, most of these resources are limited by time issues. The paper products are dated by their time of publication. Even the electronic resources have an update schedule. You, of course, will want the latest news about the giving of the foundations you are researching. Where will you look for the freshest information? You will look where you looked for fresh information about individual prospects—in newspapers, magazines, and other media resources. Foundation news is not as common to general circulation publications as news about companies and individuals is, so researchers avail themselves of publications that cover foundation news (see Exhibit 4-3). These publications are published daily, weekly, bi-weekly, or monthly, and they include the latest news about institutional giving and update readers about changes in giving priorities for many of those givers. Two resources, *The Chronicle of Philanthropy* and *The Chronicle of Higher Education,* offer articles and grant searching tools on their Web sites for subscribers. Will you find the foundation you are researching in these publications? If it is large, you will. If it is well established, you will. If it is small or new, you may not find information about it in these publications. You may find news of gifts made by those foundations in the newspaper in the foundation's operating area.

Exhibit 4-3   **Where to Find Foundation News**

Here are a few resources for news about new foundation gifts:
- *The Chronicle of Philanthropy:* http://philanthropy.com/
- *The Chronicle of Higher Education:* http://chronicle.com/
- *Nonprofit Times:* http://www.nptimes.com/
- *Philanthropy News Network* Online: http://pnnonline.org/

Source: Authors

Go Directly to the Grantees

The Internet offers researchers another place to look for news about foundations. Many nonprofits post the news about support they receive in the press release section of their Web sites. A general search for news about the foundations in which you are interested may uncover those nonprofit-based news stories. These stories are the best resources you will ever find. They often include background information about the person who established the foundation. They will outline the individual's connection to the nonprofit to which the gift was given. While you are visiting the nonprofit's Web site, be sure to check the pages about its leadership. You may discover the foundation director (or spouse, children, or siblings) sits on the nonprofit's board. You will gain a deeper understanding of the why of giving when you can make these links.

Researchers sometimes contact their colleagues at other nonprofits to ask about grants they have received. Nonprofits report their donors in annual reports similar to the reports published by foundations. These annual reports, or honor rolls of donors (often called donor rolls), are available to anyone who is a donor to the nonprofit. Depending on the position taken by each nonprofit, a donor roll may be available to anyone who requests a copy. The donor rolls report gifts in ranges and do not include details about the gift, like whether it was made outright or paid over a number of years, for example. Some nonprofits are hesitant to share their donor rolls with nonprofits they view as competitors. Many researchers hesitate to even ask for donor rolls from other nonprofits, as a point of ethics as well as etiquette. Strong relationships among colleagues from different institutions sometimes open access to sharing donor rolls. In any sharing that occurs, everyone involved must be mindful that the precise details about any donor's gift are protected by the nonprofit's stated ethical guidelines. Generally speaking, the only public information related to gifts made by individuals is that which is published in press releases or donor rolls. Public information about gifts made by foundations and corporations comes from these resources and from the institutional givers themselves.

Finding the freshest news has to be one of your highest priorities in foundation research. One of the largest foundations in existence today changed its giving priorities over a period of less than six months. With the change in those priorities came a watershed change in the size of the gifts the foundation began to give. A foundation that once gave gifts of $100,000 to $500,000 began to give multi-million dollar gifts. See how important the news over that six months or so became? Your nonprofit could have been one of those asking for $100,000 when $1 million had become the average grant. And there is one truism about fund raising that does not change: If your organization gets anything, it will be what you asked for or less. Would you rather coach your organization to get the larger or the smaller gift?

Community Foundations

Community foundations are created by groups of philanthropists who, for the most part, turn over the distribution of the funds to administrators or to a board of their members who will represent all the donors. Do you know an example of this type of foundation? Of course you do. There are community foundations in your town, the nearest city, county, or state. They have names like the Omaha Community Foundation, Community Foundation of New Haven, and the Community Foundation for Monterey County. It will be your mission to find the community foundations in your locale, discover if they support organizations like your nonprofit, and if any of the community foundation's leaders are linked (or could be linked) to your nonprofit. Simple enough, right?

Everything we have said about researching private foundations is true for community foundations. There are important differences about the grants made by community foundations, though. The giving of community foundations is less dependent on the ideas of individuals and more dependent on the wishes of the groups of donors who formed the foundation. The community foundation will be directed by its mission to support nonprofits in a specific geographic area. That area will be small, usually a city or county or two, not often as large as a state.

A new generation of donors has sought out the structure of community foundations to help them bring the collective wisdom of a group to their philanthropic decisions. Some of the new community foundations are structured so that donors have a larger role in the giving decisions of the foundation. Others are formed based on demographic qualities of the donors rather than the locality—groups of women, young technology workers, retired people, for example. It is common that, to join and retain membership in the foundation, donors have to contribute a specific amount of money each year. That money is then thrown into the collective grants pot so that, with the power of many contributions, donors can make a few large gifts to local nonprofits.

Company Foundations

Companies with philanthropic programs support nonprofits in several ways. One of the ways can be by creating a company foundation. The company foundation's sole purpose is to manage and administer the company's philanthropy. These foundations are entities separate from the company, but their giving is strictly controlled and influenced by the company. Company officers sit on the foundation's board. The foundation employees often have close ties to the company. The foundation's corpus is formed by contributions from the company. "Pass-through" foundations use money the company gives the foundation annually to make grants. If the foundation is structured to build an endowment from the company's contribution, its giving may remain stable regardless of the vagaries of the company's economic well-being.

Once again, there are a few important differences when we compare company foundations to private foundations. The foundation supported by a for-profit company has an agenda designed to help the company succeed. To that end, the company foundation will:

- Support the communities in which employees live. Better communities mean better employees—or potential employees—for the company. Improvements to the community's social and cultural services as well as to its academic offerings will attract new employees to the community and will continue to keep the community attractive to current employees. If the company has stores, offices, or factories in several communities, it may direct all of its philanthropic giving to those communities. It may enlist the assistance of the company branches to make giving decisions.

- Advance the interests of the company. Many companies use their foundations to improve their potential pool of new employees by supporting specific education programs. Company foundations often contribute to business schools and academic programs like accounting and economics. Pharmaceutical and medical equipment companies support science research at colleges and universities. The aerospace industry supports engineering research on college campuses.

- Promote the company's products, image, or global mission. National and international companies have a global community to support and enhance. They often give to causes that reach a greater number of people and that appear to be a greater distance from the product or the commercial mission of the company. Careful study will often uncover the logic behind a baby food company supporting baby formula distributions in underdeveloped countries or a software company promoting the installation of computers in inner city schools and libraries.

Your research into companies who may support your organization through their foundations will follow the same course you have now taken in your research of individuals, private foundations, and community foundations. You will closely review the age, structure, and history of the company foundation. You will review its guidelines and accumulate a list of nonprofits to which it has given and what causes it has supported. You will review the company and the foundation's leadership to uncover links to your nonprofit. All of these pieces may then come together to lead you to recommend this company and its foundation as a prospect.

Sometimes we researchers are dropped down into the middle of the trail rather than at the trailhead. When you discover that your nonprofit has an affiliate who leads a company and that company has a foundation, you will have to work your way back to discover if the individual's proximity to the foundation and to your nonprofit might add up to a major gift. You will try to uncover the importance of the individual's position and his power to influence the company foundation. The foundation may even include, in its guidelines, its commitment to supporting the causes of it executives. Or you may uncover precedents for that support as you gather the history of the company foundation's gifts. Did the company foundation make a large gift to the just-retired CEO's alma mater? Is the foundation supporting a local nonprofit on whose board the company chairman sits? Pieces of information like this will form the markers for your analysis.

Learning the Language of Foundations

The language of foundations unintentionally offers us a lesson in listening. Remember your grandpa telling you that people only hear what they want to hear? Foundation managers will testify that they get rivers of phone calls and mountains of applications for support from nonprofits that do not fit the foundation's mission. "Giving to preselected organizations only" . . . "funding healthcare initiatives only" . . . "supporting (the name of the state next to yours here) charities" . . . "letter of inquiry accepted" . . . these and other phrases from the language of foundations are intended to tell nonprofits precisely whether a foundation is the right one to pursue for support (see Exhibit 4-4).

Exhibit 4-4 **The Language of Institutional Giving**

Grantor: The foundation making the gift.

Grantee: The recipient of the gift.

Operating area: The geographical area in which a foundation or company gives grants. It is usually the same as the area in which the entity is located, does business, has plants or offices, or the area in which many of its customers live. For foundations, it may be the same community or state where the founders grew up or lived.

Letter of inquiry: A brief letter in which a potential grantee asks a grantor to indicate interest in the grantee's type of nonprofit or proposed funding request.

Assets: The total amount of money the foundation has at the end of its fiscal year, after expenses are subtracted.

Corpus: The same as assets.

Guidelines: The grantor's explanation of what institutions, causes, and programs they wish to support.

Application procedures: How to apply for support from a foundation, including format, reporting requirements, and deadlines.

Source: Authors

We are now speaking the dialect of affiliation and interest in the language of foundations. When you learned about researching prospects in general, you discovered that the best prospects are those who are already affiliated with or interested in your organization. This also holds true for foundations. What do the foundation guidelines tell you about the type of nonprofits it prefers to support? Is your nonprofit—without stretching the definition, please—that type of nonprofit? If the foundation supports community-based youth programs, it is unlikely to support a new wing for the art museum. If the foundation guidelines outline the geographic area the foundation supports and your nonprofit is not in it, move on to other foundations. Do not imagine that, because your cause is unique, the foundation will stretch its clearly defined borders to include your cause. Did the foundation say that it gives to preselected charities only? That means that the board members have a grocery list of causes they support and yours is not likely to be on it if you have not already heard directly from the foundation. Can you get your nonprofit on that list? There may be instances when you can. In the meantime, while you are spending energy trying to make your round nonprofit fit into the foundation's square hole, there is another foundation just waiting to hear from your organization, one that sees your nonprofit as a perfect fit for its philanthropic mission.

Before you go deeper into research and long before you recommend a foundation as a prospect to your fund-raising team, what restrictions on giving will you try to spot? The foundation's area of interest, the types of causes and organizations it supports, the geographic areas in which it gives, and whether it even accepts applications or inquiries at all will be the first gauntlets through which you must pass.

It is important to follow the guidelines and limitations outlined by the institutional donor. Remember, you are responsible for deciding how to spend the philanthropic dollar you were given to get the next dollar. To do so, you must decide who are the very best prospects, the most likely prospects, for your organization to cultivate. You must spend your research time identifying and qualifying those prospects. No matter how big a foundation's corpus is, none of their grant money is for your nonprofit if it does not fit their guidelines and mission. Is a foundation with a smaller corpus but with guidelines your organization fits a better prospect? Of course it is. Although your organization's mission is compelling, is it really unique enough to draw the attention of an institutional donor intent on supporting other charities? The answer is likely to be "no."

When You Can Break the Rules

Now that we have steered you away from researching foundations that do not match your nonprofit in regard to mission, we have exceptions to outline for you. This is not like learning French verbs where, for every rule, there are ten exceptions. There are only a few exceptions about researching and pursuing foundations for which your nonprofit is not a fit. These exceptions are simple and clear. You should break the rules we have set down here and pursue researching not-a-fit foundations when:

- You have an insider in your midst. You will see that sometimes foundations give to charities well outside their own guidelines. You may have thought, "Well, they gave to a _____ (fill in the type of nonprofit you work for here) once before. That means this foundation might give to my nonprofit." Actually, this is a clue to you that someone on the foundation board is linked to that not-a-fit nonprofit. The prep school that received a large grant from the foundation that only supports animal shelters got that money because one of the foundation's directors graduated from that prep school. You can bet on it. Now you must discover which foundations are led by your insiders. You can do this by carefully linking your key donors to their foundations, regardless of the limitations in giving you discover about those foundations. Although it is less likely that this will make a difference, you will also pay attention to your affiliates who are top company officers and directors able to influence the giving of their company foundations. When you have an insider in your midst, any—or even all—rules may be broken.
- When your research reveals that a foundation is rapidly shifting the types of organizations it supports. Even though the foundation's guidelines exclude your type of nonprofit, something has altered this foundation's perspective on philanthropy. The foundation has given large gifts to several organizations very much like yours. This is worth exploring.
- When your nonprofit or the foundation is brand new in the community. You and the foundation are meeting at a point of education. It is grade school days for causes and funding causes. Do the philanthropists in your area even know about your nonprofit? They may wish to add your organization to their list of charities once they learn about your nonprofit's mission. In turn, a new foundation still developing its giving plan may welcome the chance to learn about the giving opportunities your nonprofit offers. Although neither of these situations are the optimal use of that first philanthropic dollar for which you are being held responsible, they may be worth pursuing.
- When the foundation reports that it accepts letters or telephone calls of inquiry, and its mission is vague or all-inclusive. Notice that this opportunity to break the rules does not include "when its mission is clear and my nonprofit is not included." If the foundation takes phone calls or letters of inquiry, and your nonprofit or a project that needs funding might fit, call the foundation and ask. Just remember that, with the phone call, you have initiated the cultivation process.

- When a foundation is already supporting your nonprofit, it may be open to supporting other projects at your institution that do not precisely fit in its guidelines. This is only likely when the new project is within the realm of interests for the foundation or when your institution's relationship with the foundation and its staff runs deep.

The Art of Reading Federal Tax Forms
(or How We Learned to Drive Without Going Crazy)

Remember when you learned to drive a car? Remember how excited you were? If you think about it, you will realize that you weren't actually excited about learning to drive. You were excited about the idea of driving away from your parents' home, on your own. You were excited about being a driver, not learning to drive. In fact, drivers' ed was boring, sometimes even scary. It was scary when your drivers' ed classmates took the wheel for their turns on the freeway. Practicing parallel parking with your father was a nightmare. But driving—well, that was heaven.

Reading foundation 990-PF tax forms is a lot like driving. You will be happiest when you have the information you need off of the forms and into the foundation profile you are writing. Learning to read 990-PFs may not be fun, but it is the key to getting the important foundation information you need. Let's get you to the point where you are driving away from home on your own.

First, the Big Picture

Before a 990-PF is filled out by a foundation, it is 12 pages in length. After it has been completed and submitted, with its lists of the foundation's investments, directors, and grants made, 990-PFs may exceed 20 or 30 pages and often run 50 or 100 or more pages. But there are so few lines of a 990-PF to which you will attend that you will be surprised. You will be infinitely relieved, since U.S. tax forms have a terrible reputation for being difficult to read and complete. In fact, the IRS provides data about the time filers can expect to spend filling out forms. We will try to cut down on the amount of time you have to spend understanding this form. In this section, let's highlight the item lines and sections on a 990-PF that will interest you (see Figure 4-2).

990-PF, the Abridged Version

Although the 20 or more pages you will meet when you find the completed 990-PFs of the potential supporters you are researching may daunt you at first, you will soon be breezing through 990-PFs like they are grocery coupon booklets. Some pages have something you need and some pages do not. After you download a 990-PF from the Internet, you will skim it to locate the information we list next. The information will be in the same place in nearly every 990-PF you see. You may decide that it is important to print the entire

Form **990-PF**

Department of the Treasury
Internal Revenue Service

Return of Private Foundation
or Section 4947(a)(1) Nonexempt Charitable Trust
Treated as a Private Foundation

Note: *The organization may be able to use a copy of this return to satisfy state reporting requirements.*

OMB No. 1545-0052

20**02**

For calendar year 2002, or tax year beginning , 2002, and ending , 20

G Check all that apply: ☐ Initial return ☐ Final return ☐ Amended return ☐ Address change ☐ Name change

Use the IRS label. Otherwise, print or type. See Specific Instructions.

Name of organization

Number and street (or P.O. box number if mail is not delivered to street address) | Room/suite

City or town, state, and ZIP code

A Employer identification number

B Telephone number (see page 10 of the instructions)
( )

C If exemption application is pending, check here ▶ ☐

D 1. Foreign organizations, check here . ▶ ☐

2. Foreign organizations meeting the 85% test, check here and attach computation . ▶ ☐

H Check type of organization: ☐ Section 501(c)(3) exempt private foundation
☐ Section 4947(a)(1) nonexempt charitable trust ☐ Other taxable private foundation

I Fair market value of all assets at end of year *(from Part II, col. (c), line 16)* ▶ $

J Accounting method: ☐ Cash ☐ Accrual
☐ Other (specify) ....
(Part I, column (d) must be on cash basis.)

E If private foundation status was terminated under section 507(b)(1)(A), check here . ▶ ☐

F If the foundation is in a 60-month termination under section 507(b)(1)(B), check here . ▶ ☐

Part I **Analysis of Revenue and Expenses** *(The total of amounts in columns (b), (c), and (d) may not necessarily equal the amounts in column (a) (see page 10 of the instructions).)*

		(a) Revenue and expenses per books	(b) Net investment income	(c) Adjusted net income	(d) Disbursements for charitable purposes (cash basis only)
Revenue	1 Contributions, gifts, grants, etc., received (attach schedule)				
	Check ▶ ☐ if the foundation is **not** required to attach Sch. B				
	2 Distributions from split-interest trusts				
	3 Interest on savings and temporary cash investments				
	4 Dividends and interest from securities				
	5a Gross rents				
	b (Net rental income or (loss) _____)				
	6a Net gain or (loss) from sale of assets not on line 10				
	b Gross sales price for all assets on line 6a				
	7 Capital gain net income (from Part IV, line 2) . .				
	8 Net short-term capital gain				
	9 Income modifications				
	10a Gross sales less returns and allowances				
	b Less: Cost of goods sold . .				
	c Gross profit or (loss) (attach schedule)				
	11 Other income (attach schedule)				
	12 **Total.** Add lines 1 through 11				
Operating and Administrative Expenses	13 Compensation of officers, directors, trustees, etc.				
	14 Other employee salaries and wages				
	15 Pension plans, employee benefits				
	16a Legal fees (attach schedule)				
	b Accounting fees (attach schedule)				
	c Other professional fees (attach schedule) . .				
	17 Interest				
	18 Taxes (attach schedule) (see page 13 of the instructions)				
	19 Depreciation (attach schedule) and depletion . .				
	20 Occupancy				
	21 Travel, conferences, and meetings				
	22 Printing and publications				
	23 Other expenses (attach schedule)				
	24 **Total operating and administrative expenses.** Add lines 13 through 23				
	25 Contributions, gifts, grants paid				
	26 **Total expenses and disbursements.** Add lines 24 and 25				
	27 Subtract line 26 from line 12:				
	a Excess of revenue over expenses and disbursements				
	b Net investment income (if negative, enter -0-) . .				
	c Adjusted net income (if negative, enter -0-). . .				

For Paperwork Reduction Act Notice, see the instructions. Cat. No. 11289X Form **990-PF** (2002)

FIGURE 4-2
Page One of the IRS Form 990-PF (2000)

990-PF or, like many researchers, you will print only the pages you need or save the pages electronically. What information were you seeking in the first place? That is what we will review now and what you will focus on when you read 990-PFs.

Contact information: The first section of the 990-PF, in grand IRS style, is actually a pre-section. It is the demographic section before Part I. The name and address of the foundation is at the top of the first page, in the same white or "label" box where you put your name on your individual tax form. The foundation's telephone number is entered in the "B" box.

Foundation assets: The first spot where the foundation reports its assets is the "I" box just above the beginning of Part I. This box asks the foundation to report the "fair market value of all assets at the end of the year." It is the same figure you will see on page 2, line 16, of Part II.

Contributions received: Line 1 of Part I is the spot where the foundation lists the gifts and grants it received. If the foundation is a pass-through, you are likely to see a number here that nearly matches the number reported for the dollars given away.

Grants made: Line 25 of Part I is the spot where the foundation records the total "contributions, gifts, grants paid." That is pretty clear, right? This is one of the most important numbers you will retrieve.

Expenses: The line just before the grants line, Line 24, records the total operating and administrative expenses for the foundation. It is worth looking at this line because it tells you whether the foundation is a very small operation with no staff and little overhead or a foundation with paid employees with pensions and benefits. Your development team's approach to the foundation may be affected by the size and sophistication of the foundation.

Total Assets, Part II (and Part III): On page 2 of the 990-PF, the foundation reports its total gross and net assets. For the "bottom line" number, look at the bottom line on this page. Now, I bet that surprised you. Line 6 of Part III reports the "total net assets at the end of the year." That is the number that interests you.

Remember, the foundation is required by law to make grants that add up to 5 percent or more of its total net assets. You can do a quick and simple math problem to see what percentage of net assets was given away by the foundation you are researching. Here is the math problem:

Total contributions, gifts, grants paid (Part I, Line 25) divided by total net assets (Part III, Line 1) = percent of assets paid out in grants.

Sample problem:
$752,500 (grants paid) divided by $13,235,452 = 5.68% of assets paid out in grants to nonprofits.

Interesting questions: Part VII-A, page 4 of the 990-PF includes a few interesting questions. This section asks the foundation if, during the reporting year, there have been changes to its bylaws (question 3), a liquidation or dissolution (question 5), to which states the foundation reports its activities (question 8A), if anyone became a substantial contributor to the foundation (question 10), and who keeps the foundation's books (question 12). The answers to questions 3, 5, and 10 will intrigue you if they are not "no."

Directors, officers, trustees, and highest paid employees: In Part VIII, page 6 of the 990-PF, the foundation lists the directors, trustees, and employees, their titles, and their compensation. Your review of the directors and officers of a foundation will tell you a couple of important things. Who is in charge? Who appears to be related—by family or by business—to whom? Can you verify those relationships? And who among the trustees has a relationship to your nonprofit? The answers to these questions may propel this foundation to the front of your cultivation line or shove it to the back of the field. Each piece of information improves the foundation profile you are building.

Information regarding programs: In Part XV (you are delighted at our leap from Part VIII to Part XV, right?), the foundation reports whether it gives to pre-selected charities only, the contact person for applications, the format applications take, deadlines for applications, and geographical or program restrictions (2a through 2d). Foundations often attach a separate paper that outlines their programs and goals, including limitations to their giving plan. Be sure to look for that page.

Grants Paid: Line 3a of Part XV requires that, for the reporting year, the foundation lists all the grant recipients by name, the purpose of the grant, and the amount of the grant. Many times this list is assembled on separate sheets of paper, which are attached to the 990-PF. Look for those pages. The lists of grantees is often a long one, since the foundation will be reporting gifts of every size here. Line 3b is for a list of grant recipients who are already approved for future payments. This is where you may find information about multiple-year awards. It is worthwhile to review several years of 990-PFs, though, to accurately retrieve information about multi-year grants as well as to see single grants to other organizations. Some of the 990-PF aggregators have a couple of years of the reports available. You will be able to get earlier years from the IRS, of course.

That takes us to the end of our driving lesson . . . oh, we mean our lesson in reading 990-PFs. Now you can easily navigate your way through the most cumbersome 990-PFs all by yourself. We will stand on the porch and wave as you go.

Corporate Giving Programs

Some companies create corporate giving programs and give to charities directly through that program. The program may include some or all of these elements:
- Sponsorship of community events
- New or used equipment donations
- Loaning executives for fund-raising or other nonprofit leadership roles
- A matching gift program where the company donates an amount in the donating employee's name to a nonprofit
- Grants to charities

How Do I Love Thee? Let Me Count the Ways

We talked about the reasons behind corporate giving in the company foundation section of this chapter. Whether a company gives through a foundation or through a corporate giving program, the framework for giving decisions remains the same. Companies want to be located in strong, healthy communities in which talented employees want to live. Companies want to find a ready pool of well-educated or well-trained applicants when it is time to hire. Company leaders want to spread goodwill about their business. Corporate philanthropy, after all, can be a sort of advertising. It speaks well of a company. People remember who supported the middle school's computer access effort. They remember who contributed to the hospital's new wing each time they walk by the donor wall in the lobby. They never forget which companies stepped forward to help after the last flood.

So, we will expect corporations to give in their areas of operation, to causes that benefit their employees or the company directly, and to causes that promote the good reputation of the company in the community. You will draw a bigger picture of this same outline when you consider national and multi-national corporations as possible prospects. Their vision of community and need and reputation may be larger and reach farther, but it will have essentially the same aims at its core.

How to Find Companies and Their Giving Programs

For the most part, information about company foundations will be in the same places you looked for information about private and community foundations. It will also be in the same spots where you will look for information about companies and their giving programs (see Exhibit 4-5). Although companies giving through foundations report those gifts on 990-PFs, you will not find the same kind of easily retrievable records for the gifts made by companies directly through giving programs. Most companies with formal giving programs publicize that philanthropy with brochures and outcome reports. They release press stories about the company's giving. Companies with Web sites often include a link to information about their giving programs.

Exhibit 4-5	Resources for Researching Companies

Please see the appendix for a beginning list of books, CD-ROMs, and electronic databases to which you may subscribe. Here are a few Internet sites (some free, some charging a fee for premium content) that will get you started:

- CorporateInformation.com: http://www.corporateinformation.com/
  Search for companies by name, by country, by industry, or browse this site's collection of U.S. companies by state.
- Business.com: http://www.business.com/
  Search for companies by name.
- Hoovers: http://www.hoovers.com/
  Search for companies by name; site includes a fee-based section that gives subscribers more information.
- CEOExpress: http://www.ceoexpress.com/
  Find company information and other options for business research.

Source: Authors

After you visit the company's foundation or "community support" page on the Internet, you will go next to the press release section. Look for news releases about two things: the company's overall well-being and the company's philanthropic activities or that of its leaders. If the company established a foundation as its giving vehicle and the foundation accumulates assets, it may be unaffected by the financial health of the company. If the company makes philanthropic gifts directly or uses its foundation for a pass-through, the scope of its philanthropy will be closely linked to the company's financial health. You may be able to determine the company's health by reading press releases and news stories and by keeping abreast of the general news about this type of business. Some researchers analyze price/earning ratios and other features of company financial reports, but that level of detail and analysis may not be necessary or useful for most institutional giving research. Generally speaking, the profit levels that a company must reach to open the door to philanthropy are impossible to determine. Some of the wealthiest companies are the smallest givers and some small companies give more generously than anyone could expect. This sounds like we are talking about individual donors again, right?

Many things about viewing companies as philanthropic entities will parallel your experience with researching individuals. Young companies often have no philanthropic plan. They are concentrating their resources on becoming an established company. As the company grows, its philanthropic presence in the community grows, too. It is often an outgrowth of the founders' ideas about philanthropy. Initially, the company's giving may reflect causes that interest the founder, promote the company, or enhance employment for those working for the company. A company may begin its philanthropic maturation by matching employee giving, that is, giving an amount in an employee's name to the same nonprofit to which the employee gives. Some companies make matching employee gifts a hallmark of their philanthropy. Your organization will design ways to track companies that match employee gifts, or will prompt supporters to inquire at their companies and fill out the forms to get their gifts to your organization matched by their companies (see Exhibit 4-6).

Exhibit 4-6	Matching Gift Companies

Council for Advancement and Support of Education (CASE) maintains a list of matching gift companies. You will find ordering information at http://www.case.org/matchinggifts/Default.htm or by contacting CASE at the CASE Matching Gifts Clearinghouse, 1307 New York Avenue NW, Suite 1000, Washington, DC 20005-4701 (telephone: 202.478.5656; email: matchinggifts@case.org).

Source: Authors

Sponsorships

Some nonprofits offer companies (and individuals) the opportunity to underwrite events or to support elements of the nonprofit's program. This arrangement is called a sponsorship. We can all name well-known sponsorships in our communities. We have seen the product banners at the walkathons, the concerts, and the other fund-raising events we have attended. How do sponsorships differ from outright support? Sponsorships may involve goods and services rather than a cash contribution. In exchange, the nonprofit gives the sponsor "naming rights," which may involve detailed expectations for the manner in which the sponsor's name and logo are displayed and promoted.

If this relationship feels more commercial to you than the types of philanthropy we have been discussing, you are right. A sponsorship is a business arrangement. What is a prospect researcher's involvement in sponsorships? A researcher may be asked to uncover a company's relationship with other nonprofits. A researcher may have to outline a company's stance on various political issues so that coworkers considering the sponsorship can decide if the company is the right match for this nonprofit. Finally, a researcher may be asked to analyze a company's past to determine if the company's values and performance match the reputation the nonprofit touts for itself.

Stupid Things to Do When Researching Institutional Prospects

Do not worry. This is not the part where we suggest you put a rubber band on your ear or hop on one foot while you wait for 990-PFs to download. Instead, we offer you a short list of side roads that, if taken, will waste your and your nonprofit's time and resources.

1. Spend time researching and or encouraging your fund raisers to pursue prospects despite the fact that your nonprofit does not fit their guidelines. By this point, you are interpreting "prospects" to mean "individuals, companies, and foundations." We now promise not to

remind you one more time about identifying the best prospects. Cross
our fingers. Oh, we mean cross our hearts.

2. Consider creating a program to fit the guidelines of the foundation or
   company that is a big giver in your geographical or philanthropic
   community. If we had a list of all the nonprofits that have done this,
   we would not be rich, but we would have an awfully long list. What is
   the fatal flaw in this approach? First of all, it is a variation of Stupid
   Thing No. 1. It is you and your organization trying to squeeze your
   Size 5 mission into a foundation's Size 2 mission. But that is not the
   fatal flaw. The fatal flaw is that you might get the grant. Once you get
   it, you have to use it the way you promised. In the end, that may cost
   you more than you gained. After this foundation finishes starting your
   program, who will support its continuation? If it did not exist as a
   part of your organization's plan in the first place, will anyone be interested in continuing it? What message does abandoning a program that
   a foundation supported give this and other foundations watching
   your nonprofit's performance?

3. Contact foundations with guidelines that state, "giving to preselected
   charities only" or "does not accept applications." They will be polite
   enough not to say, "Can't you read?" But, guess what? That is what
   they will be thinking.

A Few Smart Things to Do with Your Free Time

Since you will not be busy wasting your own time or that of foundations, or
your fund-raising team, you may have a bit of time left over for a few smart
foundation tracking and advocacy moves.

1. Keep your eye on changing guidelines. Add tracking foundation news
   to your daily or weekly routine. It is no exaggeration to say that foundations of all sizes change their guidelines. The life events of the
   founders, changes in a community's needs, and the expansion or
   shrinking of assets all play a role in altering the course of giving for
   foundations. If you are connected to information that will report
   these changes, your organization can be one of the first to jump
   through the newly opened threshold the changes may create.

2. Link your board members and volunteers to the foundations and corporations in which they hold influence. These individuals are your
   nonprofit's best advocates. They believe in your nonprofit's mission—
   that is why they are volunteering. But, amazingly, it may not have occurred to them that they can bring financial support to your nonprofit
   through the influence they hold with a foundation or company. It may
   take the coaching that your fund raisers can provide to reveal that
   route to gifts. You can identify the institutional prospects to which
   your closest supporters are "related" for the fund-raising team.

3. Watch who is dancing with whom. Your nonprofit's closest supporters also support other causes. Sometimes you will discover that those causes bear an uncanny similarity to your nonprofit's causes. By paying attention to which organizations your best donors support and, conversely, from what corporations and foundations your peer institutions garner support, you may open a few more pathways to new support for your nonprofit.

Remember the Four and a Half Rights? Well, Here We Go Again.

In chapter 3, we outlined Karen Osborne's Four and a Half Rights for fund raisers. We linked research's functions to each of the Four and a Half Rights. It is delightful to see how clearly the Four and a Half Rights concept (four out of four and a half anyway) fits corporate and foundation research.

- Right amount? Other gifts given will help you answer this "right."
- Right time? See the institutional prospect's guidelines to learn when to apply.
- Right purpose? Back to those guidelines—that is where you will clearly see what the institutional giver supports. Be sure to gather fresh news about the foundation or corporation's giving, too, so you can see if the course has changed dramatically.
- Right person? When we talked about individual prospects, this meant, "Have I sent the right person to ask for this gift?" It still means that, but getting grants from foundations and corporations may involve more people than individual cultivation and solicitation takes. So, there are more "right person" appraisals for the fund-raising team to make. The grant writer, the development officer assigned, the leaders of your nonprofit, key volunteers affiliated with the corporation or foundation—we have filled a conference table, have we not? Usually the development officer assigned to the institutional prospect will be the person to coordinate all who have roles in this cultivation.

Sometimes all of these people are really one person—and that one person is *you*. If you work for a small nonprofit where researching, grant writing, cultivating, and asking are all among your assignments, you will have a lot less coordinating to do. Okay, so that is the only good point about being alone with all those chores. But you would be surprised how often the harried fund raiser with four or five colleagues and volunteers to apprise and appease would trade places with you. Even for just one day.

Government Funding

Throughout the 1960s and 1970s, the U.S. government expanded its forays into funding nonprofit programs that supported the government's goals. In the 1980s, the office-holders changed and the government switched gears. Funding for the arts diminished and funding for social services was deeply cut. Gradually, programs reorganized and found new funding resources. Generally speaking, government funding is philanthropy that supports the initiatives of the administration in power. It is important to stay in close touch with the ebbing and flowing tides of the leadership's ideas about nonprofits if this kind of funding is important to your organization.

Government funding often comes in the form of grants for specific programs and initiatives. Funding for science, health care, childcare, the arts, education, the environment—the range of funding types is vast. Researchers have a range of experience in looking for support for their organizations from governments. Some researchers in higher education spend little time researching these funding possibilities. Professors often write proposals for support for their research or for academic programs. They stay closely connected to proposal deadlines and funding priorities. Individual program officers solicit support from state and city governments. In some nonprofits, a researcher's job becomes trying to coordinate and record all of these efforts. In others, the researcher works closely with faculty and with program officers to identify prospects.

Researchers in some nonprofits closely monitor government funding opportunities. They rely on federal, state, and local funding programs to support their causes. Their organizations may operate programs that are regularly funded by a government agency or two. Some researchers almost exclusively spend their time identifying government funding opportunities, managing application deadlines, and overseeing reporting requirements. Let's take a look at how to connect to information about support from government.

National Support

The opportunities for funding from the federal government are so diverse and numerous that we cannot begin to cover them in this book. Instead, we will give you a few tools that will help you locate the opportunities available to your nonprofit.

The federal government has moved whole-heartedly into using the Internet to communicate grant opportunities (see Exhibit 4-7). All government information continues to be available in paper form, of course, but the Internet makes searching tens of thousands of government documents an easier enterprise. The International Society of Research Administrators (SRA), a group of professionals who oversee research projects, offers an extensive collection of government funding links at **http://www.srainternational.org/newweb/grantsweb/index.cfm**. Their site is a good starting place for researchers of all types who are looking for government funding.

The SRA recommends that those new to government funding begin their education at the U.S. government's "Catalog of Federal Domestic Assistance." This is the campfire around which all the federal programs gather. The searchable database of opportunities is a first stop for researchers looking for government support. If Internet access is not your route to this information, the General Services Administration offers a printed, CD-ROM, or disk version of the catalog. The catalog of information is searchable by several factors, including applicant, subject, deadline, and other indices. More than 50 agencies and almost 1,500 assistance programs were in the 2000 catalog. The programs include both financial and other programs, and the assistance opportunities are for nonprofits and other entities (individuals and companies, for example). Grant opportunities for nonprofits are linked, of course, to the initiatives of the current office-holders. They cover the entire realm of possibilities: education, healthcare, social services, research, and the environment.

Exhibit 4-7	Federal Funding Links

Catalog of Federal Domestic Assistance
Federal Domestic Assistance Catalog Staff (MVS)
General Services Administration
Web Site: http://www.cfda.gov/
Order a paper version of the catalog for a fee at
http://www.cfda.gov/public/COF99.htm or at 1-888-512-1800.

Review the Notices of Funding Availability (NOFAs) that appear in the
Federal Register at http://www.gpo.gov/su_docs/aces/aces140.html:
First Gov is the U.S. government's Web portal to nonprofit information
offering visitors links to many agencies and grant opportunities:
http://firstgov.gov/Topics/Nonprofit.shtml.

Source: Authors

State, County, and City Support

Finding state, county, and city support for your organization follows the trail that we have mapped in this chapter. Nonprofits seeking support for their programs from state and local governments connect to the state, county, and city offices giving away money for their type of program, cause, or mission. Those offices will have clear application procedures, including format, deadlines, and reporting procedures. Researchers may contact government offices directly and wade through the layers of departments, sections, and divisions. Researchers with Internet access can visit the state, county, or city home page. By drilling down through the agencies represented on that page, you will find the program support you are seeking. Some state and local government Web sites offer advanced search tools and some offer little more than phone numbers for various departments (see Exhibit 4-8).

Exhibit 4-8	Links to State, County, and City Web Sites

- U.S. Census Information: http://www.census.gov/
  Find the latest census data for the location you are researching here.
- The Grantsmanship Center: http://www.tgci.com/
  The State Funding links give visitors a map of the United States, which sends you to the state you choose with a click of your mouse. You will be at the state's home page so you will need to search for the appropriate agencies and offices.
- Search Systems: http://www.searchsystems.net/
  Search Systems has created an ever-expanding collection of links to state offices throughout the United States. The collection includes links to each state's home page as well as links to any state offices offering database-searching.
- U.S. Geological Survey (USGS) National Mapping Information: http://geonames.usgs.gov/pls/gnis/web_query.gnis_web_query_form
  Learn the name of the county for any city, township or even landmark entered.
- National Association of Counties (NACo): http://www.naco.org/counties/counties/index.cfm
  NACo provides profiles for counties, including elected officials, county seat location, link to the county Web site, and a list of cities located in each county.
- USA Citylinks: http://usacitylink.com/
  This relocation Web site includes hot links to cities, organized by state.

Source: Authors

Trail Report

Now that you found all the significant information about one or many institutional prospects that may support your nonprofit, what will you do with it? You will assemble the information in a foundation or corporation profile similar to the profiles you created for individuals. There are some distinct differences between institutional donor profiles and individual profiles—and some important similarities.

Like the individual profiles you build, the institutional prospect's profile will outline the prospect's past and present relationship to your nonprofit. It will report the philanthropic nature of this prospect. It may not include detailed financial information about any individuals, although it may reference other profiles for the individuals (the ones who are your nonprofit's affiliates) associated with the company or foundation you are profiling. The financial information it includes will be about the assets of the institutional prospect or the annual pass-through total.

After you have built many donor profiles, you will form opinions about what should and should not be included. It is wise to wait until you are experienced with profile building before you make wholesale changes in your organization's profile format. As you develop your own style and begin to adapt profiles to it, remember what you are trying to accomplish and you will know what to include. You wish to create a capsulized portrait of this prospect. You hope that the member of your fund-raising team who reads it will easily pick out the salient points. You organize the document in a routine way, so that your audience—that fund-raising team—knows where to look for information time and time again (see Exhibit 4-9).

Profiles of institutional prospects capture key information about who the potential donor is and how to make contact. They include background information that tells the history of the institutional prospect and outlines the history of that prospect with your organization. The giving history, noting the purpose of the gifts, will be listed. Gifts to other nonprofits, including the purpose of those gifts, will be listed. Many researchers include a suggested Ask or a giving range, based on what peer institutions received.

You will find sample profile formats for institutional prospects in the appendix section of this book.

| Exhibit 4-9 | Institutional Prospect Profile |

An institutional prospect profile includes:

- Name of organization, company, or agency
- Contact information (mailing addresses, phone numbers, Web site address, email and facsimile) for the institution and for key people
- Institutional prospect's history, if appropriate (if it is a foundation, include who established it and what year, for example)
- Demographics about the prospect—gross sales, number of employees for a company; total assets and gift range for a foundation; total grant budget and average grants for a government agency
- Institutional prospect's affiliates who are affiliated with your nonprofit and how
- History of giving to your institution
- History of giving to other institutions
- History of contact with your organization (outline proposals submitted and their outcomes)
- Important news about the institutional prospect
- Recommendation, including capacity, Ask amount, and any cultivation strategies that emerged during research

Source: Authors

Now That You Know How to Do It, What Do You Do with It?

We began this chapter by suggesting that you relax. Now we are near the end and your head is spinning again. Our hope is that you are excited about the new tools you have and eager to begin the work ahead of you. Our greatest fear is that you have reached this point ready to ask, "Whatever do I do now?" To allay our fears, let's outline what you will do in the line of researching institutional givers.

1. Project-defined research: The grant writer at your organization (it might even be you) has projects that need funding. The next initiatives your organization wishes to complete, or a need in the community, requires funding. It will be up to you to find likely institutional prospects for that funding.
2. A link in the chain: Now that you know where to find information about institutional givers, you will be checking to see if your individual prospects have foundations or lead companies with corporate giving programs. Knowing that individual prospects have this additional option for making gifts will enhance your nonprofit's chance of getting a gift.
3. Patchwork: Members of your fund-raising team will receive pieces of information, and they will ask you to complete their half-finished pictures. "I heard that there is a new foundation in town. Let's find out if we fit their guidelines." "Did you know that our annual fund chair's company is now matching employee gifts?"
4. Funding for the future: Now you are plugged into news about institutional givers. You are reading about the grants they are making. Your nonprofit's mission and overarching goals are on your mind when you see articles about institutional givers making grants to nonprofits like yours. You will save information about these possible prospects. You will toss these future funders into your pool of prospective donors, so that you can pull them back out and research them later.

Now that the tools and concepts you need for institutional giving research are in your hands, do not go crazy on us. Remember what we told you at the start of this chapter. Ideally, institutional donors will make up about 20 percent of your support. You will now have to find a like-number balance when you look at the percentage of your time that you spend researching these prospects. It will be up to you to concentrate your research on the most likely institutional prospects, following the same rules that we outlined earlier in this book to predict who those prospects will be. Create a research time hierarchy to wedge, by affinity (or "most likely fit"), the institutional prospects you identify. Set up ways to get the information you need about these potential prospects coming your way. When you do these things, you will begin to effectively add solid institutional prospects to your team's cultivation lineup.

CHAPTER 5

Research Math

"Well, you'll get to know me! Look me up in Who's Who,
Dun & Bradstreet*!"*
      —American millionaire Leland Davis, a character in the 1966 film *How to Steal a Million.*

Warning: Do Not Skip this Chapter

We can hear you groaning. We can hear you, that is, if you even showed up for this chapter. Perhaps you have thumbed ahead to chapter 6. Maybe you are lingering at chapter 4, afraid about what is coming in this chapter. Or you may be in the break room by now. We know what is going on. Researchers reading this book, haunted by nightmares of high school math classes, will try to skip this chapter, this part of becoming a great researcher. Unfortunately, there is no avoiding it because in the next hour or day or week, a fund raiser will be standing in front of your desk, asking, "Can you tell me how much stock Jane Smith owns and what it's worth?" Or that fund raiser will tell you, "John Jones sold his company to that giant retailer last year. How much did he get for it?" Or she might say, "A trustee told me that Mary Brown is wealthy. She was one of the first investors in that startup that went public about six months ago, I'm told. How are the company's investors doing?" Then that fund raiser will wait for an answer from you, for a sign of intelligent life from your side of the research desk.

So, no matter what you do to avoid it, you are trapped in the math vortex. You have to get these research math skills—better labeled as financial research and analysis skills—under your belt. Miracle of miracles, here is your chance. And we promise that, by the end of this math work, you will have the preliminary tools to answer the types of financial questions development officers will bring to you and the questions your own research will raise.

Can you do it? Can you master the analytical skills necessary to move research to a higher function at your institution? Of course you can. We are testimony to that. We had never read financial reports and proxies the way we read them now. We, like most researchers, were inexperienced financial data evaluators, unskilled at transforming information gathered from financial resources into opinions and ideas about philanthropic potential. With a bit of practice, a dose of faith, and a lot of information from other researchers, any researcher can add prospect math skills to the set of talents he brings to a nonprofit's advancement efforts.

The Rules of Engagement

Let's lay down the rules of engagement, a framework for what we will do in this chapter. This chapter is called "Research Math." That is not a school of math that you will find in a college course catalog. It is a relatively informal collection of methods and formulas researchers apply to the financial information they find about prospective donors. The financial reckoning that we will describe as research math is the process by which real estate and stock holdings, salaries and bonuses, giving histories, and other dollar data are analyzed to make (hopefully) reliable conclusions regarding both the potential for a gift (capacity) and the predicted size of that gift (capacity rating and the Ask).

In this chapter, we will outline what financial information is available, what you do with it once you find it, and what it then means in terms of your goal to identify and qualify major gift prospects. We will call these three elements of research math our "Research Work Bench." The three elements are:

1. Locate: Find the financial information available through public documents. We will create a road map to this information and, most of the time, you will find the information in the same place from prospect to prospect.

2. Calculate: Apply mathematical formulas to the information retrieved to facilitate conclusions. The formulas applied will be both standard formulas and ones that researchers and fund raisers have developed after years of evaluating financial capacity.

3. Amalgamate: Combine the financial information gathered with other background data, as well as with the calculations made from the information, to make recommendations to the development team.

You will see these three words—locate, calculate, and amalgamate—throughout this chapter, after the heading "Research Workbench: Salary." They will become signposts for how to handle the financial information your development team needs to secure major gifts.

Art or Science?

The things you have learned about the prospect research field up to this point are important to remember. Prospect research is a young field. The wealth of information available to professional financial analysts is not available to researchers and would, in fact, lend little to our goals of setting capacity thresholds and philanthropic Asks. Over the short history of this field, researchers have developed formulas, mathematical expectations, and opinions about donors and capacity (we like to call them 'fund-raising adages') that form the framework for much of what occurs throughout the prospect cultivation process. Research math helps in:

- Evaluating constituents' financial well-being to determine if the individual or company is a major gift prospect
- Promoting the assignment of freshly identified prospects for cultivation
- Setting a ranking for prospects in the cultivation hierarchy
- Moving the cultivation process along (when new financial information is added through ongoing research)
- Motivating development officers (when numbers can inspire a more aggressive approach)
- Calculating capacity ratings for prospects based on their economic growth, personal holdings, investments, income, and other factors
- Recommending the Ask for prospects based on analysis of financial details coupled with other historical and relational information
- Suggesting planned giving opportunities based on the financial resources and life stages of prospects
- Monitoring the information stream to re-evaluate the prospect's financial well-being as other relevant factors (age, life stage) change

After finding solutions to traditional story problems like the ones we describe here, researchers apply fund-raising adages to the mix to make conclusions that will help advance fund-raising goals. This is the part of the equation that is more art than science. The fund-raising adages are based on the experiences of many nonprofits over many years. They are assumed to be *generally* true—which means that you will find exceptions to these adages at every turn. As you use these formulas at your nonprofit, you may adapt them to better fit what you discover after you witness the outcomes of cultivation after cultivation. The path you then take to estimate gift capacity and the Asks made of new prospects may become more and more reliable. That is the word of the day, by the way—estimate. Remember that the art part of this equation can only create estimates. Remind your development team of this every time you have an opportunity. Do not let their expectations and their experiences with your success transform your estimates and predictions into fact. There are only a few facts in this part of prospect research, and the most important fact will be the actual gift that arrives at your nonprofit after all of your research, estimates, and predictions are finished.

The Research Wallflower: Net Worth

In fund-raising circles, you will hear the term "net worth" bantered about (see Exhibit 5-1). You may be asked, in fact, to estimate the net worth of prospects. Many researchers resist this directive since there is no way to accurately make such an estimate. A few clever researchers have even renamed net worth estimates as "known assets" or "wealth indicators" estimates. Even that, however, is inaccurate since we cannot know all of a prospect's holdings and investments, just like we cannot know all of a prospect's expenses or debts.

Exhibit 5-1	Net Worth and Fund-Raising Adages about Net Worth and Gift Capacity

Net Worth: The monetary value of a prospect's holdings after all expenses and debts are deducted. The net worth of a prospect is unavailable to fund raisers since the details of the prospect's precise income and expenses are not available.

Fund-raising Adages about Net Worth and Gift Capacity:
"Salary represents 10 percent of net worth."
"Stock holdings represent 20–25 percent (or 30–35 percent) of net worth."
"Real estate holdings represent 20–25 percent (or 30–35 percent) of net worth."
"Prospects have the capacity to give about 2–5 percent of net worth (or known assets) to charity."
"Prospects have the capacity to give 10 percent of the value of stock options of $1 million or more to charity."

Source: Authors

Some nonprofits, eager to rate prospects accurately or to make precisely the right Ask, require researchers to make net worth estimates and, therefore, doing so may be unavoidable for you. It would be unfair of us to withhold from you the formulas that those researchers are using, even though we share them with trepidation. We plead with you to remember the dangers inherent in this course—if you try to estimate net worth, you cannot ever be right; you are doomed to be proven wrong. A development officer from a small nonprofit with no research staff once came to visit, to learn the basics of research. In these circumstances, with no more than an hour or two to explain everything about research, we often try to give individuals tools that will help them identify and qualify prospects easily. In this case, we began by outlining what one of this fund raiser's affiliates held in stock and earned in salary and what this might mean in terms of gift capacity. As the information unfolded, as we quickly gathered dollar figures and stock holding numbers, we began to form an opinion about gift capacity based on the fund-raising adages we outline here. We tossed around gift capacity ranges like $100,000 to $300,000. Then, suddenly, our visitor said, "But in an article in the newspaper recently, this prospect said he gave away $11 million to charities last year."

Did we feel foolish? Of course we did. But that was not the most important element of this story. This story points out the futility in trying to gauge giving and capacity based on the numbers you will generate in this chapter. If there are newspaper articles, including interviews with your prospect, that better outline her wealth and capacity, use them. But if gathering and analyzing the numbers we outline here is all we have, we plod forward, hopeful that the members of our team never forget two things. We hope they remember that we are deep into the art part of prospect research. And we hope they remember to use the net worth estimates and the other numbers that emerge from that math as mere *starting points* that will be amended and enhanced by the information they gather through cultivation. And of course we hope that they share what they know with us from the start.

Researchers write cautions and warnings that they attach to net worth estimates so that the fund raisers who read the material will put it in the correct perspective. A qualifying statement, placed at the top or bottom of the page, may read something like this:

"This document includes an estimate of net worth. Because an accurate accounting of expenses as well as income or assets is not available to the research department, this estimate must be viewed as speculative. It must not be taken as true or accurate, but only as a rough guideline that may contribute to estimating gift capacity for the purpose of rating a prospect or setting the Ask."

So, you are now fully armed to enter the net worth arena. If you use the formulas you see here that involve estimating net worth (or estimating known assets), do so with all the armament we are giving you. Better yet, show this chapter to your development staff to let them know that no net worth estimates you can make will equal the information they uncover through cultivation. Maybe then they will stop asking for net worth estimates.

Evaluating Wealth Indicators

In chapter 3, we briefly discussed prospects affiliated with public companies, private companies, and those who gained wealth by inheritance, by real estate investments, and by other avenues. In this chapter, we will explore in detail how to evaluate these routes to wealth . You will get the tools you need to make recommendations to fund raisers about assigning and rating prospects and about concluding and timing an Ask.

Public Company Affiliates: Salaries, Stock Holdings, and Other Compensation

As we learned in chapter 3, the Securities and Exchange Commission (SEC) regulates the information available regarding publicly held companies. Because these companies accept support from the public—in the form of stock sales—they must report their use of these investments. This use includes the salaries and other compensation of the top officers of the company. It also includes the stock holdings and options of the company's directors and others who hold 5 percent or more of the company's stock or who are key decision-makers. And, finally, it includes detailed remuneration information, such as loans, signing bonuses, incentives, and other opportunities for great wealth. This information is reported annually in the company's proxy statement.

Proxy Pointers

The proxy statements for public companies are available by telephoning the company and asking that a copy be sent to you. They are also available on the Internet at the Securities and Exchange Commission's Electronic Data Gathering, Analysis, and Retrieval system (EDGAR) Web site and at other financial sites that are collecting EDGAR documents (see Exhibit 5-2). EDGAR documents were first posted on the Internet in 1994. Publicly filed documents are posted on the SEC's EDGAR site 24 hours after they are filed. Proxy statements are called "DEF-14A" documents in the EDGAR database. You will find a "Guide to Corporate Filings" that will explain the naming convention at the SEC Web site at **http://www.sec.gov/edaux/forms.htm**. The SEC's EDGAR Web site also includes information about how to search for documents, qualifying information about what corporations must file, and updates about changes in the EDGAR project. Each of the commercial EDGAR Web sites provides the SEC information to visitors in a slightly different way. Try them all to find the interface and search process that suits you. To see proxy statements older than those released in 1994, researchers may contact various SEC document sellers, libraries, or the company itself.

One of the simplest Internet resources for how to read proxy statements is at the AFL-CIO "Executive PayWatch" site, on the page called "How to Track Down Executive Pay" at **http://www.aflcio.org/corporateamerica/paywatch/**.

Exhibit 5-2	EDGAR Internet Links

- Securities and Exchange Commission Search EDGAR: http://www.sec.gov/edgar/searchedgar/webusers.htm
- EDGAROnline: http://www.edgar-online.com/ (fee-based)
- EDGARScan: http://edgarscan.pwcglobal.com/servlets/edgarscan
- 10K Wizard: http://www.tenkwizard.com/
- FreeEDGAR: http://www.freeEDGAR.com/

Source: Authors

Proxy statements are long documents, and it is unlikely that you will find the entire document useful for your purpose. Researchers frequently copy and paste the relevant sections into a document that they then save or print. The easiest way to do this is:

1. Use the "find" feature in your browser to locate all the references to your prospect in the proxy statement.
2. Copy and paste those sections into a page of your word processing program. Besides the sections that outline your prospect's salary and stock holdings, other sections will explain the reasoning behind those awards—be sure to review and copy the relevant portions of those sections. Include the headings and footnotes to tables. It is also wise to note the breaks between sections where you have eliminated text or tables. Be sure to include the identifying information about the document, including type, date, and the Web address where you found it.
3. Researchers have discovered that, by setting a word processing page with a font such as Courier and a font size of 10 or less, the tables in the proxy statement will align well, despite the loss of tabs in the conversion. It is necessary to change your page to a "landscape" orientation instead of the "portrait" orientation that is usually the default format.

Some EDGAR document providers now give visitors the choice to download these massive documents as text or in an html format. Try both versions to see which suits you and your equipment.

It is important to save this information in the prospect's electronic or paper file. This is historical information that will be handy later, when you are asked to trace the prospect's professional growth or when you must review a prospect's financial life after he retires. It will also serve as "backup" if you are asked to re-examine your calculations later.

Exhibit 5-3	Proxy and Stock Terminology

Here are the definitions for a few of the terms associated with public company research that we are using in this chapter:

Insider: One of the chief officers, all directors, and any person who holds and controls 5 percent or more of a company in the form of publicly traded stock. Insiders have access to information about the company that other stockholders do not.

Chief officer: One of the top officers of a company. The hierarchy of jobs is usually chairman, president, chief executive officer, chief operating officer, secretary/treasurer, executive or senior vice presidents.

Director: A member of the board who oversees operation of a company. The board is usually made up of leaders of other companies, large investors, and the employee who heads the company.

Stock holdings: The number of shares of a company's (or companies') stock that an individual owns.

Option: A benefit of employment or board service that gives the individual the right to buy a specific number of shares within a designated period of time.

Option price: The price per share of stock that a company officer or director will pay for shares granted as a benefit of association with the company.

Exercising an option: The act of buying shares of stock that are outlined as available to a company officer or director at an established price within a specific period of time.

Find the definitions for other terms at these (and other) Web sites:
- AFL-CIO (Proxy) Terms and Methodology:
  http://www.aflcio.org/corporateamerica/paywatch/ceou/ceou_terms.cfm
- Bloomberg.com Financial Glossary:
  http://www.bloomberg.com/money/tools/bfglosa.html
- Investorwords: http://www.investorwords.com/
- The Motley Fool Glossary:
  http://www.fool.com/school/Glossary/glossary.htm

Source: Authors

Proxy statements are dense documents that may seem daunting at first. There are many resources to help you understand the terms and concepts related to public company employment research (see Exhibit 5-3). With practice, you will learn how to find the information you need with few bumps or bruises. Occasionally, you will meet new pieces of information relating to a prospect that will have you saying, "Well, that's a new twist on compensation." Sometimes you will see things that are difficult to decipher. Remember that help is usually nearby—researchers are a friendly lot and your peers and colleagues can brainstorm the translation of that new information into easy-to-analyze terms.

In this section, we will look at proxy information from the fictitious corporation called XYZ Company. In doing so, we will occasionally encounter oddities that will, we hope, demonstrate the fluid nature of reading and evaluating proxy information. We will not be consistently or thoroughly researching any one officer or director, but instead highlighting the type of information researchers seek.

Salary

Under the section of the proxy statement called "Executive Compensation," the annual salaries of the top officers are listed. The salary for the year of the proxy report and the salaries for the previous two or so years are outlined. In addition to salary, the employee's bonus and stock options granted or stock awards are also listed (see Exhibit 5-4). The salary and bonus are added together to represent the total *cash compensation* for the individual.

In the XYZ Company proxy, Jane Able, the chief executive officer, earned $700,000 in salary in 1999. She earned no bonus that year, but earned a bonus of $250,000 with the same salary the year earlier. This inconsistency in year-to-year remuneration should prompt you to search the proxy again for additional information. Why did Ms. Able earn around $250,000 less in 1999? A search for the term "bonus" in the proxy statement uncovers that bonuses are linked to the company's overall performance. Our fictitious proxy reports:

"For fiscal 1999, the Company's committee for compensation established performance targets based on the achievement of specific levels of income for the Company. At the end of the fiscal year, it was determined that these targets were not met. Therefore, no annual bonuses were awarded for this year."

So, XYZ Company's chief officers did not, for the most part, make their performance-based thresholds and thus received no bonuses in 1999. That drop in personal income, real or anticipated, would make a difference in the amount or timing of an Ask, would it not?

The "Executive Compensation" table will include footnotes at the end of the table outlining details about the salaries listed. For example, if the officer joined the company in the middle of the year, the relatively lower salary he received that year will be explained in a footnote corresponding to the footnote number by the individual's name. This is the case in the XYZ compensation table. A footnote explains that the salary difference of $300,000 for 1998 and $104,000 for 1997 for Mr. Can is because he joined the company in August 1997. He therefore received only a part of a year's salary paid for that position in 1997.

In that same compensation table, there may be a column named "all other compensation." This is often the dollar value of other benefits, such as supplemental insurance policies, the use of cars, airplanes, and other amenities. Compared to the salary and bonus, this amount is often negligible. The XYZ

Company proxy has a footnote that explains the negligible amounts and what they covered for each of the executives.

| Exhibit 5-4 | Executive Compensation |

This table will outline the salary, bonus and other compensation for the company's top officers. It will outline the annual compensation (salary and bonus) and "long-term" compensation (stock options granted and "all other compensation," for which there will be footnotes). It will look like this:

		Annual Compensation		Long-term Compensation	
Name and Position	Fiscal Year	Salary	Bonus	No. of Stock Options Granted	All Other Compensation[1]
Jane Able	1999	$700,000	0	25,000	$4,000
	1998	$700,000	$250,000	50,000	$4,000
	1997	$650,000	$500,000	50,000	$3,900
Tom Best	1999	$500,000	0	20,000	$4,000
	1998	$500,000	$120,000	20,000	$4,000
	1997	$450,000	$200,000	20,000	$3,900
Rob Can	1999	$300,000	0	10,000	$3,000
	1998	$300,000	$90,000	10,000	$3,000
	1997	$104,000[2]	$150,000	10,000	$2,800

This is where you will check the footnotes associated with the table to see explanations of things in the table. They will report, for example:

[1] The company provides each named executive with group life, health and other non-cash benefits available to all salaried employees and not included in this column. The amounts shown in this column represent additional insurance premiums that the company provides for certain employees, as well as other insurance covered by the company, such as automobile insurance.

[2] Mr. Can joined the company in August 1997.

What will the salary and bonus numbers tell you? This is when the work you have done to study wealth and to establish a threshold for a major gift for your organization pays off. You will decide if an individual with a salary and bonus of $185,000 a year has the makings of a major gift prospect. You will decide if it will take an annual salary and bonus of, say, $750,000 or more to generate a major gift to your organization. Your decisions will be based on your organization's history of gifts, what other researchers use as benchmarks, this particular donor's philanthropic nature, and other factors.

As you may know, some religious groups promote tithing—giving 10 percent of your income—as the charitable goal for their adherents. *The*

Chronicle of Philanthropy analysis we referred to in chapter 1 reported that individuals with incomes over $200,000 gave closer to 2–3 percent of their income in 1998 (August 10, 2000). Many fund raisers predict that philanthropic Americans can give in ranges of 5 to 10 percent of their annual income over three to five years (2 to 3 percent in a single gift) to all of their charities—or, at least, that the Ask should be in that range. This serves as a guideline—a fund-raising adage—for researchers. The individual with a cash compensation package of, say, $300,000 would make gifts totaling $15,000 to $30,000 to all her charities in the time period described (see Exhibit 5-5). If your nonprofit defines a major gift as $25,000 given over three to five years, this individual might qualify as a major gift prospect. Of course, the other factors we have been discussing until now—how your institution ranks in the prospect's philanthropic plans, your prospect's age and life stage, other draws on the prospect's resources, for example—might alter your recommendation.

Exhibit 5-5   **Gift Capacity Math Adages**

Fund-raising Math Adage: An individual has the capacity to make philanthropic gifts in the range of 5 to 10 percent of his or her annual salary and bonus over three to five years (2 to 3 percent in a single gift).

Formulas:
(annual salary + bonus) x .05 = gift potential
(annual salary + bonus) x .10 = gift potential

Example based on cash compensation of $250,000 (salary) plus $50,000 (bonus) per year:
($250,000 + $50,000) x .05 = $15,000
($250,000 + $50,000) x .10 = $30,000

Estimated giving potential: $15,000 to $30,000 over three to five years

Source: Authors

Research Workbench: Salary

Locate: Find salary information under "Executive Compensation" in the proxy statement filed by a public company. The proxy statement can be obtained by calling the company to request a copy or by visiting an EDGAR site on the Internet. Be sure to retrieve all the information you need from the proxy to make your knowledge complete.

Calculate: Add the salary and bonus. Using the 5 to 10 percent fund-raising adage, figure the dollar amount your potential prospect might be able to give to your organization over three to five years (or annually, using 2 to 3 percent).

Amalgamate: Review other important factors you have learned about the prospect, such as age, life stage, draws on her resources (children in school, for example), and your organization's rank in the prospect's philanthropic priorities. Include information about increases or decreases in compensation from the proxy. Based on this review and your calculations, form an opinion about this individual's likelihood to make a gift, the size of that gift, and even its timing. The opinion will be to qualify the individual as a major gift prospect, to rank the individual's giving potential, or to set the Ask amount. It will be a preliminary opinion, with modifications to occur as we look at stock holdings next.

Stock Holdings

Many employees of public companies receive stock benefits as an additional feature of their compensation. These benefits may involve the opportunity to buy stock at a reduced price, to receive stock as a part of the company's profit sharing plan, and to receive stock as a part of the company's performance incentives. The only public company employees for whom stock buying, selling, and holding information is available in the proxy statement are the top officers, often the top four or five. Stock holding information is also available in the proxy statement for the company's directors and for other individuals who hold 5 percent or more of the company's stock.

To find stock holdings and option information, go to three distinct tables in the proxy. They are:

1. Stock Ownership table
2. Executive Compensation table
3. Stock Exercises table

We will look at the first table in the Stock Holdings section and all three tables in the Stock Options section of this chapter.

Stock Ownership Table

The "Stock Ownership" table appears early in the proxy, and it outlines how many shares each officer and director owns (see Exhibit 5-6). In the XYZ Company example, Executive Vice President Tom Best owned 450,000 shares at the close of the company's fiscal year.

As you can see, the table lists the number of shares held and the number of options held for each chief executive and each director or other insider (see Exhibit 5-6). The footnotes, once again, will include explanations about those holdings and options. Some of the stock held, for example, may be held jointly with the individual's spouse or held in trust for the officer's children. In the case of Ms. Able, the second footnote tells us that 500,000 shares held by the nonprofit Able Foundation are not included in Ms. Able's totals since she has no monetary interest in the foundation. If we did not already know about the Able Foundation, we do now.

The "Stock Ownership" table also outlines stock options, shares that may be purchased in a prescribed period of time. We will look at this in a moment.

Exhibit 5-6	Stock Ownership

Stock Owned by the Directors and Officers of XYZ Company

In this section of the proxy statement, the company outlines the shares owned by the officers and directors and the shares that may be acquired during an upcoming period of time. The stock ownership table will also include the percent of the outstanding shares that each person holds. The information in the table is associated with a date, usually the same date shown throughout the proxy for the other financial data.

Name	Aggregate Number of Shares Beneficially Owned[1]	Shares Acquirable within 60 Days	Percent of Shares Outstanding
Jane Able	3,195,000[2]	5,000	1%
Tom Best	450,000	10,000	—
Rob Can	15,000	5,000	—

The footnotes that follow the table will further delineate the details of the information in the stock ownership table. The footnotes may include information like:

[1] The number of shares listed here includes shares both individually and jointly owned, as well as shares over which the individual has sole control or voting power.

[2] Does not include 500,000 shares held by the Able Foundation, a charitable nonprofit corporation in which Ms. Able has no pecuniary interest.

Source: Authors

Researchers estimate the value of stock holdings in a few ways. All of the approaches involve a series of assumptions and once again point to the unreliability of estimating the value of assets. Some researchers think the stock holding report made annually in the proxy statement contains the most reliable information about holdings. These researchers apply today's stock price to the total proxy statement holdings to arrive at a value for the stock, adding a clarifying statement that the resulting number is an old holdings number times a new stock price. Or they use historical stock quotes to estimate the value of the stock at the time the proxy statement was released. Some researchers are more interested in estimating what the stockholder has today. They use resources to get what they hope is current stock holding information. We will discuss these resources in a moment. The approach you choose to outline the value of stock holdings may depend on details about the prospect you are researching. If the prospect is no longer an insider and is, therefore, no longer required to report holdings and trading activity, you will look at a proxy statement as a financial moment "frozen in time." The last proxy statement that includes your prospect will report his holdings at that moment. Information about what happened to these holdings since then will be unavailable.

To create a *snapshot* of the prospect's holdings—a picture or "still life" of what the prospect held at the end of the company's fiscal year—multiply the number of shares by the market price per share at the date of proxy. Some researchers use the market price of the shares today and include a qualifying statement in the report like, "If the prospect still holds these 45,000 shares, they would be worth $675,000 at the time of this report (based on a price of $15.00 per share at the close of trading today)."

Prospects may hold shares directly or indirectly, generally indicating the prospect's power to dispose of the shares without consulting others who have interest in the shares. They may hold different classes of shares, carrying different voting rights. They may hold common stock, purchasable by nearly anyone, or preferred stock, which has a special dividend associated with it. Sometimes the stock holdings of insiders are converted to stock units, as defined by the company and with a unit price attached. As you can see, there are simply too many terms, concepts, and possibilities to cover in this book. Keep a financial terminology dictionary in your office or use the Internet definition resources listed here (see Exhibit 5-3). Remember to turn to the resources you have—board members, volunteers, other staff or faculty members, and prospect research colleagues—to help you understand the range of stock holding scenarios you will encounter.

Researchers usually quote direct and indirect shares separately in their reports and profiles since the prospect has a different level of control over these two types of holdings. For the stock price, researchers use the previous day's closing price. This number can be found in the stock pages of the newspaper or in one of the resources listed in Exhibit 5-7. A report of a prospect's holdings might look like this:

- No. of shares held at the time of proxy (03/15/2001): 45,0000 direct, 20,000 indirect
- Value of shares held: Direct shares: $450,000; Indirect shares: $200,000 (share price of $10.00 at the time of proxy)

Exhibit 5-7 **Where to Find Stock Prices**

Use these Web sites to find stock prices for public companies. Each site may include other features like stock price charting, historical quotes, company profiles, and stock symbol look-ups. Visit them all (and others you find) to see which interface and features suit you best.

Yahoo! Finance	http://finance.yahoo.com/
Quicken	http://www.quicken.com/
TradingDay.com	http://www.tradingday.com/
Big Charts	http://www.bigcharts.com/

Source: Authors

Options

Public company insiders often purchase stock at a price that is well below the market price of the stock. This is called an option price. The price may be set at the time of employment or board service and it acts as an incentive for the employee or other insider to help the company perform at a level that generates a stock price above the option price. Often the option price is well below the market price; sometimes the option price exceeds the market price. It is important to compare the market price, the current stock price that outsiders must pay, with the prospect's option price. In the difference between these two numbers you will calculate an estimate of your prospect's profits.

Although options—the opportunity to buy stock within an established period of time—are a benefit of employment, the employee is not obligated to take advantage of, or exercise, an option. A table in the proxy statement will tell you the total number of shares that the prospect had an option to exercise (buy), and what options he exercised during that time.

Optioning for Riches

One of the ways public company employees become wealthy is by exercising options (buying stock) when the difference between their option price and the market price is large, and then immediately selling the stock (see Exhibit 5-8). By making these timely purchases and sales, the individual may accumulate great wealth very quickly. So, in addition to the wealth building from salary and bonus, riches are stacking up from smart trading. Not all prospects aggressively buy and sell stock to create wealth. There are many reasons why—the company's stock price and the prospect's option price do not allow that sort of wealth-building or the company is young or there are restrictions on trading, for example.

| Exhibit 5-8 | Sample: Shares Bought and Sold in a Six-Month Period |

Math formula: (no. of shares sold x sales price) minus (no. of shares bought x option price) = gross profit

No. of Shares	Date Bought	Price	Date Sold	Price	Gross Profit
10,000	01/04/2001	$30.00	01/06/2001	$80.00	$500,000
10,000	03/15/2001	$30.00	03/16/2001	$75.50	$455,000
8,000	06/20/2001	$30.00	06/22/2001	$92.00	$496,000
			Total Gross Profit=		$1,451,000

Source: Authors

It is important to examine the stock history of a person who has or had an association with a public company as an insider. Great wealth is built by both holding stock and by exercising options and then selling that stock. The prospects for whom you will wish to review optioning for riches are:

- Current public company officers, directors, and other insiders
- Former public company officers, directors, and other insiders

- Retired public company officers, directors, and other insiders
- Deceased public company officers, directors, and other insiders (when their heirs are your prospects)

If your prospect is buying and selling stock to create wealth, it is important for you to analyze that stock activity so that you can knowledgeably evaluate the giving potential that activity may be creating.

What is the stock history, where is it, and how will you review it? The stock history is the holding, buying, selling, and gifting record of an individual's stock holdings. All individuals who are officers, directors, or other insiders of public companies are required by law to file a report with the SEC when they take any action on their stock *as long as they are active with a company*. When the individual ceases to be active in the company (quits, is fired, retires, or dies), he is no longer required to report his stock activity. When you research a person who is no longer with a public company, you will be looking at a snapshot in time, frozen at the date of the individual's separation from the company. For others, though, you will be reviewing a changing history.

So, where is this history? Researchers find current stock holdings for top employees, directors, and other company insiders via a number of sources. Several free Internet financial sites offer insider trading information (see Exhibit 5-9). Commercial information sellers also offer information about the stock buying and selling history of individuals. The free Internet sites offer information covering a six month to two year time period. It may be difficult to get all the information you need from these sites, since searching may be by company and not by individual, and since the posting timeline for the information provider may not be as rigorous as that of the information sellers. To create nearly as complete a picture of your prospect's stock holdings and activity as possible, you will have to know all the public companies with which she is associated. To overcome the posting timeline problem, you will have to check several resources and compare the trading and holding reports at each. The commercial information sellers allow searching by the individual's name, timely new data postings, and they often provide more years of stock history. In other words, you often get what you pay for.

Sometimes you may be able to retrieve the entire history of trades a person has made while with a public company. Sometimes you will only be able to review a specific period of time, and so your evaluation will simply outline the way the individual handled her stock option opportunity. The breadth of information available will be related to which resource you are using, the time period the person was associated with the company, whether she continues to be active with the company, and the efficient allocation of your time in building the type of prospect portrait you will need regarding this constituent's holdings and stock activity. Whether you are identifying the individual for initial assignment, rating the prospect for gift capacity, or setting the Ask will also dictate the scope of this assignment. A narrow, brief look at holdings may serve to identify someone as a new prospect with major gift potential. When the prospect has become engaged with your institution and the development team is nearer to an Ask, a deeper—and current—review of holdings and activity will be necessary.

Exhibit 5-9 **Insider Holding and Trading Resources**

The most thorough and direct way to get holding and trading information is from stock history information sellers (see the appendix). Each of the Web sites listed here includes a combination of stock symbol lookups, company profiles, stock performance charts, and more. Generally, you must enter a stock symbol and then find the hot link that takes you to insider trades. Some of these sites include "members only" areas, additional information for subscribers or sometimes for a single-use fee. This is not a comprehensive list of all insider trading Web sites. Visit each site to see which interface suits you and which provides the information you are seeking. If you find other useful sites, be sure to share them with the development research community.

- PCQuote.com: http://www.pcquote.com/
- CBS MarketWatch: http://cbs.marketwatch.com/
- Quicken.com: http://www.quicken.com/
- Yahoo! Finance: http://finance.yahoo.com/
- Lycos Finance: http://finance.lycos.com/

The most direct way to find the other public companies in which your prospect has stock rights is to buy the information from insider trading information sellers. The Web sites listed here offer searching by an individual's name or a simple word search where you may enter any words (the name of your institution, for example).

- 10K Wizard Financials Online—use the "Word Search" feature to search by an individual's name or by the name of your higher education nonprofit (which may be mentioned in the individual's proxy biography)
  http://www.tenkwizard.com/
- EDGAR-Online: From the menu bar, choose a People search under SEC Filings
  http://www.edgar-online.com/

Source: Authors

Research Workbench: Analyzing the Trades

The stock buying and selling table in Exhibit 5-8 is the type of table you will create from the information you gather. The free insider history sites will generally offer information in this format:

1. The names and titles of the officers, directors, and other insiders who have had stock activity in the time period covered. The officers' list often goes deeper than the proxy statement and includes vice presi-

dents and others not listed in the proxy. A click on an individual's name will bring forth a list of that individual's activity in the time period.

2. The type of activity being reported—a buy or sell or other type of activity. You will find a legend explaining the types at the Web site, usually at the bottom of the table.

3. The number of shares involved in the activity being reported, the date of the activity, the transaction price, the total holdings after the transaction, and whether the transaction involved direct or indirect shares.

The transaction price is often your clue to the prospect's option price. You may also find the option price outlined in the proxy statement. The buy price will usually be the prospect's option or strike price, the price at which the prospect may buy stock as a benefit of employment. The sale price will be the market price for the stock on the day the sale was made. You will now be able to create the type of table you see in Exhibit 5-8. You have the dates of the activity, the buying and selling prices, and the number of shares traded in each event. The gross profit, the amount the prospect made from the trades, not including his expenses for brokerage fees and other costs, will be another element in the financial profile you are building.

It will be important to complete this same math problem and table for the stock your prospect is buying and selling in other public companies in which she is an officer, director, or other insider. For chief officers and directors, the individual's role in other companies is usually listed in the biography for that individual in the proxy statement. By looking at proxy statements for earlier years, you will find companies in which your prospect had a role in the past.

Unrealized Options
Researchers often state the value of options not yet taken. Individuals affiliated with public companies are granted options as performance and retention incentives. The options have at least three limitations: a number of shares limit, a time limit, and a set price. A specific number of shares must be optioned by a specific date or the option to buy the shares ends (or expires). The options offered to the prospect may be taken in the time between the granting of the options and their expiration. Using the option to buy those shares at the price named is called *exercising an option*.

There are many reasons why a prospect may neglect to exercise an option. One of the primary reasons may be that the market price of the stock remains lower than the option price throughout the option period. Other factors, like the prospect's own financial well-being, the health of the company and the industry in which the prospect works, the strength of the stock market, also come into play when prospects evaluate the benefits of exercising options.

Executive Compensation Table
The "Executive Compensation" table includes a column called "Long Term Compensation" with a sub-heading like "Number of Stock Options Granted."

In our example, XYZ Company, stock options were granted to the three officers we are reviewing in 1999 (see Exhibit 5-4). The XYZ Company compensation table also shows the number of stock options granted in earlier years. As we have outlined, you may find the exercise of these options in the stock history of the individual you are researching.

Since unrealized options are speculative and may have a different value based on the time they are exercised, research reports generally include a statement about the number of options available to the prospect but do not place a dollar value on those options. You will be delighted, though, the first time you are researching the prospect's current stock activity and you spot the moment she exercised options that you first found in the proxy statement.

Option Exercises Table
The third spot in the proxy statement providing information about stock holdings or options is the "Stock Exercises" table (see Exhibit 5-10). In our example, Mr. Can took his option on 25,000 shares in the time period covered by this table. The table outlines the "value realized upon exercise." The footnote explains that value realized is calculated by subtracting the exercise price from the fair market price. The dollar figure you see in this table for the value of options taken is an important part of your prospect's wealth.

In our example, you will also see the number of unexercisable options and a dollar figure for the "in-the-money" options not exercised. "In-the-money" options are the unexercised options with an option (or "strike") price lower than the market price at the time of the report. Unexercised options are those shares to which the prospect has an option but which have restrictions that prevent the taking of that option in this time period. You will find the definitions for these and other terms you will encounter in your proxy work at the Web sites outlined in Exhibit 5-3. You may find your prospect taking those options in the months following the date of proxy when you review current stock activity.

Whatever Does It All Mean?
We know how you feel. By now, your head is swimming with numbers and concepts. If a door opened to get out of this part of prospect research, you might run through it. But wait, do not run away yet. The information you are gathering from proxy statements turns out to be the clearest, most thorough financial portrait you will be able to draw for any of your prospects. Your development team will be delighted with the hard numbers and factual histories you will create in your prospect profile for public company affiliates. You will be able to quote several years of salaries, months or years of stock holdings and trades, and even the prospect's pension plan or separation agreement with the company.

Remember our cautions about estimating net worth at the beginning of this chapter? Now we will take you down that dangerous path. Remember that, on this trek, we are using art and not science to map our way. We are

Exhibit 5-10   **Option Exercises**

The Option Exercises section of the proxy will look like this:

Option Exercises and Values for Fiscal 1999

The table below sets forth the option exercises during fiscal year 1999 by each of the named executive officers, as of April 20, 2000:

- the number of shares of common stock acquired upon exercise of options during fiscal year 1999;
- the dollar value realized upon exercise of the options;
- the total number of exercisable and non-exercisable stock options held on April 20, 2000; and
- the aggregate dollar value of the in-the-money exercisable options.

Aggregated Option Exercises during Fiscal Year 1999 and Option Values on April 20, 2000

Name	No. of Shares Acquired Upon Exercise of Option	Value Realized Upon Exercise	Number of Unexercised Options 4/20/2000		Value of Unexercised In-the-Money Options, 4/20/2000	
			Exercisable	Unexercisable	Exercisable	Unexercisable
Jane Able	50,000	$1,100,000	10,000	100,000	$150,000	$2,000,000
Tom Best	0	0	75,000	50,000	$1,000,000	$900,000
Rob Can	25,000	$500,000	0	30,000	0	$500,000

Here you will see the formula used to calculate the value of the shares. For example, the text might say:

"In accordance with SEC rules, values are calculated by subtracting the exercise price from the fair market value of the underlying common stock. Fair market value is deemed to be $25.00 per share, the average of the high and low price of the stock reported in transactions on April 20, 2000."

divining predictions about gift capacity and wealth, predictions that are likely to be proven wrong by extensive contact with the prospect. The predictions sometimes may be useful in making initial judgments and recommendations about planning fund-raising efforts and motivating development officers. Researchers often look at the numbers we are generating in these public company examples and estimate gift capacity using the art part of research math. As long as everyone in the fund-raising mix understands the "art" part of these conjectures, all is good in the world of prospect research.

Exhibit 5-11	**Doing the Math: Stock Holdings and Net Worth Estimates, Adage-Style**

Fund-Raising Math Adage: The value of stock holdings represents 20-25 percent (or 30-35 percent) of an individual's estimated net worth.

Math Formula: $\dfrac{\text{(No. of shares x market price)}}{\text{either .20, .25, .30, or .35}}$ = Estimated Net Worth

Example: $\dfrac{\text{(15,000 shares x \$40.00 per share)}}{.20}$ = \$3 million

$\dfrac{\text{(15,000 shares x \$40.00 per share)}}{.25}$ = \$2.4 million

$\dfrac{\text{(15,000 shares x \$40.00 per share)}}{.30}$ = \$2 million

$\dfrac{\text{(15,000 shares x \$40.00 per share)}}{.35}$ = \$1.7 million

In this exercise, the prospect's net worth might be estimated at \$1.7 to \$3 million.

The example of valuing stock holdings outlined in Exhibit 5-11 demonstrates the range created by applying the fund-raising adages we have described in this chapter. As you can see, the range created is large. By adding in other things you have learned in your research—the prospect's age and giving history to other nonprofits, for example—you may decide to lean toward one end of the range instead of the other.

Research Workbench: Stock Holdings

Locate: Find stock holdings and option prices in the company's annual proxy statement. Find the last 6 to 18 months of stock trading by insiders at free Internet financial sites. Find several years of stock history for individuals through commercial information providers.

Calculate:
1. Multiply the number of shares reported in the proxy by the price of shares at the time of proxy to create a snapshot of the prospect's holding.
2. Review the prospects' stock history of buying and selling activity. Calculate the gross (not net) gain or profit by subtracting the purchase at option price from the market sale price.
3. Review the prospect's options as outlined in the proxy statement. Make a plan to watch for stock acquisitions under the options plan outlined in the proxy statement.

Amalgamate: At this point, it will be critically important to review all the information you have gathered. Place the salary information and stock calculations you have assembled in front of you. Lay the stock activity table you built on your desk, too. Stack the background information about the prospect's giving to your and other nonprofits in front of you. There is no need to worry if the pieces of information do not seem to match and gel. It is your job to use the pieces of information to make conclusions, to discount some information because of what other information is telling you, or to value other pieces because of the things you have learned about your prospect.

Retirement Compensation and Other Proxy Information

Are you researching a public company insider who retired in the last few years? You may be able to compute the retirement pay for that individual from the information provided in the proxy statement. You will need to know the length of time the person had been associated with the company and the person's salary in the year he retired. The individual's proxy profile will outline when he joined the company. The proxy of the last year he was actively employed will reveal his salary. Follow the clues the proxy gives you: The XYZ Company proxy tells you that the "average annual base (salary)" considering the "highest five consecutive years" is the first number you will seek (see Exhibit 5-12). The next number you need, in this example, is the number of years of "credited service." You may not be able to accurately arrive at this number, but you will probably come close. Once again, we enter the art wing of the research palace. Be sure to read the paragraphs near the "Retirement Plan" table—they may offer the answers you are seeking. In this example, the base figure you need is spelled out in the paragraph following the table.

Other information that is valuable in the financial portrait you are building might be found in the proxy, provided you do a thorough job of looking for it. Proxies often contain the terms of an individual's employment in detail. Did your prospect unexpectedly leave the employment of a public company? The details of separation might be outlined in the proxy. Look in the proxy statement released after the separation and the earlier proxies. You may find the separation agreement the employee and the company made when the employee was hired.

Other benefits granted to the individual, such as special low- or no-interest loans so that the individual can buy company stock, will be included in the

| Exhibit 5-12 | **Retiring from a Public Company** |

Retirement Plans

In this section of the proxy, you will find detailed information about XYZ Company's retirement plan for salaried employees. The details will include the minimum length of time the employee must have been with the company and will describe the basis for the compensation plan. For example, each employee's retirement may be set by the highest five years of compensation during the 10 years prior to termination or retirement. Part of the retirement may be based on a dollar amount, and another portion may be based on years of service.

The table below illustrates the estimated annual retirement benefits of the top employees of XYZ Company. The table assumes a normal retirement age of 65.

Retirement Plan					
Average Annual Base Compensation (Highest Five Consecutive Years)	**Years of Credited Service**				
	15	**20**	**25**	**30**	**35**
$150,000	$45,000	$55,000	$65,000	$75,000	$85,000
$250,000	$75,000	$85,000	$95,000	$105,000	$115,000
$350,000	$100,000	$120,000	$140,000	$160,000	$180,000
$500,000	$150,000	$175,000	$200,000	$225,000	$250,000
$800,000	$200,000	$230,000	$260,000	$300,000	$350,000

Look here for qualifications about the specific retirement plans offered to the company's officers. The paragraph you see here will indicate the number of years that each officer has with the company and may even outline the specific dollar benefit each employee can anticipate. For example, it might say:

"The estimated annual retirement payments would be based on the average compensation of $650,000 for Ms. Able, $500,000 for Mr. Best, and $400,000 for Mr. Can. Ms. Able has 38 years of service. Mr. Best and Mr. Can have 20 years of service."

Source: Authors

proxy. Your prospect's rise to a directorship may be explained in the proxy. You will be interested to discover that your prospect became an officer or director because she sold a private company she founded to the public company whose proxy you are reading. The sale price will be included in the public company's annual report that same year. Look for this and other important information related to your prospect in the proxy statement and other public documents filed with the SEC.

IPOs and Your Prospects: A Breed of Their Own

Peculiar to public company research are the prospects who are working for or directing a company as it "goes public" or makes an "initial public offering" (IPO). This means that a company was private and, on a specific day, the company will be inviting investors on the open market to join in supporting the company. The initial filing document, named S-1 and S-2 in the SEC set, will outline the history of the company, who the founders and major investors are, and other valuable information about your prospect. You will find salary and stock holding information, including the option or "strike" price for officers, directors, and other insiders. You may find the other things we describe here, such as employment and separation agreements.

If an initial offering is successful, the stock price may quickly exceed your prospect's strike price. Insiders will have a period of time where they cannot sell stock, called the lock-up period. Knowing this window will be important as you recommend the timing of an Ask.

Much of the research of IPO affiliates is the same as researching other public company affiliates. The primary difference is that you are meeting your prospect at the infancy of his company's growth and development, at a time of volatility and, sometimes, exponential growth. Great gifts to nonprofits have been born out of IPOs. Great expectations that do not reach fruition have also been borne by nonprofits. Your caution and thorough research will help you take the wise course. Press releases and news stories will be important tools to help you make your conclusions, since they will track the progress of the initial offering and its success or failure. Use the Internet resources listed in Exhibit 5-13 to access IPO information.

Exhibit 5-13	Internet IPO Resources

Use these resources to learn IPO terms and processes as well as search for individual IPOs.

- IPO.com
  http://www.ipo.com
- Hoover's IPO Central
  http://www.hoovers.com/ipo/0,1334,23,00.html
- Alert-IPO!
  http://www.alertipo.com
- Bloomberg.com IPO Center
  http://www.bloomberg.com/markets/ipocenter.html

Source: Authors

One Last Time: A Few (Public Company Affiliate) Things to Remember

Now, just in case you skipped over sections of this chapter, we will now hammer in a few of the important things for you to remember:

- Throw up the red flags and flares when you wander into the realm of net worth estimates. The truth is that researchers use these formulas. The equally important truth is that they are unproven and unreliable.
- You do not have all there is to get if you only looked at one public company affiliation. Your prospect may be involved with more companies (and have stock options and holdings in those companies, too).
- Check the salary history for your prospect for several years. You may find a significant spike or drop that will be important in your calculations.
- Look at the stock activity history of your prospect in all the public companies with which she has an affiliation. She may be buying and selling highly valued stock to get rich.
- Keep talking to your research colleagues about how this type of analysis fits—or does not fit—in their work.

Private Company Affiliates: Researching Without a Net

Prospects who own private companies, who are in key leadership roles as employees of private companies, or who are the members of a family with ties to a private company attract researchers even more often than those who are affiliated with public companies. Why more often? Because there are many, many more of them. There are several thousand public companies in the United States and several million private companies. It is easy to conclude that your prospect is more likely to be affiliated with a private company.

There are four relationships that interest researchers about prospects involved with private companies:

1. Is the prospect an owner or founder of the company?
2. Is the prospect an investor in the company?
3. Is the prospect employed in a top position in the company?
4. Is the prospect a close relative of any of the above?

As you can imagine, the strength of the prospect's financial position may depend on which one of these relationships she has with the company. But the precise relationship—the combination of the four possibilities outlined here—is often difficult for a researcher to determine. Sometimes news stories or information the company releases will profile the company's history, key investors and founders, and the relationship top officers have with the company. Often that information does not include the prospect's precise ownership position. Does the prospect own the company outright or have a 30, 50, or 75 percent interest? News stories will sometimes report a person's investment in a company at the time of a buyout, during financial struggles, or in other moments of change, such as one generation passing the company to the next.

The company's Internet site may include some of this information. Secretary of State corporation registry records in many of the 50 U.S. states will include the names of the boards of directors and chief officers of companies. Some state offices have placed their corporation registries online. Some corporate information may be available at your local library or by phoning a Secretary of State's office.

There are no public investors in private companies. Private companies are owned by individuals, families, unrelated individuals, or even by other companies. They do not offer stock that can be bought and sold by strangers on a public or "open" market. Those who own the company invest their own resources or find investors who are willing to have a clearly defined voice in the company, usually based on the scope of their investments. Since no money (in the form of stock) is requested of or offered to the public by the company owners, the government has little interest in regulating the distribution of investment capital in private companies. There are no public disclosure documents for private companies—proxy statements or annual reports—like those required of public companies.

What Information is Available?

The first answer to this question is "not much." It is important to understand what is available and who provides it so that you can make smart choices about how you evaluate the information.

The most basic private company information available can be found at the Secretary of State's business registration database in the state in which the company is located. This bare-bones information will include the name of the company, the address, and the chief officers who are listed in the company's "annual report"—actually a one page document that includes the information just outlined here. This information is available to the public and some Secretary of State offices now offer Internet access to these records.

In-depth information about private companies is available from information sellers. Companies—both large and small, public and private—do business with one another based on their good credit history and financial reliability. For example, Company A will sell Company B 500,000 cogs for the widgets Company B is making. Company A will produce and ship those cogs with little money down and with full payment pending, based on Company B's good credit reputation. The world has become too large for the leaders in Company A to actually know the leaders of Company B very well, so they must rely on other devices to make an assessment about Company B's stability. Several companies offer this service, but the two best known are Dun & Bradstreet and Standard & Poors. These companies provide credit ratings upon which other companies rely when making decisions about trusting one another to pay bills, lend and borrow money, and fulfill commitments. To provide reliable ratings, Dun & Bradstreet and Standard & Poors survey companies about the details of their business—number of employees, gross sales, number of days bills are outstanding, names of chief officers, and more.

Exhibit 5-14	Company Profile Resources on the Internet

- Thomas Register
  http://www.thomasregister.com
- Business.com
  http://www.business.com
- Corporate information
  http://www.corporateinformation.com/
- Multex Investor Market Guide
  http://www.marketguide.com/

Source: Authors

This information forms the core that prospect researchers use to evaluate the well-being of the private companies with which their prospects are associated. Researchers believe that the performance of the company is an indicator of the financial well-being of the individuals who own or run the company. Some of this information is available for free at Internet sites or in Dun & Bradstreet and Standard & Poors directories researchers purchase or find in most public libraries (see Exhibit 5-14). When researchers purchase this information, the least expensive (and most commonly used) "company profile" provided by these and other services consists of the company name, address, year founded, type of business, number of employees, gross sales, and the names and titles of the chief officers (see Exhibit 5-15).

Exhibit 5-15	Private Company Citing

Citing company's code (Duns number, for example)
The Smith Company
5000 Company Road
Anytown, USA
Year founded: 1950
Type: headquarters
Type of business: manufacturing
Gross revenues: $24,000,000
Number of employees: 75
Chairman: Robert J. Smith
President: Chad Smith
Vice President: Marilyn Smith
Treasurer: Gail Smith

Source: Authors

More details about private companies are available from these same information providers for a greater fee. Most researchers do not pursue these expensive, detailed business reports until the fund raiser assigned is nearer to asking the prospect for a gift, if they find a need to get them at all.

Researchers with advanced analytical skills sometimes try to use price/revenue ratios or other formulas, or to compare similar companies for which other information—such as sale or appraisal data—is available. Once again, the goal of these efforts is the same: to determine the financial success that the prospect enjoys from her association with the private company. We will not cover advanced theories and formulas in this book. They are, for the most part, highly speculative, and they require a deeper understanding of private company analysis than beginning researchers acquire.

Salary Surveys and Other Rabbits

Researchers look for information or analytical tools they can use in regard to private company employees, ones that will replace public company tools like proxy information. What prospect researchers have done is to creatively apply tools intended for other uses to the analysis of wealth and capacity. In case you did not notice, you have just walked back into the artistic part of the job. But research is not performance art. We are not magicians with hats full of tricks—that is important to remember. Nonetheless, when we are thinking about artistic applications, the Internet has been a boon to researchers.

This is particularly clear when we think about compensation for prospects who work for privately-held companies. Job hunters and recruiters meet on Web sites that include comprehensive salary surveys. Industry trade journals that were not readily available to prospect researchers in years past now post salary surveys on the Internet (see Exhibit 5-16). The surveys cover most of the careers in which researchers find prospects: insurance agents, accountants, stock brokers, bank executives, lawyers, doctors, architects, and others. Researchers using salary surveys always indicate the source of the information in their reports and include a few sentences outlining the limitations of these surveys. The information must be considered a guideline only. Does a broker with five years of experience who works for an East Coast firm in a large city earn enough to make a major gift? What salary range has been reported for lawyers in Midwest cities who are partners in medium-size firms? This information cannot tell you precisely what your broker or lawyer prospect earns, but it may indicate a broad range of possibilities. The income possibility you help your team visualize can aid them in deciding whether or not to cultivate an individual.

Exhibit 5-16	Salary Survey Internet Resources

- JobStar Salary Surveys
  http://jobstar.org/tools/salary/sal-surv.cfm
- Workindex Compensation Page
  http://workindex.com/extsubcats.asp?CATID=697
- Salary.com
  http://www.salary.com

Source: Authors

Prospect researchers who have been in the field a long time sometimes look at the way other professions evaluate a company's productivity and then test the limits of applying these theories to their prospects. They study the ways that business appraisers, bankers, and other evaluators rate and value businesses. There is no way to measure the success of these applications since the conclusions researchers reach have not been measured or verified. The difficulty in using any of these theories is that, as prospect researchers, we do not have all the pieces of information necessary to fill in the formulas. Researchers who try to apply these formulas must speculate about portions of the formulas to make up for this deficit. These formulas will remind you of the other research and fund-raising adages we are outlining in this chapter. Examples of these formulas or adages are:

- The profit for owner/operators of new car dealerships is in the range of 1 to 5 percent of gross sales.
- Chief executive officers (CEOs) of private companies with sales of less than $5 million earn in the range of $120,000 to $200,000 per year. CEOs leading private companies with sales in the range of $5 to $10 million earn $125,000 to $250,000 per year.
- Grocery store owner/operators earn approximately 2 percent of gross sales.
- After earning out their advances, writers earn 7 to 15 percent of list price, with escalation clauses after the first 2,000 to 5,000 copies sold.
- Bonuses for investment bankers are linked to the fee income generated. Bankers with $200,000 in fee income are awarded 20 percent of the fee, with bonuses increasing with income, up to 50 percent for those generating $1 million in fee income.
- Portfolio managers typically earn about 1 percent of the annual return on the fund.

These theories are examples of those shared by researchers at meetings and seminars and on PRSPCT-L, the prospect researchers' listerv. Some theories may be more accurate than others. Remember that they are simply guidelines. As you are exposed to other researchers and their theories, and as your prospect pool continues to broaden, you may see opportunities to apply some of these theories or to develop your own theories. We like to think of these theories as "fun with math." That light-hearted reference reminds you that these theories and formulas are unproven. They are flawed by the holes in the information you (and the researchers who use them) have. You may find some of them to be useful in setting thresholds in your research. Many of them will never be of use to you. Our only attention to these types of formulas in this book will be this brief explanation since they are highly speculative and they involve a skill level and breadth of experience that beginning researchers do not have. Do not worry—you will encounter them throughout your career in prospect research. It will be up to you to evaluate their worth. Evaluating resources is something at which you are going to get very good, believe us.

Do not forget that the salaries of employees in a few professions sometimes become public information because of the high visibility of their work. The salaries or income of actors, professional athletes, politicians, and others are often found in news stories or other sources. Elected officials are required to release income information by public disclosure laws. You may remember reading news stories around April 15 last year about what the president of the United States paid in taxes. Many incomes that come under arbitration are outlined in news stories. The real thing, as they say, is always the best thing—so when an actual salary is available, it is better information than any collection of speculations.

What Does It All Mean?

The things that were available while researching public company affiliates simply are not available when researching private company affiliates. So, what does a company profile like the one outlined in Exhibit 5-10 tell a researcher? The first important information this profile suggests is that the company is family-owned. All of the chief officers share the same last name, and it is the same as the name of the company. That information alone is significant. It may mean that most—if not all—of the company profits are distributed between family members and that younger members of the family stand to inherit the company as older family members retire. This may seem like a lot of assumptions but, remember, that is the landscape when you research private company prospects.

The second detail to which researchers pay attention is the year the company was founded. It is standard lore that the older a company is, the more likely it is that its debt ratio is smaller. Most of the costs of starting a business have been recovered. Equipment and land costs have been paid. An older business is likely to be in a period of larger profits than a younger, similar business would be. These are the details about profit and financial well-being researchers try to surmise.

The third item researchers evaluate is actually three pieces of information taken together. They are the number of employees, the gross revenues, and the type of business. We are now moving back into the art wing of research. How does a company with many employees and low gross revenues compare with a company with few employees and large revenues? If the company's line of work were heavily dependent on expensive processing or equipment purchases, how would its revenues compare with a company that is, for example, a service firm with few equipment or parts expenses? All of these conjectures are, of course, informal conclusions that researchers develop and make through exposure to information involving private company after private company.

Other Sources for Private Company Information

Since no information about salaries, stock holdings, or other indicators of wealth is available, effective research involving prospects with private company affiliations is dependent upon other pieces of information. Company press releases and news stories play a key role in evaluating whether a prospect is

successful in a private company affiliation. There are critical moments in the life of a private company that draw the attention of development researchers:
- Buying or selling the company
- Significantly expanding (or downsizing) the company
- Turning the company over to the next generation
- Taking the company public
- Closing the company

These events may be covered by the local newspapers or, in the case of large private companies, by national news agencies. The articles will often include financial numbers that are news to the researcher. If a public company is involved in a sale or purchase, for example, more details about the private company will be available in the public company's annual report following the transaction.

Company press releases will be available through the company, and they are usually found at the company's Web site. Other information at the company Web site may surprise you. The Web site may include a detailed history of the company's founding, outlining the key players and their roles. One family company was so proud of the legacy they had built that their Web site included a link to a five-generation family tree. You would be delighted to find it that easy to connect a prospect to the company's founding family. The company Web site will also profile the chief officers of the company. It may outline the scope of the business, its operating areas, and what the company's charitable giving involves. In many cases, a prospect who owns a private company will support nonprofits through the company's philanthropic plan. Sometimes the company will match the gifts made by employees. All of this information might be found on the company's Web site.

Another source for private company news is the annual "top" lists. Local newspapers, city and regional business journals, and national business magazines publish annual lists of the largest private companies. They also publish lists of the wealthiest families, many of whom built their wealth through private companies. These resources often provide wealth estimates and are considered to be useful indicators by researchers.

Industry trade journals provide information about the prominent companies in a particular industry. Publications like *Dairy Today, Construction Monthly,* and *American Banker* portray industry leaders and report the latest contracts and advances among the companies they cover. Even companies that do not attract the attention of the general media may be covered by trade and industry journals and publications.

Research Workbench: Private Company Affiliation

Locate: Find private company financial information through the Secretary of State database of company registrations, private company profile sellers, the company's own Web site, and news stories.

Calculate: Evaluate the likelihood that the company's owners are doing more than making a living by comparing the type of company with the number of employees and the gross revenues. Look at news stories, press releases, and "top" lists to evaluate the company.

Amalgamate: Bring other indicators of wealth, such as real estate information, giving to other nonprofits, and giving to your nonprofit to the evaluation table. Use these other indicators to determine the weight you will place on the individual's private company affiliation.

Wanted: Real Estate Appraiser (Foolhardy Need Not Apply)

As you learned in chapter 3, prospect researchers often look at real estate holdings when there is little other financial news to collect. This will be the case when you are researching long-retired prospects, prospects associated with private companies, prospects who are not at the very top of the hierarchy of public company employees, and other prospects whose wealth is obscure. It will also be the case when you research prospects who build a career around real estate development, investment, or management.

There are three areas of real estate research that prospect researchers examine. They are:

- Residential real estate
- Businesses that involve real estate
- Real estate as a business

As we outlined in chapter 3, counties and townships assess the value of real estate all over the United States for tax purposes. That information is made available to the public through the township or county assessor's offices. Most counties can be telephoned for the assessed value of properties. Some counties that process many calls require that requests be made in writing and submitted with a small fee. Many assessors have established Web-based searchable databases of property valuation information (see Exhibit 5-17).

Exhibit 5-17   **Internet Resources for Real Estate Assessor Databases**

Portico: Offering many resources for researchers, including links to county, township, and city assessor sites across the United States.
http://indorgs.virginia.edu/portico

Northwestern University's Assessor Database: Links to assessor offices, including telephone numbers for those without Web sites. This site also gives visitors the multipliers that will bring assessed values within a range that approximates market value.
http://pubweb.acns.nwu.edu/~cap440/assess.html

Source: Authors

Market value, the true value of a property, is established by one thing—the sale of a property. The sale price is the market value at the exact moment the property is sold. It does not represent the value a year earlier or a year later—the real estate market is too volatile for that breadth of time. The only people who are qualified to make valid market value estimates are real estate appraisers. They complete education requirements to be certified by their professional organization to do so. They have rigid rules about how they complete valuations. They methodically compare a property with similar properties that have sold recently in the immediate area, making mathematical adjustments for differences they find in the property or the improvements at the property. They may also complete complex comparisons based on a replacement approach—what would it cost to build this building again? And finally, they often estimate the value of the property based on its return to an investor who would lease the property over a period of time. Appraisers then reconcile the values they conclude from these methods.

You may believe that real estate agents also estimate market values. Actually, that is not true. Real estate agents estimate the likely sale price of a property, or more accurately, they estimate the asking price. As anyone who has sold a home can tell you, the asking price and the sale price are two different birds. Sale price approximates market price. Real estate agents are not generally qualified to estimate the market value of real estate.

Is estimating the market value of real estate something that prospect researchers can do? No. This is important to remember as you dabble in evaluating the importance of the real estate holdings of your prospects. The best course for researchers is to simply report the assessed values of the properties held by prospects, and to include information in that report about the assessment rate and the frequency of assessing in the county in which the property is located. Is this where most researchers stop? No. Researchers are usually asked for an opinion beyond this bare reporting of the facts. As you know, researchers turn information into knowledge. How researchers handle real estate information is a good example of that mandate.

A Prospect's Castle: Residential Real Estate

Home ownership can be one attribute of wealth. What does real estate value tell a researcher? It can indicate a type of lifestyle your prospect enjoys. But there are limitations on what interpretations a researcher can reasonably apply to real estate values, and some of these have become prospect research truisms. If a prospect's home does not reflect significant wealth, it cannot be assumed that the prospect is not wealthy. People handle wealth in different ways and some people do not use their resources for big houses or expansive estates. Conversely, some people buy homes beyond their means, so a large home does not mean that a constituent has the resources to support your organization. Different areas of the country have enjoyed—or suffered from—volatile real estate markets. Some areas have seen property values skyrocket, while other areas have sat on stagnant values or even watched property values decline. The overall economic health of an area is an important factor in evaluating the assessed value of real estate. These are a few of the research truisms about evaluating real estate.

Researchers who look at real estate assessments have to deal with another tough issue. Transforming assessed value into something close to market value is a difficult exercise and can only be described as an artful attempt. Each homeowner, even those who are prospect researchers, knows that the assessed value of a property must not be equated with market value. Some states do not rely on real estate taxes to build their coffers. Assessed values for properties in these states may be based on rates of assessment as low as 10 percent of projected market value. In states drawing a great deal of their tax base from real estate, assessors often value properties in a range of 80 to 90 percent of market value (see Exhibit 5-18). One state that diverges from all others in the way properties are assessed is California. In 1979, Proposition No. 13 in California rolled back assessed values and capped the permissible annual rate of increase for properties that do not change hands. This tax initiative made it nearly impossible to deduce the market value on the basis of assessment. These are just a few examples of the pitfalls you will meet when you try to convert assessed value into something approaching market value.

Exhibit 5-18	Real Estate Assessment Math

Formula: Assessed Value divided by Rate of Assessment (or multiplied by a set multiplier) = Something Sort of Close to the Assessor's Idea of Market Value

Example: In Colorado, residential properties are currently assessed at 9.74 percent of what the assessor approximates their market value to be. This represents a multiplier of 10.25. The very rough estimated market value of a residence assessed at $50,000:

Assessor's Value x Multiplier = Approximation of Market Value
$50,000 x 10.25 = $512,500

Source: Authors

Some assessors include a "market value" figure with the assessment values for the properties in the areas they cover. This number is rarely an actual estimate of market value for a property since *market value is the price that a willing buyer and a willing seller agree upon for a property.* Some researchers try to close this gap by concurrently looking at asking prices—the sale price listed—for properties in the prospect's neighborhood. This is a risky avenue for a couple of reasons. As most home sellers know, asking price and market or sale price are rarely the same. Further, comparing the asking price or even the sale prices for other properties in the prospect's neighborhood does not consider the significant and subtle differences in properties. Significant differences like the size, age, the quality of the improvements, and the specific location or amenities of the property cannot be fairly valued from a distance or by an amateur appraiser. Does the prospect's property enjoy a territorial view? Are there access or infrastructure issues that alter the value? Are there encumbrances on the "similar" properties that are not apparent in a sale's listing?

Sometimes researchers actually find the sale price a prospect paid for a property. Assessment records in some counties include information about the last transaction, including price and date. This, of course, is the best information you will ever get about your prospect's real estate holding.

But when a property has not sold for years, when sale price is not included in assessor records, what are researchers to do? Researchers, as usual, get creative and aggressive about collecting and analyzing the information that is available. They study real estate values and track the prices of expensive homes in their area and in the other areas in which their prospects live. They learn which neighborhoods are the wealthy ones, the ones with the most expensive homes. They track changes in real estate values as the economy of the areas where their prospects live rises and falls. Researchers keep a quick reference of the apparent relationship between assessed value and market value in each area that draws their attention. Fellow researchers in other states can be good resources for building this quick reference, since they know the usual relationship between assessed value and market value in their own areas. Researchers find out how recently properties were valued by assessors, since that timeline will be linked to quickly changing economies. These activities turn researchers into near-experts on evaluating the importance of real estate assessments within the context of the information they are analyzing about each prospect.

Businesses That Involve (Big) Real Estate

Some of your constituents own businesses that include significant real estate holdings. Ranches, farms, factories, warehouse complexes, and other businesses are a few examples of "real-estate heavy" businesses. The value of these holdings may be significant. Many times the assessed value for these types of properties is considerably lower than the potential sale price. Nearby commercial and residential neighborhoods may be encroaching on these types of properties and, with that development, the value of the property would rapidly change.

Although these properties are not likely to be liquidated to make a gift to your organization, they are other indicators of the financial resources in your prospect's control. You will collect these assessed values and include them in the research profile you build. Understanding the real estate holdings your prospect controls or to which your prospect may be an heir helps your development team with the cultivation process or with setting the Ask. This information will be significant at life transition points—when the prospect sells the company and liquidates holdings, for example, or when the older generation passes the company to a younger generation.

Real Estate as a (Big) Business

Researchers remember the first time they drove by an office building or shopping center under construction and thought, "I wonder who is behind that project." After spending time studying wealth, prospect researchers begin to realize that the many paths to wealth include real estate investing, developing, holding, and selling. Real estate magnates might be those who build and rent apartment and office complexes, those who purchase undeveloped land and transform it into neighborhoods full of houses, and those who buy and hold land until encroaching developments turn parcels of sagebrush and grass into gold.

The path to information about real estate magnates is often circuitous. Parcels of land may be bought in partnership or deal-specific names as elusive as the "53rd Street Development" or "Three Oak Trees Project." Once again, news articles are often the most direct routes to information about who is behind a local project or the value in the speculation unfolding. Trade papers or business journals might outline the project in detail, even naming the project's completion time, the financial investment, the partners involved, and other details that help a researcher pin down a prospect's involvement.

Even when researchers find some or all of the property development projects in which a prospect is involved, pegging the range of profit coming to the investors is another hurdle. Trade journals may shed light on the margins of profit in building subdivisions, renting office buildings, or selling shopping centers. Gathering as much information as you can from news sources and real estate records maximizes your opportunity to present a compelling picture for or against cultivation. Development will then have the chore of delineating the depth of the prospect's involvement and success.

Stirring Net Worth Ingredients into the Real Estate Mix

We know you have not forgotten the flashing caution signs we erected about making net worth estimates. But, as we told you, we do not believe it would be fair to have you leave this chapter without all the tools that other researchers have. As you develop your own style as a researcher and as you learn more about the opinions of other researchers and your own development team, you will find the proper spot for these formulas. You will, above all, know that what your team learns from the prospect during the cultivation process brings the best information forward.

Saying all that, let's look at how researchers evaluate real estate holdings. Some researchers have abandoned real estate assessments as a gauge of anything and no longer even collect the information. Some researchers make net worth estimates based on real estate holdings (see Exhibit 5-19). That represents the two ends of your options. If you decide to estimate net worth based on real estate holdings, do not forget to add cautionary explanations about the estimates in the reports to your development team. Give the team the same flashing "danger" signs we are giving you.

Exhibit 5-19	Real Estate and Net Worth Estimates, Adage-Style

Fund-Raising Math Adage: Real estate holdings represent between 25 percent and 30 percent of a prospect's net worth.

Formula:
Estimated Market Value of Real Estate Holdings divided by .25 or .30 = Estimated Net Worth

Example: $\dfrac{\$3.5 \text{ million}}{.30} = \$11.67 \text{ million}$

$\dfrac{\$3.5 \text{ million}}{.25} = \$14 \text{ million}$

Conclusion: This prospect's estimated net worth, based on estimated worth of known real estate holdings, is $11.67–$14 million.

One Last Time: A Few (Real Estate) Things to Remember

What seems like a simple directive—"find out what Mr. Smith's house is worth"—involves more of the art aspect of prospect research than most development people anticipate. We know it is difficult to tell your team that you are only guessing, but it is imperative that you surround your estimates with warnings when it comes to real estate, if you do anything more than report the assessed value of properties. Prospect researchers are not professional appraisers and must not give the impression that they can conclude the market value of real estate. What other limitations will you meet in researching real estate?

- You are unlikely to uncover all of a prospect's property holdings since we cannot search for properties nation- or world-wide and since properties are often held in names other than the prospect's name.
- You will have difficulty establishing the value of properties in areas of the world where real estate is not assessed for tax reasons or where this type of information is not made publicly available.
- Your estimates of market value will only be rough estimates. They will not represent true market value, a figure which is arrived at by special computations and comparisons performed by professional real estate appraisers.

- You will not be able to reliably estimate the value of properties with extraordinary features, and those features are commonly found in the properties of the very wealthy.
- Estimating a prospect's net worth based on real estate holdings is just one more way for researchers and development teams to hone in on an Ask amount. It should be taken in concert with other research. It must take a back seat to the first-hand information the development team builds through cultivation.

So, have we erected enough warning signs?

Research Workbench: Real Estate

Locate: Find the real estate holdings of a prospect by contacting the assessor's office in the county in which the prospect lives, by searching the assessor's property database on the Web, or by using a commercial real estate assessment information provider.

Calculate: Use assessor information about the rate of assessment, news reports about the local real estate market, and suggestions from researchers who live in that area to estimate the approximate market value of real estate.

Amalgamate: Apply the real estate research data you have collected to a review of the other information about the prospect. Use real estate information to support conclusions you are making. Do not use real estate information to refute other data. Real estate is not the best indicator of wealth.

Heirs Apparent (and Not So Apparent)

We are sorry to report that there are not any fund-raising formulas that apply to inherited wealth and that this area of prospect research is at once the hardest or the easiest research task you will assume. Great wealth often walks hand-in-hand with great hiding places. Blind trusts, subsidiaries, estate, company, and collection hand-me-downs, and more descendents than seem divisible by the original windfall are sometimes the chief markers on the research trail regarding inherited wealth. And, on the other hand, old money just as often walks life's path with a tremendous spirit of philanthropy and an organized and forthright approach to charitable giving. Which trail is your prospect traveling? You will know rather soon after you begin researching him. It may be as simple as this: Has the family established one or several foundations to propel their philanthropic giving? In the last 20 or so years, the number of private foundations has doubled, according to Constance Casey's report in *The Chronicle of Philanthropy* ("Where Small Foundations Can Learn the Ropes," May 18, 2000, p. 9). Part of this explosion can be attributed to the exponential growth in wealth opportunities that we discussed in chapter 3.

Those families who have been wealthy for generations often turn over the management and distribution of that wealth to professionals. Who has how much, who sits at the head of the family table, and who makes distribution decisions can be dependent on the whim and wishes of the family heads. There is no formula to apply that unravels that dynamic. And the answer is not often found in directories or databases. It is sometimes found in newspaper and magazine articles, family-specific biographies, or in wills and other legal decrees. Wills and divorce decrees are public documents and some prospect research departments review these documents at county courthouses with the hope of clarifying family relationships and wealth distribution issues. Some researchers feel that reviewing wills and divorce decrees is intrusive and disrespectful to the relationship the nonprofit is building with the prospect. You and your nonprofit will have to decide where you sit in this debate. Whatever you decide, remember to follow the course that honors the high ideals of your organization and the respect you have for your constituents.

Researchers tune into other relatively subtle clues about inherited wealth. Does your prospect run the family company or an important subsidiary? When you review the list of individuals who sit on the family's foundation board, is your prospect's name among them? Is your prospect's investment company managing the family's wealth? How many members of your prospect's family are linked to your organization? The more, the merrier, since a family of major gift donors may fold your organization's well-being into their own family's success story.

How will you place a prospect on the genealogy tree of a prominent family? As we reported earlier, national publications are producing "who's wealthy" lists each year. Many of these lists include families as well as individuals. That may be a good starting point for locating your prospect's relationship to a wealthy family. Other sources for family links are "who's who" publications (see the appendix section). These directories may list parents and their offspring. By tracing an individual back through the years, you can discover who is whose father and who is whose brother or sister. The Internet has been a boon to genealogists, and prospect researchers profit from this resource, too. Genealogists are posting their family trees on Web sites; sometimes the branches of these trees are entangled with your prospect's tree. One researcher became a fan of genealogy sites when he found that the name of the prospect he was researching had been handed down through several generations—a common naming rite in many families. This distinctive name appeared in the family trees of distant relatives on several genealogy Web pages. The sites placed this prospect's family in a specific industry and in a particular locale. These links established a good starting place for this lucky (and skilled) researcher who was trying to uncover the source and scope of the prospect's giving potential.

The greatest tool you have for researching inherited wealth is your development team and their adept interviewing skills. What cannot be found in books or directories or Web sites will be found in conversation after conversation that a development officer records in contact reports. You may then use the other tools you have acquired in this chapter to analyze the giving capacity of your heir prospect.

Collections

Cecilia collects snow domes, those cheap plastic domes with scenes of Mount Rainier, a San Francisco streetcar, or a Maine lobster anchored in a watery bubble raining plastic snow. The co-author of a book about snow domes, in describing himself, coined a wonderful term for serious collectors of anything: he called himself a "dedicated accumulator" (*Snow Globes,* 1993, back jacket).

Your prospect may be a dedicated accumulator. He will probably collect things more valuable than snow domes. He may collect art, cars, horses, coins, antiques, boats, or nearly anything you can imagine. The folly of strapping baseball cards from the 1950s and 1960s to the spokes of bicycle wheels became clear in the 1980s and 1990s. When those very cards were selling for hundreds and thousands of dollars, former bicycle riders everywhere groaned in hindsight.

What sort of attention should you pay to your prospect's collections? Simply knowing about the collection and including it in your prospect profile as another indicator of wealth might be enough. When a collection becomes an object of gift-giving, the appropriate appraisers are called in to value it. Sometimes, though, development people want research to attach a value to a collection. Clever researchers find information that may lead to a guess, not really an educated guess but a superficially informed guess, about the value of the collection by exploring publications for collectors, manufacturers, or dealers of that item. How much are Piper Cubs selling for? What is the market for 1940s-era radios? We can hear you saying, "Oh, the art part of research again." You are getting wise to us.

One Old (and New) Money Adage You Need

There is one fund-raising adage that we did not examine in this chapter yet. We have outlined such benchmarks of wealth as salary, stock holdings, real estate, and company revenues. We have clearly stated that not all—or even any—of these characteristics of wealth necessarily become the charitable gift itself. Where does a charitable gift come from then? We are clear about who gives a major gift. Now we need to appreciate from where most major gifts arise. Major gifts come from assets, not income. "What?" you say. Well, what we have been talking about here is precisely that—assets. Stock holdings, property, money invested in art collections, foundations—these are the assets from which major gifts usually come. Knowing this will help you when you "amalgamate"—when you value the benchmarks of wealth both in terms of qualifying a prospect and, later, in recommending the amount and the timing of the Ask.

Prospect Research and Einstein's Theory of Relativity

We hope you gasped at this section heading. Now we hope you will laugh with us. Guess what? Prospect research is not rocket science. The real math part is simple multiplication and division. It is a few fractions and decimal places to manage, some rather large numbers to move around. The art part of fund-raising math is percentages, odds, a sort of hedging game. And foremost in our minds by now should be this idea: The first purpose of research math is to begin the prospect portrait. When augmented by the information returned by the major gifts team, research math can help define the timing and the amount of the Ask.

As you use these formulas and apply these rag-tag theories, you will add and subtract them from the research equation you create for your nonprofit. Do not doubt for a second that plenty of organizations raise millions without ever making one net worth estimate. But it is unlikely that many organizations raise a respectable amount of the money that is available in their donor pool without identifying the top prospects through asset research and without setting Ask amounts through the analysis of *all* the information gathered by research and development's cultivation process.

6

Building a Pool of Potential Prospects

*"I also bought a new pair of sneakers and a car and
I have been making investments in other Internet startups."*
—William Peabody, age 27, about what he had been doing since making about $10 million
when he sold his company to Lycos, *Forbes*, August 24, 1998, p. 22.

If you walked past a major donor on the street, would you know it? Would there be dollar bills peeking out of his pockets? Would there be a gift receipt stuck like a wet leaf to his shoe? Would a bespectacled secretary follow in his wake, rattling off appointments with important people? Would he jingle as he walked from all the change in his pockets?

You should not count on it.

That woman in the expensive suit who parked her $60,000 BMW next to your Chevy outside of the bank—is she a major gift prospect? Maybe she is. Or maybe she is on her way to get a second mortgage to help finance an overextended lifestyle. A gift to her favorite nonprofit—if she has one—is the last thing on her mind.

Just like our mothers always told us, outward appearances are often deceiving. Major gift prospects are often as subtle as they are flamboyant. And the flashiest members of society are not always the richest. But there is one truth about major gift donors: Your best prospective donors are already in your database. You may not know who they are, but they are lingering there among the mass of constituents, giving well below their capacity. A prospect researcher's job is to find them. The job of the development team together is to draw them deeper into your organization, connect them in a personal way to your nonprofit's mission and values, and motivate them to exercise their capacity to give.

Prospects Quietly Getting to Know Your Nonprofit

How did they get into your database, these quiet philanthropists who are lingering in wait for their first major gift cultivation? There are many ways. They are participants in your nonprofit's programs. They attended an event your organization sponsored and then filled out a registration card. They gave $25, the smallest amount on the response card, when they returned one of your nonprofit's direct mail appeals. They contacted your nonprofit for an information packet, a schedule of upcoming programs, or other service your organization provides. However they got there, 99.9 percent of the time, they came to you of their own accord. It is unnecessary to look outside of your own nonprofit's constituency for major gift donors. Believe us, they already know you. Now you need to get to know them. That is, after you find them.

Why are we encouraging you to look for major gift prospects you already have rather than looking for brand new ones who do not know your nonprofit? Acquiring new donors is much more expensive than keeping and upgrading old ones. That millionaire in the next city or two states over who does not know your nonprofit will require special care and a long cultivation just to get to the point where your annual fund donors already are. The person already in your database is getting a degree of care and cultivation and has been for as long as she has been affiliated with your nonprofit. She has been receiving your newsletters, attending events, and participating in your surveys. Most important of all, she has been giving your nonprofit gifts, albeit small ones. She has already jumped the first and most difficult hurdle. She has voluntarily affiliated with your organization. Strengthening that tie is easier than forging a new relationship with a stranger quickly enough to ask for a large gift. Remember, the efficient use of the first philanthropic dollar to raise the next dollar is actually the mission of all the members of the major gifts fund-raising team.

Not everyone who has jumped that first hurdle is willing to run the full race with you. The fund raisers at your organization may never be successful in bringing that capable person to the point of a major donation. Then again, they might. But cultivating the already affiliated makes getting a gift much more likely than cultivating strangers.

The Major Gift Donor Composite

So, there are quiet prospects in your database. How can you sharpen your sight to find them? We have discussed many of the characteristics of major gift donors in the preceding chapters. Now we will apply these pieces to finding the right constituents to research, those who are most likely to become major gift donors. In your efforts to populate the pool of potential prospects, you will don those special glasses that allow you to see what the wealthy in your database look like.

You may begin by focusing your lenses on the major gift donors you already know. This close examination will not be a scientific trial or a statistical analysis. Your development team can name characteristics that your major gift donors share. From this information, you can form a composite picture of your typical major gift donor. The picture you create may be different from that of another nonprofit. The age, location, and mission of your nonprofit as well as the type of fund-raising efforts you have relied upon may affect that picture. As the composite picture of your organization's typical major gift donor emerges, you will begin to see other individuals in your database who share these characteristics.

The Composite Experiment

Let's draw an example of a typical major gift donor composite. In a brief and lively discussion about the composite idea held at the symphony orchestra's development office, the fund raisers and researcher agreed that the following characteristics are typical of their big donors:

- They are season ticket holders.
- They are over 55 years of age.
- Their children are grown and some of them are also season ticket holders.
- They serve on one or more of the symphony's boards and committees or have volunteered in significant ways.
- If the team plotted the annual giving record of the major gift donors over a number of years, the graph would show consistent giving with gifts that gradually increased in size.
- They have significant appreciated assets, assets that they have held for a long time such as real property, stock, or collections.

In a sophisticated effort to see who else among their constituents has these same characteristics, the symphony staff decided to carry out a database experiment. They used as many of these characteristics as they could to match other constituents who had the same look. In other words, they picked season ticket holders over 55 years old who serve on committees and boards and who have grown family members affiliated with the symphony. They picked only those constituents who were regular donors (of any amount). They were unable to gauge steadily increased giving in this first experiment. They were also unable to measure wealth indicators at all since this information is not in the database for constituents who are not major gift prospects already. While this seems like a marginal approach to finding the next major gift donors, this group distinguishes itself by having characteristics that are most similar to major gift donors.

So, you will build your composite and then search your database for constituents who mirror the composite in appearance. Will those you find be immediately assigned to your fund raisers as major gift prospects? No, they will not be ready to be assigned. You selected them based on characteristics recorded in the database—age, consistency of giving, participation, and even the extent of their affiliation. In other words, these constituents have passed through the affiliation and interest gateways we outlined in chapter 3. They have not passed through the capacity gateway. You do not know if they have the financial capacity to be major gift donors. You have not qualified them financially. It is likely that there are few financial characteristics recorded in your database. There may be no financial characteristic record like "has appreciated assets." You could use another measure of the likelihood of wealth. You could look at your constituent's zip codes to roughly draw out those who live in wealthy neighborhoods and who meet the other characteristics that make up your composite. But even those who emerge from this second pass would require further research to make sure that you are pointing the fund-raising team in the direction of the most likely major gift prospects.

Most researchers do not add constituents to the pool of potential prospects—the suspect pool—until they show a sign or two of capacity. After all, capacity is the key piece of the major gift puzzle. The signs of capacity are usually straightforward, though. A job promotion that might lead to wealth, a property purchase in an expensive neighborhood, or news of a connection to family wealth—any of these factors would qualify a constituent for suspect pool membership.

Peripheral Vision

Developing a vision for the characteristics of major gift donors and applying that new sense to researching other constituents should not mean that you fitted yourself with a pair of blinders. Not all future major gift donors will match the profile of your past major gift donors. All researchers quickly learn this: Imagining that there are rules for prospect research means accepting that, for each rule, there are many exceptions. Even our mandate that you look among your own constituents first for donors has a small, ragged hole in it. There are people who give to high profile causes whether they have an earlier affiliation with that nonprofit or not. If your cause can attract those donors, it will be worth it to add them to the suspect pool you are building.

And despite everything we have said, there are some wealthy philanthropists who are not in your database but who might one day support your organization. Should you spend the better part of your time researching them? No, not now. That can happen when you are finished looking at the potential donors who have already affiliated with your nonprofit. Never forget that those who already love you make much better partners than that wealthy stranger across town (or across the country).

Our experiment in database segmenting simply offers you a starting point for narrowing the field of constituents who you will research (see Exhibit 6-1). It forms the masses of constituents into a manageable approach to prioritizing whom you ought to research. You have looked at your database, developed a composite of your typical major donor, and you have begun to create a pool of constituents for further research (suspects). Is that all there is? Not by a long shot. You have other places to look for constituents who can join your pool. Some of these places will offer us a chance to see donors who do not fit the composite. Let's review a few of these places.

Exhibit 6-1	Segmenting

Segmenting the database is breaking the constituents in the database into groups with similar characteristics. Database segmenting allows researchers to approach their research tasks in a more directed and productive way.

Source: Authors

Volunteer Prospectors

There are discoveries about your constituents that purchasing every prospect research tool on the market would not buy for you. One well-connected volunteer is worth hundreds, even thousands of dollars in prospecting tools. A well-connected volunteer who wants to tell your organization where the wealth and inclination to give are worth even more. After all, who knows your constituents better than other constituents? Who knows who is wealthy in town better than those who move in the same circles?

Your well-connected volunteers will be motivated to help your nonprofit for several reasons. They want to help a cause they believe in. As major gift donors themselves, they already know the positive effects giving has on a person. They want to help their friends and colleagues have a similar chance to make a positive impact with their discretionary funds. If they believe in a nonprofit and trust its leadership, a well-connected volunteer may be happy to direct the nonprofit's fund raisers to other potential major gift donors.

In the dialect of winter baseball chatter, discussing ballgames and players and trades and the prospects for winning in the spring is called hot stove baseball. Imagine a group of baseball lovers arranged around a wood stove on a cold December night, excitedly sharing stories of the great opportunities a new season may hold. Which up-and-coming players show the most promise for maximum performance? Which well-known players will "step up to the plate" and lead the team with important hits and runs in the spring?

Now imagine a fund raiser and a beloved supporter doing the same thing, but in this scene they are talking about the "next spring" that is the nonprofit's upcoming capital campaign or just another season of raising money. Who can help the nonprofit meet its goals? Who do they know who can step up to the plate with a big gift? The development officer and the well-connected volunteer are hot-stoving it, fund-raising style.

Does this sound like telling tales out of class to you? If it does, you are misunderstanding the context and meaning of fund raising and research. The fund raiser is not interested in scouring the volunteer's mind for details that are unrelated to gift-getting. There is no imagined or real benefit for either member of this conversation in passing over the boundaries of propriety. The same ethical standards that are guiding the nonprofit and its employees each day will hold fast in the fund raiser's relationship with in-the-know volunteers, too.

There are several ways that volunteers share information with fund raisers. Contact reports that development officers write after a visit with a volunteer often cite the constituents that the volunteer recommended for additional attention. The fund raiser will suggest that research look into this constituent or that committee member, since the volunteer mentioned during the visit that there is a possibility of capacity and major gift support. A volunteer may agree to review lists of constituents they know. They may agree to attend a formal peer screening session. We will discuss these opportunities later in this chapter. Regardless of the way the information comes to the nonprofit, it will be important to capture it in a permanent place. You and your fund-raising team should check to be sure that the information meets your ethical standards and is relevant to the fund-raising process. Then you will file it, either electronically or on paper, or both ways (just to be safe).

"Top" Lists

Forbes magazine does it. *Fortune* magazine does it, too. Your local newspaper probably does it. Business journals around the country do it. What do they do? As we have mentioned before, newspapers, business journals, and professional publications compile "top" lists or, what some researchers call, lists of superlatives. The largest private companies in Atlanta, the highest-paid public company executives in Minnesota, and the top women in technology are examples of the types of lists you will find. When a researcher looks at those lists, what does she see? If she finds a match between someone on one of the lists and a name in her database of constituents, she usually is looking at a major gift prospect.

In chapter 2 we talked about the compulsion to collect that inflicts prospect researchers. The "top lists" represent shining gems at the center of a researcher's collection. The trick to collecting anything is to collect the *right* thing, the valuable or useful thing. Picking the lists that are likely to contain a name or two from your constituency will not be difficult. If your nonprofit is locally based, the lists produced by your local newspaper and business journal will interest you. If your nonprofit is national or international in scope, you will find top lists that cover the wealthy, the successful, and the philanthropic across those domains. If your constituency is filled with lawyers or architects, you will be interested in the lists of top law or architectural firms.

The Big "Top" Lists

Here are a few readily available lists. By reviewing these, you will begin to see the value in top lists. You will be stirred to locate the lists that will matter most to your fund-raising team. The worth in checking the names on these lists for matches in your database is increased when you begin with the lists that are likely to include the wealthy in your area or in the professional field your constituents populate.

- *Forbes* People Lists (**http://www.forbes.com/people/**):
  Here you will find the *Forbes 400* richest americans, top CEOs, top celebrities, and the world's richest people. You can search for people by name, geography, and several other indices. Often the alma mater for each person listed is given, but the Web version does not index this data, so the printed version is actually better for browsing for a school name. If you have not looked at a top list like this before, begin by checking the *Forbes 400* and the *Top CEOs* lists for people who live in your state. Are they in your database? We will be able to hear you hooting from here when you get a match, you know.
- *Fortune 500* (**http://www.fortune.com/fortune/fortune500**):
  This list of the top companies in the United States actually profiles 1,000 businesses. They have conveniently provided a CEO browser, so you can check to see if one of your constituents is at the helm of one of the engines of capital.
- *The Book of Lists* (**http://www.bizjournals.com/bookoflists/**):
  For many major U.S. metropolitan areas, there is a book of lists marketed by BizJournals.com. If you have a subscription to the printed version of the business journal in your area (and you should—remember what we said about reading), you probably get a copy of the *Book of Lists* annually. However, if you want a handy electronic version for ease of sorting and selecting, or if you have constituents in another region not covered by your local business journal, you can buy the list in a database form. The list includes the top officer's name. The lists generally are not available without paying a fee, but they may be available at your local library.

Newspaper and Regional Magazine "Top" Lists

Most of the newspapers in major U.S. cities and many regional business magazines publish annual lists of the top companies in the area or the rankings of the highest paid public company executives. Many of these lists are published on the newspapers' or magazines' Web sites, often under a heading like "Special Reports."

Donor Rolls

Nonprofits publish lists of donors, categorizing them by the size of the gifts and with the gifts falling into ranges. Researchers call these donor rolls, honor rolls, or tributes. You will read our urging that you collect these lists many times throughout this book, we are afraid to say. They are currently the most direct way to tune into giving, and that can lead to some reliable conclusions about capacity and even inclination or interest. If one of your constituents can give $50,000 to the local hospital, he might be able to give your healthcare nonprofit a major gift, too.

The playbills, annual reports, and newsletters from other nonprofits will be important resources for you. You try for matches with the names on those lists with the names in your database, usually setting an arbitrary cutoff that approximates a major gift or a large annual gift at your organization. Some researchers actually enter all the top donors on those lists in their own databases. They believe that if they enter the names when they encounter them, noting the gifts to other organizations in the person's new electronic file, they will be ahead when this individual joins their constituency in the future. Other researchers simply save the playbills and annual reports and, when a new prospect surfaces, the researcher rechecks those materials for a match.

Event Attendance Rosters

When your nonprofit holds an event, do you review the list of attendees? Is the information that a constituent attended an event added to each attendee's electronic record? If you are nodding your head up and down, you are giving the right answer. Constituents who attend events are further deepening their affiliation with your nonprofit. Many of the parties, auctions, fairs, and shows are fund-raising events. When someone shows up and makes a purchase, it says two things: First, this constituent has enough money to spend it on things that are enjoyable or interesting to her, and second, she is interested in your organization.

Paper, Paper Everywhere

Now you have single names and lists of names everywhere. The names are on slips of papers, in news articles you have saved, on pages from programs and playbills, on notes scratched on memo pads. The pieces of paper might report:

- A brief news story about a constituent selling her company
- A letter from another constituent who writes about his golf adventures at the course near his winter home in a swank warm weather location
- A copy of the check that is a substantially larger gift—but still under major gift level—from a constituent who has given steadily for years
- A clipping from a social page reporting the recent marriage between two constituents from prominent families—he was an affiliate, but she was not
- A short note written by a fund raiser about another affiliate who recently founded a company of her own
- A copy of a page from the theatre's playbill where the donors supporting the latest season are listed

Each of these slips of paper represents constituents who display a hint of financial capacity. Some of these constituents may actually be ready to move

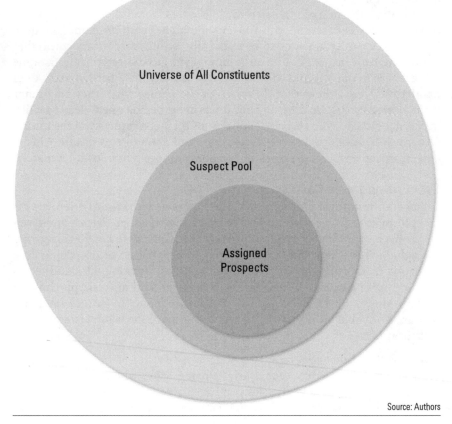

Source: Authors

FIGURE 6-1
Segmenting the Universe of Constituents

to prospect status. If, for example, the sale price of the company the constituent sold was included in the news story, there may be enough financial signs to point toward assigning that individual for cultivation by a development officer. The constituent's age, life stage, and other factors would also be considered, of course. But some of the names on the slips of paper could be fast-tracked to prospect status, if enough information surfaces. Not all research projects are tedious, after all.

Some of these constituents need to be set aside in a sort of holding place to see how their capacity-building activities develop. Like the woman who recently founded a company, there may be more elements to their financial story, factors that will make waiting to cultivate them a wiser course. This is the definition of a suspect, is it not? Remember, that word is development shorthand for someone we *suspect* could be a major gift donor. The pool will be a great place to hold them until you can take a closer look at capacity as well as other factors (see Figure 6-1).

Where to Put the Pool

What are you going to do with those slips of paper? Not too many years ago, the pool would have remained in an in-tray on a fund raiser's desk. You can still maintain the pool that way, if you have no other options. But if you keep the pool on slips of paper in a file or desk drawer, an in-tray, a binder or in a fund raiser's head, you lose a few options. The number of names in the pool only gets larger. Before you realize it, there are too many names to manage in a drawer or in a person's head. You will not be able to select affiliates needing special attention from the pool without missing a few. You will not be able to consistently add them to invitation lists, special fund-raising events, or other efforts to engage their interest in your nonprofit.

The era we live in offers us better options than desk drawers or head storage. We can now save names of people (and foundations and corporations) electronically. We can save special features about those names, such as their status in our prospect research program.

There are easy and rather complex ways to keep a pool of potential prospects electronically. Some organizations use very simple databases or spreadsheets and list the members of the pool there. Because the list is electronic, the staff can search for names using either the "find" feature in the program or another elementary search tool. Creating a separate database of the occupants of the pool like this one means that you cannot relate your actions for these constituents very easily with the rest of their electronic constituent record. You will have to hand-enter any data in the two places you are keeping these names. It is likely that you will begin to keep one record and not the other. Many researchers call these "orphan databases" because they are not related to the other (usually primary) database. Most researchers will tell you that this is a frustrating and unreliable course to set upon. You would only choose this elementary way of keeping your suspect pool if you have no other options. Some young or resource-limited nonprofits will find that this system is better than the alternatives: no system at all or the slips of paper system.

Tagging Suspects: Why and Where

Once again, the era we live in offers even better options. The databases designed for fund raisers allow researchers to "tag" constituents who they wish to place in the suspect pool. If you are working with one of these systems, it is likely that your suspect pool is already filled with constituents who will be your organization's next major gift prospects. If you are just beginning to build your suspect pool, you will decide a few things about what you want the system you create to be able to tell you. Nonprofits design ways to not only "tag" constituents as suspects in the pool, but also to provide the answers to a few other questions with similar electronic markers. These markers (or codes) can include anything that is important to your nonprofit. The usuals are:

- *Why* the individual was recommended for the suspect pool
- From *where* the information came

The why and where can be included in the portion of the electronic record that represents the suspect pool.

A news story reports that your constituent owns one of the most expensive homes in your county, according to assessor records. You now have the *why* and *where* of this equation: real estate assets (why) and a public report (where). What other reasons to add an individual to the pool would your organization want to note? They will be the same characteristics of wealth that we outlined for qualifying prospects in chapter 3. They include:

- Real estate
- Giving (to your or another organization)
- Compensation (salary and bonus)
- Family assets or future heir
- Future success or up-and-comer (a young constituent who may one day be a major gift prospect)
- Other assets (stock holdings and collections, for example)

What are some of the choices for *where* the information comes from? The information that someone belongs in the pool might come from:

- Volunteers
- Staff members
- News stories or other information from a print source
- Self-identification (through contact, a survey, or through giving)

Back to the slips of paper. The constituent who founded a company would be coded "Suspect, future success, volunteer." The newlyweds would be coded "Suspect, family assets, news story." Look at the other examples we listed and decide how they would be coded. If you design your own coding system, you are certain to think of other codes you will want to use in addition (or instead of) the ones we listed here.

You have a few other decisions to make. Will you need to use special coding to connect spouses or life partners with the suspects in the suspect pool? Many databases apply the same information to both individuals in the marriage or life partnership. Some do not. If you need it, you can create a code for spouses or life partners of suspects. You may even have a code for suspect couples. By coding both members of the marriage or life partnership, you will be able to accurately follow those two constituents if something—like divorce or death—interrupts their relationship.

You may decide to enter constituents in the suspect pool at varying levels, based on the amount of information you have when you put them in the pool. For example, by applying a special code to those who can be moved to assigned prospect status with minimal research, you will create a ready set of "next to research" suspects.

The last piece of the suspect pool involves decisions you must make about coding constituents who do not reach the Ask stage or who do not give a major gift after a period of cultivation. You may even wish to create a special code for constituents you have researched but who you are not going to recommend for major gift assigning. You may tag these constituents' records as:

- Not interested in supporting your nonprofit
- Cultivated but did not give
- Giving to other nonprofits
- No major gift capacity

Once again, you will think of other reasons you encounter at your nonprofit. The few listed here are only meant to give you an idea or two about how to set up this coding.

When designing your suspect coding system, you may decide to use the first letter initials as the code or you may devise a numerical system. Your database may already include adequate coding. Whatever system you design or elect to use, you will have thoughtfully considered the things you want to capture about constituents who are being elevated out of the larger group of affiliates and placed in the potential prospect, or suspect, pool.

Foundations and Corporations Need Attention, Too

As usual, all of our attention has been directed toward individuals, but you also will be adding corporations and foundations to your suspect pool. Everything you have learned about building a suspect pool for individuals applies to corporations and foundations. Many of the codes we suggested work for these entities, too. You may add other coding that is particular to foundations and corporations. Some of the language for making or not making grants will work here. For example, "out of area of operation" and "pre-selected charities only" cover the why of dropping a corporation or foundation from consideration.

Pool Maintenance

An annual checkup for the pool will help you maintain it as a well functioning part of your prospect research efforts. Are there names in the pool that do not belong there any longer? Many schools add the names of prominent or wealthy parents to the pool. If these parents have not been moved into the cultivation stream by the time their children graduate, it is unlikely they will become major gift prospects after their connection to the school has faded. These parents can be either removed from the pool or coded as "not interested" or "no longer affiliated." There may be other groups like this who can be removed from the pool during your annual pool cleaning.

During the pool checkup, you can evaluate how smoothly the pool is working in general. Are you using the pool to find your next prospects? Are you adding the new suspects you find in your daily reading to the pool? Are the fund raisers using the pool to look for people to fill their visit lists when they travel? Are the members of the pool being invited to events? In other words, is the entire team working to "field research" these potential prospects? The "next to research" list will grow quickly if these steps are a part of the fund-raising plan.

What's Next? Research, of Course.

Once you have begun to populate the pool, you will experience a feeling of relief. All those names that were swimming in your head are now swimming in the pool. You do not have to try to remember them anymore. Now you can select them for research, as you will.

Well, actually, your selections will be slightly more directed than that. The members of the suspect pool have some characteristics in common but they have many others that make them distinct from one another. If you are working for an academic institution, the suspects will affiliate with different departments or major fields of study. If you work for a health care facility, the suspects may fall into distinct groups based on the origin of their link to your nonprofit. Are they doctors or other staff members who work for the nonprofit? Which ones are patients who have supported the institution in the past? Your answers to these questions will help you now segment the pool so that you can begin qualifying new prospects. Your goal will be to find the right prospects for upcoming fund-raising initiatives.

Peer Screening and Rating

"You know, you ought to visit Dave. He has been telling me for years that one day he wants a scholarship at your school named for his father. And he recently hit it big with a company he invested in. This might be just the time to contact him about that scholarship."

"Have you ever met with Marie? She bought that property near the lake last year and, when I ran into her at the season premier for her new exhibition, she said that she had been selling some of the jewelry she designs in Europe. I think she would be interested in that art program you started for the preschoolers."

"I do not think Frank is the guy for you this year. He took a bath on those Death Valley lots he was developing when the water rights didn't come through. You know he loves your organization, but you might want to give him a year to recover."

Fund raisers are experts at conversation. After all, cultivating relationships is a part of their work. Fund raisers are on a mission: Just like researchers, they are looking for the next supporters for their nonprofit all the time. They are also looking for ways to connect the constituents they are cultivating to the nonprofit. Every experienced fund raiser knows that asking for and accepting advice—when the advice will be seriously considered—is one of the important ways that they can make a deeper connection with their prospects.

Committed volunteers—and major gift prospects fall into this category—are also on a mission. They often believe in your nonprofit's purpose so deeply that they almost form an amateur team of researchers themselves. They are savvy. They know what a major gift is at your nonprofit. They understand the nuances of fund raising, including who makes a good major gift prospect. They know your organization's history, and they may have even been among the founding donors. They often know many of the philanthropic people in the community and among your constituency. Instead of calling them volunteer researchers (as we would like to), we will call them peer screeners and raters.

That is a portion of what prospect researchers are doing, after all. We are screening constituents and rating them for an Ask. When volunteers enter this ballpark, they are joining the fund-raising team in a unique and important level. Their commitment to the fund-raising mission has reached a new position of trust. These volunteers become an integral part of your fund-raising program.

Peer screening is the examination of a number of fellow constituents by a volunteer to uncover which among them are likely to be major gift prospects. The screener shares general or specific information they have that will help the fund-raising team focus on the constituents who are most likely, if cultivated, to make a major gift soon. Rating constituents is the circumstance when a volunteer tells the fund raisers what range of gift they should ask the constituent for or what size gift the constituent is capable of making. In addition to gift rating, some volunteers dabble in rating wealth. The volunteer can indicate her impression of a constituent's wealth by placing that individual in an income or wealth range.

Peer screening and rating can enhance your efforts to segment your constituent universe. We hinted at peer screening when we talked about the well-connected volunteer—usually a major gift donor or donor-to-be—who shares the names of other potential major gift donors with you. That same volunteer may offer capacity information about the constituents she knows. When she does this, she is screening prospects. Now, take this one step further. Add a list of constituents and a group of volunteer screeners or a one-on-one screening with a fund raiser, and you are conducting a peer screening session.

Designing a Peer Screening Session

The types of peer screenings conducted by nonprofits vary nearly as much as the constituents themselves. Some fund-raising teams plan group-screening sessions. Some sessions are conducted with one volunteer at a time. Some screening sessions are held in the homes of volunteers and some are held at the nonprofit.

You can design an effective group screening session for your nonprofit. You will begin by creating a list of constituents who match the major gift donor composite you constructed. Tighten the characteristics until the list only includes about 200 to 300 names. You can do this by narrowing the characteristics, such as picking constituents with a larger giving history. Now choose 10 to 20 well-connected volunteers who are willing to act as peer screeners. Your nonprofit's board of directors will be a good place to look for screeners. Others who are particularly close to your organization, like key staff members or committee members, may also wish to participate. The volunteers who have long associations with your institution will have the most insight into the capabilities and interests of its constituents. Ideally, your volunteer screeners will be a lot like your potential donors. They will attend the same functions, belong to the same clubs, or do business with one another.

The format of the session we are designing here will involve the volunteers reviewing a list of names and indicating knowledge (or a lack of knowledge) about those people. Each screener will respond to written statements about the constituents on the list. The statements will be prepared before the session, taking the form of a questionnaire, and will be based on the information the fund-raising team is seeking from the volunteers (see Figure 6-2).

Getting Volunteer Screeners Ready

Some organizations prepare a handout for volunteer screeners. The handout may begin by instructing volunteers about how the screening session will be conducted and what is expected of each screener. It explains what a major gift is for this nonprofit (including multiple year payments), the ways the screening results will be used, and what kind of information the nonprofit hopes to receive through the screenings. It may include information about upcoming fund-raising initiatives that will benefit from the screening results. The handout usually explains the extraordinary value of the screener's participation in the screening and issues a thank you to the volunteers.

Volunteer screeners are counseled that they should only screen constituents they actually know. Some screening questionnaires even ask screeners to qualify how well they know the individuals they are screening. Checking statements like "I have known this individual for many years," or "I only know this individual casually," or "I have been involved with this individual professionally" can help the nonprofit's staff gauge the value of the screener's rating when compared to later information.

Screeners are usually instructed to assume that the constituents they are reviewing would be motivated to make a gift. In other words, they are not expected to consider the donor's state of mind or the degree to which he affiliates with the nonprofit. Even if a screener feels that she knows the constituent's state of mind, most screening sessions are disrupted if screeners

The volunteer may fill out the questionnaire himself or staff members attending the screening session may fill out the form as the volunteer comments on each name being screened. An explanatory handout will outline the reason for the screening session, what the development team expects, and how the results will be used. The form might include statements like these:

Please check the appropriate box.

I know this constituent well.
Over a three to five year period, this person could make a gift of:
- ❑ $10,000
- ❑ $25,000
- ❑ $50,000
- ❑ $100,000
- ❑ $250,000
- ❑ $500,000
- ❑ $1 million

While not a candidate for an outright gift, this person is a good candidate for a deferred gift.

While not a candidate for a major gift, this person would be a great volunteer.

I would be willing to contact this person on behalf of this nonprofit.

Other comments: _____

Source: Authors

FIGURE 6-2
Screening Questionnaire

focus on this aspect. As you can see from the screening questionnaire, the statements are simple and direct. There is not time for long discussions when volunteers are screening dozens of names in one sitting. Further, assigning prospects is not based soley on the third-party information about whether the prospect likes the nonprofit or not. Capacity can sometimes outweigh attitude. Most fund raisers believe that they have a chance at changing a prospect's attitude by educating him about the nonprofit. Development officers are usually willing to make a few contacts with a major gift prospect to evaluate the person's hesitancy and to see if additional information might bring about a change.

Shaping the Screening Session
The type of screening session we are describing can be carried out in several ways. Some institutions invite a group of volunteers who are available for a

screening to an evening together, complete with light refreshments and inspirational words from one of the fund raisers or a key volunteer. There is a lot to accomplish in a group session, so the evening progresses quickly and efficiently. The energy in the group adds to each volunteer's effort.

Alternately, the list of names to be screened and the questionnaires can be mailed to volunteers who will then return it to the nonprofit. This variation would be the most difficult format to manage. Getting the volunteers to finish and return their screenings promptly would become a management task in itself.

In another and more common approach, fund raisers take the screening tools with them when they visit volunteers and prospects. They will, of course, prepare the volunteers before their visits so they know what to expect. Then, the one-on-one screening session will go quickly and be productive since the fund raiser will leave with the screening results. Development officers may see this as a chance to draw a screener (who also may be a prospect) closer to the nonprofit.

What to Do with the Results

You may have noticed that we prepared a single list of 200 to 300 constituents to be screened. In a group session, all of the volunteer screeners might screen the same group of constituents. The results of several screeners reporting about the same constituents are immeasurable. The results, when compared, can generate consensus. If several volunteers rate a constituent in the same range, it is likely that the fund raisers will place greater weight on that consensus of opinion.

Some screening sessions segment the constituents to be screened by characteristics about the screeners. Screeners may be asked about other constituents in their age group. The lists might be divided geographically or, for an educational institution, by class year or major course of study.

When the results from the screening sessions are back in the office, the real work begins. You and the fund-raising team must have a plan for dealing with the results. Will you add them to the database? Many fund-raising databases have sections designed just for that type of information. The screening or rating section on the database requires that you enter the date of the screening, the screener's name, and the rating that emerged from the screening. By recording the results in the electronic database, you will begin to build a collection of ratings for each constituent rated. In their preponderance they will begin to tell you a few things about the range of gift capacity and more.

The fund-raising team might convert the dollar ranges we described in Figure 6-2 to codes. The codes make an evaluation even easier: Bob received one A ($1 million) and seven Cs ($250,000). Coding is shorthand that helps us focus on the key information. By this estimate, the Cs have it. The accumulation of screening results will help you cull confusing results. Volunteer screeners will give you good leads for your next research projects in the comments they write on the screening questionnaire. That research may add support to the screening conclusions.

Now that the screening results are in, do not forget your original intent. You were looking for more people to add to the suspect pool and, ultimately, more potential prospects to qualify through research. The screening results establish a clear lineup for you. The individuals who consistently received ratings in the major gift range will be added to the suspect pool. The individuals who consistently received the highest ratings will be researched first.

Electronic Screening

Our screening model involves people and pencils and paper. There is another type of constituent screening that involves segmenting a nonprofit's database electronically. Professional screening companies apply their methods of lifting constituents up out of the universe for special attention from the prospect researchers and fund raisers. The advantage of using an electronic screening company is that your entire database, or any portion of it you choose, can be screened in one process. The screening will not be based on the personal perspective of volunteers who actually know your constituents, but on matching your constituents with publicly available information about the wealthy or with the screening company's model of wealth. We will deal with electronic screening in chapter 7.

Assigning Names for Cultivation

In the past and in the present at some nonprofits, these four words, "assigning names for cultivation," may present a minefield for the prospect research office. The minefield is laid by issues that have little to do with prospect research itself or with fund raising. The minefield distracts those present from the difficulties the institution has switching the fund-raising motor on. Or the minefield gives those present a chance to awkwardly practice ancient exercises in trust, hierarchies, and posturing. Moving on to something productive can be difficult in these circumstances.

In a small nonprofit where the fund raisers and the researcher know one another and appreciate each other's work style, problems are either minimal or very clear and solvable. Researchers are free to talk to the fund raisers about the new prospects they identify. They can adapt their reporting formats to meet the needs of the staff, to maximize the name assigning process. Fund raisers and the researcher can talk about the way prospects are being qualified. There are ongoing opportunities to build a successful relay relationship. Passing the prospects from research to the fund raisers becomes as smooth as a relay race where the baton is never dropped.

Large nonprofits may be characterized by fund raisers and researchers who are separated both physically and bureaucratically. Researchers at large nonprofits may prepare reports about new prospects for fund raisers who they have never met. They may never hear the outcome of the cultivation process. It is not uncommon for a researcher at a large institution to read about the outcome of the cultivation, the gift received, in the nonprofit's press release or in the newspaper. It might be difficult to move new prospects identified through screenings or by other means into the cultivation process. The reasons for this are unique to each situation, but might include some of the following:

- Fund raisers feel that they have a full plate with the prospects already assigned to them.
- A relationship of trust has not been built between the fund raisers and the research office.
- Volunteers (often board members) have come forward with different names than those suggested by the research office, and the fund raisers feel obligated to respond to the volunteers first.
- The name assigning process became stalled and has not been reviewed or renewed for some time.

These examples demonstrate that it is crucial for the fund raisers and the researcher to be in agreement about the prospect needs of the organization. They can make conclusions and develop a plan for prospect research and assigning and cultivating prospects through the managers of these departments. Before volunteer screening and rating sessions are arranged or before an electronic screening is considered, the managers of the development and research sections will determine how the newly discovered prospects will be assigned. Once the team leaders are committed to the new plan, they can coach their fund raisers and researchers about how to add new research or new prospects to their workloads. The politics of managing your way through the hierarchy of a large nonprofit can be complex and fragile. If you are the manager who has to create a welcoming place for prospect research, you will form the foundation of that place with the alliances you make among the members of the fund-raising team.

What Does a New Prospect Report Look Like?

We have known development departments that have researchers writing elaborate research reports—full profiles—for brand new prospects who no one has ever telephoned. We have seen slumping researchers sadly fingering four and five and six page reports as the assignment manager balks at assigning the subject of that report. We have met assignment managers who will not assign a new prospect unless they believe they know everything there is to know. It is no matter that the prospect may not even take the fund raiser's phone call. It is not important that the researcher has spent hours and hours gathering and analyzing information about a prospect who recently suffered financial setbacks that no news story has reported.

What do these scenarios have in common? They are pointing a flashing neon sign with three words: "Keep it simple." The first research report, the one written to outline why a newly identified prospect should be assigned and cultivated, is supposed to simply identify and qualify. A fund raiser does not need a full profile to make a first contact. What does he need, then? He needs good contact information. He needs enough capacity information to demonstrate that the prospect actually has capacity. This usually means outlining the basics of the prospect's financial resources (job, real property, or inheritance). The fund raiser also needs to know, very specifically, how the prospect is affiliated with your nonprofit. He needs to know the affiliation in detail. Does the prospect serve on a board? Has he named the nonprofit in his will? Is he a former employee? Is he related to other constituents? The affiliation information is integral to how the fund raiser begins a relationship with the prospect.

As you learned in earlier chapters, the other information can be outlined and analyzed later. It is likely that the fund raiser will bring fresh information back to the researcher after a contact or two with the prospect. Researching and writing detailed profiles for all the suspects who are being recommended for assignment creates a bottleneck. Research gets stalled researching and writing reports, and some of those reports will be for constituents who will not turn out to be major gift prospects because of issues unknown by or unavailable to the researcher. Research's efficient use of its resources will be diminished by this agenda.

Brief initial reports might not be the choice fund raisers would make. It is much more comforting to have a full profile on the person they are about to meet for the first time. However, everyone on the team must remember that the primary activity of the fund-raising team—including research—is to raise money, not write reports and protect one another from unexpected encounters. Major gift money is raised by cultivating relationships with donors. Those relationships cannot even begin if the research section is trapped in report writing, the fund raisers are trapped in reading long, complex reports, and no one is on the road meeting prospects.

How Many Ways Can an Assignment Be Made?
Let Us Count the Ways

Researchers prepare reports about newly identified and qualified prospects in very similar ways, no matter what type of institution employs them. They use similar resources and cover similar topics in their reports. There are differences, but they are subtle. A researcher working for an art museum may list a prospect's collections in greater detail than a researcher working for a children's organization would. A researcher working for an animal rescue nonprofit might list the names and breeds of a prospect's pets, while researchers working for a hospital will not be interested in that detail.

But, when it comes to turning those reports into prospect assignments for fund raisers, the wide range of approaches begins. Some nonprofits put the research section in charge of making the assignments and managing the progress of those assignments. The research section is viewed as Switzerland, a neutral place to begin what can become an emotionally charged event. Other nonprofits put the development manager in charge of making the prospect assignments. The development manager is often a good choice for motivating and monitoring the progress of the fund raisers she is supervising.

There are nonprofits that ask the researcher to present a report about the new prospects at a strategy or prospect management meeting. The researcher makes a short report that includes the prospect's affiliation to the organization and a brief overview of the indicators of capacity. You might say that the oral portion of this report is "the facts, Ma'am, just the facts." The researcher will have a written report, which includes more details, ready to distribute. This format gives members of the development team a chance to add their stories to the mix. The downside of this approach is that it challenges the researcher to be a good presenter. It can also become a version of "Let's Make a Deal," where the researcher is negotiating for what is behind Door No. 2, a development officer who will take this assignment, while trying to ignore the distractions of those who wish to challenge the researcher's conclusions.

Another way to present new prospect names frees the researcher from occupying center stage. A researcher can prepare the new prospect reports and simply pass them to the person in charge of making the prospect assignments. That person can assign the prospects and then let the researcher know who is assigned to whom. If the prospect assignment manager decides not to assign a prospect, the researcher will be told why. The researcher may pursue additional information that will help convince the manager of the worthiness of the assignment. Or the researcher may return the almost-prospect to the suspect pool and wait for better days for that constituent. This format takes the performance element out of assigning prospects. If the assignment manager is good at giving feedback, this format maintains the "small nonprofit" benefits of clear messages about outcomes between researchers and fund raisers. The drawback for this format is that there is no limelight for research. Limelight is sometimes essential to keeping a budget, a program, or an employee.

New Name Quotas

Some nonprofits set a schedule for new prospect identification. The leadership asks that the researchers on the fund-raising team identify and present (or submit) a specific number of new prospects each week or month. This schedule ensures that the researchers are moving through the pool. It ensures that new prospects are moving into cultivation, to replace those who have reached the stewardship stage or those who are being dropped from assignment because a gift is not forthcoming. Filling the stream with prospects and keeping the fund raisers' assignment lists full—it sounds like a good thing, does it not? It is. Research managers can carefully evaluate the time available for researching new prospects. They can balance this against the special tasks, such as research requests and event reports, that researchers must complete. With an eye on the reading, copying, filing, and general upkeep that a research job involves, a reasonable quota for new prospects can be set. In a perfect world, the quota is a guideline based on trust.

Some researchers are expected to identify one or two new prospects each week. Some researchers spend almost all of their time identifying and qualifying new prospects. Some researchers identify one or two new prospects a month. The number of new prospects identified is affected by the other tasks the researcher has to complete each week. Researchers refer to this balance—and how far the scales tip in either direction—as working in a reactive or proactive research office. A reactive office has researchers spending the bulk of their time reacting, working on projects others have asked for (research requests and event reports). A proactive research office spends the majority of the time acting of its own accord, that is, identifying new prospects.

While the concept of a proactive office has been the rage in the prospect research community over the last five or ten years, there are reasons for each type of office. And the reasons that cause a researcher to be reactive or proactive change with the nonprofit's stage of development. A young or growing nonprofit needs prospects. The researcher who works for a new nonprofit or a nonprofit launching special fund-raising initiatives will spend her time identifying new prospects and keeping the fund raisers busy with plenty of people to meet and visit. An older, established nonprofit that is not going into a capital campaign may have fund raisers with prospects in the advanced stages of cultivation. Those fund raisers will be asking the researcher for deeper, more complex information about their prospects. They may have an agenda of annual events that have become traditions. The researcher at an older, established nonprofit might spend a great deal of her time working on analytical reports that help set the Ask and the timing of the Ask. She may be preparing event reports that reflect her insight into the prospect relationships to advance during the event. While her time is spent in reactive research, it is not any less valuable than the time that a researcher spends identifying new prospects.

Houston, We Are Ready for Liftoff

Once the managers and the researchers establish a pattern, the process for assigning new prospects will become familiar and expected to the entire fund-raising team. As you already know, researchers like benchmarks. Development managers who establish contact and cultivation benchmarks for their fund raisers are researchers' best friends. Benchmarks such as how soon first contact should be made and how long an average cultivation ought to take, for example, help the fund raisers stay on track and help the researcher see the progress that arises from his hard work. And, most important of all, those benchmarks help the nonprofit add major gifts to its fund-raising totals.

Even with a cultivation schedule in place, some prospects will remain uncultivated. It is difficult for researchers to accept that hard-found prospects may languish on fund raisers' assignment lists. It happens though and, in reality, the better part of the researcher's job was finished when the new prospect's name was passed to the fund raiser. The researcher has moved on to researching another prospect or two. But even the most forward-thinking researcher is happiest when he knows that fund raisers have a framework of expectations about contacting and cultivating prospects. You will learn more about this in chapter 8.

Electronic Screening

"I explain it that I've been hit by lightning. You can make it pretty likely that you will be hit by lightning by standing on the highest hill with your feet wet and hanging onto a piece of metal. You can increase the odds."
—Retiree Rebecca Allen, not yet 30 years old, who began working at Amazon.com in 1996, *The Seattle Times*, March 21, 1999, p. A1.

"There must be a better way to do this." That is probably what Henry Ford thought just before he applied the assembly line concept to his first automobile factory. He must have looked out across his Model T production area and thought, "I have to be able to speed up this process."

We imagine that the first researchers who pecked away, name by name, at uncovering the wealth in their databases thought the same thing. Some days they worried that they didn't have enough solid prospects for upcoming fund-raising initiatives. They couldn't imagine how they could work any faster at identifying and qualify prospects. Other days, they simply shrugged and tossed new suspects into the pool, realizing that they will only ever brush by a fraction of the names in their databases. "There must be a better way to do this," they probably thought.

Early in this book we told you about the long-time arts patron who commented on the new, young theater-goers. She complained that she did not know who the wealth-holders are in the audience (or in town) anymore. In chapter 6 you learned how fund raisers and researchers rely on constituents just like that arts patron. Through peer screening, the constituents who are most intimate with the institution help identify the next major gift donors. The information those "most affiliated" constituents share helps the fund-raising team rate prospects. We can think of this approach as the first screening efforts, an approach that did not rely on electronics. Fund raisers still use this approach. It is particularly valuable in identifying the relationships between known supporters and prospective donors. But a peer screener cannot be expected to review more than a few hundred names in one sitting. And peer screeners can only help with constituents they know through their affiliation with your nonprofit, in the community, at work, or through other nonprofit work. As you can see, this approach would never allow you to screen your entire database. A human screener cannot reach deeply and broadly enough into your database to help you discover all the wealth that you are unable to see.

With thousands, tens of thousands, and sometimes hundreds of thousands of names in a database of constituents, researchers and their fund-raising colleagues face a dismal task. Sure, we can find a new prospect here in a news story about a successful company and another there among the new gifts our nonprofit received last week. But how can we find 50 or 100 or 1,000 or 5,000 new prospects all at once? How can we find enough potential donors to populate projections for the number of prospects the development team needs to meet a fund-raising goal?

Campaigns and Other Hungry Beasts

Looming campaigns, or any fund-raising initiative that means a great deal of money must be raised, often are the catalysts for the search for more donors. Untapped donor pools, a new major gifts unit, or a strong economy calling fund raisers to get their nonprofit's piece of the pie are other catalysts for finding new prospects. Actually, a weakened economy even calls for new donors, does it not? When institutions have to raise a great deal of money in a specific period of time or for special causes, wise development leaders assess the gift possibilities among the known major gift prospects. The initial assessment may come up short.

Fund raisers know the speculative count of gifts is coming up short because, like researchers, they have math formulas they have created to assist them in their work. Like the research math adages you learned about in chapter 5, most of the fund-raising adages are based on the experiences of these professionals, not on scientific study. But they are based on years of experiences across a broad group of fund raisers and consultants. Some of the math formulas associated with campaigns are based on the careful study of the outcome of campaigns at many institutions (see Exhibit 7-1).

Exhibit 7-1	Campaign Survey Resource

About 300 educational institutions were surveyed about their campaigns for the annual *CASE Report of Educational Fund-Raising Campaigns 1999–2000* (Washington, DC: Council for Advancement and Support of Education (CASE), 2000). The report can be ordered from CASE's website book section at http://www.case.org.

Source: Authors

One of the important numbers fund raisers must generate is an estimate of how many major gift donors it will take to meet a specific campaign dollar goal. Skilled fund raisers do not enter a campaign without this estimate. The total number of major gift donors in this estimate matters and, at another level of detail, the number of donors who will give at a specific level is just as important. You might think of this as measuring the depth and breadth of the potential donor base for a specific project in a precise period of time. What sort of campaign can your donor pool successfully complete? One fund raiser calls this measure "capturing reality." Its importance cannot be overstated. The morale of a nonprofit's best volunteers, closest constituents, and staff depends on it. When told about a new funding initiative or plans for a campaign, a responsible fund raiser will sharpen her pencil, pose it over a piece of paper and say, "Where will the lead gifts come from?"

The list that begins to take shape becomes an outline for the progression of the campaign. It will be a measurement of what, in the way of giving, can be done and by whom. The illustration of this measurement is a *campaign gift table*. While the table is constructed during pre-campaign periods, it is also useful for any fund-raising initiative a nonprofit faces, no matter what the size.

Campaign Gift Table

The campaign gift table dissects a campaign goal by the size and number of gifts needed for success (see Figure 7-1). It is rooted in the donor giving model you learned about earlier in this book, the one that estimates that 90 percent of the gifts will come from 10 percent of the donors, the wealthiest donors. With this in mind, 90 percent of a campaign goal will be mapped out and "assigned" to 10 percent of the donor pool. Further, many fund raisers believe that the lead gift, the largest gift that will be given during the campaign, will be equal to about 10 percent of the campaign goal. That lead gift slot is the place to begin building the campaign gift table.

There are other formulas that fund raisers use in estimating the amount a nonprofit can raise in a multi-year campaign. Remember, we are on the art side of the hall again. The campaign goal may reasonably be estimated at twice as much as a nonprofit normally raises in one year, multiplied by the number of years of the campaign (see Exhibit 7-2). So, if the children's theater raises $3 million each year, a five-year campaign of $30 million is a reasonable expectation for a campaign goal. The composition of the theater's best supporters, its trustees, the condition of its donor pool, and the fund-raising staff's skill and readiness must all be considered and may alter this estimate.

Exhibit 7-2	Setting the Campaign Goal

(Total raised annually x 2) x no. of years of the campaign = campaign goal
Example: ($3 million x 2) x 5 = $30 million

Source: Authors

The campaign leadership determines the size and number of the lead gifts by identifying the biggest known donors and what they will give to the campaign. Those donors, often trustees who will lead the campaign, will be asked to review the preliminary gift table. The fund raiser managing the campaign will ask these insiders where they see themselves in the campaign and if, in fact, they see themselves in the lead gift positions. In this way, the campaign gift table has more than one function: It is a cultivation tool and it sets the bar for the biggest donors and those who follow. We might say that the slots on the campaign gift table become leadership spots where major gift donors can envision their own names.

The campaign goal and the lead gifts are now taking shape. What is next? Many fund raisers actually draw the other top slots on the table name by name. How many of our donors can give $1 million? What are their names? Capacity is one element in these decisions. Inclination or likelihood to give becomes an equally important factor. During the momentum of a campaign, it is not uncommon for donors who are highly motivated to stretch to give more. At the same time, some of the constituents with the greatest capacity may never be inclined to give at that capacity. Two groups of prospects, the "unlikelies" and the "willing to stretch," shape and reshape the prospect list during planning for the campaign and throughout the campaign itself. Research adds a third group: the "not-yet met" (or not-yet identified or qualified). These new prospects added to the equation by research keep the gift table full of potential campaign donors.

So, the high end on the gift table is identified as the campaign goal is set. The low end on the table will be set at your organization's minimum major gift. All gifts below that level, the other 10 percent of the campaign goal, will come from the rest of the constituents (through direct mail or phonathon efforts, for example). Just like the 90/10 illustration earlier in this book, the donor gift table is sometimes drawn as a pyramid. When it is illustrated in that form, fund raisers and researchers call it a campaign gift pyramid.

The $10 million campaign we are illustrating in our gift table calls for two donors who can give $1 million each, four donors who can give $500,000 each, and six donors who can give $250,000 each. Figure 7-1 outlines the number of donors required for the other major gifts. Now we will apply another fund-raising and research adage to this equation. To actually get two $1 million gifts, an organization needs six—not two—donors *who are prospects for gifts of $1 million each*. Fund raisers and researchers estimate a nonprofit needs three prospects for each gift on the campaign gift table. This "breathing space" gives fund raisers and researchers room for the unpredictables. Those unpredictables include prospects who have been qualified or rated incorrectly, prospects who decline to give, and prospects who cease to be affiliated. In our example, the cultivation of six $1 million prospects will result in the successful closing of two $1 million gifts. Once again, we are in the art quadrant, not the science quadrant, of the fund raising universe. These ideas are based on the experiences of many researchers and fund raisers.

No. of Donors Needed	Gift Amount	No. of Prospects Needed	Total Anticipated	No. of Known Prospects
2	$1,000,000	6	$2,000,000	6
4	$500,000	12	$2,000,000	10
6	$250,000	18	$1,500,000	20
15	$100,000	45	$1,500,000	36
20	$50,000	60	$1,000,000	64
40	$25,000	120	$1,000,000	100
Total = 87		Total = 261	$9,000,000	236
All the rest	various		$1,000,000	
		Campaign Total =	$10,000,000	

Source: Authors, with Beth Herman

FIGURE 7-1
Campaign Gift Table: $10 Million Campaign

The gift amounts, the numbers of donors, and even which donors fall into which categories are targets or goals. These goals are based on a deep analysis of the prospect pool and an assessment of the inclination of the wealthiest prospects who have been identified and qualified and who are already in the cultivation stream. Of course, the actual gifts received may be larger or smaller or may come from a different number of donors. Some of them will come from donors research will identify during the campaign. No one will mind if the nonprofit gets three $1 million gifts instead of two or if new major gift donors emerge, will they? The gift table is a guideline for development's leadership, not stone writing, but it is an important tool in shaping the entire course of the campaign. As you can see in this example, the $10 million campaign will need 87 major gift donors who have the capacity to give gifts during the campaign period at the outlined levels. To expect to get those 87 gifts, the nonprofit needs 261 prospective donors.

Where are those 261 prospects? As we said, some of them are well-known. Others are in the prospect or research pipeline already. In our example, some are unknown. The last column of the gift table in Figure 7-1 indicates how many prospects have been identified. Some of the totals fall below the number of prospects needed at the gift levels outlined. In order to find many prospects quickly, the nonprofit may need another prospect identification tool. We are now crossing into the world of electronic screening. Electronic screening is the en masse examination of specific characteristics of a database of constituents in order to identify the most likely gift prospects. Electronic screening intends to give a nonprofit new prospects or, with the information provided, to further qualify known prospects. To do this, electronic screening uses both internal and external characteristics of wealth-holders.

The First Electronic Screeners: Prospect Researchers

Think of the type of screen that you used in a sandbox when you were a child. As you shook the screen, most of the sand particles fell through, back into the sandbox. What remained in your screen were the larger objects, a shiny marble, a pebble, or a once-buried toy treasure. Researchers are continually searching for treasures, for new prospects. More accurately, they are looking for new suspects who, with further research, may be elevated to prospect status. With this aim, prospect researchers design their own simple screens. From the database, a researcher may shake out a list of constituents who have job titles such as president, vice president, owner, or director. That researcher might select records based on constituents' zip codes, focusing on zip codes of wealthy neighborhoods. Or the researcher may sift the database inhabitants by lifetime giving, single largest gift, most consistent giving, or other giving factors (see Exhibit 7-3). This type of screening might generate many new prospective donors. Further research can determine if the presidents and owners are in wealth-building positions and if the most consistent givers are good candidates for major gift cultivation.

Exhibit 7-3 **Constituent Characteristics Screened by Researchers**

A few of the characteristics by which researchers screen and segment database constituents:

  Address (zip code, town)
  Age
  Job title (president, vice president, partner, owner, co-owner, founder, director, trustee)
  No heirs
  Lifetime giving
  Single largest gift
  Consistent giving

Source: Authors

But we are still searching the database in a rather small way. The success of this sort of screening is dependent on the integrity of the information entered for each constituent. The information must be current. It must consistently include items like job title. There are several important wealth indicators that we cannot access with this approach. We have not really flipped the switch on that conveyor belt that will deliver dozens of prospective donors yet, have we?

Meet the Professional Screeners

The mission of professional screening firms is to identify new prospects for nonprofits. That is only a portion of what screening firms do, but it is what draws nonprofits to them. Screening firms also offer consultations, assessments, custom donor rankings, ongoing prospect information, alert services, and more. In this chapter we will concentrate on the prospect identification and qualification part of their business.

There are many electronic screening companies and even more appearing on the horizon each year. The surge in information availability and the increasing sophistication of fund-raising efforts by nonprofits around the world is contributing to this growth. Improvements in technology, particularly with regard to the volume of information that can be stored and retrieved, also encourage these changes. All of these developments have heralded a range of donor identification services for electronic screening firms to market to nonprofits. The electronic screening firms offer one or a combination of the services we are listing here. For the purposes of introducing the basic concepts of electronic screening to you, we will concentrate on the following services and the way they are used together to generate new prospects:

- Matching your constituents with information from other databases
- Matching your constituents with a model of a wealthy person or a major gift prospect created by the screening service
- Analyzing the information you share from your database to select the most likely major gift prospects

Matching Your Constituents with Information from Other Databases

All electronic screening companies need information from your database to screen, of course. They need your constituents' names and addresses and any other identifying information you are able to share. They often ask for each donor's giving history, too. How each screening company applies the information and what results they return are as individual as the companies themselves. By understanding the range of applications and results, you will be able to do a better job of choosing the screening service that meets your information goals. There is terminology to learn and there are concepts to grasp (see Exhibit 7-4).

Exhibit 7-4   Electronic Screening Terms

Algorithm: A procedure for solving any problem; usually applied to math problems.

Household-level data: Information about groups of residences generated by surveys and U.S. Census information; the information may include home values, family size, income range, and other data.

Individual-specific data: Information that is particular to a single individual, such as place of employment, stock holdings, real estate holdings, and other data.

Predictive modeling: Using a mathematical algorithm to analyze certain characteristics and past actions of a prospect for the purpose of predicting future behavior.

Proprietary: Owned by one entity; not available to be copied or reproduced in precisely the same way by others.

Ranking: The place in a hierarchy where a unit falls; the act of placing individuals in a hierarchy of value based on a set of characteristics.

Segmentation: Dividing objects (or, in this case, people) into clusters of common traits or characteristics.

Source: Authors

Some screening services make a one-to-one match between information you have about your prospects (her name and employer, for example) and information that they find in commercial databases. To what, precisely, are the screening companies matching your constituents? Part of the information is from the same databases that researchers use to qualify prospects. What is different then? Researchers usually fish with a rod and reel for this information, plunking one donor name into the information pool to see if some bits of information attach to that name. An electronic screening service casts a net of names and then trawls them through a sea of information. What information? It is information about:

- Public company officers and insiders
- Private company owners
- Public and private company directors
- People profiled in Marquis *Who's Who, Dun & Bradstreet,* and other biographical or professional databases
- Yacht and airplane owners and others who own the accoutrements of wealth
- Trustees of foundations and nonprofit organizations
- Philanthropists
- Real estate owners with large holdings

There are many other sources the electronic screening firms use, but this short list gives you a sharper picture of where the data begin. To put it simply, the screening service matches the information in those sources with your constituent names. Rather than applying one name at a time to the information sources, the screening firm applies an entire group of sources to all the names you give them to screen. The screening firm can generate many matches between the information sources and the names in your database.

Using that trawling net, the screening company will compare your constituents with databases of thousands and tens of thousands of names of individuals who are exhibiting signs of wealth. The screening service will be *electronically* looking for matches. They will use the names, addresses, and any other distinguishing information that you have shared with them to establish matches. We will discuss the veracity of the matches, but reputable screening companies tell customers that the work is not finished when the screening results match some of your constituents to wealth-indicating sources. Screening companies urge nonprofits to have researchers further verify that there is, indeed, a valid match.

The types of matches we are describing here are individual-specific matches. You will see in a moment why this is an important distinction. Information matched to the individual is a person-to-person match. It is job, professional or nonprofit leadership, real estate, stock holdings, or other information that is linked to a real person with a name and address. The screening company is telling you that they believe that the real person they are naming is the same real person found among your constituents. The screening company expects that the Jane Smith in Richville who is the president of Richville Industries is the same person as the Jane Smith in Richville who is one of the constituents in your database. It will be a happy day for both you and the screening company if this is fresh news for you. The screening firm will have done the job they promised to do (times hundreds or thousands of names), and your nonprofit will have a new prospective donor to research and cultivate.

Matching Your Constituents with a Model (or Predictive Modeling)

There is a lot of data about what a wealthy person looks and acts like. There is information about where wealthy people live, what types of cars they drive, and how old they are. Magazines tout who their typical subscriber is to those interested in advertising in an issue. The answer might be something like this: The typical subscriber to *I Love Adventure* magazine is a married, upper middle-class male, age 32-48, with a sport utility vehicle, two computers, a DVD player, skis, a mountain bike, and two children. He takes two vacations a year and travels for business. He plans to buy a new home in the next three years. Check the section of your favorite magazine's next issue or its Web site to see these types of profiles. Do you remember the last product survey card you filled out when you bought a stereo or a leaf blower? The card asked you what magazines you read, how many people live in your house, their ages, the total household income, and other details about your lifestyle. Those surveys and other information-gathering efforts create profiles. We will call this type of information *direct marketing data.* Direct marking data tell us something about behavior, another word for lifestyle.

The U.S. Census collects information, too. There are many uses for census information, and one of those uses is to create neighborhood and household profiles. Visit the U.S. Census Web site at **http://www.census.gov/population/www/** to review the profiles the government creates from their 10-year data. The census statistics create a profile of a neighborhood or an entire town. It generates details about the size of the homes, the number of people living in the homes, the income of a neighborhood, and other details. Marketers use census information to identify consumer groups for their products.

Electronic screening companies take the type of information we are describing here, the direct marketing information and the census data, and they apply it to the constituents in your database. You might say that the screening firm creates profiles of groups of people by demographics and by behavior and then matches your constituents with these profiles. For example, your constituents living in a particular neighborhood in Chicago might be described as:

Urban, ages 40 to 65, married with children, affluent with a household income in the $100,000 to $300,000 range.

The screeners will even name these groups. This one might be called, for example, the AU40s (Affluent Urbans over 40). They will apply a name, a score, or other code to each one of your constituents that matches one of these groups. The range of descriptors will cover nearly all the possibilities that your donors will present. These matches are matches at the household level, rather than at the individual level that we described earlier. Your constituent is *assumed to be* similar to the people in his neighborhood. If most of his neighbors are wealthy, there is a good chance that your constituent is wealthy, too.

Understanding your prospect's demographic characteristics is a big step toward understanding his wealth profile. However, you would like to know more. You would like to know if he gives away any of his wealth. We have just moved from a demographic profile of your prospect to a profile that folds in lifestyle or behavior. In that short step we entered the world of predictive modeling. Screening services involved in predictive modeling use complex formulas applying a wealth of information from several sectors. Some of the information is provided by you. Some of it comes from census data. Some of it is from direct marketing databases. The screening company crunches all of that data from the various sources, including your data, through its formulas. At the other end, a shiny drop of distilled extrapolation comes out. That drop—a drop for each of your prospects screened—will be a prediction of how likely that prospect is to make a gift of a particular size.

You can see that there is a significant difference between the product you will receive from a company that matches your constituents with public information and the product you receive from a predictive modeling firm. The matching process yields specific, verifiable research data about the gift capacity of a small percentage of your database, usually 1 to 5 percent. The predictive modeling process gives you a "score" or a prediction about the gift probability of virtually every person who is screened. Of course most of those people will be returned with a low probability of being a major gift donor. Some—perhaps as many as 10 percent—will return with scores that draw the attention of the research or fund-raising team.

Are the predictions accurate? The screening firm hopes that the model and descriptors or "scores" they have created will be right, of course. Their business depends on it. But every researcher who has been through an electronic screening can tell stories about the one that slipped out of or into the trawling net. They can tell you about the major donor who lives in a rural area who escaped accurate coding in this type of model. They will talk about the teacher living in an apartment on the edge of the wealthy neighborhood. She is not wealthy, but she generated a wealth code based on her address. Does this mean the screening firm failed? No. There will be a few that get away and a few caught that should not be. Those errors will be a minor issue when you see the names of potential donors who you did not know, the ones who were caught in the screener's net. Depending on the effectiveness of the model the screening company uses and the integrity of your database, the screening company will attach a major gift score to a number of constituents who you had not noticed before the screening.

Database Integrity

The results of the screening will be a beneficiary or a victim of years and years of database integrity established (or not) by your nonprofit. By database integrity, we mean the veracity of the names and addresses and other details about your constituents contained in the database. Were the names entered carefully, with attention to details like spelling, middle name or initial, and other name features? Were addresses entered accurately, with the correct directionals and other details? Have addresses and telephone numbers been kept current? When mailings come back "return to sender," are the new addresses for those supporters pursued while the trail is still fresh? Do many of your constituent records contain "lost" addresses, former addresses at which your constituents no longer live? Does your nonprofit have an established plan for maintaining deliverable addresses and solicitable names and telephone numbers? The answers to these questions may tell you that there is database housecleaning work to do before you enter a screening process. Many screening firms offer database cleanup services for an additional fee. Other firms specialize in this kind of housecleaning.

Analyzing the Information You Shared

Some screening companies use the model they create to review giving patterns in your database. With this type of application, they can offer even more services to nonprofits. They may use their models to add a ranking to your constituents, creating a hierarchy of prospective major gift donors. By applying their model to your donors, patterns you were unable to detect may emerge. The screening company may, in a broad way, compare your database to the databases of similar institutions. That comparison may help you evaluate the depth of your donor pool.

The screening firm has, without a doubt, fine-tuned its model as it trekked through hundreds of thousands of records from the many nonprofits that have used its services. The firm can provide feasibility analyses to help the nonprofit's leadership resolve many issues before a major fund-raising effort even begins. The screener can, for example, help the leadership decide what is a reasonable dollar goal for a campaign.

As you can see, there are important decisions to make. Your leadership will have to choose the right screening firm by considering the type of results that will be returned. Individual-specific matches, household- or neighborhood-level groupings, or a combination of services that includes these types of matches and predictive modeling will be one of the early decisions. The type of rankings based on your donor giving data that a screening firm might generate will be another option to evaluate. These decisions will separate the screening firms from one another to some degree. Those that do not offer the type of screening that your team wants will drop from contention. Now, there are other decisions to make.

Choosing a Date for the Prom

You have now passed the crash course in electronic screening services. Are you ready to sign a contract with a screening firm? No, not yet. Let's outline what you must do before you sign on the dotted line and wind up with a pile of results and no place to put them.

What Do You Want?

We have dramatically simplified screening services here. This pared-down description does not address the additional services firms offer, such as ongoing prospect updates, access to Internet databases, annual fund and planned giving help, and more. You, the researcher, may be designated to ferret out which of these resources will benefit your nonprofit. The electronic screening firms will be happy to share information about their products and services with you.

When you think about what we have outlined, you can see that you have big decisions to make. Precisely what do you want? Do you want to know which of your constituents is an insider or public company officer? Do you want to compare your constituents to the model of wealthy people or wealthy behavior that a screening service has created based on algorithms of several commercial and governmental databases? Do you want someone to help you analyze the giving patterns among your constituents? Answering these questions will begin to pare down the list of screening services you will consider.

How Much Can You Spend to Get What You Want?

Here we are again, back at using that first dollar raised to effectively raise the next dollar. What you want will be modified by what it costs. Many screening services have a base price and then a per-record price that is added to the base price. To contain costs, nonprofits can segment their databases and drop the "least affiliated" from the process before it begins. Some screening firms have additional fees for auxiliary services. You will be able to evaluate the costs when you contact the firms.

How Effectively Can Your Data Be Screened?

We described how researchers conduct their own small screenings of constituents by searching the database for specific information. A researcher's ability to screen a database is only as successful as the integrity of the information in the nonprofit's database. You will find this to be true for the most complex screenings available, too. Many nonprofits consider this well in advance of contracting with an electronic screening service. Database housecleaning before the screening occurs can be a valuable first step. Some nonprofits hire companies who can add current address and telephone numbers to lost constituent records. Better addresses will improve the characteristics that will be used by the screening services to identify (and match) constituents. The more identifying characteristics your nonprofit can share, the more likely those matches will actually be valid. Constituents with no identifying characteristics other than name are unlikely to be matched to anything. They certainly cannot be matched to neighborhood data since they have no address. Remember that adding database housecleaning to the chores will increase the costs of this project.

Where Exactly Will the Results Go?

This is not a rhetorical question; it is a question of location. Each service will have a unique process for adding, or *appending*, their results to your database. You must be sure, before you select a firm, that your database is compatible with the screening firm's plan to append the results. Will it work? There are researchers who will tell you tales of data that did not append. They can tell stories about post-screening appending projects that turned into time-consuming tailoring jobs to notch out electronic spots for screening results. They can also tell you about team members who resisted adding the information to the database, fearing that it would compromise the integrity of the information that was already there. Some screening services do not add anything to your database, but instead provide you with a supplementary database containing their results. Those results can be manipulated within that database.

We will not tell you which of the many options available is the best solution for your nonprofit. That answer will lie in an analysis of the appending possibilities your database accommodates. It lies in examining the format the results will take and your team's level of comfort in that format. Screening firms can provide you with detailed information about this element of your decision. You will be able to see samples of screening results. You will be wise to talk to others who have used the screening services you are considering. You will be able to ask them how the results phase of the screening process worked at their institutions.

Will You Want to Do It Again?

The segmentation and ranking processes used by electronic screening firms are *proprietary*. They are designed by each screening company and are owned by them. They cannot be duplicated by another screening company with exactly the same information set or model. It is important to keep this in mind when you choose a database screening service. With good planning, you will be able to make a few predictions yourself. Would you like to repeat the same screening in a couple of years? Remember that you will have many new constituents then and some of your existing constituents will have major life changes in that time. Will you be more interested in investigating a distinctly different screening service then, one that might match with constituents not elevated by the screening service you are considering now? This type of long-range planning can only benefit your nonprofit.

After the Dance (or the Screening) is Over

You may be disappointed to hear that, after the screening is over, your work has just begun. If you want the screening to be successful, you must consider this element as you are selecting a screening service.

What are you going to do with the results once you have them? Do you imagine that you will thumb through pages of results, picking out the prospects who you do not know? Are you going to send development officers out to meet the top names that emerge from the screening? "Yes, of course" is the wrong answer. An electronic screening is a *preliminary* indicator that a constituent *might be* a prospect. Think of the most likely major gift donors named by the screening firm as *suspects*. Now the work begins.

The most successful post-screening stories involve a detailed plan for what will happen with the results. The four key elements of the plan are:

- Training
- Researching
- Visiting
- Measuring

Training

How well your staff is trained to interpret the results will become linked to your impression of the screening company your team chose. All reputable companies have a training element. Most come to your location to review the results with the fund-raising leadership. They may then hold a session for a portion of the team where they share the results and show team members where to find the information in the database and how to interpret the screening company's coding or scores. In addition to the presentation, there are usually handouts. These are important since your team will refer to the results for months—sometimes years—to come. New employees who were not with your nonprofit when the screening took place will learn about it when they arrive. Keeping these materials accessible is vitally important. Some screeners link customers with others who have used their services so that they can hear about the successful way the results were handled at another institution.

After the screening company leaves, training of your own design will begin. The members of the fund-raising team who will be—or should be—using the data will be involved. Who are they? Depending on which screening service you chose, the post-screening team may include representatives from research, the annual fund, planned giving, major gifts, and database management. The new ways that constituents have been grouped and segmented by the screening will interest each one of these divisions. Each division can outline goals for using the data. It is likely that the screening company began that process, but this is an opportunity for the fund-raising team at your nonprofit to tailor the goals to the way your team functions. The plan each division forms can be sensitive to time and money resources while it addresses the original goal— to identify the potential for new gifts in each fund-raising division.

But have we not been concentrating on major gift prospects? Did the results not just produce major gift prospects? Yes, but it is likely that the screening results grouped your nonprofit's constituents in several levels of potential and at many life stages. For example, the annual fund can corral the group just beneath the top group. This "second tier" of constituents will be good tests for appeals at the highest annual fund Ask. Constituents who respond favorably may even be candidates for further research. The appeals may be tailored to the descriptors the screening brought to this group (or groups). For example, a mailing to that urban Chicago group of middle-aged parents might look different than one to a group of older constituents who live in a rural setting.

The demographic information that forms the core of many screening models will form a windfall for the planned giving team. Once unnoticed, constituents who are now congregating in groups by age, projected income level, and other wealth indicators can receive planned giving mailings or information about bequests and trusts.

The plan each division of your team develops to apply the electronic screening results to their next fund-raising efforts will be the first test of the success of the screening process.

Researching

As each division is making plans to use the screening results, notice that the plans we outlined as examples are all about mailings to groups of constituents. We did not suggest a plan that involved contacting the individuals who fell into the top groups. By now you have a good idea about what you are not going to get with an electronic screening. You are not going to get a set of new, ready-to-solicit prospects. You will not get a set of already-researched prospects. You are likely to get an intriguing and exciting set of something. That something will be the names of constituents who your fund-raising team does not know well. And research will be the first place to go to learn more about those constituents.

Earlier in this chapter we mentioned that the screening companies would urge your fund-raising team to turn the results over to prospect research. The screening firms have indicated matches between their resources and the constituents in your database. But are the matches good ones? Will they stick? Are the individuals the screening firm thinks match your constituents *really* matches? Prospect research will be able to determine if the matches are accurate. By picking a few reliable resources to check, a researcher will be able to further link the constituent in the database with the screening firm's information.

The same routes to information that we have discussed throughout this book will serve the researcher well post-screening. Donor and constituent files may contain a clue to the links to public or private companies that have now percolated up through the screening process. Researchers are a cautious lot, so it is likely that the hundreds or even thousands of constituent names now in focus will be further reduced by a researcher's review. Some of the constituents in the screening's top group may drop from the focus list because no information verifying the standing emerges. Information demonstrating that the screening rank is erroneous may push a name down into the depths of the database again. Most important, the constituents for whom verifying information is found will become the very first prospects to visit.

Visiting

There are two reasons why we list visiting prospects as the next stage of the post-screening plan. First of all, the screening results will not mean much if the new prospects identified by the electronic screening, and then verified by research, are not visited and cultivated. The value of the screening process comes in actually getting these new prospects into the donor stream.

Second, there will be "field research" to do. There will be some qualifying of constituents that only the development officers can do. Research may find enough pieces of information to cause the team to lean toward assigning the constituent as a major gift prospect. But the information may not be conclusive. The vast group of constituents who are not public company officers, who do not own private companies, who do not hold real estate in their own names may elude many of the screening slots. But the demographic profile or predictive model created for these constituents may draw them to the top of the results. There will be little for a researcher to find. After all, a researcher is using many of the same resources that the electronic screening service is using. These are just the constituents for development officers to add to their visit lists. These are the constituents who become prospects only through a well-oiled research-development partnership.

Measuring

How will you know if the electronic screening is a success? Will the number of constituents who the screening firm names as top prospects tell you that the screening money was well spent? By now you know how we will answer this. The success of the screening will depend on your development team as much as it depends on the screening service's good work.

Did the screening accomplish what you set out to do? Did you find enough new donors to launch a campaign, begin a major gift program, or fund a new initiative? Were you able to elevate to major gift status a significant number of constituents who you did not realize were wealthy? Did the screening results help the research section add valuable information to the files of known prospects? Was research able to further qualify an acceptable percentage of those who the screening company named as top prospects?

It will be worthwhile to create a report that summarizes the results of the screening. That document should contain the results of the research that was completed from screening data, including the number of prospects assigned from that research. While it will not be a measure of the screening itself, it would be interesting to track how many of those assigned prospects become major gift prospects.

The screening is not just about numbers. There are other things that your nonprofit can accomplish through an electronic screening. Did you learn something new about your database of constituents? Do you have a greater understanding of the depth and breadth of those constituents as a group?

The other divisions of the fund-raising team will have screening results to report. The annual fund and the planned giving divisions can report whether the screening helped them meet their goals or to develop new plans for the next few years. Did the annual fund receive new or larger gifts from constituents who rose to the top of the field through the screening process?

Measuring the results and creating a report about those results will be invaluable the next time your nonprofit considers hiring a screening company. The next decision-makers—and that might include you—will have the story of this screening, its steps and missteps, and the outcomes. That information may ensure the success of the next electronic screening.

You will find a starting point for contacting screening firms in the appendix of this book.

8

Prospect Tracking

"Why not give some of it back to the community? To me, it's so basic. If life's good, then you share the wealth. It's kind of a no-brainer."
— Pearl Jam bass player Jeff Ament, on the band's philanthropy. They raised $500,000 for 10 charities in two concerts, adding that to the $1 million the band has already given away to local charities, *Seattle Post-Intelligencer,* July 21, 1998, p. A1.

Whenever the number of development officers exceeds one, there is a potential that the right hand will not know what the left hand is doing. Which development officer is working with which prospect? When can we expect to receive their donations? For each development officer and funding priority you add, the potential for confusion multiplies. A good prospect tracking system can help clear away the confusion and open lines of communication among the development staff. In some offices, the preferred terminology is "prospect management" or "relationship management." In many places, however, these terms are used interchangeably.

With prospects to manage, a nonprofit needs a manager. A job title like "director of prospect research and prospect management" is not unusual to see. These duties may belong to you since, even when it is not implied in a researcher's job title, prospect tracking sometimes falls in the domain of the prospect research office. Regardless of the tracking duties you have or do not have, you are, like all researchers, trying to promote prospects and see the ones you have identified reach the end of the cultivation cycle. In this chapter we will help you understand prospect tracking and management.

What is Prospect Tracking?

Prospect tracking is the process of planning, recording, and reporting significant moments in the relationship between the prospect and your organization. Not every organization explicitly includes the planning aspect in their prospect tracking system. Even without this feature, most tracking systems are up-to-the-minute historical records of the institution's relationship with the donor. Systems that employ the planning feature have both a historical and a future orientation and fit more properly in the category of "management" systems. Both systems require a high level of commitment from fund raisers and the organization's management in order to work. But we will get to that in a moment.

The Goals of Prospect Tracking

There are four goals of prospect management or prospect tracking:
- Coordination of the development effort
- Management of prospects through the development cycle
- Accountability for development officers
- Creation of a historical record of donor relationships

We will examine each of these goals in detail in this chapter.

Coordination

A development officer for the engineering school of a major university had been carefully cultivating a major gift prospect over an extended period. At what seemed like the right moment, the fund raiser arranged a meeting with the prospect and laid a proposal on the table for a six-figure gift. The prospect shifted uncomfortably, and then asked, "Didn't you know that the music department already asked me for a gift of a similar size?" The development officer was stunned. Because he was clueless about the activities of his colleague in music, both he and the prospect suffered a moment of embarrassment. Fortunately, that was the only lasting damage done in this true story. The consequences of this kind of miscommunication, however, could be far more serious. They could include offending the prospect ("what are you trying to do, milk me dry?"); undermining the nonprofit's credibility with the prospect ("don't you people know what each other is up to?"); or losing the relationship with the donor altogether ("I'd prefer to deal with an organization that has its act together").

In smaller organizations with just a few fund raisers (or only one), this kind of problem may be rare. In institutional environments with many development staff members, it will happen eventually unless there is a system in place that promotes communication about donors and prospects and coordinates cultivation and solicitation activities.

A prospect tracking system assigns one prospect to one manager. The prospect manager is responsible for the overall relationship between the prospect and the organization, including solicitations. Each manager can work with many prospects, of course. But when you look at the organization from the prospect's point of view, there is one primary point of contact to the development office, and that is the prospect's manager (see Figure 8-1).

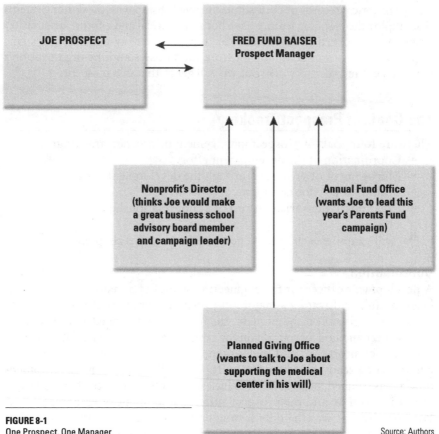

FIGURE 8-1
One Prospect, One Manager   Source: Authors

That basic understanding of "one prospect relates to one manager" can be taken in different directions, depending on the policy and procedures adopted by the organization. And believe us, this is one area where you will want to write down your policy and procedures to keep everyone on the same page. Even if your nonprofit is small, with only a handful of staff members, written policies about prospect assignments and management will help everyone stay on track.

There are several ways to approach prospect management. One approach gives the prospect manager sole authority to solicit a prospect. Other development staff members are barred from approaching the prospect for fund-raising purposes or including her in their fund-raising plans. This policy has the advantage of simplicity. It is easy to tell who is working with whom. It has a number of disadvantages, however. First, it has little to do with the real world. In the real world, development officers (sweet and generous people though they are) live in a competitive environment. They have goals to meet and a limited universe of prospects with the gift capacity to help them meet those goals. Each development officer is naturally inclined to view her own proposal as worthier of the donor's attention, and more likely to succeed than others. Under this kind of system, competitive pressures can cause a development officer to attempt to collect a stable of prospects who can only be solicited by her. The result can be a group of high-capacity prospects whose potential is not being fully realized because the manager has collected more assignments than she can realistically handle. This problem can be mitigated if there is a strong administrator or committee that approves and balances assignments.

It is also unrealistic to expect the prospect to relate only to one staff member, especially if the organization is large and multi-faceted. A prospect may well have interests that reach beyond a single unit or program. Consider Joe Prospect, one of Cedar University's prospects with the following connections:

- His bachelor's degree is from the business school.
- His law degree is from Cedar's law school.
- He works as an executive in a high-technology engineering company.
- Cedar's engineering school is engaged in research that has direct bearing on Joe's business.
- Joe's father received life-saving treatment in the university's medical center.
- His daughter is enrolled at Cedar now and is majoring in math.

Whose prospect is this? Because this individual has natural ties to several different departments, the development director in each area will legitimately feel that he should receive the assignment. How can we solve this problem? We can solve it with a well-documented prospect tracking system.

There is an alternative to giving one manager sole clearance to solicit a prospect. It takes into account situations like this one. In this version of prospect management, the manager is responsible for the overall relationship of the organization to the prospect, but the manager can delegate responsibility for a particular Ask to another development staff member. We could describe this as a "donor-centric" policy because it gives the donor the ability to let her own interests dictate how the organization responds.

The donor-centric system has two possible types of staff assignments for any single prospect: *manager* and *responsible staff*. The job description of the manager is much as we have already described it. The manager oversees every aspect of the prospect's relationship to the organization. The difference is that the manager does not necessarily have "dibs" on the prospect. The job description of the responsible staff is to handle all details associated with a particular solicitation. The responsible staff member is in charge of the cultivation activities, submission of proposals, and supervision of volunteers who interact with the prospect. The roles and responsibilities of the manager and the responsible staff are summarized in Exhibit 8-1.

Exhibit 8-1	Prospect Manager and Responsible Staff Duties

Prospect Manager:
- Is aware of all aspects of the prospect's relationship to the organization
- Has overall responsibility for all cultivation and solicitation activities with the prospect
- Files contact reports for all substantive contacts
- Updates the prospect tracking system when information about the prospect changes
- May delegate responsibility for a specific solicitation process to another person who acts as responsible staff

Responsible Staff:
- Has responsibility for closing a specific gift
- May also be the prospect manager
- Consults with the prospect manager about all activities with the prospect (if the prospect manager is someone else)
- Updates the prospect tracking system on behalf of the prospect manager when information about the prospect changes
- Files contact reports for all substantive contacts

Source: Authors

With most prospects, the same person acts as both manager and responsible staff. That is because most prospects do have one or two relatively clear interests in the organization. For example, a grateful patient may give to the department of the hospital where her surgery was performed. In this case, the development officer for that department is both manager (overseeing all aspects of the relationship between the prospect and the department) and the responsible staff (planning, cultivating, and closing the Ask for a major gift to the department).

When the prospect has multiple interests or very great capacity, two or more development officers may be involved with the prospect on more than one gift opportunity. Take our hypothetical case of Joe Prospect, Cedar University's mega-affiliate. Based on what we know about him, there are at least five different departments that would like to place a proposal before Joe. Interested departments might include the undergraduate department, the law school, the department whose activities closely match Joe's professional activities, the university's medical center, and the math department where his daughter is now involved.

The way your organization chooses who will serve as prospect manager will be determined by those written prospect tracking and management policies we mentioned. One way to get started on making the manager assignment decision is to look over the history of the prospect's relationship with the organization. That evaluation can lead your leadership to grant manager status to the development officer or department with the strongest ties. Notice that this policy favors those who file contact reports. To the meticulous go the riches. But any policy requires certain conditions. One of the important features of this approach would be the presence of a benevolent and unbiased arbitrator, someone who will be able to resolve conflicts among the interested divisions. The arbitrator is usually your organization's director, senior administrator, or in the more enlightened circles, the director of research who has prospect tracking and management among his duties.

How prospects are assigned is often in the domain of the organization's senior administrator or the head of development. An alternative is that assigning can be done by a non-partisan (which usually means multi-partisan) committee that will mete out assignments equitably. We talked about assigning prospects in chapter 6 when we began to build the prospect pool.

The prospect manager must take the big picture perspective in regard to the cultivation path for each prospect. He must be committed to the ideal that the greater good will be served when the donor gives at the top of his potential, even if it is not the cause closest to the prospect manager's heart (or assignments). If you, the researcher, are in charge of assigning prospects and monitoring gift potential across several interests, you will get to help everyone keep in touch with the big picture.

Management of Prospects

From the time a constituent becomes an assigned prospect until she gives a major gift and enters the stewardship phase, she is "in the prospect pipeline." Do not start imagining the Alaska tundra and miles of pipe. The prospect pipeline has four distinct stages and it is only about 24 months long (see Exhibit 8-2). On the inlet side of the pipeline is the Great Pool of Suspects, where research began. As a prospect moves through the pipeline, she passes through other stages. It ends with the prospect tumbling into stewardship after a major gift is given.

Prospect tracking is designed to make sure a prospect moves with all due speed through the pipeline, through a series of cultivation activities, to solicitation and finally, to giving the gift. This is, of course, a textbook version of a constituent's philanthropic course. In real life, prospects may enter the system at any point along the development cycle. Sometimes prospects go straight from identification to solicitation because their interest is so clear and strong. Sometimes they move forward then backward through the cultivation stages. If a solicitation is rejected, for instance, they could go back to the cultivation stage until the right project or right time is identified. No matter what the actual course, the pipeline gives us a tool to evaluate how close our prospect is to making a gift and for managers to manage the course of cultivation. Let's look at these stages in detail.

Exhibit 8-2	Pipeline Stages for Assigned Prospects

- Identification
- Cultivation
- Zero-to-six months from the Ask
- Solicitation
- Stewardship

Source: Authors

Identification

A constituent enters the pipeline at the identification stage, theoretically. We say "theoretically" because the constituent may spend almost no time at all here, or he may remain in this status for a matter of months. The constituent, now a prospect, may be identified by the research office, a development officer, or as a result of a screening process. By placing a prospect in the identification stage, we are saying that this individual looks like he has major gift potential. He has enough potential that we think he should be assigned to a prospect manager so that we can make sure he receives attention. The prospect stays in the identification stage until the manager makes contact and starts to create a solicitation strategy.

Although we hope that a prospect will move quickly from identification to cultivation, it is possible that he will exit the pipeline at that point. The manager might make contact and discover that the person who looked wealthy from a distance does not look quite so wealthy up close. Or the prospect may disqualify himself by saying that he is not interested in your organization. For one reason or another, some prospects will drop out early in the process. Some of the dropouts will be returned to the suspect pool. An individual who appears to have limited major gift capacity now may develop capacity later. Others who leave the pipeline at this point will be coded as "not a prospect" since they have indicated that one of the pieces of our triad—affiliation, capacity, and interest—is not present and will not be.

As we said, the initial identification stage should be completed in short order. It often takes just one telephone call or visit. But this stage sometimes is the toughest one to pass through. If a prospect languishes in the identification stage of the pipeline for more than six months or so, it may be time to call in a development plumber. Something is clogging the pipes. A prospect manager with too many prospects may not be able to handle another one right now. Or the blockage could indicate that the manager does not think the prospect is worth attention. This opinion might have the manager giving the prospect a low priority on the "to do" list. Whatever the reason, if a prospect remains in the identification stage for too long, it is time to revisit the assignment to see if it is still appropriate. A fresh look at this assignment will tell us if the problem is the prospect, the assignment load, the manager, or another factor. Whatever the answer, we will have the chance to shake loose the clog to open the pipeline again.

Cultivation

The next stage in the pipeline is cultivation. This stage can take up quite a bit of pipe. A prospect entering this stage has been contacted by a development officer or a volunteer. The development officer has qualified the individual as a major gift prospect. To say a prospect is "qualified" means that the development officer has confirmed that the prospect probably has the ability to give at the major gift level (capacity), feels connected to the nonprofit or could become connected (affiliates), and is or may be inclined to support this nonprofit (interest). These are the same qualifiers that you, the researcher, used to get the prospect assigned in the first place. This first contact now verifies your conclusions, for the most part. Contact and qualification are the two major requirements for moving into this stage in the pipeline.

Some prospects bypass the identification stage and start their journey through the pipeline at the cultivation stage. Usually this is because the development officer has already contacted the prospect—often accidentally—at a function of some kind, or via an introduction by a volunteer. Alternatively, the research office may have found enough information about the prospect to fully qualify the prospect. Once contact has been made, cultivation begins immediately.

The prospect will travel through the cultivation section of the pipeline for a period of time. When we talked about who is a prospect, we outlined a few guidelines. In addition to affiliation, capacity, and interest, we said that a constituent is someone who can give a major gift within 18–24 months. We are now in that two-year window of time. Prospects who are in the cultivation stage should move through this section of the tracking system within two years.

The cultivation stage is the time when the development office attempts to strengthen any natural ties that exist between the organization and the prospect, and to forge new ties where none existed before. Usually, this means increasing your prospect's involvement with and awareness of your organization by engaging her in meetings, activities, and committees, for example (see Exhibit 8-3).

Exhibit 8-3 **Examples of Cultivation Activities**

- Have lunch or coffee with the prospect
- Invite the prospect to visit the nonprofit
- Organize a meeting with the organization's leadership (president, director, or any leader who is closest to the prospect's area of interest)
- Invite the prospect to serve on a board or committee
- Invite the prospect to attend an event (reception, lecture, or production, for example)
- Invite the prospect to teach a class, address an audience, or otherwise share her knowledge
- Ask the prospect for advice
- Ask the prospect to serve as a volunteer

- Ask the prospect to ask others for gifts
- Send the prospect informational material and ask for feedback

Source: Authors

The suggestions in Exhibit 8-3 do not form an exhaustive list of cultivation activities. Planning and carrying out cultivation activities is in the development officer's area of expertise. However, as a researcher, you may be in a good position to suggest cultivation activities to the development officer. Some of the things you learned about the prospect during research may suggest opportunities to cultivate this prospect. Did you find out that this prospect just published a book? Perhaps she could give a lecture to your constituency on the subject of the book. Does that prospect have an art collection? He might be willing to host a gathering that shows off his collection. Has the prospect founded a successful company? He might be an excellent candidate for a slot on your board of directors.

Although most researchers do not design or carry out cultivation plans, they have important information to share. This is where the random pieces of information are transformed into knowledge and analysis. A researcher who practices this talent will stay engaged with the entire cultivation process all the way through the prospect pipeline. Your research will put the team leagues ahead in regard to insights about the prospect's interests. You may know that the prospect spends part of the year in another locale, for example. You may have discovered that the prospect is interested in Aztec ruins or ancient tapestries. Each piece of information can facilitate and enhance the cultivation process. There are two more reasons to keep yourself in the mix: Sharing your good ideas will contribute to a successful solicitation and will increase your visibility and importance on the development team.

The purpose of cultivation activities is not just to keep the development officer and the prospect busy. In fact, the cultivation activities are carefully planned by a skilled fund raiser and will have established purposes. Each activity should serve one or more of these purposes:

- Enhance the prospect's appreciation and understanding for your organization
- Strengthen the prospect's personal involvement with your organization and its leadership
- Determine the maximum gift (the right amount) that the prospect is likely to make to your organization
- Ascertain the right time and the right purpose for a gift and the right person to make the Ask
- Move the prospect one step closer to making a gift

Did you notice the word that led the last example of an activity? That word is "move." Remember our conversation about insider language? Fund raisers have insider terms, too, and one you may hear is "move." The cultivation strategies that a fund raiser puts in place, the planned activities for drawing a prospect nearer to the Ask, are often called moves. Like all insider language, it is shorthand, in this case for the concept in our last point, "to move the prospect one step closer to making a gift."

No major prospect should spend more than six months in this stage without some kind of cultivation activity taking place. This is where a good prospect management report can really help the development officer focus on the prospects who need attention. We will discuss reports later in this chapter.

Zero-to-Six Months

This stage ought to be called six-to-zero months instead of zero-to-six months. It is a countdown stage, measuring how close the prospect is to the Ask. The prospect is fully cultivated. She knows all that she needs to know about your organization. She has attended events, joined a committee, or offered to solicit other affiliates. There is nothing else (that is relevant to her gift) than can be learned by taking the prospect out to lunch one more time. As the prospect nears the end of the cultivation stage and makes the transition into the zero-to-six-months stage, the development office must determine the answers to the four and a half rights, first described in chapter 3.

- What is the right Ask amount?
- What is the right gift purpose?
- What is the right time to make the Ask?
- Who is the right person to make the Ask?
- What other details are relevant to the Ask?

The involvement of the research office may increase during the zero-to-six-months stage. This is a time to refine and refresh the prospect data. Earlier in the pipeline, it was enough to know the prospect had the capacity to make a large gift. As you prepare for the Ask, it is now time to pull out all the stops and learn all that you can, with as much accuracy as possible, to estimate what gift this prospect can make. We have already pointed out in chapter 5, Research Math, that the perfect Ask amount is not necessarily something that can be determined with scientific precision. Nevertheless, it is time to give it your best shot. At the same time, the prospect manager will be mustering all of his information resources so that collaboration between development and research results in the best possible Ask.

During the zero-to-six-months stage, the manager or responsible staff will be in relatively frequent contact with the prospect. It is the time when the responsible staff member will begin to prepare the prospect for the Ask. The prospect should not be caught completely off guard when a proposal is laid on the table. It is the prospect manager's job to make sure that the prospect is ready for the Ask when it comes. The research office can analyze the history of the organization's relationship with the prospect, pointing out potential solicitors and appropriate gift purposes, and suggesting possible solicitation strategies.

As implied in the name of the stage, the prospect should not remain in this section of the pipeline for more than six months.

Solicitation

We can almost see the light at the end of the pipeline now. The zero-to-six-months period ends when the solicitation is made and the prospect says "yea" or "nay." If it happens like that, there is little need for a solicitation stage. It all happens in one meeting, and, bang, you go straight from "zero-to-six-months" into "stewardship."

Sometimes it is not as neat as that, however. The answer may not be either "yea" or "nay." It is not uncommon for the prospect to say something like, "I want to make this gift, but I'm involved in something else right now (or I need my stock to appreciate, or my business is taking up too much of my time right now, or I just made a large gift to someone else and I'm not ready to give again yet), so I'd like to wait until such and such a time." When this happens, your prospect goes into a kind of limbo where the Ask has been made, the prospect is willing, but all the pieces have not yet fallen into place. Welcome to the solicitation stage.

If it were a perfect world, this would not happen. All of the prospect's issues and needs would have been identified in advance and factored into the solicitation strategy. However, we cannot anticipate all the factors weighing on the prospect's decision to make a gift, no matter how hard we try. Sometimes unanticipated issues arise for the fund raiser, the nonprofit, or the prospect. Therefore, our tracking system must be prepared to deal with unexpected contingencies.

Once the prospect is in the solicitation stage, there should be regular contact with the prospect, not to pester her, but to let her know that the development office is ready to go the final step whenever she is. The research office may have unique duties during this time as well. You may be asked to monitor the price of the stock that has to go up before philanthropy begins for this prospect. If she is waiting for the stock to go over a certain threshold, the researcher can ring the bell when that moment comes.

Pipeline Variations

Some prospect tracking systems include both the suspect and the stewardship stages in the mix. Sophisticated fund raisers see opportunities to nudge constituents through the suspect phase with special solicitations that ask them to stretch beyond their usual gift. Nudged or not, the act of stretching can signal that changes in capacity have occurred. The annual fund team may have volunteers in place to make these special Asks. An active approach like this to the suspect pool helps a researcher prioritize the next suspects to move toward assignment.

Prospect tracking systems that continue to track and plan activities with major prospects after the gift has been given offer fund raisers even more opportunities to cultivate donors. During the stewardship stage prospects are actually being prepared for their next gift.

Stewardship

Once the prospect says yes, she moves out of the pipeline into the Great Pool of Stewardship until a new project is identified that fits her interests and capacity. A stewardship stage ensures that this important relationship with your prospects, the one where they are honored and cherished, is not inadvertently overlooked. Good stewardship tells a donor that you love her (not just for her money, of course, but for her commitment to this nonprofit). And stewardship helps prepare a prospect for the next trip through the prospect pipeline.

Stewardship contacts need not be as frequent or regular as cultivation contacts, nor do they have the same goals. The purpose of stewardship is to thank the donor, to keep her affiliated with your nonprofit, and generally to continue a positive relationship. Whether or not a donor reenters the donor pipeline, every major gift donor deserves ongoing stewardship. These contacts should be annual at least.

To and Fro Momentum in the Pipeline

A prospect's optimum progress in the pipeline is forward, of course. But a prospect can move back a stage at almost any point. Some prospects skip a stage and leap forward. And some prospects drop out of the pipeline altogether. New information and new circumstances are the most common reasons for prospects to drop out of the pipeline. Prospects who drop out may be returned to the suspect pool for later consideration or they may return to their pre-suspect status as a constituent.

As we said, solicited prospects who give move into stewardship. At some point, a prospect in stewardship may return to the pipeline for another cultivation and solicitation. This prospect is unlikely to return to the earliest stages of the pipeline since he is already fully cultivated. But he can return to the zero-to-six months stage. We can imagine that a prospect might even return to suspect status when, many years after his last gift, a brand new research effort must be launched to requalify and reassign him to the prospect pipeline. Figure 8-2 illustrates the forward and backward movement through the pipeline.

Pipeline Planning

A great prospect tracking system does more than record the history of activities with the prospect. It will also anticipate activities in the future. A great deal of planning must happen in order to guide a prospect through the pipeline

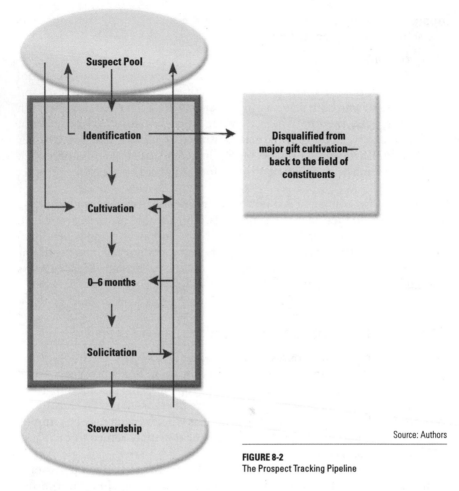

Source: Authors

FIGURE 8-2
The Prospect Tracking Pipeline

stages. The development officer will often coordinate the efforts of several people—volunteers and members of the fund-raising team—in order to give the prospect the best possible experience to move her toward making her gift. The prospect management system becomes the central reference point for all those involved in cultivation and solicitation activities.

The planning tool included in a prospect management system can be as simple as a list of anticipated events on the way to a gift. If the system can support it, that list can be made more useful by adding dates and the names of all staff and volunteers involved in each event. Ideally, the cultivation and solicitation plan will be linked to the calendars of all staff members involved. A sample cultivation planning tool is shown in Exhibit 8-4.

It is conceivable that a planning tool like the one in Exhibit 8-4 would be modified after every contact with the prospect. It is, after all, a worksheet. A

Exhibit 8-4	**Cultivation Strategy Worksheet**

Prospect Name: _____ Plan Date: _____

Manager: _____ Responsible Staff: _____

Volunteers: _____

Right Amount: _____

Right Purpose(s): _____

Right Solicitor(s): _____

Right Time: _____

Long Term Goals (Ultimate gift from the prospect): _____

Short Term Goals (Next Ask): _____

Moves:

Activity	Person	By When	Expected Result
1.			
2.			
3.			
4.			
5.			
6.			
7.			

Notes:

Source: Authors

development officer will create a series of plans for each prospect as he discovers new information and hones the cultivation and the solicitation plan.

Accountability

Not every gift arrives because of the efforts of a development officer. Some gifts are *unsolicited*. Some lucky organizations attract money the way a planet attracts meteors. They exert a gravitational pull on donors for various reasons. Educational institutions have alumni, some of whom decide to make a gift just because they want to share their success with their alma mater. Hospitals have grateful patients. Certain high profile organizations like the Boy Scouts or Habitat for Humanity have such a clear and compelling mission that some people are moved to give their support, even though they have not been asked. A donor may be related to a volunteer or an employee of the nonprofit and make a gift to honor that relationship. Whatever the source of these "pennies from heaven," they can contribute significantly to the bottom line of money raised.

Why should you care whether the gift was unsolicited or solicited? The fund raiser cares because careful tracking of cultivation and solicitation activities can help him learn which of these efforts are the most effective. It can also help demonstrate, in the unfortunate case where large gifts are not being made, that the development officer is actually doing a good job of working with prospects, but the fruits of his labor are still in the future. A fund-raising supervisor cares because information from a prospect management system can be valuable in evaluating the performance of individuals and the entire team. The donor cares because when a gift is properly cultivated, solicited, and stewarded, the relationship to the organization is strengthened and the donor is more likely to make repeat gifts. Directors and supporters of the organization care because development is an expensive process. They want to be assured that the people they employ to raise funds for their organization are using their time effectively.

Nuts and Bolts of Prospect Tracking Systems

Most prospect tracking systems use a database to record information and make reports. Accountability for one's prospect activities is demonstrated through those reports. These reports do more than just track accountability. They are a useful way for senior managers to measure the status of the development activities across the board. They help the individual development officer organize his work by showing which prospects are ready for a contact or a move to the next stage.

There are two basic options when it comes to tracking databases: homegrown or purchased from a vendor. The homegrown tracking system can be as simple as a spreadsheet or a relational database application like Microsoft Access or Corel's Paradox. It can be as complex as an integrated development database, which combines the data entry, storage, and reporting capabilities needed for gift processing, biographical records, contact reporting, and prospect tracking. Keep this in mind: The simplest tracking database is still a complex piece of programming. Do not expect to be able to throw together a great tracking database after a couple of software classes. The cost of a homegrown system comes in the time and expertise required to create it as well as the cost of the database-building application used and the time and expense spent training staff in its use.

A vendor-supplied database has a higher up-front cost but comes with the benefit of the vendor's experience with many clients. Each vendor system is a little or a lot different from the others. But most of them have the necessary fields and tables for recording prospect management data. The problem sometimes lies in getting the information back out again in the form of useful reports.

Straight Talk About Reports

Any prospect tracking system lives or dies by its reports. It is well and good for a development officer to carefully record a prospect's movement through the pipeline. Unless the data can be shared and analyzed, however, it is just a lot of record keeping with no useful product. Even in the smallest organizations, a development officer doe not work in total isolation. There are other administrators she works with and board members to whom she is responsible. In larger operations with many fund raisers and layers of administration, the importance of clear communication about prospects is multiplied many times. Good reports help facilitate that communication.

When you purchase a database from a vendor, it is likely that it comes with some "canned" reports. Those reports, the ones designed by the vendor trying to anticipate what clients will need, should be reviewed carefully. It is likely that those reports will not meet all of your needs. Do not be upset about this. It is not surprising. No vendor can anticipate the reporting requirements of all of its customers. In a sense, the database comes to you unfinished. It is up to the customer to define the reports needed. Anyone planning to purchase an integrated development database should include budget dollars for designing and programming custom reports.

The simplest report, and usually the first one requested by a fund raiser, is a list of the prospects assigned to her. Because that list does not remain the same forever, it must be updated regularly. By adding a little bit of information (like pipeline stage and date of most recent contact, for instance), that report becomes even more useful.

Sample Reports

We have provided examples of three of the most useful reports that we have encountered. They are the stage aging report, the counts and moves report, and the contact activity report.

Stage Aging Report

The purpose of the stage aging report is to show development officers and their managers how long a prospect has been in a particular stage of the pipeline (see Exhibit 8-5). A separate report is created for each development officer, and it includes all the prospects for which the officer is prospect manager or responsible for staff. Notice that the gift rating is coded to make reporting easier. It presents a snapshot in time, accurate as of the moment the report was generated.

Exhibit 8-5	Stage Aging Report for Prospect Manager Marie Curie

Report date: 3/1/02

Name	Days In Stage	Prospect Manager	Responsible Staff	Last Contact	Contact Type	Next Action	Gift Rating
Stage: *Identification*							
Elton John	54	Marie C.	Marie C.	4/21/02	Phone	7/25/02	B
Jimmy Buffet	12	Albert E.	Marie C.	6/19/02	Visit	8/1/02	C
Stage: *Cultivation*							
Neil Diamond	157	Marie C.	George H.	11/22/01	Visit	8/1/02	A
Yoko Ono	93	Marie C.	Albert E.	1/15/02	Visit	7/15/02	D
Stage: *0–6 Months*							
Amy Grant	45	Marie C.	Marie C.	5/17/02	Email	7/15/02	A
Carlos Santana	95	Marie C.	Marie C.	3/7/02	Phone	9/4/02	B
Stage: *Solicitation*							
Jennifer Lopez	15	Marie C.	Marie C.	6/16/02	Visit	9/15/02	E
Johnny Cash	38	Marie C.	Marie C.	6/1/02	Phone	8/1/02	B

The Gift Rating indicates a code that this nonprofit established for expressed gift capacity ratings. In this example, the codes are A = $1+ million; B = $500,000–$999,999; C = $100,000–$499,000; D = $50,000–$99,000; E = $10,000–$49,000.

Source: Authors

Counts and Moves Report

The counts and moves report displays information about a specific period of time. It is a spreadsheet with two axes showing pipeline status and anticipated gift level (see Exhibit 8-6). Each cell reports the number of prospects in that cell (for example, the number of people who are at the solicitation stage and who are prospects for a gift in the $1 million+ range), and how many moved into that cell in the previous month. Variations on this theme are counts and moves for prospects assigned to specific officers (shown) or counts and moves for all development officers. You could also show the names of prospects in each cell when the report is just for one development officer.

Exhibit 8-6   Counts and Moves Report for the Prior Month

Manager: Marie Curie

	Identification (added)	Cultivation (moved)	0-6 Months (moved)	Solicitation (moved)	Stewardship (moved)
$1 million +	8	3	24	5	17
	(1)	(0)	(0)	(0)	(2)
$500K–999K	4	0	24	9	5
	(0)	(0)	(2)	(3)	(1)
$100K–499K	19	5	46	8	23
	(2)	(0)	(1)	(0)	(3)
$50K–99K	2	1	10	2	15
	(0)	(1)	(0)	(0)	(0)
$10K–49K	7	24	4	1	35
	(1)	(4)	(0)	(1)	(2)

Source: Authors

Contact Activity Report

The Contact Activity Report summarizes activity with prospects within a certain time frame (see Exhibit 8-7). Notice that not everyone has the same goal for contacts. Some fund raisers work part time, others have additional duties that reduce the time available for contacting prospects. Nevertheless, this report clearly outlines expectations and progress.

Exhibit 8-7   Contact Activity Report for Fiscal Year 2002

Period: Fiscal Year 2002

Report Date: 3/1/02

	Prior Month		Year to Prior Month	
Staff Person	Contacts	Goal	Contacts	Goal
Marie C.	32	30	49	60
Albert E.	15	20	37	40
George H.	7	30	38	60

Source: Authors

These three reports are a good foundation for communicating prospect information. There are many other ways the prospect tracking data can be cross-tabulated, of course. Your own unique situation will dictate the kinds of reports you create. They should always serve one or both of these purposes: demonstrating accountability and showing progress. Reports help to assure the managers of the development operation that staff members are doing their jobs. They help the staff members focus their energy where it will raise the most money.

To be effective, the reports have to be used. To be used, they have to be easily obtained. They should be provided one of two ways: on a recurring basis so that members of the development staff know when to expect them, or the staff should be able to generate the reports on their own schedule, whenever they want an update. The content of the report and the capabilities of your system will determine which of these two methods is used. The stage aging report, for instance, could be generated on the fly, since it is a snapshot of the situation at a particular point in time. The counts and moves report, on the other hand, would be generated once a month because it summarizes information that relates to the prior month. Under no circumstances should it be difficult or complicated to obtain reports. The fewer barriers there are between the development staff and the tracking reports, the more likely it is that they will be used, and by extension, the entire system will be successful.

Creation of an Historical Record

The last goal we listed for the prospect management system is to record history. The pipeline stages and reports we have been describing do just that. Fund raisers who participate in the prospect management system become major gift historians. The fund-raising team is holding each donor's philanthropic history in its central file records. Many of the details of that cherished history of giving are found in the prospect tracking system. The events attended, the gift negotiations, the proposals rejected and accepted, and more, are all recorded in the prospect's tracking record. Having a tracking system puts the entire team in the role of maintaining and recording the events surrounding the cultivation of each prospect. No slips of paper stuffed in drawers for this blue ribbon team—they have a prospect management system to keep them on track.

The Point Is

Every development office engages in prospect management. It might not be called that. It might not be systematic. Maybe it resides on somebody's calendar. But one way or another, every development officer has to have some way of keeping track of his assignments. Every senior administrator needs to know that the staff is paying attention to the organization's prospects appropriately. Every organization needs to be able to forecast gift expectations. By systematizing the management of prospects, the organization benefits from a development program that is more coordinated, focused, efficient, and accountable. With that profile, this fund-raising team will raise more money. Let's remember: That is the ultimate goal, raising more dollars to support the organization's mission.

Walking the Talk (or How to Be a Prospect Researcher)

"Your desk is not your bed. And your khakis are not your pajamas."
—Consulting company OnVia, in an ad campaign directed at entrepreneurs,
Silicon goldberg, January 20, 2000, p. 1.

You have arrived at this point outfitted with many of the tools you need to be a researcher. You know how to build a prospect pool, how to identify the rich folks in it, and how to evaluate the sources of their wealth once you find them. You even know how to estimate the size of the gift they could give to your nonprofit and how to keep track of their involvement with your team. Now what? What precisely are you going to do with it all? Let's spend this chapter discovering how you, now equipped, will pilot the research program at your organization.

The Way You Do the Thing You Do

Strap on your seat belt because we are going to tour prospect research offices today. We will visit three offices: one at a large university, one at a museum in a major city, and one at a young environmental organization. We will navigate. You take the flight recorder's seat—your job is to map the significant differences in the research positions we are going to see.

Tray Tables Up: We are Off to the Big Show

Frannie is one of six researchers at State University in the Northeast. She has been a researcher for five years. Frannie's division is called Advancement Services. Her supervisor, the director of the department, reports to the vice president of University Relations. On an organizational chart, Frannie's boss is a peer of the director of development who supervises 40 fund raisers. In addition to overseeing Frannie and her five research colleagues, the director supervises five gift processors, four data entry people, three file clerks, and one prospect tracking manager. The University has 300,000 constituent records: alumni, parents, and friends who have an affiliation with the University are housed in that database. The researchers and the paper prospect files—called central files—are located in the same office space.

State University is a large, comprehensive school with academic colleges, four graduate programs, and a law school. The law school has its own development and research team. The university is located four miles to the northwest of the complex where Frannie's office is. The research team and the data entry staff are housed in a corporate office park. No other university offices are located here, but seven other divisions are housed at off-campus locations. The University's growth throughout the last two decades left the school short on space. In fact, the research team is in the "pre-campaign" phase of a $450 million eight-year initiative with goals that include adding scholarships, faculty, and the construction of two buildings. The campaign will be publicly launched in two years. In the pre-campaign phase, the mandate is to flush out possibilities for support that will help the university meet its campaign goals. Frannie's boss had an electronic screening of a portion of the database completed about a year ago. Since then, Frannie and the other researchers have added sifting through the screening results to their duties.

The responsibilities of the six researchers are divided by type of prospect and by region. Frannie researches individual prospects in the Western region, which includes the university's prospects living in California, Nevada, Utah, Oregon, Washington, Montana, and Idaho. One researcher is exclusively responsible for researching institutional prospects. Each researcher is expected to develop an "expertise" about a particular aspect of wealth. Frannie's area of expertise is private company analysis. When the other researchers are researching prospects who have bought or sold privately-held companies, or when they need to estimate the financial benefit of leading or sharing ownership in private companies, they ask Frannie to help.

The researchers also divide their reading responsibilities. Frannie reads, in addition to the leading newspapers and business journals in the region she covers, *Forbes* and *The Chronicle of Philanthropy.* She routes important articles to interested researchers and files others.

It would be difficult to think of a resource to which Frannie does not have access. Most of the resources she uses are electronic, facilitating quick data sorting and searching. The tools she has for research are important because Frannie's mission would be daunting without them. Frannie's pre-campaign chore is to qualify the people from her assigned region whose names rose to the top of the electronic screening. There are 2,300 names in that group. She has rolling deadlines for this project. In addition to that ongoing task, Frannie must meet the research needs of the fund raisers assigned to her region. There are eight fund raisers who ask Frannie for:

1. New prospects
2. Additional information and analysis about known prospects
3. Recommendations for Ask amounts

The fund raisers each carry an assignment load of 120 to 160 prospects. At any time, each fund raiser has about 40 prospects in active cultivation. The fund raisers are not located in Frannie's office complex. In fact, Frannie has never met three of the eight fund raisers with whom she partners. Two are "in location" staff members: they live in the regions they cover. All of the fund raisers communicate with Frannie primarily by email. They post their contact reports to her by email, and she sends them the research reports they request the same way.

Because prospects are moving through the pipeline, the fund raisers need a steady supply of new prospects. That is another part of Frannie's job. With the campaign approaching, Frannie's research of the top names from the electronic screening fills this need. Usually, Frannie is required to identify six new prospects each month. With the screening project and its quotas, Frannie is surpassing this expectation.

Frannie attends one meeting each month, a general staff meeting within her department. In that meeting, workloads and special needs are reviewed and updates about research process, tools, and training options are covered. New initiatives, bottlenecks, and the progress of the current initiatives are discussed. Frannie has heard about researchers who meet with their development team on a regular basis; she cannot imagine what that would be like. She is used to sending new prospect names out into the hinterlands and calling that the end of the process. She is unlikely to hear about the progress of cultivation, unless the prospect gives a large gift for which a press release is written. Frannie does not mind this: The end of research is the identification and qualification of prospects. It is not the same as the end of the process for development officers, cultivation reaching a successful conclusion. Frannie believes that researchers do not have much influence over the initiation, progression, or outcome of cultivation.

Layover: Paintings, Pots, and Prospects

Now we wing our way to the Midwest to meet Kayla. She is the sole researcher at a 125-year old art museum located in a Great Lakes city with a long tradition of supporting the arts. The museum has been formally raising money to support exhibits and expansion for 20 years, but it has employed a researcher for only 12 years. Kayla has held the position for eight years. Her title is director of the research department, but she is actually the entire research department. There is a gift processor, a data entry staff person, and a file clerk in the office across the hall, in the ground level offices of the museum. Kayla is their manager. The six fund raisers who Kayla supports are located down the hall. The director of gifts and stewardship oversees the fund raisers, and the museum's director sits at the head of the table. He is also thought of as a fund raiser, although his administrative duties limit his time to final cultivation of the biggest donors.

Kayla manages her research budget and decides which resources she will need for the coming year. She has a mix of mid-priced electronic and paper resources. She is unable to get the most expensive resources because her budget does not allow it. She is pleased with the range of resources she has, though, and feels like she can meet the needs of the museum with them. The person who set up the research office at the museum was hired one-third of the way through the museum's last capital campaign. That first researcher was brought on board when it began to look like the prospect pool was not deep enough for the fund raisers to meet the campaign goals. The value of research became clear immediately, and there never was a question of retaining the position after the campaign ended. Kayla came to the museum the year after the campaign ended. The museum's database of constituents includes about 45,000 names. The prospect pool has about 2,500 names, and the fund raisers are managing a total of 780 prospects.

About 80 percent of the museum's constituency live in the metropolitan area that comprises this Great Lakes city. Because the city is surrounded by farmland, the fund-raising team's reach extends into the three neighboring states. There are a few names on the prospect list who Kayla thinks of as expatriates: museum lovers who grew up in the region but who now live in other parts of the country or the world.

Kayla stays in touch with the latest advancements in prospect research. She enjoys finding new prospects for the museum, so she consistently tracks local and regional news. She keeps the potential prospect pool freshly stocked and feels happiest when the fund raisers' appointment calendars are full. She estimates that she devotes about 50 percent of her time to "proactive" research"—to finding new prospects unknown to the museum. The development team is thrilled with Kayla's approach. This dynamic approach has helped nurture a team concept in their suite of offices. It makes it easy for Kayla to advocate for prospects she believes are worth the extra effort. It also keeps her in the loop about unexpected outcomes and sidetracks that the development team encounters. Kayla likes to think that, on her team, there is a lot of mutual cheering and nudging going on: Fund-raiser heads frequently poke into Kayla's office to say, "Wait until I tell you what happened when I called that woman you told me about yesterday!"

There are ongoing fund-raising initiatives to make purchases for the collection, special exhibitions, and a visiting artist series, but there are no capital fund-raising goals for the museum right now. The museum is about five years away from another campaign, so it is a small conversation at this point. The fund-raising team meets every other week in prospect strategy meetings. Kayla organizes and attends those meetings. The group strategizes "next steps" and Kayla brings new prospects to the table for assignment. Kayla is asked to help develop cultivation strategies, to recommend Asks, and to keep the fund raisers in touch with the latest developments in prospects' lives.

To meet all these needs, Kayla has devised a rigorous schedule of tasks and a dedicated approach to managing time and resources. She maximizes her performance by eliminating tasks that will not lead to major gifts: She does no research to support the annual fund, for example, and she is not involved in event preparation reporting.

Kayla has friends in both big and small nonprofits. She is happy to be in a spot where everyone is closely linked to the fund-raising process from beginning to end, but where there is enough of a budget to support clearly defined tasks. The museum's size precludes Kayla from getting to do some types of research, and she regrets that. There is sometimes a scramble for major gift donors because the museum's initiatives are regional at best. So, there is not the "star quality" of the prospects Kayla hears her peers tout. Kayla knows that the balance within the team is closely linked to the leadership and to the personalities of those employed by the museum. It is sort of like going to a small school, Kayla thinks. Everyone knows everyone and there is no room for anonymity or distance. The power of each personality and intellect is building the course of the next fund-raising effort. So far, so good, Kayla thinks. The balance has prevailed.

Flaps and Wheels Down: Winging It

As we fly west, we cross the Missouri River, the Rocky Mountains, the Tetons, and finally the prairies and deserts beyond, where Paul works. Paul is the first researcher at a 10-year old environmental agency. Although the agency's mission is to save bird migration habitats in six nearby states, bird lovers around the world have stepped forward to support this nonprofit. The agency has a total of 40 employees, and many are involved in an aggressive phone and mail marketing effort. That is where Paul began, before the agency decided to add a research component to its staff last year. The agency head and three other people are the major gifts fund raisers.

Paul is called "researcher," but this is something of a wishful title, a title for the future. The agency is struggling to dedicate Paul's hours exclusively to research. His old duties in the annual fund arena spill over into his research tasks. Database updating, record maintenance, identifying annual fund and fund-raising event attendee prospects still pull Paul away from research time. And the agency asks that Paul aggressively research foundation and corporate support possibilities, too. Paul even writes grant proposals. The agency has a constituent pool of about 10,000 supporters, but no comprehensive screening of the database has been done. So, it is up to Paul to segment the pool himself. In fact, Paul does not have a research budget yet. He uses the Internet to find information, and he has been lobbying to purchase a foundation directory and a CD-ROM that profiles businesses.

The director, the fund raisers, and Paul meet each week. They discuss the immediate objectives and the agency's long-range goals, which include funding a major bird survey and purchasing a tract of land to protect it from commercial development. The latter goal may become urgent if the county council approves one land developer's plan next month. Paul's team estimates that the two projects would total $2 million or more. Paul's success in identifying major gift prospects has the director hoping that a prospect or two interested in buying that land to preserve it will soon surface from Paul's efforts.

Paul spends almost every day at work under a sense of urgency. He cannot complete all the chores he has been assigned, and research seems to fall to the bottom of that unfinished list. He needs an assistant, another researcher, or a volunteer who would like to learn how to research. And he needs to let go of the duties that were a part of his old job in the annual fund division. The agency recently hired Daisy to take on some of Paul's annual fund duties. Once Daisy is trained, Paul might get a chance to find major gift donors for that sanctuary and bird survey.

Paul is excited about working in the "startup" phase of research and fund raising at this agency. He identifies himself as an environmentalist and was delighted to get a job where his work would make a difference. He is overwhelmed by projects most of the time and worried that he cannot get to the research work. Paul has grand hopes for the days to come, when the work he can turn over to a helper will allow him to get down to research.

Flight Report: Soft Landing, Long Look

Can you see how Frannie, Kayla, and Paul are spending their workdays? What are some of the similarities? All three are reviewing incoming information, researching prospects, and writing reports. How much time they do that seems to be directly linked to the time they spend on non-research tasks. And that seems linked to the age of the research position. Where would your position fall in comparison to these three? Ask yourself these questions:

- What are the benefits of working in each domain? The large non-profit has every resource a researcher could want. The smaller organizations give their researchers freedom to design and manage their own work.
- What is the downside of working as a researcher in each venue? The answer to this question may have as much to do with you and the way you like to work as it does with the actual scenarios drawn here. Do you like to know what you will be doing every day or are you happiest when you get to create the day yourself? Do you enjoy patching and pasting and making something fly or would you rather have a ready-made kit?
- How could each work situation change for the better? Once again, how you see this will say something about you and the way you are happiest and most productive at work. We can be sure that the small nonprofits would be delighted to have more resources. That is not usually an option. There are increments of improvement in this and other areas that begin larger changes in productivity. One or two new resources—the right resources—along with the time to use them may leapfrog a small nonprofit's prospect identification efforts.

Take a few minutes to consider these and other factors emerging from the brief pictures you now have of three distinct nonprofits and how researchers might work in each. These are just three examples; you can imagine the variations from these three in terms of mission, budget, staffing, and resources. The range of experiences is interesting to consider. It is easy to think that we are all in the same predicament. It is a surprise to discover that we each face distinct problems and issues. While we sometimes find unique solutions to those problems and issues, it is intriguing to realize how often we can share solutions. Learning about the issues other researchers face sometimes changes the way your own difficulties feel. Hearing about how others pilot their course can bring new ideas for solutions to your own problems.

Height x Width x Depth = A Well-Designed Research Department

Let's talk about dimensions. The size and shape of your job as a researcher are directly linked to your ability to be successful at finding and qualifying major gift prospects. We believe that you can have an impact on the dimensions of your job. Some of the boundaries of your work will be set in stone. Others may be the kind you can recalculate over time. Let's visit the elements of a well-designed research department that will facilitate your prospecting. But first, let's visit the not-too-distant past.

Research Time Travel

It is 1982 and the researcher at the local hospital is asked to produce a list of potential donors for the new surgery wing in the planning stages. She has few options for gathering information. The fund-raising section does not have an electronic database of donors yet, although the leadership has been looking into buying one. In the meantime, one of the staff members maintains oversized index cards about each major gift donor. To begin building the prospect list for the new wing, the researcher sorts through these cards by hand. She adds to the list the names of those who gave large gifts in the last five years and those who are currently giving gifts of $250 or more each year to the hospital. That list is too short, of course. The names of prominent people in the community, the founders and leaders of the old, established companies, are added, too. The researcher knows many of those names already. She does not worry at this point about whether these people have had any association with the hospital.

Next, she will go to the public library to check the news clipping files maintained there. She will find a few more names she did not know to add to the list. These include a handful of names belonging to prominent, local families. The researcher then searches the city directory to verify the correct spelling of the names, to add spouse names, and to get home addresses. Next, she makes a trip to the county assessor's office to gather the assessed values of the homes of the people on the list. The property assessments will form the most important piece of supporting information for the list she compiles.

Two years earlier, the development staff began to maintain files on the most important donors. The files include correspondence, giving histories, and brief visit information. They also include tally sheets that staff members use to note a donor's attendance at events. Most of the information in the files has emerged as development officers were encouraged—prodded, actually—to move the files they keep about their prospective donors to a central area accessible to the entire fund-raising staff. There are about 300 of these files now. The researcher will manually check these files to add to the information set she is building about each prospect for the new wing. She plans to add any additional names she finds in the files to the list.

Back to the Present: Information Manager, Knowledge Maker

That 1982 researcher had few resources for qualifying prospects and even fewer for identifying them in the first place. Treks out of the office to retrieve information were common. Sifting through piles of papers was the norm. For some nonprofits, the distance between the 1982 story and today is small. Organizations just beginning a prospect research unit have few in-house resources, plenty of paper piles, and may have fewer prospects.

Actually, even for young or established nonprofits, the distance between this 1982 research picture and today is a gulf. The flow of information into the research office has been a river. In 1995, or a little later for more youthful research programs, the data flow became a torrent. The Internet and easy communication by email brought down the dam. Researchers must now manage more information than anyone could have ever predicted (see Figure 9-1). Manage information? Does that mean simply channeling the information toward your data entry people or into your central file system? No. That will not advance your prospecting plans, will it? Effectively and efficiently managing information involves three stages:

- Stage One: Sift
- Stage Two: Weigh
- Stage Three: Ship

Stage One: Sift

The range of information available now is literally immeasurable. It includes rich, varied, and even odd bits of information. We have gone over the rich end of the scale—salaries, stock holdings, company profiles, and biographies. The varied and odd end of that scale is the part that challenges your information management skills. You may learn to which computer user group

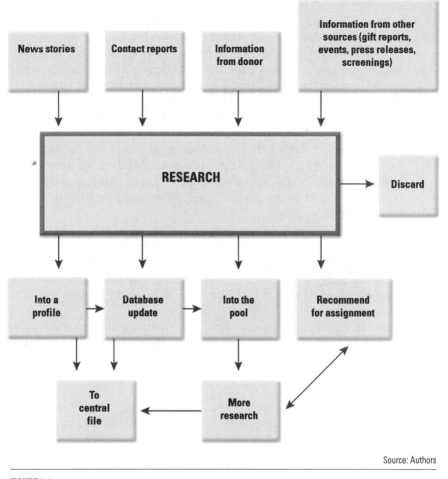

Source: Authors

FIGURE 9-1
The Information Trail

your prospect belongs, his running time in nearly every marathon he's entered in the last four years, and where he and his family spent their summer vacation (photos included). Here is the rub: You will find that same information about constituents who are not prospects. At first, you may think that finding any information about any person signals you to complete more research. It does not. Part of the art of managing information will be to determine if the information is about someone who can be a major gift donor. Your job will be to sort through the torrent to find the information that is valuable to major gift prospecting. It requires a researcher to abandon hope of handling *all* the information. Remember your directive—to use the first dollar efficiently to get the next major gift dollars. You cannot keep up with the entire database of constituents. You will have to let some information flow by. You will also have to evaluate the worthiness of prospect information. You will ask yourself:

- Does this information further the fund-raising teams' cultivation or gift closure goals? Your organization's mission and your fund-raising teams' goals will help you decide if those running times or summer vacation photos move the prospect closer to giving a major gift.
- Does this piece of information invade the privacy of the prospect? Yes, we know that it appears that it was public information if it was on the Internet. The Internet is teaching us that the opposite of "private" may not be "public." As information compilers, we must stay current about concepts of privacy and data aggregating, that is, bringing pieces of seemingly unrelated information together to create comprehensive profiles.
- Does the information respect the prospect? Keep in mind that your organization has a friendly relationship with prospects, that you are not a detective compiling intelligence on individuals. This frame of mind will help you stay in touch with the idea that the information you collect—the entire prospect file you build—must respect the prospect.
- Does saving the information respect the mission and reputation of your nonprofit? If you are comfortable with the answers you gave to the other questions here, you will be in good standing in regard to stewarding the reputation and mission of your organization.

Loretta was a prospect researcher for ten years before the Internet arrived at her workplace. When her nonprofit hard-wired her computer to the Web, Loretta was more intimidated than thrilled. She sat in one of the front pews in the church of Internet doubters, those who saw this untamed electronic party as a passing fancy with which people would soon tire. She was adept at finding information through several fee-based electronic resources, and her large collection of print resources was nearly equal to that at larger nonprofits with bigger budgets. At first she ignored the Web, but when her colleague began excitedly telling stories of information he had found on the Internet, Loretta realized that she would have to investigate this new resource.

Loretta began her forays slowly and, unfamiliar with the unstructured nature of the Web, she decided to print nearly everything she found about her prospects. She found information she had never encountered in her standard resources—data about hobbies and genealogy, for example. The novelty of the type of information she found made it difficult for Loretta to estimate its value. Everything seemed valuable in its rarity. Loretta did not worry about whether the information was filling in blanks about her prospect named Robert F. Johnson; she would decide if this was the *right* Robert F. Johnson later. In the meantime, it would not be right to send this information to file where someone might misinterpret it, so Loretta began stacking the papers in a box under the table in the corner of her office. When the first box filled, Loretta pushed it into the closet, knowing that she would have more time in the summer to deal with the information. She kept looking for data on the Internet and she kept finding it.

In three months, Loretta had three boxes full of papers from Internet hits. Her anxiety when she turned on her computer in the morning had become palatable. She had never before let sets of information pile up, unattended. She realized that the information would be as useful in the trash as it was in boxes in her closet. But to sort through it all to try to determine what was useful and what was marginal or useless would involve abandoning her regular duties for at least a month.

Loretta could not sift through the information she encountered. Instead of acting like a funnel, Loretta was a channel. The channel was open between the computer's printer and the box in the corner, with no filter between the two. Loretta's inability to pick and choose created a dam in her closet, with information that might be useful to her nonprofit's fund-raising efforts trapped behind it. You must choose the right information from the cascade you encounter each day or week. You must set parameters for what you have the time to collect. The sifting you do at the start of the information collecting cycle positions you for the next stage in knowledge management. It facilitates the process you will establish for efficiently weighing information.

Stage Two: Weigh

Now that you are choosing the right pieces of information, the ones that move fund raising forward at your organization, you have another task. You must transform that information from something singular into a facet of the bigger picture about your prospect. The prospect has been promoted to president of a company. What does that mean? How big is the company? Is it public? Should this prospect now move up the cultivation priority list? Should this prospect be nearer to an Ask? Often, each piece of information seems to require another piece to come alive. It may require a bit of research math. Some information is collected now for use later. Significant events in a company's history, promotions on the way to prospect-hood, even births and deaths of near and distant relatives may sometimes be filed away for later reporting.

Here are a few of the pieces of information you may be asked to review or manage on a daily, weekly, or monthly basis:

- From newspapers, magazines and journals: job change announcements, obituaries (paid funeral notices), social news, philanthropy news, and articles profiling individuals and companies.
- From internal sources: names of donors who give new gifts above a specified level; new information about prospects and potential prospects garnered from correspondence, constituent updates, and contact reports.

- From other sources: donor roll data from other nonprofits; board lists from for-profits and nonprofits, and club rosters.

As you can imagine, some of these information bits are more perishable than others are. News of the death of a prospect or a member of the prospect's family will require immediate attention, since the fund raiser assigned to that prospect may wish to go to the funeral or send condolences. Other pieces of information can sit idle until they are needed, and they will not sour. You will have to evaluate the perishability of the pieces of information you collect and establish a set of priorities for managing them.

Nathan begins each workday reading the local newspaper. The constituents who support the food bank where he is the researcher generally live in the city and nearby suburbs where the food bank is located. On this day, as he does each morning, Nathan sat down at his desk, logged into the constituent database, and warmed his hands on his coffee mug as the machine whirred awake. In the meantime, Nathan cracked opened the paper. Shedding it of its advertising inserts, he pulled the local section and the business page to the top of the pile. A story about the rate increase planned for garbage customers was the centerpiece of B-1. Nathan quickly skimmed the headlines and then turned to the obituaries. He typed each of the ten names listed in the paid notices into his database, listening for the quiet "ding" that meant no match was found.

But when he typed in the fifth name, Harriet Wilkerson, there was no familiar dinging sound. Nathan glanced at the screen to see that Harriet was a member of the food bank's supporters. He quickly checked the giving screens and found that Harriet was a regular donor. She had given the institution $500 or so each year for the last eleven years. Harriet was assigned to Tara, the planned giving officer for the food bank. With so many things to manage, Nathan could not remember if Tara had mentioned Harriet as a prospect in the active stages of cultivation recently. He flipped to the prospect tracking section of the database to find that Harriet was a "Stage C" prospect, in cultivation but she had not been asked for a major gift yet. The record also noted that Harriet had the food bank in her will. Nathan skimmed the obituary, focusing on the last paragraph, where survivors usually list the deceased's wishes for memorials and remembrances. There it was: "In lieu of flowers, please send gifts to the Jefferson County Food Bank."

In the family relationships listed in the obituary, Nathan could see that Harriet was the surviving spouse of a couple who had founded a large construction company about fifty years ago. A quick search of the local newspaper's archives uncovered the story that the company was sold when Harriet's husband died three years ago. The obituary indicated that Harriet and her husband had one son. More accurately, the son appeared to be a son from a first marriage, since he had a different last name. By typing the son's name in the database, Nathan discovered that he, too, supports the food bank, but only recently. And he was not linked to his mother's record. Nathan decided that, since the son's name was different, the nonprofit probably never knew he was a member of this prominent family. Nathan did a bit of digging and discovered that the son ran his own successful development company, a spin-off from his parents' firm. Two newspaper articles touted the son's interest in homeless issues and one outlined his drive to improve resources for the community's poor. He had worked on three building projects for nonprofits where he donated some of his company's time and materials.

Nathan felt his heart beat a little quicker; this discovery could mean a good match for a philanthropist-in-the-making who seemed to be looking for the right cause. He imagined that Harriet's son might easily move into the kind of leadership role at the food bank that Harriet herself would have enjoyed seeing. Nathan assembled the pieces of information he had collected in less than an hour, forwarded them to the central file room, added the son to the suspect pool, and summarized the important points in an email to Tara. Later, he intended to recommend that the son be assigned as a major gift prospect. He would recommend that Tara get the assignment, keeping these prospect management tasks in the family, you might say.

Nathan quickly zeroed in on the important pieces of information that transformed an obituary notice into response-readiness for his team. Tara would alert her staff to anticipate memorial gifts. Since Harriet and her husband had been leaders in the community, there could be many gifts and some may be large. Tara would send condolences to Harriet's son. Nathan anticipated that Harriet's son might move into a position of prominence among the food bank's leadership, with the additional information this researcher had garnered and with Tara's attention.

Stage Three: Ship

Simply sending the new information to file or to the data entry staff will not make that piece of information dynamic. You have to do that. After sifting and weighing, you will decide what to ship where. Is this an information bit that your fund-raising team needs to know immediately? Be hard on yourself as you make this judgment—do not send them things just to show that you can find cool information. They are busy people and, unfortunately, a large part of your reputation will be based on the quality and timing of the information you share.

Can you expect that the fund raiser assigned will see the information if you simply send it to file? When will the member of your team (or you, when you are asked to assemble new information into a report) see the information in file? Will it be at the right time? In many cases, it will. So, shipping information to file may often be the route to go.

Does the information involve a change that should be noted in your database of constituents? If it is a job change, a marriage, a death, or a new residence, it will be up to you to forward that change to the data entry staff. There may be others who will learn about that change, but you must not rely on that. Your relationship to current and reliable database information is one of the most pivotal ones on the entire fund-raising team. Address and other information will be used to screen and build your pool of potential prospects. Name changes may determine whether you even find an individual in your database when important wealth news comes your way.

Master of Time

The river of data is flowing. You have the dams, channels, and canals built to catch, evaluate, and distribute the information stream. Life is good, right? Actually, for most researchers, life is a little frantic these days. As you can see, there is a lot to manage and it does not stop, not for a single day. The best researchers become disciplined masters of time. Each workday is carefully scheduled. Each day holds in it the balance of keeping up with river maintenance or falling behind. Since the flow does not abate, any snag created by resources overlooked or skipped only seems to get worse. The resources that yield fragile, time-sensitive information are handled every day. They become an appointment of sorts: Every day at 9:00 a.m., for example, you will skim your newspaper's business page, obituaries, and front and local pages for news about your donors or prospects. When gift reports—printouts or database alerts of the gifts received the previous day or week—hit your desk, you skim them for the gift threshold that tips you toward researching someone or adding that name to the suspect pool. The best researchers do not follow the "wait until you hear the crying" approach: they put that baby—information management—on a schedule.

There are truisms about managing time that fit prospect research well. Do not handle something twice. Set up funnels and landing places for papers based on priority ("today," "this week," "this month" boxes, for example). Informally measure the amount of time you spend on time-hungry tasks and rank the value of them. If you spend one hour a day reviewing a publication that yields few bits of information or information that is not major gift-driven, drop it from your routine. Do not forget the point of the pool: It is a holding place for potential prospects and information about them that you will deal with later. Use it. Are your fund raisers busy? Do they have good prospects to cultivate, even more than they need? Then you are on the right track.

More Snag Clearing: Keeping the Flow Going

Let's look at a few of the elements of running a research office that will challenge your time management and information processing skills but are essential to identifying new prospects and qualifying assigned prospects. These are knowledge-making opportunities that:

- Put information about new prospects in front of you
- Put knowledge about known prospects in front of your development team
- Enhance the communication flow for the entire fund-raising team

These knowledge-making opportunities will give you the chance to identify new prospects and to add potential prospects to the pool. They will allow you to add information and analyses to your conclusions about already-identified prospects. They give the entire team the chance to stay on track with the progress of fund raising at your organization. We have briefly mentioned most of them in earlier chapters. Let's look into these knowledge-making pieces in greater detail so that you can fit them into the mix of information you review or create during your workweek.

Gift Reports

Gift reports are paper or electronic assemblages of the donations made to your organization each day or week. These donations will come from Asks made by the development team, gifts that came from phonathon or direct mail efforts, and gifts that came independent of any initiative on the part of your nonprofit (unsolicited gifts). Your organization's gift processing section should be able to create printouts of gifts received and share those printouts with you. If you have a bang-up database, you can do it yourself. Whatever way you review these gifts, the report format will be the same. Each will include the amount of the gift and who made the gift. Other gift details like the prospect's spot in the cultivation cycle, whether a company matches the gift, or the prospect's link to your organization, may be included.

As you develop the habit of reviewing gift reports, you will begin to set a threshold for the gifts that will catch your eye. If your organization has established $50,000 as the minimum major gift, you are likely to pay attention to out-of-pocket gifts of $2,000 and up, for example. If your organization is small, all gifts above $250 may interest you. When you see the gift report, you will quickly skim it, paying attention only to the dollar numbers at first. You have a few choices about what you do with the donor names that draw your attention. You can do a little research before you code them to join the pool of prospective donors. You may set up a few "filters" through which you will quickly pass those names: real estate assessment, an Internet search engine, and a look at total giving, for example. Or, if your pool is small or you are particularly busy, you can toss those names into your suspect pool and research them later.

Contact Reports and the Reading File

Large or small, how will your team keep each other apprised of the latest developments about the prospects in active cultivation? How will you find out that one of the development officers discovered during a visit that the new prospect you think owns one business actually owns four? How will you hear that a prospect told a fund raiser that he has three brothers who are also interested in your nonprofit? The poking-a-head-in-the-doorway approach to communication will not work in large institutions and cannot be relied upon to work consistently in small nonprofits.

Contact reports and the reading file take the place of a casual form of communication. As we have said, a contact report is the story of each formal encounter with a prospect. Development officers write contact reports when they complete a telephone or face-to-face meeting with one of their prospects. The contact report includes the date, time, and place of the contact. It includes who was present. The development officer writes the story of the meeting. In the early stages of cultivation, the story might focus on how the prospect feels about the institution, what the prospect's next business or personal goals are, and reflections on the prospect's experiences with the nonprofit or with her philanthropy in general. Later, the contact report will outline the presentation of a proposal for support made to the prospect, the other details of the Ask, and new events in the prospect's financial life. The contact report becomes an ongoing journal of the prospect's philanthropic relationship with your nonprofit.

The reading file is the collection of that week or month's contact reports, proposals, and other important communications gathered into one convenient place. If it is a paper version, it is quickly circulated among the development and research staff. Many nonprofits require that the reading file spend no more than one day on anyone's desk. A reading file may take an electronic form: It may be posted on an Intranet or passed among team members via email. The reading file gives the entire team the chance to share what is happening with the prospects in active cultivation. Each team member will be sure to hear about proposals, gift closures, the outcome of major events, and other significant developments. The annual fund might include samples of their latest mailings. Other departments affiliated with the development team—the public relations department, the education team, the administration of the nonprofit—might include materials in the reading file. All of the materials included are there because they are related to advancing the cause of fund raising.

Research Requests in the Queue

As fund raisers ask you for additional information about those prospects, you will create—or maintain, if it already exists—a system for dealing with their research requests. Large operations deal with research requests in a formal way. Fund raisers fill out a form (paper or electronic) that outlines what they already know, what they hope to learn from this "second-stage" research, and by which date they hope to receive a report. Research request forms can ask fund raisers to note that they have already checked the prospect's central file to see if the answers to their questions are there. The form has a place to include any new information that prompted the research request ("she recently bought a factory") and a place to note the time frame for completing the request. Some researchers outline reasonable deadlines for research requests on the form by creating a hierarchy for the various types of requests. For example, researchers may need a few days to complete a simple request, a week to gather and analyze complex financial information, and even longer to create a full profile about a prospect with a long association with the nonprofit. You, the researcher, will place the research request on your calendar, estimate the time it will take, and schedule it with a deadline that satisfies the fund raiser and the demands on your time.

If your organization is small, you may be dealing with research requests in an informal way. Fund raisers walk across the hall to your office, send you an email, or telephone you to ask for additional research. If your nonprofit has a casual communication system, it is still important to set up a tracking plan for research requests. It is common to have a conversation across a desk with a member of your team and not realize that the chat included a research request. Each time a fund raiser communicates with you, evaluate whether there was a research request imbedded in that dialogue. What appears to be a chatty recounting of a recent visit with a prospect might actually include a fund raiser asking you to find out more from the wealth or philanthropy indicators that the visit uncovered.

Is it up to the fund raiser to communicate requests clearly? Sure it is. Will your life be better or worse if you spend your time, instead of researching, in "he said-she said" arguments? It will be worse. A short list of open and completed requests and a plan to let the requestors know when they can see results will not interfere with the casual way small organizations operate. You can create a research request form for your team, even if they will not use it often. The form will let them know what you hope they will do before they turn to you, and it will outline the typical turnaround for responses to their requests (see the appendix section for sample research request forms).

Event Preparation Reports

Researchers are often asked to prepare fund raisers and organization leaders for events by giving them concise information reports that will facilitate the cultivation of prospects who will attend the event. The events might be, for example, building dedications, annual donor recognition receptions, or regional fund-raising parties. The guest list might be restricted to major gift donors or it may include a mix of constituents. Your event preparation task will be defined by the leadership. It may involve simply updating your team with the latest news about the biggest prospects coming to the event. It may mean that you will write brief profiles about all the assigned prospects who plan to come. Some researchers are able to download the pertinent information in a readable format from their databases. The information could include each donor's name, affiliation with your nonprofit, latest gift, total giving, recent events attended, and family members who are affiliated with your nonprofit. Many researchers produce event reports with a word processing program. Most researchers create a boilerplate for event reports.

We have heard stories about researchers who are expected to prepare event reports covering as many as (gulp) 100 or 200 attendees. We wonder who could even read this much information and what its value would be to the development team. We suspect that the decision-makers on the team are failing to trust that the researcher can pick the major gift names from the list. Researchers who spend their time writing about people who are not major gift prospects are not functioning as major gift researchers. The mandate (first dollar gets next dollars efficiently) has been lost, probably in the shuffle of papers that writing about 100 attendees takes.

Are you are a researcher who is being asked to research and write about too many event attendees? If you are, speak to your team about the value of this approach. You may discover that they are unhappy with that many pages of information prior to an event, too. They may say that they cannot remember anything about anybody after they wade through that stack of information. They may rejoice when you volunteer to pick the top 20 or so prospects or potential prospects from the list for research.

Researchers who have met resistance to their attempts to change this assignment have found other ways to cope with it. They have abbreviated the information they assemble on the 100 attendees. Instead of gathering as much information as we outlined here, they might include name, company name, position, spouse's name, and not much more. The report becomes a collection of name tags in narrative form. It does not seem to have a great deal of major gift value, but it does make the assignment almost manageable for the researcher. It may satisfy the development team's need to see some information about *everybody*. It will not usually advance major gift-getting, though.

When designing and producing reports, know who your readers are, and try to anticipate their needs. If the report is going to be shared with key volunteers or committee people who are not members of your professional fund-raising team, you may wish to withhold giving records or information about outstanding proposals from the report. When we talked about ethics, we mentioned that, although members of the public can see each other's giving in annual donor reports, the giving appears in ranges and not in the level of detail commonly found in internal reports like the ones that we are describing here.

The best way to find out if your nonprofit's format for event reports is working is to ask your readers. Is the information they want clearly and quickly available in the format you are using? Are you including the information they want to see? Are the right people covered in the report? After you gather this feedback, you can adapt your report format to include the new ideas.

Family Trees

Earlier in this chapter we mentioned reviewing obituaries. You probably thought, "How morbid." Let's face it—the sports page is more fun to read. But here is what we discovered about obituaries:

- They help us keep track of important events in a prospect's life, like the death of one of the members of a prospect couple or the death of an uncultivated prospect. If your fund raisers and your institution are close enough to the prospect, news of the demise may reach your office in a more direct way than seeing it in the newspaper. But, if you begin following obituaries, you will be surprised to learn how often you are the first one at your nonprofit to learn of a death.
- If a significant percentage of your nonprofit's constituents lives in your geographical area, you will discover that you are an important piece of keeping the database current through the news you find in the local newspapers. Noting life changes is a part of that database maintenance. You may find many important constituents in the obituary pages each year.
- Linking your suspects and prospects to the wealth that was created in an earlier generation or two is the first step in assessing inherited wealth. Obituaries frequently outline family relationships and tout the accomplishments of the deceased. Obituaries of prominent people in your organization's geographical community give you a chance to see if any of their relatives are "related" to—affiliated with—your nonprofit. This is a first step in building a family tree.

Family trees are tools for organizing and linking related individuals. Family trees come in handy when the number of individuals related to one another and linked to your organization reaches a "critical mass:" too many to remember and too many to keep straight. Married names, third generations, subsequent marriages and divorces will be too much to handle in your head or in a narrative format.

The family tree you construct can be as complex as those included in a purchased genealogy software program or as simple as drawing boxes and lines on a piece of paper. What you come up with in the end might look like the tree we have built in Exhibit 9-1. Notice these features:

- We do not know whom Edward Alder married.
- We do not know the birth date of Greta Pine.
- We do not know several middle initials, but we would have included them if we did. They would help us distinguish between generations and between people with similar names who are unrelated to this family.
- We do not know the birth dates of the youngest generation of Alders.

We are including birth dates because, like middle initials, they help us distinguish between the generations. There is a Thomas Alder in the oldest generation and in the third generation, and there is a Beth Alder in the third and fourth generations. As we all know, repeating names from generation to generation is common in families.

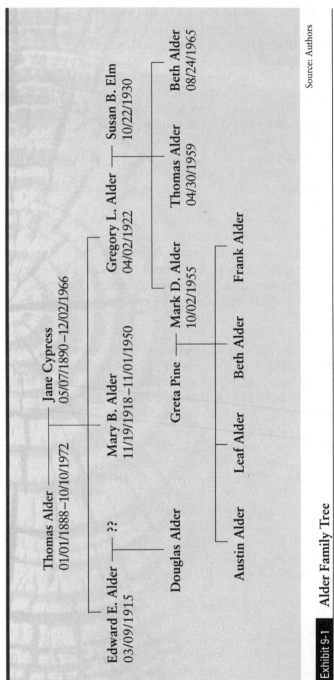

Exhibit 9-1 Alder Family Tree

The trees of famous families often are included in books about those families. Families that are responsible for settling an area or whose members are the founders of companies that shaped an area's growth may have been the subject of biographies. If the relationships among family members are not outlined in a tree in the book, there will be enough information about those relationships to help you get started on building the tree yourself. You can then copy the tree to the files of all the members of the family who are affiliated with you organization. Most important of all, you can link the family members with one another in your database. As the wealth passes from one generation to the next, your fund-raising team will be ready to cultivate the next prospects among those family members.

You can give the chore of reviewing obituaries to someone identified to help you—a volunteer, a staff member, or a part-time helper. It is a tedious task that can pay off with important dividends. But then, that defines a lot of information-gathering tasks in many research offices.

Profiles: Traditional and Alternatives

A profile is an outline of demographic, biographical, financial, and contextual facts. Those units of information are then analyzed and the conclusions and recommendations are added to the mix. We talked about profiles in several chapters and you can find examples in the appendix section of this book. Profiles are not the same at every institution, and every institution does not use a profile format to report the findings and conclusions of research. Decisions about the composition and use of profiles evolve from their functionality at each institution. Before you suggest profile changes to your team, evaluate the functionality of your organization's profile format by writing a few of them. Heavy equipment operators talk about "time in the seat:" the time an operator has spent on the seat of a tractor, with each hour adding wisdom and experience to the operator's skill level. There is no substitute. If your nonprofit has an established procedure about using profiles, you will be wise to follow it until you have enough "time in the seat" to conclude how profiles are adding to or impeding your nonprofit's fund-raising efforts.

A Brief (Surmised) History of the Profile

The profile has been a mainstay of research reporting for many years. Some institutions have raised profile writing to a fine art. Researchers talk about generating profiles that are nearly a dozen pages long. They review the prospect's electronic and paper file, gather new information, and compile all the relevant data into an outline format from a standard boilerplate, ensuring that the development team is able to find the information they want in the same place time after time. Some organizations ask their researchers to update profiles of major prospects on a regular basis. Some researchers only update profiles when a research request or a major event prompts that work to begin.

The tools available for profile building limit each researcher to some degree. Researchers who can build profiles in their constituent database by copying and pasting or uploading information into a prescribed format invariably use that time-cutting tool. Some of the databases allowing this type of profile building have a companion feature that permits the researcher to append notes to the profile. That formula seems to cover nearly all the angles on assembling a usable profile. Researchers with this option have one more benefit: Changes in the profile, such as new giving totals, changes in address or job title, will be automatically updated when that new information is added to the database (often by others on the team). Other researchers must build profiles with a word processing program. They save these profiles in an organized way on their computers so that, when they must update them, they can work from the profile they built before and simply add new information.

Profiles differ in fundamental ways from institution to institution. They differ because:

- Institutions tailor profiles to meet their needs. One institution may need its researchers to outline proposals in profiles, but a proposal-light nonprofit may not. A nonprofit may require researchers to organize their financial conclusions in a table within the profile. Another may require that net worth or giving capacity estimates be included in every profile.

- Some researchers have the option to tailor profiles for each subject. Researchers generally maintain a boilerplate and then add and subtract categories of information. For example, if a prospect lives a great distance away, you may not have access to his gifts to other nonprofits. You will not then need a section on the profile to report donations to other institutions (unless your team needs to see a string of "don't knows").

- Some nonprofits have tested other ways to collect and disseminate information, so the profile format has faded into the background at those organizations. As information retrieved from fee-based information providers and Web sites has become both more accessible and more readable to novices, some researchers simply attach these documents to a brief narrative where they outline their conclusions. These institutions are concluding that profile writing, particularly those profiles that are pages and pages long, is not the best use of their researchers' skills and time.

Researchers store profiles in electronic databases, on shared hard drives, and in paper files that are accessible to the entire team or to part of the development team. They create rules about who can update or change the profiles. They adapt profiles in response to the specific role it will be taking; a volunteer solicitor may not receive the same information that a development officer sees in a profile. But, above all, researchers write profiles which are respectful celebrations of the philanthropic lives of their donors and prospective donors.

If your organization encourages you to distribute profiles electronically, it will be worthwhile to establish who amends or changes profiles. Since you are the one completing research, you may ask your team to pass new information to you and you will add it to the profiles. That way, a series of distinct profiles created by other staff members will not begin appearing in the prospect's file.

Is your profile format serving your development team well? To find out, ask them. Before you do that, ask researchers at other institutions to share their profile formats with you. Offer your team a few examples of what other institutions are including in profiles. Comparing your profile format to those used by other researchers will be worth the time. You will learn the trends in profile making. Remember that changing the content of your profiles will alter the time it takes you to update older profiles. You will have to change them to match the new format when they arrive in the queue for updating. See sample profile formats in the appendix section of this book.

Special Reports

When it comes to researching and writing reports, a researcher's favorites have to be the ones we will throw into the category of special reports. Remember when we talked about researchers becoming "best in field" on a topic? We wrote that, after their work requires them to learn everything they can about classic car collecting or San Francisco real estate investing, for example, they are the prospect research experts on analyzing that type of wealth. Those research efforts are usually driven by research requests or new prospect identifications. They often require a special report format, to give the researcher room to explain her assumptions and conclusions.

Researchers are asked to prepare special reports about many topics. Some requests—or slight variations of ones you will get—are:

"Of all the prospects we have assigned, who are really the richest among them?"

"John Smith is a wheat farmer. What do wheat farmers earn? What is the value of a wheat farm?"

"What foundations might support a new work training initiative at our nonprofit?"

"Can you figure out what a winery earns for its owners?"

"I just found out that Rachael Jones owns race horses—and one of them won the Preakness! What does that mean, wealth-wise?"

As you were about to say, many of these requests will take us deeply into the "art" realm of prospect research. We are so glad you have caught on to us. You remember that we outlined the Land of Supposing for you in chapter 5, the Research Math section of this book. How you report what you find will depend on the level of detail your development team likes to see. A general format for special reports is:

- Identify the prospect by name and any other distinctive database coding.
- State the research problem.
- Outline the prospect's history or the relevant background information for this problem.
- Briefly summarize what you found to support your conclusions.
- Show your math.
- Outline your conclusions.
- Make recommendations.

Each special report might include a few of these categories. Some will include all of them. You will design special reports that are clear, concise, and that accomplish the initial goal of the research assignment. You will keep in mind the style and format of reporting that your team is used to seeing. That will make it easy for them to pull the information important to them out of your report.

Other Duties as Assigned: "I'd Be Able to Research Prospects, If Only I Didn't Have to . . . "

Throughout this book, you may have noticed assumptions we make about prospect researchers. We place certain tasks within the domain of other members of the fund-raising team. As you now know, we are firm believers in "highest and best use" for nearly everything, including researchers. There are some fund-raising tasks that appear to be related to research but, in fact, they support the entire team. Researchers are sometimes identified as the people to complete these tasks. If your organization really wants you to find new prospects for cultivation, the researcher will get to spend her time researching. Regardless of our high-minded attitude about being goal-directed, researchers are asked to perform database-updating chores, oversee central file systems, and even process gifts. Researchers sometimes write grants and steward donors. Why does this discourage us? If researchers are doing these things, they will not be researching. Over and over again, research will fall by the wayside. It will be the last thing on the "to do" list. It will have to wait until Friday, when that researcher has time, when all the gifts have been booked and all the donors have been thanked. Friday comes and goes and then it is Monday again. An organization can get by for a while without identifying new prospects. Can it grow without new prospects? No. Can it support its programs in lean times without new prospects? No. Can it sustain its current level of service without new prospects? In the long term, it cannot.

You may be lucky enough to have a job that allows you to focus on prospect research. If you do not, help your organization by lobbying for that job to be valued and protected as a research position. You may work at a nonprofit where dedicating full-time resources to prospect research simply cannot happen anytime soon. The nonprofit may be young and small, and it may take most of the current resources and employee hours just to keep the organization on track with its mission. Are you reading this book because you already sense that your organization is missing chances to identify potential supporters? If so, you may be ahead of your colleagues. The good news is that you have nothing to lose by adding a few prospect identification processes to your workday. If you have too many duties and research trails in the pack, you have to move it up to the front. Pick a day and name it "Pure Research Day." Let everyone know about it. Before long, you will build an army of supporters. With each piece of information you bring to the fund-raising table, you will gain a research advocate among your team members.

Other Duties, Part Two: "I'd Be Able to _____ (Fill in the Blank), If Only I Didn't Have to Research Prospects."

Some research offices have profile-writing or new prospect-finding quotas. Researchers or their supervisors estimate the time it takes to identify and qualify a new prospect. They then decide that researchers ought to direct a certain portion of each week to finding new prospects. Many researchers believe that it takes an average of 8 to 12 hours of work time to research a new prospect and write a profile reporting the findings.

When the other information management duties research handles are considered, it may not be reasonable to expect more than two or three days a week to be allocated to researching and reporting new prospects. Some research offices have nearly abandoned all other types of assignments and encourage their researchers to spend the bulk of their time researching new prospects. Some offices concentrate their research time on updating the profiles of known prospects and completing research requests.

Proactive and Reactive Research Offices

As we mentioned in chapter 6, researchers have named these two types of approaches proactive and reactive research. Your office is likely to fall somewhere on this continuum. Your output may be shaped by quotas. You may have little time to proactively look for unidentified prospects. You may be expected to establish your own mix of proactive and reactive research. The expectations you meet will be influenced by the needs of your organization. If your fund-raising team is actively cultivating a strong group of prospects, you will be getting plenty of new information that requires second-stage research. But during the early stages of a campaign, there will be a stronger push for new prospects. The fund-raising leadership may even use your production level—the rate at which you introduce new, viable prospects—to help estimate the campaign goals. It will be important for you to stay in close touch with how reasonable these expectations are. As a valuable member of that team, adjustments should be considered and respected. It will not help anyone—you, the team, or your nonprofit—if you are dissipating your energies to worrying about quotas instead of spending that energy researching prospects.

The Research Log

Here is the bad news. Nearly every researcher has witnessed a fund raiser burst into a room, saying, "I got the gift! She said 'yes' to $ _____ (thousand, million—fill in the amount)!" What is wrong with this picture? We will give you a minute to think about it. Okay, time is up. Here is the answer: *You* were not in it! Fund raisers do not get gifts; *fund-raising teams* do. Unfortunately, the nature of fund raising leads the front-line staff to think they did it alone. After months of cultivation, juggling volunteer solicitors, strategizing the approach with their colleagues, the entire process can boil down—well, vaporize—to the Ask and who on the team was present at that moment. That is where the credit will fall.

Development officers even add their fund-raising totals to their resumes. They report that they raised $50 million during their tenure at a job, for example. Do researchers add dollar totals to their resumes? No. But research is full to the brim with dollar figures. Do researchers add up the gift potential, the estimated wealth, the real estate holdings, the gross sales of companies, or the salaries of the prospects they identify? No. These numbers would have little value in the fund-raising culture because they are not "in the door" dollars. Do researchers total a different figure, one comparable to the one the fund raisers tout? No, researchers rarely track the outcome of the cultivations of the prospects they identified. Why? Such a total would not represent the truth about the work the researcher did. The prospects who were identified but not cultivated, or whose cultivation did not result in a major gift, would not be included. The outcome is out of research's hands, right? Researchers can find prospects, but they are not usually in charge of kick-starting cultivation, pushing fund raisers toward closing the gift, or securing a gift from a reluctant prospect. Totaling the what-might-have-beens is not likely to happen. But the what-might-have-beens, uncounted by the healthiest researchers, can be a considerable part of the work.

What shall we measure and count then? We have plenty of things to count: new prospects identified, research requests completed, and event preparation reports, to name a few. One of the ways you can keep everyone current about your production is by keeping a research log (see Exhibit 9-2). This log will be the report of everything you accomplish each year. It will include new prospects identified, research requests fulfilled, special reports, and any other research work you complete. You will set the log up in such a way that it can be viewed by its various features. By creating the log as a spreadsheet, a word processing table, or in another sortable format, you will be able to review and measure several bits of information. With the log, you have the option to:

- Track the opening and closing of research requests by date
- Track the frequency of requests by each development officer
- Track research requests by prospect name
- Total the number of various reports written

A research log keeps the value of research in focus for the fund-raising team. The log becomes a quiet advocate for staffing and resource needs. And, when the team celebrates the next major gift, you can check the log to see when you first identified the prospect, qualified her giving capacity by analyzing financial information, added new information to the mix with news you monitor, and when you wrote the final report, recommending the Ask. You will then certainly be a part of the celebration.

Exhibit 9-2 Research Log

Prospect Name/ Request	Requestor/ Assignee	Date Requested	Date Completed	Type of Report	Notes
Smith, James update profile	VP	03.22.2001		profile	
Jones, Mary new prospect	DO	n/a	09.01.2001	new prospect	
Top Donor Event	DO	07.15.2001	08.15.2001	event	Brief write-ups on 25 major prospects attending.

Source: Authors

Back Me Up: A Central Filing System

The nugget-filled stream of information you are now sifting and weighing needs a permanent residence, an address, where current and future employees can find it. The prospect histories you are building through your research must be retrievable. The other information that accumulates about a prospect or a prospect-to-be, such as gift records, event attendance information, correspondence, and news articles, needs a home. Welcome to the central filing system.

In the brief period before a nonprofit has a development program, but when the organization's leaders begin raising money, files begin to form. They are kept in the desks of the people raising the money or in nearby filing cabinets. Those files hold the first recorded history of the nonprofit itself. They tell the story of the nonprofit's founders, of the first gifts given that built the main building or funded the first programs. It is imperative that these files be kept in a central place that is accessible to those who follow those first fund raisers. If they are not kept in a central place, the nonprofit's history will be lost. And the fund raisers' efforts will be for naught.

If your nonprofit has an established filing system, you are in luck. An established system, with written policies and procedures in place, solves these problems:

- What type of information can be found in each file
- Where each file is all the time
- Where information can be found in each file
- Who has access to the files
- Who maintains the files

Your organization's filing system is likely to be the paper kind. Some large nonprofits with extensive resources have moved to electronic filing systems by adding data imaging and other technology to their options. In the years to come, these options may be available to a wider range of nonprofits. It is the most efficient form of storing files. It eliminates physical space issues, and it makes all the information in the files accessible with a few keystrokes. The information in the files is accessible to more than one person at a time. It even makes the information available to staff members when they are not in the office. And it eliminates the problem of missing or misfiled data. It requires more data entry resources, since all the materials that are not electronic have to go through the imaging process to be added to the electronic file. This means it requires greater commitment of time and money.

If you work for a small nonprofit in the beginning stages of establishing a fund-raising program, there may be no centralized filing system. If your organization does not have an established filing system, you can be the one to start it. You will be our hero, if you do. Do you hate to file as much as we do? Are you as confused by the filing systems you encounter as we are? Take heart— we will try to break out of the land of lost papers now by outlining a few simple filing tips. We will give you only the rudimentary formula for a central file. It will be up to you and your team to adapt it to your nonprofit's needs.

10 Easy Steps to a Central Filing System

We are exaggerating when we say that you can create a central filing system for your constituent, donor, and prospect files in 10 easy steps. But these basic steps might simplify the task and get you started. You will adapt these suggestions to fit your organization's characteristics. If you work with someone who is proficient at organizing materials and creating filing systems, tap into that person's wisdom to help with this project. The 10 steps are:

1. Build a house: Okay, you have to start somewhere. First, find a geographic place to keep the files. It has to be a secure place, since the in-

formation contained in the files is confidential. At the same time, it has to be accessible to the people who will need the files.

2. Check local and national laws: In chapter 2, we discussed the confidentiality policy that you, by now, have written. This is a brief reminder of that longer discussion. As you wind your way through the process of creating a central filing system, it will be important to document the policies you hope to establish and to make sure that they conform to the rules already established for your type of institution. Your state may have open record laws that affect publicly-funded organizations. As you write the filing policy, you will include who has access to the files, the procedure for sharing a file with a donor who requests access to his file, what should and should not be filed, and who has responsibility for monitoring the content of files.

3. The Name Game: Establish a process for naming files. Make rules about how to alphabetize hyphenated names and the names of foundations. Will you file the John Smith Foundation file under S or J? Decide when you will need to cross-reference files to one another. You may not need to separate information about an individual from the information about the company she owns, if the individual is your sole prospect in this mix. But, each time you make that choice, you will need to place a "dummy" or "refer to" file in the spot where file hunters will look for the corporate file. Establish a procedure for starting new files. Some file systems do not establish files for prospective donors until a critical threshold of paper for that donor is reached. You and the fund-raising team will decide what is best for your organization.

4. File what? The reports you write, the contact reports written by development officers, correspondence with the prospect, news stories, and other materials will go in each file. It will be important to check the tax regulations for your nonprofit, if the central files you establish are going to be the donor files that track your constituent's gift-giving.

5. As simple as A, B, C: An index system will get central file users to the right files quickly. It might be as uncomplicated as an alphabetical list of all the files in your system. It may be on paper or it may be electronic. You decide.

6. What's the password? Decide who needs access to the central filing system and how their use of the files will be noted. A simple "out" card procedure works well. A place card put in the spot occupied by the file notes the file name, the borrower's name, and date the file was removed.

7. File maintenance: Make a plan to review the files periodically. Files can be spot-checked to see that the right materials are getting to file and that they are being placed in the file properly. All things sent to the file must be dated, of course, with the source of the material

noted. The name of the file to which the piece of paper is intended must be placed prominently. The periodic file check can uncover errors in filing, files not being returned to the central file area within a reasonable time, and missing files for which no user card was placed.

8. Archive and disposal: When a constituent does not give, dies, or ceases to be affiliated with your organization, the constituent's file can be archived or destroyed. If a period of time that you and your team designate passes with no activity in the file—no news items, no visits, no correspondence filed—the file probably does not need to be close at hand or maybe maintained at all.

9. One for All, All for One: None of what we have written here will matter if your fund-raising team has not committed to the procedures you formulate. At each stage of the process, the fund raisers and support staff must be educated about the plan and must agree to follow it.

10. Find a mentor: Other researchers who work at nonprofits like yours will be your best resource for instructions about setting up a central filing system. You will save yourself time and increase the likelihood of getting this right the first time by collecting the good ideas of your peer researchers. Your local research group may be able to help you find just the right person. Later, when you are an ace at this, you can return the favor for another new researcher.

Simplifying the process for setting up a central filing system is not meant to be a short cut to the important decisions that must be made. We only hope that creating a handful of steps for you will prompt you to begin this important task. Your nonprofit will make a leap forward in information management when you do. You will find a sample central file procedure in the appendix section of this book.

Frequent Flyer Miles

Remember Frannie, Kayla, and Paul, the researchers at the beginning of this chapter? Those three researchers were piloting their nonprofits to new donors with the tools and resources at hand. The particular set of riches and problems they faced can shine a light on what you may encounter as you establish or improve the research function at your nonprofit. Just like these three, you will find that the size, resources, and mission of your organization will influence the course you set.

A few math formulas and a map to resources only begin the research course you are navigating. The integral pieces that will make this plan as far-reaching as its potential presages are the systems you devise for collecting and sharing information. The most important navigation you bring to your team will be the way you transform information into knowledge. The report formats, the balance of new and second-stage research, and your team's efficient access to information will set the course for the accomplishments that are next for your nonprofit's fund-raising team and donors.

Creating a
Research Plan

"Almost everyone backs into philanthropy. You don't go to college and sit in class and think to yourself, 'I want to be a philanthropist.' It's a folklore business. You learn from other people's stories."
—Jane Justis, Leighty Foundation, *The Chronicle of Philanthropy*, May 18, 2000, p. 9.

Can you guess at what point many nonprofits begin to think about prospect research? If "when they need to raise more money" popped into your head, you are right. What began as a great idea—a new art museum, a facility for homeless children, a stream reclamation effort—quickly experiences growing pains. Before the staff and volunteers know it, the nonprofit is bursting out of its donated quarters. It cannot purchase the materials and supplies it needs. Or, more fortuitously, an unexpected gift arrives. That gift is a signal that there is more support to be had, if those who founded and run this nonprofit only knew how to find it. The man who donated the building has been asked for money. The woman who arrived one day with a pickup truck full of clothes for the children has been asked for money. The soil testing company that lent equipment and resources has been asked for money. Did we ask for enough? Did we ask for too much? Who shall we ask next? Who else cares about museums or children or water?

What these nonprofits need is information. They need to know who their next big donors will be. They need to know how to find those next (or first) major gift donors. They need a way to track those donors through cultivation and the Ask. And they need a plan with which to accomplish this.

The first research plan at many nonprofits is often borne out of need. It is an informal plan—many would say that it is no plan at all. It is simply to get information, to identify a few major gift donors. That uncomplicated plan may arise during a crisis (need money, no donors). Many nonprofits begin their foray into prospect research when someone interested in gathering information joins the staff, the volunteer group, or the leadership. Or the nonprofit hires a grant writer, someone accustomed to researching foundations and corporations. Or a new donor or board member with a reputation for philanthropy emerges. That presence begs for more information. The nonprofit's fund raisers tell one another, "We could ask her for a gift, if we only knew how much to ask for."

Some nonprofits begin their relationship with research in a formal manner. They see what their peer institutions are gaining through research. It is surprising how quickly news of a new researcher in town spreads. Press releases about large gifts to a peer institution raise eyebrows. Lunch conversations among fund-raising colleagues from neighboring nonprofits include questions like "how did you know that the Fresh Water Foundation had begun giving grants in our region?" or "I see that Jane Smith gave your organization $100,000—when did she get an interest in children?" It is hard to keep something this big of a success a secret, and it may be worth touting. Yes, we hired a researcher. It is a mark of an institution reaching a new plateau in fund-raising sophistication.

Some nonprofits arrive at the decision to add research with the help of a fund-raising consultant or database screening service. Those professionals determine that the next step in the organization's growth requires a research department. In these circumstances, the evolution of the research function may be planned out in logical, incremental stages. Before the door to the new research office is unlocked, the cost of hiring a research staff, the budget for resources, and the plan for what research will accomplish are evaluated. And, paramount to the formal plan, the entire organization—including the board of directors—supports the addition of research to the fund-raising equation.

Regardless of what is pushing your organization to add research to its fund-raising effort, there are six questions to answer. We will spend this chapter posing these questions. You will have to answer them.

Here is a way to track and quantify your answers to these questions. Create a table to record the questions that follow here. Mark the top of the columns with a scoring system, like -3, -2, -1, 0 (neutral), 1, 2, 3. If you have a ready answer to a question, put the answer in a box (like "$45,000"). Each row will represent a question. Feel free to pick and choose the questions that apply to your circumstances. If, for example, space for a research department is not an issue, do not add a response or mark "0" (neutral) for that question on your table; simply do not answer that question. You get the idea. This table will help you quantify your answers as you work your way through this chapter (see Figure 10-1). You will notice that we are not inviting you to total your answers. We believe that, without needing totals, you will have a sense of what your next steps are by making yourself quantify each answer. So, make a copy of the table and mark your answers as you read through the series of questions in the next section.

	-3	-2	-1	0	1	2	3
Q1: Timing							
Campaign							
Screening							
Other Projects							
Pool Depth							
Natural Growth							
Q2: Type of Research Unit							
Freelance							
Part-time							
Full-time							
Q3: Cost of Research							
Space							
Compensation							
Training							
Equipment							
Resources							
Q4: Expectations of Research							
Research Only							
Grant Writing							
Stewardship							
Database Mgmt							
Tracking							
Other							
Q5: Research's Expectations							
Outcomes							
Advocacy							
Q6: Resources for Research							
Resource Budget							

Source: Authors

FIGURE 10-1
Decision Work Table: Adding Research to Your Nonprofit

Creating a Plan: Preliminary Decisions to Make

1. Is it the best time to add a research component to your fund-raising efforts?

This question is not answered with "only if we are ready," although there are elements in that simple answer that we will address in this chapter. This question refers to the activities of a nonprofit enhanced by a research component.

There are several periods in a nonprofit's life when prospect research is the right addition to the mix. Research is a valuable component throughout a formal fund-raising campaign, but it is the key to identifying new donors at the beginning of a campaign. By "beginning," we mean when the nonprofit's leadership begins to consider and plan for a campaign, not when the campaign is announced to the public. As we said, sophisticated nonprofits believe that almost half of the targeted amount should be raised by the time a campaign is announced publicly. Years before the first gift is booked, plans for a campaign are formulated with the organization's leadership. That is the time to decide if research can be a strong contributor to meeting the campaign goals. Your leadership can analyze the depth of your donor pool, how fresh that pool is, the number of major gifts needed to make the campaign goal, and the likelihood that a researcher can identify new prospects to make those gifts. They may conclude that research is exactly what will help the fund-raising team reach the campaign goal.

The looming fund-raising effort may not be a campaign, but it may involve raising money for a special project from a pool of potential donors that appears to be too shallow to make the goal. The effort, for example, may stem from a challenge grant offered by an individual or a foundation. Challenge grants are named aptly: They set the stage for more fund raising by making the receipt of the gift contingent upon raising money from others. So, the ABC Foundation will give your nonprofit $500,000 if you raise $500,000 from individuals by a specific date. The effort to raise money may emerge from plans for a new program or facility or other financial needs that can be met by a short, intensive fund-raising effort with the right donors and the right Asks. Prospect research can be the place to start.

Does your leadership feel that the organization is simply tapped out of donors? A young nonprofit may have yet to identify a pool of donors. An older institution may be going back to the same donors over and over again, creating donor exhaustion. In either case, nonprofits improve their donor pools by adding a prospect research component. The fundamental function of research is identifying and qualifying potential donors.

Some organizations meet the shallow pool problem by hiring a database screening service. You learned about this option in chapter 7. The results from any screening are preliminary. All good screening firms will tell you that. After the screening company parses your database of affiliates and returns results that point out individuals who are likely candidates for major gift cultivation, a prospect researcher can further qualify this information. Because many screening services use predictive modeling, the results are just that—a prediction, not a fact. Prospect research will turn this information into conclusions about which individuals in the results are actually prospects for your nonprofit—who ought to be cultivated by development. There is our old friend again, the concept that the best use of the first dollar is to raise the next dollar.

Many organizations grow rather naturally into prospect research. Remember our outlines of the evolution of a nonprofit? Remember reading early in this book that many organizations begin their first years of fund raising by soliciting foundations? Well, after that vein of gold has been tapped, successful nonprofits look for the individuals in their pool who can support the mission. The first look is usually easy. A little database mining will return individuals who have given the largest annual gifts or whose giving has been consistent, if unspectacular. With that elementary effort, the nonprofit has identified two important groups: those whose giving is noteworthy and those who give routinely. Next they ask, "Who are these people? Of the _____ (pick a number: 100, 1,000, or 10,000) possible prospects we have identified, who should we cultivate first?" Enter the researcher. The nonprofit taking this course is responding to a natural urge to grow in size, dollars raised, efficiency, and sophistication.

Now return to the table where you are scoring your responses to these questions. Mark your answers to these questions about timing, or motive, if you like.

2. What sort of research component should your nonprofit consider?

You have decided that you want to add prospect research to your fund-raising efforts. Before you consider the details of adding research, even before you consider what you can afford, you must decide what that research department might look like at your nonprofit. We ask you to design the look of research at your institution before you consider the cost of it. We want you to picture what prospect research would be if you had unlimited resources. From that picture you can carve out the research component that you can afford. By using this approach, you will get two plans: the ideal plan for research at your institution and the practical, more immediate plan that you can affect. You may think of the idealized plan as a goal for what the prospect research unit might become over the next few years.

The first decision you must make is one of duration. Is the need for prospect research immediate and short-term? Will your nonprofit need a researcher only to see it through a campaign? Or has your nonprofit reached the point where prospect research needs are ongoing? After the campaign is over or after the database screening results are analyzed, will you continue to need a researcher? Or can you imagine using a researcher for a period of time and then bringing the research effort to an end?

Let's approach this question from a couple of angles. We will begin by applying something similar to our artful approach to math. Many nonprofits use a couple of formulas to determine the shape and size of the research component they need. Here are some numbers you may either already know or that you need to know. The typical researcher in an established, well-functioning nonprofit supports five to seven full-time fund raisers. For this illustration, we will say that the typical fund raiser carries a workload in the range of 100 to 150 prospects. Of course, in reality, the number varies from institution to institution. But now you may wish to create a few math problems out of the numbers you are crunching. You know the number of potential major gift donors the screening service identified for you. You can roughly estimate the number of new prospects each development officer needs annually to maintain a full workload. With these numbers, you can project what you need a researcher to do and in what period of time this work can get done.

Once you are generating a few numbers and you have decided the long- or short-term nature of the research function you are designing, you will be able to answer the next questions that arise. Do you need to hire a full-time researcher? Will a part-time researcher be able to do everything you hope to accomplish? A research effort tied to a campaign or to qualifying the potential prospects identified in a recent screening may be short-term. Would hiring a freelance researcher meet the needs of those circumstances?

The duration or longevity of the prospect research function at your nonprofit might be hard to imagine. Keep in mind that many nonprofits are on a formal or informal cycle of campaigns, mini-campaigns, database screenings, and other efforts that call for a researcher. Further, prospect researchers are involved in much more than sorting through a single pile of potential donors. Their contribution to strategy, planning, and ongoing efforts to both qualify and set the Asks for known supporters is immeasurable.

Return to your decision table again. Mark the table with your answers about the longevity of the prospect research component you are designing. Don't worry if you are thinking about the immediate and not the long term. You can return to this exercise again later, after the pressures that are driving your nonprofit right now have eased.

3. Does your nonprofit have the money to add a prospect research component?

All of us who work in nonprofits know how important it is to be frugal, to use judiciously the resources we have, and how to accept the limitations of what is possible on the budget we are given. Adding a prospect research position is sometimes a difficult leap for a nonprofit to make. When an organization hires a fund raiser, the leadership imagines that the gifts the new fund raiser secures will more than offset the cost of adding the position. What some boards don't realize is that the same formula works with research. The first few major gift prospects a researcher identifies pay for the research position, the resources, and more. The hitch is that those prospects have to be cultivated and asked for a gift. If they are, those few gifts to your institution—maybe as few as one or two, depending on what you set as a major gift—may equal the entire cost of adding the research unit. And then there is the rest of the year of prospect identification to follow.

In regard to costs, you must consider:

- Space to house the research office: Is there room? Will you be giving space that must go to another use? Prospect research needs a quiet place. As you know, the work involves a great deal of reading. It requires an atmosphere that is conducive to completing mathematical analyses.

- Salary and benefits for the researcher: The Association of Professional Researchers for Advancement (APRA) is a good source for prospect research salary information in your area. APRA conducts surveys of its members and the surveys include the compilation of salary data. Nonprofits in your area or those with a mission similar to yours in other areas are also good sources for salary and benefits information. There are issues about the way you construct the first research position at your institution that will establish the position's veracity from the beginning. At many institutions prospect researchers are placed in the same job classification as development officers. A close examination of these issues will be valuable to your organization.

- Training expenses: Let's face it. In many localities it is difficult to hire an experienced prospect researcher. It is not uncommon for people to come to this profession from other arenas. Library workers, corporate researchers, and others find their way to prospect research. An individual new to prospect research will need immediate training. All researchers need ongoing training. Since the profession has a strong link to electronic resources and information availability is changing rapidly, researchers must have formal opportunities to learn about the latest techniques and resources in their profession.

- Equipment costs: Every experienced prospect researcher is shouting, "Give me a new computer and a faster Internet line." That simplifies the issue, but it is to the point. You may expect that a prospect researcher's electronic needs will require equipment that is updated or replaced on a more frequent schedule than their fund-raising colleagues who are, for the most part, word processing.

- Research resources: In addition to an Internet connection, a prospect researcher will have to have subscriptions to fee-based databases, CD-ROMs, directories, and other resources. This is so important that it gets its own question in this exercise.

As you analyze the costs of adding research, you may decide to formulate several plans. The first plan may answer your immediate research needs. The second plan, with a timeline, may address your organization's long-term needs for a prospect research component.

4. What will your organization expect of research?

This question is about the design of a research department that you are creating. Your answers to this question will have a significant effect on what the research department is charged with accomplishing. There is no standard set of responsibilities for researchers. Some researchers are in charge of prospect tracking. Others are in charge of database maintenance. Some researchers do a bit of grant writing and even stewardship. Some prospect researchers spend their time doing only research. Just like any job, prospect research cannot do it all. As we said, a researcher who has many non-research tasks each day will find it difficult to get to the research tasks. What tasks will your research position include? Will you use this new position to cover other (non-research) tasks that have been neglected? Will you be asking someone who is on your staff now, doing something else already, to add prospect research to his tasks?

So, the first element of defining expectations is taking a realistic approach. After you decide what duties research will have, you may wish to create production levels for the research component. Your organization may have visit quotas for development officers. You may have a schedule of proposals that your grantwriter hopes to complete in the next year. Creating a framework of expectations for the research office may be difficult, but it may help you keep that realistic approach. What are the "measurables" for researchers? Some research offices focus their production expectations on tasks like the number of profiles researched and written, the number of new prospects identified, the number of research requests completed. There are several things to keep in mind with this approach. Setting up a new research unit will take some of the time the researcher is supposed to spend producing. So will learning new skills, if your researcher is inexperienced. If you designed the research position to include non-research tasks, you will have to estimate the time the researcher actually has remaining to do research, and what priority you and your colleagues have given to the range of tasks. Is stewardship more important than research? If a proposal deadline approaches, will research time be set aside? Of course, it will, if the researcher is the proposal writer, too.

How does your decision table look now? Have you added your responses about the expectations of research you may realistically have?

5. What will research be able to expect from the fund-raising team?

It would be logical for us to tell you at this point that, if your fund-raising team is not ready to deal with the new prospects the researcher identifies, do not bother to add a research component to your fund-raising plan. But we are in search of a higher logic. We will say this to you instead: Go ahead. Add research to your program. Whether your fund raisers are ready or not, the new prospect names will come. They will come like a trickle at first. If your pool of affiliates is deep enough, they will come like a river. That in itself ought to be enough for the leadership in your organization to turn the fund-raising engine on.

Researchers get frustrated when they identify major gift prospects and those prospects are not cultivated. They should not, of course. Their initial work is finished when they have identified and qualified the prospects. They are not generally in charge of getting the fund raisers to begin cultivating the prospects. But researchers are a dedicated lot and they get excited about the new opportunities for support that they are uncovering. The corollary of excitement and dedication is frustration, unfortunately. You can help the researcher-to-be at your institution by making sure that you have enough fund raisers to need a researcher and that you have a system in place that encourages your fund raisers to manage their prospects well.

If the research section is in charge of prospect tracking and the prospect strategy meetings, they have a greater role in the management of the prospect pool. As you learned in chapter 6, some nonprofits revisit prospect assignments on a regular basis and those prospects who are languishing in the pipeline are reassigned. Some researchers are the monitors for these actions. An involvement at this level of prospect tracking often gives the research department a formal attachment to outcomes.

Who will be in charge of the research section? Who will be the researcher's boss? Everyone needs an advocate, including research. As the function of research at your institution grows, the budget will need to be increased. The demands on the research department may grow in complexity and volume. Everyone needs someone to help them stay on track, to monitor the expectations and the realities of work. Is there someone who can readily add overseeing the research function to his duties?

6. What resources will the prospect research unit have?

This question is inseparable from both the budget question and the expectations question. We have it standing alone here because it is often overlooked. It stands alone because we want you to envision the resources your newly hired researcher will need to find and qualify the prospects that your fund raisers will develop into donors.

Throughout this book we have discussed what researchers use to find information. Some of the things are already available at your nonprofit. Your database of affiliates, your central files, and other in-house tools are the beginnings of resources for researchers. But they are only the beginnings. For a researcher to identify the next major gift donors to your institution effectively and efficiently, that researcher will need tools. Some of them may be available at the local public library. Some of the ones that must be purchased are low-cost. Some of them can be acquired in stages. Some of the tools researchers need are expensive.

It is unrealistic to ask a researcher to meet the expectations of your nonprofit—whatever they are—without tools. So, while you are making a plan to add a researcher, plan to add an annual budget for resources. Your peer institutions will be the best source for guidance about what a preliminary budget should be. They can provide a list of "first resources" the research department will need to begin work. This is a good initial task to assign to the researcher you hire. In researching the resources needed, the researcher will have an opportunity to make contact with his colleagues at other nonprofits. He will also get a range of opinions about the value of particular resources. That will be useful when it is time to buy resources.

There are few research departments that have every single resource they need. Some of the big universities have most of the resources small nonprofits dream of, but even researchers at those institutions will tell you about this or that new product they wish they had. While the researcher you hire researches what is available, he can begin building a "wish list," a list of the products that he may lobby for in later stages of the growth of this new department. When you design the research resources budget, it would be useful to plan one, two, and three year increases, since the productivity of both the research department and the fund raisers will be increasing at a similar rate.

The Internet Myth (a Myth for a Few More Minutes Anyway)

Many small nonprofits are attracted to the idea of hiring a researcher because of "this Internet thing." What is the Internet thing? It is the myth that everything anyone wants to find is on the Internet. You would think that, with billions of Web pages, this would be true. It is not true. Not yet, that is. There is plenty of useful information on the Internet that a skilled researcher will find. But there is information that can be found only in books and directories, particularly historical data. Some information is not available for free on the Internet, but can be purchased for a relatively small fee. Information-for-a-fee seems to be an Internet trend. You can expect that trend to grow, so you will have to plan your information retrieval budget accordingly.

Do not create a research department with the idea that all the researcher will need is a computer with a fast Internet connection. We give you fair warning that a resource budget that only includes access to the Internet will be inadequate. This is true for all nonprofits, but it is particularly true for nonprofits whose affiliates are locally based, and who are not the prominent people featured in newspaper stories or found at the very top of company hierarchies.

What does your decision table look like now? Is it full of boxes with notations? Are there plenty of 2s and 3s? Are there areas sporting negative numbers? Use the table to give yourself an overall impression of your organization's readiness for a researcher. Use the table to get a sense of what areas need changes before a researcher can be effectively added to the fundraising team. And, finally, use the table as a tool to formulate your plan for promoting research to the rest of the leadership at your nonprofit.

How to Hire a Prospect Researcher

The time has come. You are ready to hire a prospect researcher. The ideal candidate for the job will be able to leap tall buildings . . . oh, wait, that is a different job description. The researcher you hire will, ultimately, be able to do prospect research. That is the most important aptitude the individual will bring to the job. It is entertaining to hear all the ways research managers and development directors have devised to screen applicants for prospect research jobs. Since there is no formal training that leads to this position, the folks who call themselves prospect researchers come from all sorts of backgrounds. They share several qualities though, and that is what those who do the hiring try to ferret out. These qualities include an extraordinary sense of organization, curiosity, strong writing skills, an analytical mind, adequate math skills, and the ability to evaluate information quickly to extract what is valuable.

Those who hire researchers often create research and writing opportunities for the job interview. Some of us were asked to review a stack of papers about prominent individuals and then write summaries of what we had learned during a 15-minute period in our prospect research job interviews. Other researchers were asked what magazines they read, what sections of the newspaper interest them, and what hobbies command their time. We have not heard about prospective researchers being asked what they think about the designated hitter rule or whether Elvis is really dead, but it would not surprise us. These questions are all designed to reveal a person with a lust for information who can dissect and reassemble data into a meaningful story and who can analyze information and form a responsible opinion.

It is common to hear that those hiring researchers have difficulty in finding applicants with experience in this profession. It is a small and growing field, so there are few people with the depth of skill that you might hope to find for your organization. It may be necessary to hire someone who has done one or more pieces of the prospect research job in another career and then get training for your new hire.

If you need help creating a job description for a prospect researcher, contact nonprofits with a mission or size that is similar to your nonprofit's and ask them to share their research job description with you. Many will also share the researcher's salary range with you. For sample job descriptions, go to the files on the PRSPCT-L Web site, where you will find sample job descriptions posted by researchers. You may find guidance about salaries and other issues by contacting the Association of Professional Researchers for Advancement (APRA) for its salary survey results. You will find directions for getting to both of these resources in the appendix.

With or Without a Researcher: Creating a Plan for Research

Once you have made a plan for adding research to your nonprofit's fund-raising efforts, you will sit back with your feet up on your desk and wait for the big gifts to pour in, right? Actually, quite the opposite is true. Adding research to the fund-raising effort will create more work for everyone. In turn, there will be more gifts, without a doubt. But roll up your sleeves, because there is plenty to do.

You can choose from a buffet of plans for what your research component will accomplish. Any plan you devise must consider whether you have hired a full-time researcher and what non-research tasks you have given the researcher. We will outline two plans here. We will consider whether you hired a researcher, but we will not be considering that the person you hired has been assigned non-research tasks. As you know by now, we do not really approve of giving researchers too many things to do that are not, well, research. We know that a researcher can be busy enough just trying to manage the information flow, turning it into something useful to securing major gifts. We also know that the real value in prospect research is realized only when researchers research. If you have elected to hire a researcher, you may already know who will be doing research, and you have probably devised a schedule of when that research will get done. If you have not, believe us, no research will get done. Everything else will always come first. Maintaining the status quo is easier than moving into the future, right? But it is not better.

One of the plans we outline here is casual and the other is formal. You will notice that elements of the two plans overlap. You will be able to use these plans to build a research plan that suits your nonprofit.

Plan One: Foraging

The foraging plan sets a goal simply to find new prospects or qualify known prospects for your nonprofit. This may not even mean adding a full-time, professional researcher at first. That is not ideal, but it is all too common and so it is workable. You or one of your colleagues may be the person who has demonstrated an interest in looking for information. If this describes the situation at your nonprofit, there is good news. You have a research plan and you did not even realize it. It is a plan to get some prospect research done, even just a little bit. It is a plan that will work like foraging for berries. You will meander on a path you have to clear yourself. Sometimes you will find what you are looking for and sometimes you will not. Sometimes you will not even find a path. But a bit of research will get done. Everyone will be excited about what you or your staff member or the freelance researcher you hire finds.

In this plan, you may have a very small research budget. Even with a researcher, you may be limited in what tools you can provide. Despite these drawbacks, you can establish a plan for what the research function will accomplish. The plan may be as simple as this:

- Use the resources in this book to establish a system for reporting what the researcher finds. Use profile forms or design a simple way to record and file the information found.
- Create a set of rules (procedures) for information-seekers at your nonprofit, including a confidentiality and ethics policy.
- Set a target goal for the number of prospects that the person doing research will identify or qualify in a specific period. For example, you may decide that two new prospects will be identified and qualified each month. That means the researcher will move two new prospects into position in the pipeline.
- Track the work accomplished by research. This information will come in handy later, when you want to demonstrate to the board of directors why they should authorize more money for research.

Plan Two: Farming

You have hired a full-time researcher. The researcher has set up the research department; she has purchased resources, carved out a workspace, and reviewed the access of the central file and database resources. You are farming in rows, heading with determination for the harvest. The next steps in this plan are:

- Establish systems: Add research forms for profiles and other reports to the plan.
- Add standards for informational retrieval, including a policy of confidentiality and central file procedures.
- Establish research procedures. Make a plan for the return on research requests. Some research departments further qualify research requests by the depth of research and the time required to complete the task. For example, a full profile may take a day to complete. Development officers should know when they can expect an answer to their research requests.
- Set up a way to track the prospects that research identifies by using some form of a cultivation pipeline.
- Outline core projects and set timelines. If you recently completed a database screening, you have a ready pool for the researcher to begin

qualifying. If you do not have a ready pool, the researcher can begin creating one.

- Develop a calendar of annual reports that will require research. Many organizations have events that occur each year. Now that you have a researcher, you may wish the researcher to review the event attendance lists. The researcher will be able to pick out major gift prospects who are attending the event. Nonprofits fold researchers into the trustee process. A researcher can make trustee recommendations or simply research and write profiles on trustee candidates.

- Invite the researcher to attend (or lead) the prospect strategy meetings. Once the researcher is gathering information about prospects and donors, he will be one of your best contributors when it comes to strategizing plans for cultivations and Asks.

- Track progress. Keep a record of research reports, profiles written, new prospects identified, and whatever else you want to be able to measure later. This will be important when you wish to expand the research department or its resources.

- Leave room for rows of flowers. By this we mean leave time in the schedule you are creating for the researcher to just do pure research. As we have said, many refer to this as proactive research. This is research that does not begin with a research request or a scheduled report. It is research from the pool of prospects or from the daily uncoverings that come the researcher's way by reading newspapers, magazines and other materials. It is the kind of research that often yields the best prospects. All of the elements we have discussed in this book come together in the kind of research that is actively seeking out prospects.

Forage or Farm, You are Harvesting a Crop (of Prospects)

Which path you take to add research to your nonprofit's fund-raising efforts will be directed by your organization's financial resources, its readiness to accept and support research, the immediacy of the need to identify and qualify prospects, and other factors. Here is our best advice: Take a path. Either one will move your organization ahead. Make a plan to add research to your fund-raising efforts. If you do, the success that comes to your nonprofit in the possibility—and the actuality—of new gifts will be significant. A plan to forage will, almost without exception, lead to a plan to farm before you know it. The prospects found, even in a casual or part-time research effort, will expand the depth and reach of your fund raising. Those first few prospects will become an indelible sign of the value of research to your nonprofit. A day will come when you will wonder what you ever did without prospect research in your organization's fund-raising equation.

Development and Research: Living in the Development World

"The most successful person in the first half of the next century will be the storyteller. The value of future products will depend on the story he tells."
—Alf Nucifora, *Puget Sound Business Journal,* June 26, 1999, p. 19.

Prospect researchers who work at large institutions can tell you about the organizational charts at their nonprofits. The levels of administrative leadership and their work groups unfold like a family tree. Prospect research is often a few branches out from the trunk, a second or even third generation cousin in the family of fund raisers.

The prospect research branch on the organizational tree might be headed by someone who began as a researcher. It is often led by someone who holds a variety of skills, an assortment of those you have been reading about in this book. The head of research may be in charge of the constituent database, stewardship, gift processing, or any combination of these branches of the fund-raising tree. The head of research is, in a sense, a Jill- or Jack-of-all-trades. Regardless of which fund-raising tasks besides research were placed on that branch of the tree, our Jack or Jill must know a lot about all fund-raising duties and goals. As you learned in chapter 1, prospect research touches upon all of them. Do all the branches know a lot about prospect research? No, they do not. Many in the fund-raising family wave their arms like magic wands when talking about prospect research. They deem us with the powers of Merlins. In the meantime, researchers have to know precisely how everything else in fund raising is working, where information being gathered is going, how it is getting there, and what happens next. Those details are a part of what makes our jobs function well.

Here is the odd thing. While prospect research does not sit close to the trunk of that fund-raising tree, it often holds an important role in shaping the tree's growth. This influence goes well beyond identifying new prospects or keeping the team informed about known prospects. It often reaches into the pace and scope of the fund-raising effort. It reaches into the established procedures for moving information and for sharing information with one another and with volunteers. Prospect research touches several branches of fund raising.

We think of research's influence as quiet leadership. The placement of the research section on the organizational chart may not always reflect that leadership, but it is occurring nonetheless. Let's look at the places where it happens and how you will nurture the role of research at your nonprofit.

Establishing Policies and Procedures

Information is on the move. It never stands still. It does not lie on one desk or computer screen for long. If it does, it is on the verge of being lost forever. Information is valuable when it is linked to other bits of information, analyzed, and then shared.

Everyone on the fund-raising team has a chance to collect new information almost every day. From the return address details that appear on an envelope, to wedding and death news from the newspaper, to a prospect's promotion, information is passing from one location to another. That return address has to get to the data entry worker so a constituent record can be updated. The wedding report goes to data entry, too, and probably to the central files. That news may change a suspect or prospect's placement on the priority list. The news may need to reach a development officer if the individual is or was an assigned prospect. The job change notice is shared with data entry. If the promotion made the individual a chief corporate officer, research ought to hear about it. If the nonprofit's grant writer is tracking the prospect's company, the news that your nonprofit now has someone of influence at that company must reach that grant writer. News can change solicitation plans. All of this news must get to research; it is likely that most of it opens an opportunity to gather and analyze new information about these prospects.

None of the paths that information takes in this example happen without policies and procedures. How will we differentiate policy from procedure? Policy is the opinion. Procedures are the step-by-step actions that cause adherence to a policy. Let's think of procedures as the *who, where, when,* and *how* and policies as the *why* of any distinct event or process.

There are few development team members who innately realize that the chain of information only remains intact and effective if the information moves to the right places. Who will be concerned about how information moves about the entire fund-raising team? Each development officer is interested in his own prospect list, for the most part. That is enough to manage. The data entry and gift processing teams are busy with the constant flood of paper coming their way. But there is one team member who understands that the even flow of information, particularly that related to the identification and qualification of prospects, benefits everyone. It is research.

Research often writes—or suggests—the information flow policies and procedures. Research outlines where new constituent information needs to go (to file and to the data entry people, for example). Research wants to know why a never-heard-of foundation gave our nonprofit a gift of $5,000 this week. Is it a matching gift in recognition of one constituent? Were those two records—the foundation's and the individual's—linked on the database when this gift was recorded? Is it a gift from a newly established foundation, one set up by a constituent or her family? Research is interested in the information getting to the files of the family members and in making sure that the family members and the foundation are linked in the database.

Research is interested in the particulars about the database, in fact. How is the database being used? Are there features of the database that would help research? Are there tracking or information-housing elements that are not being used? Why? Is it a staffing issue or is it the bad habit of not incorporating those features into a way of operating?

These are a few elementary examples of how research is connected to the paths that information takes through the fund-raising team. As you can see, you will construct these paths with the policies and procedures you write. The paths have a chance to be well tended and used, beyond the presence of one or two key people at the nonprofit, if they are mapped. In the writing, each task gets a person or job duty attached to it. Whether the proper transfer and recording of information happens is no longer left up to a whim or one person's dogged pursuit. The policies and procedures become the interest of the entire team, the individuals here today and those who will be here in the future. The policies and procedures are institutionalized, and that is a good thing. Here are a few procedures and policies that the research section may write, review, facilitate, or augment. The creation and use of each is essential to a high-functioning research unit.

Central File Policies and Procedures: We outlined a basic approach to creating a central filing system in chapter 9. We have talked about the confidentiality and access issues that must be addressed with a policy. We have sketched a basic approach to filing and indexing. After the central file design is created, each step has to be written and shared with anyone sending things to or taking things out of the central files. Who has access to the files will even be a part of the written policies. A process for monitoring adherence to the procedures will be designed and implemented. It, too, will be written. All of these tasks will be assigned to individuals, to positions, within the fund-raising team. Each section of the development team will have input about these procedures. It will be important for each member of the team to understand how the filing system works and how they can support its smooth operation. It is likely that the research section will have a lead role in creating these procedures. You will find a sample central file procedure in the appendix section.

Data Entry Procedures: Updating and maintaining constituent records accurately are the first steps in an effort to stay in touch with constituents. And, in case we forgot, constituents who do not hear from us may forget to give to our nonprofits. The procedures created for data entry will establish how new information about constituents is added. They will outline who passes what information where. The data entry procedures will be linked to the capabilities of the nonprofit's database. How contact information is written and abbreviated, how many addresses can be kept electronically for each constituent, and how the addresses are updated and from what sources are only a few of the details that will be outlined in data entry procedures.

You may remember that we said the database and the data entry staff are often under the domain of the same person who is managing the research section. Why? Data entry and research seem to be wedded to one another from the start of their relationship in fund raising. The growth of prospect research paralleled the advances in database technology. These two areas of the fund-raising effort are distinctly technological, in ways that other areas are not. The research section has an effect on constituent records, and the database workers have an effect on the progress of research. Research is managing an unending trail of information about constituents and can only do so when the first bits of information about those constituents are entered accurately and updated in a consistent manner.

Gift Processing Procedures: The gift processing section needs detailed procedures for recording gifts received by the nonprofit. These procedures will be responsive to tax reporting and other requirements as well as to the ways that the fund-raising team will want to retrieve gift information. In order to analyze giving, the information must be retrievable in many ways. For example, all foundation gifts must be linked to the individuals in whose name the gifts are given. The same holds true for matching gifts given by companies. Nonprofits refer to hard and soft credit for gifts. Hard credit is credit given for a gift actually received from a constituent. Soft credit recognizes gifts given by other entities in the name of the constituent. The other entity gets the hard credit and the constituent in whose name the gift is given gets the soft credit. Details like this have to be outlined in written procedures that are consistently followed. It becomes nearly impossible to backtrack to fix errors made due to a failure of procedure.

The research section is looking at donors who give gifts, measuring details like the size of the gifts, the consistency of giving, and to what specific causes the gifts are given. Another detail for researchers is *how* the gift is given. Was it a pledge? Was it a gift-in-kind? Donors who have foundations are particularly interesting to researchers. Donors with foundations offer researchers an easy opportunity to gauge the size and the direction of an individual's philanthropy. As you have learned, foundations spell out what causes they support and report the size of the gifts they have given in previous years. By reviewing daily or weekly gift reports, a researcher can see the names of the new foundations giving to the nonprofit. Another way to see those gifts is to pull a database report of foundation gifts given over a specific period of time. This example of the link between foundations and individuals illustrates one significant feature of the steps in processing gifts. There are many more steps that written procedures will outline.

Research Procedures: What draws the time and attention of researchers? Prospects and everything about them consume researchers. Every stage of identifying, qualifying, documenting, and assigning prospects will require written procedures. How fund raisers request information about prospects will be a good example of the written procedures that will serve both the researcher and the fund-raising team. Research offices that delineate the timeline to fill research requests by the complexity of the tasks will spell out those details in written procedures. Full profiles, a complex financial analysis, a file review, or brief update each become distinct research jobs with their own timelines. Requests may be further prioritized by other factors like the backlog of other requests. Fund raisers asking for additional research can be realistic about when their request will be filled when timelines and complexity issues are outlined in written procedures.

The way constituents are added to or dropped from the pool of potential prospects will be a part of the research procedures. If prospect tracking is in research's domain to oversee, and it frequently is, the procedure for beginning a tracking module for a prospect will be outlined in the procedures.

How will freshly identified prospects become assigned prospects at your organization? New prospects might be assigned by region, by gift capacity, or by other characteristics like age, links to other constituents, or specific affinities to your organization. There is no rule about how prospects are assigned. Each organization will choose a way to assign new prospects that works well for the composition and budget of its development team, the structure of the team's management, and the demographics of the constituency.

There are other issues about assigning new prospects. You may not be surprised to hear that development officers have been known to vie for prospects. The development team manager will design a procedure for equalizing the assignment loads in regard to the number and type of prospects assigned to each development officer, keeping in mind any other duties that the fund raisers have. For example, fund raisers who are in charge of the planned giving program at an organization frequently carry a smaller prospect load. They have additional duties like complex stewardship, proposal writing, and a direct mail program to run that other development officers do not have. Some of these procedures may fall under the prospect tracking procedures, depending upon who is in charge of the tasks. Nevertheless, research-reporting procedures, the management of the suspect pool, and the way new prospects are identified and assigned will all be addressed in the procedures written.

Annual Fund Solicitation Policy: You know our opinion that we researchers do not pay much attention to annual fund prospects. Well, that is partially true. We are interested in annual fund donors who give major gift-sized gifts to the annual fund. We actually pay attention to annual fund donors giving gifts at a size that is a portion of a major gift, if the major gift were given over a few years. Each institution sets the threshold for when annual fund gifts ought to attract the attention of research. They set this threshold by looking at the range of gifts typically received and then naming what is an *atypical* gift. Are $100 to $200 gifts received often, but $500 to $1,000 gifts to the annual fund are somewhat rare? That establishes the threshold for the gifts research notices.

Who asks for annual fund gifts at your nonprofit and how high can they go? If you have a phonathon crew or volunteer solicitors, are they permitted (following our example of a large annual fund gift) to ask for $1,000 gifts? Do annual fund volunteers ask for gifts larger than $1,000? Do solicitation letters include the check-box option to give $1,000? Following our example, you can see that it will be important for research to know these details about the annual fund. Many institutions create donor clubs. In some locales, United Way's Alexis de Tocqueville Society identifies constituents who give $10,000 or more so that they are recognized in donor rolls as members of that giving group.

The giving clubs or groups, the solicitation levels for volunteers and others, and even the frequency of mailings and other contacts should be documented in written procedures. The major gifts program and prospect research can then assess the response to those solicitations. There are other reasons to document the nonprofit's approach to the annual fund. The annual fund campaign seems to be under close examination for improvements almost every year. By writing a standard approach that can serve as a baseline, the success of new approaches can be measured accurately.

Prospect Tracking Procedures: Constituents who become assigned prospects begin a new relationship with the development team. Each stage of the cultivation that began with the assignment will be recorded. That is the point of prospect tracking, after all. There may be details like the timing of the changes in status, the plans for the solicitation, or the way volunteers are folded into and prepared for a solicitation that the development team wants to standardize. You already learned about expectations for the time that a prospect will spend in each stage of the pipeline. These details will form the core of the prospect tracking procedures.

Development teams offer new employees a clear set of expectations when they have written procedures for the steps (and even methods) in moving a prospect through the stages of the tracking process. Many of these stages will affect the research section, too. When an assigned prospect is dropped from tracking, the reason for the change must be documented. Knowing (or being able to discover later) why a prospect's status changed helps research make important decisions when the prospect's name emerges as a possible assignment again, when financial or other circumstances change. Creating a form (or an electronic process) for recording changes in a prospect's status and the reason for the change will be a valuable tool for both the research section and the fund-raising team.

Fund-Raising Procedures: In a broader sense, the leaders of the fund-raising team will create procedures for the development officers. These procedures will cover expectations about writing contact reports, visiting prospects, writing cultivation plans, and attending events. They will include many other activities in the domain of development. By now you know how important promptly filed contact reports are to researchers. Establishing written expectations for each of these duties removes any confusion or debate.

Procedures Spell Relief

Great freedom reigns with the creation of policies and procedures. Staff members no longer have to wonder how to handle specific situations. It is as if an organization has received an antidote. The chronic discussions that ask those present to reinvent a course of action each time a new employee joins the team are over. The helter-skelter way that information is sent to file (or not), recorded in the database (or not), and shared with members of the team (or not) is over. The time it takes for each member of the team to write the procedures for their section is small when compared to the time wasted finding lost bits of data or missed opportunities with prospects because information did not get to the right place. Do not neglect to give yourself and your fund-raising team this gift of freedom.

In addition to its role in the establishment or enhancement of policies and procedures, prospect research's influence will be found in other unexpected areas of fund raising. Several of these areas are related to growth and performance. They are feasibility studies, starting a major gifts program, campaigns, and special fund-raising efforts like planned giving.

Feasibility Studies

Nonprofits sometimes stall and sputter. They reach a plateau, a point where things stay the same and where the amount of money raised remains unchanged. The organization's leadership realizes that, if things stay the same, there is little chance in expanding programs and services. Ultimately, an organization stalled on a plateau runs the risk of slipping backward. It is not a very big step from "staying the same" to "doing less."

But a nonprofit's leadership cannot always decipher what is causing the stall without help from someone who can look in from the outside. That someone will often be a consultant, usually someone with extensive experience in nonprofit development. The consultant might be a former development director, an agency president, a fund raiser, a grant maker, or a screening company owner or employee. The consultant can evaluate the dynamics of the nonprofit's fund-raising efforts. Taking a measurement of the nonprofit's functions, and holding those measures up to comparable institutions may help the leadership move toward new approaches.

The consultant may arrive at the nonprofit during a period that is not a plateau but, instead, a time of vigorous growth. In this phase the nonprofit has new initiatives to enact, buildings to construct, and programs to begin. How to fund those new initiatives, programs, and buildings is the question that the consultant will address. An analysis of the fund-raising process, the donor pool, and the processes used to get annual and major gifts will give the nonprofit's leadership a complete picture of what needs to happen next.

In a most basic sense, that evaluation and measure of a nonprofit's performance and the recommendation about what ought to happen next are the primary elements of a feasibility study. A feasibility study may be defined as the analysis of a specific goal that the nonprofit's leadership wishes to reach. The consultant helps the leadership determine if the goal is attainable and may recommend the course to take to reach it or may recommend a different goal.

Research Looks at Feasibility

It is likely that any fund-raising feasibility study will have a significant impact on the prospect research division. Has there ever been a feasibility study that did not call for the identification of new prospects? Has a consultant ever told a nonprofit that the pool of prospects is adequate and well cultivated? One probably has, but we have not heard about it. Consultants and feasibility studies rarely amount to "well child" checkups for a nonprofit. Whatever the conclusions made by the consultant who visits your nonprofit, prospect research can be in a good position to help with the analysis and to help meet the consultant's recommendations with new initiatives. By keeping track of all the research requests, the new prospects identified, the event preparation reports written, and the other research projects completed, you will have a ready set of statistics to share with your nonprofit's leadership and the consultant. You learned about this in chapter 9 when we discussed keeping a research log.

If you are asked to participate in discussions with the consultant, you will be able to share information about how long it takes to identify and qualify new prospects and to complete other research tasks. You will be able to outline the ongoing chores that the research section is performing. These measures, statistics, and reports will clearly define the role of prospect research at your organization. This will be invaluable to the consultant who is trying to get an accurate idea about the way that fund raising occurs at your nonprofit. It will give the consultant a better chance to reliably predict what is feasible for your nonprofit.

Beginning a Major Gifts Program

You may be reading this book because your organization is beginning a major gifts program. Your leadership may be soliciting large gifts from a small group of donors, but everyone realizes how haphazard that effort has been. Hiring a director of development is on the horizon. If you have read the earlier chapters here, you know what we will say next. That development team your new director hires will have a tough time soliciting major gifts if they do not have major gift prospects to cultivate. Prospect research is now too sophisticated an operation to expect someone to squeeze it in among other duties.

The design for the new fund-raising program at your nonprofit must include a prospect research component. Yes, there are nonprofits raising money without a researcher. Are they raising the real potential in their donor base? No, they are not. They do not even know what that is. Organizations that have hired a consultant or an electronic screening firm usually hear about prospect research. There are donors in the pool of constituents that research will help you locate. Do not miss the chance to meet them by failing to invite research to the team.

Campaigns

When an organization has a goal to raise a specified amount of money for named purposes in a prescribed amount of time, it is conducting a fund-raising campaign. While the amount of money that is raised annually will be included in the campaign total (and it actually is a campaign in itself each year), the development team will be making an extra effort throughout the campaign to raise large gifts to meet the campaign goal. In other words, the campaign goal will be more than what the nonprofit can be expected to raise each year. We outlined formulas for determining campaign goals in chapter 7.

Prospect research is the starting point for many campaigns. Do we have the donor pool we need to hit the targeted goal? Do we know who can give the first large or lead gifts? Do we know enough about the capacity of those top donors? Can we find more prospects throughout the campaign? Can the research section keep the development team well stocked with new prospects as others on their list move into stewardship after gifts are received? We discussed the campaign gift table and a campaign's need for identified and qualified prospects earlier, so you know how critical these numbers become during campaign planning.

The high energy and clear motivation of a campaign wanes if the fund-raising team finds that they are unable to fulfill their goals. Careful planning that includes a close review of research's potential to identify and qualify prospects is a good starting point for any campaign.

Planned Giving

It may seem odd that we have set one division of fund-raising distinctly apart like this. There is good reason to do so. Throughout this book we have discussed gifts that a nonprofit receives from a major gift prospect at the end of a cultivation period. The donor gives the gift; the nonprofit receives the gift, and technically, the giving relationship (for that gift) is over. The stewardship relationship begins. The nonprofit maintains the donor's constituent relationship. These types of gifts, the ones where the donor's financial interest in the gift ends with the giving, are known as outright gifts.

There are other ways to make a gift. Some gifts even take a lifetime to give. These gifts involve extensive planning to execute. They are gifts that take a great deal of thought and careful consideration of one's financial plan. One planned giving expert points out that every gift except the coin tossed into a kettle during the holidays fits this definition. The distinction for most of the gifts we will examine now is that they include a period of waiting for the nonprofit, with one exception. During the waiting, the nonprofit will maintain a close relationship with the donor as the gift is anticipated and unfolds over many years.

Headline: Donor Gives Local Nonprofit a Strip Mall

Therese had a successful career as a professional soccer player. For about 10 years she has been involved with a nonprofit called Girl Power, a social service agency offering at-risk teenage girls tutoring, athletic, and self-esteem programs. Therese is crazy about this nonprofit. She has volunteered as a tutor, funded a soccer camp, and she is now serving as a trustee for Girl Power. Therese has two grown sons, and they are also successful professional athletes. Therese is single now, but has several nieces, nephews, and friends who she will remember in her estate plans.

Therese bought a strip mall about 15 years ago. The strip mall has been a successful investment and now Therese is thinking about giving the mall to Girl Power. How will she choose to give this gift? She may:

1. Sell the strip mall and give Girl Power the proceeds from the sale. After Therese gives Girl Power the cash from the sale, her interest in this particular gift will be finished.

2. Give the strip mall itself to Girl Power and leave it to the nonprofit to sell or manage it. Therese's dealings with this gift will be finished when she signs the title over to Girl Power.

3. Give the income from the strip mall to Girl Power. Therese can send the check from the income to Girl Power each year or she can put the income in another investment (an annuity, a trust, a life insurance policy) and designate Girl Power as the beneficiary (see Nos. 5–7).

4. Name Girl Power in her will as the beneficiary of the strip mall at the time of her death.

5. Set up an irrevocable remainder trust (a unitrust) using the strip mall as the asset that funds the trust and name Girl Power as the trust's beneficiary. At the time of Therese's death, Girl Power will receive the remainder in the trust. During her lifetime, Therese (or whomever she names—it could even be Girl Power) receives a percentage of the value of the trust on a regular basis.

6. Set up a gift annuity, which will pay a fixed amount to Therese or her designee during her life and will give Girl Power the remainder at the time of Therese's death.

7. Establish a lead trust, either an annuity or a unitrust, using the strip mall as the asset that funds the annuity. Girl Power will get a fixed amount or a percentage of the value of the lead gift on a regular basis. At the end of the gift (a designated term or the donor's life) the beneficiary named by Therese (or Therese herself) will receive the remainder.

Therese has many choices about the way she gives this gift to Girl Power. How will she decide? What features about each gift should she consider in her decision? Luckily, Girl Power has a planned giving officer who can help Therese choose the best way—the way that maximally benefits Therese and the charity—to support Girl Power with this wonderful gift.

Outright or Deferred Gifts

The gifts described in numbers 3 through 7, those gifts for which a nonprofit waits, are called deferred gifts. The nonprofit's access to and use of these gifts is suspended until a future point in time. Features about each gift define when that time is, but these gifts can easily be separated into two groups: those gifts that are revocable and those that are irrevocable (see Figure 11-1).

Revocable Gifts

Revocable gifts are those that a donor can rescind. They are promises of gifts and, like all promises, these promises can be taken back. Bequests and beneficiary designation gifts, such as life insurance policies, are examples of revocable gifts. When a donor names a nonprofit as the beneficiary of a life insurance policy or for a gift in the donor's will, the donor retains the option to change the direction of the gift. The donor can, in fact, change whether the gift is a gift at all. If Therese thinks her passion about Girl Power may change or that she will need full control over the strip mall's income or disposal in the future, a revocable gift is a good idea.

Bequests: Bequests are after-death gifts. A bequest is made when a donor names a nonprofit in her will, for a specific portion of the estate or for the entire estate. An estate is all property (real and personal property), stocks, and cash owned by an individual at the time of her death. Estates are both large and small. Bequests may name several entities, including several nonprofits, which will divide the estate. The division will be outlined in detail

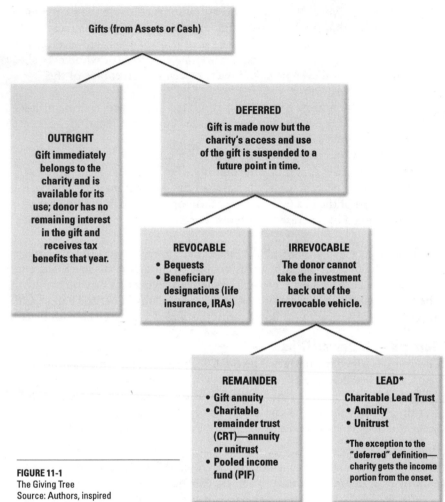

FIGURE 11-1
The Giving Tree
Source: Authors, inspired
by Steve McGlone

in the will. Most estates are liquidated—that is, the property is sold and all assets are converted to cash—before distribution of the estate is considered to be complete when nonprofits are among the beneficiaries. Some bequests are only realized after the demise of other survivors. If Therese gives the strip mall to charity in her will, it is a bequest.

Beneficiary Designations: In much the same way that a bequest works, a donor can name a nonprofit as the beneficiary of a life insurance policy or an investment retirement account. As you know, the designation for these assets can be changed at any time. If Therese turns the income from the strip mall into a beneficiary designation (say, an insurance policy), she will retain the power to change the designee, Girl Power, to another charity or to her nieces, nephews, and friends. She can also simply cancel the policy or shift its assets to another investment, removing it from consideration as a gift.

Most nonprofits do not count bequests and beneficiary designations as gift until the donor has died and the proceeds are transferred to the charity. They may count the gift in their bequest expectancy list and will include the prospect in their planned giving cultivations and stewardship efforts, but the gift has not been made to the nonprofit yet.

Irrevocable Gifts

Irrevocable gifts are those that must stay charitable gifts, no matter what change of heart a donor suffers. Depending on how the agreement is written, a donor may retain the right to change which charity will receive the gift, but the donor may not remove the gift from the domain of philanthropy. In exchange for giving up control of the gift, the donor gets tax benefits.

Irrevocable Gifts: Remainder or Lead

There are two types of irrevocable gifts. Charitable remainder gifts, gift annuities, and pooled income gifts are referred to as life income gifts because they create an income, an amount of money, that a donor or charity receives each year. Lead trusts provide payments to the charity, typically for a fixed period of years.

Remainders

A remainder gift offers a donor the chance to set cash or an asset in an investment vehicle and receive a prescribed return from it. The donor or other beneficiary receives a periodic check and also receives income tax benefits.

Charitable Remainder Trust: A charitable remainder trust (CRT) is an investment vehicle that provides the donor or the donor's designee with a percentage of the value of the trust or a fixed dollar amount on a regular schedule. The trust continues to grow under good management and, at the time of the income beneficiary's death, the charity receives the remainder. A nonprofit plans that the payment the donor receives comes from the trust's total return. A charitable remainder trust is managed by a trustee, who may or may not be the nonprofit. The trustee manages the asset, makes the payments to the donor, and distributes the remainder in the end. Therese can use the strip mall to establish a charitable remainder trust. If she is concerned about her retirement income, a remainder trust might be attractive to her. When she establishes the charitable remainder trust, she will not be able to alter the trust's ultimate destination to charity. However, if the agreement is written to give Therese the ability to change the specific charity, Therese may choose to leave the remainder to Girl Power or to change the recipient to another charity. If the agreement does not leave Therese with this control, Girl Power will receive the remainder after Therese dies.

Gift Annuity: A gift annuity is a contract between a donor and a charity. The donor receives a specific return each year, not a percentage of the value of the asset set aside. The remainder at the end of the income beneficiary's life goes to the charity. The set annual amount might be just what Therese wants to augment her retirement income. Therese is unlikely to choose this option, unless the income from the strip mall is enough to make the annuity payment.

Pooled Income Fund: A pooled income fund (PIF) is a giving vehicle for donors who have little to give or amounts below the levels found in CRTs and annuities. The donor's gift is added to a larger investment vehicle. The PIF is usually established with a minimum amount for initial entry and annual or incremental minimums. Since Therese's gift is real estate, she will not be interested in a pooled income fund.

Lead Gifts

The exception to the "deferred" concept, the idea that a nonprofit waits for the gift, is a lead gift. In this scenario, the nonprofit receives the income each year and the donor (or the donor's designee) waits, getting the remainder of the gift when the lead gift ends. Lead gifts are usually a term of years.

Charitable Lead Trust: A charitable lead trust may be a unitrust, with a percentage of the trust's value paid to the charity on a scheduled basis, or an annuity lead, with a fixed payment to the charity on that schedule. If Therese chooses this option, Girl Power will receive either a specific amount of money or a percentage of the value of the trust each year. At the end of the lead trust, Therese (or those nieces, nephews, and friends) will receive the remainder of the trust.

What Makes Planned Gifts Special

Both revocable and irrevocable gifts offer donors opportunities to fold philanthropy into their financial and estate plans. Donors can plan to help both their heirs and their favorite philanthropies through these giving vehicles. They can plan their future, even the income they receive at retirement, through planned gifts. At the same time, they may lessen their tax burden. Giving in this way involves anticipating the future and predicting the outcome of a gift over a period of time.

Nonprofits have specific policies about establishing charitable remainder trusts with donors. A charitable remainder trust only benefits a nonprofit if there actually is a remainder when the trust ends and if the time value of money (the gift) is considered in the plan. The value of managing a gift over time becomes a part of the requirements a nonprofit establishes for planned gifts. The nonprofit must consider the value of managing a planned gift over the number of years it anticipates the gift will be tied up in the remainder trust, annuity, or lead gift. Age limits, the rate of return, and other factors are addressed by these procedures or guidelines for planned giving officers.

We have given you only a brief overview of planned gifts. Development officers who specialize in planned giving are well versed in the details of these giving vehicles. They are able to take many factors about a donor into consideration when they recommend a giving opportunity to the donor. The donor's goals, both philanthropic and financial, the donor's age, number of heirs, timing of the gift, and income at retirement help the planned giving officer develop the best proposal for the prospect. The planned giving officer's explanation of the gifts and their relationship to these characteristics of an individual's life may even help a prospect see a philanthropic opportunity that she did not know existed. In fact, whenever a solicitation is met with a refusal, the fund raiser should evaluate the reason for the refusal, with the idea in mind that there may be alternative ways to give that the prospect does not realize. Constituents who thought that they could make only small gifts or who thought that they could not make large gifts at the time of the Ask realize that there are greater possibilities when a well-versed planned giving officer outlines the options. The benefits to the donors are considerable: help with estate planning, an annual income through a life income gift, tax savings, and an opportunity to be philanthropic.

Research in the Planned Giving Story

As you read this section, keep in mind everything you have already learned about identifying and qualifying major gift prospects. At the same time, we will ask you to reevaluate your conclusions about how you are defining wealth. To the assets plus income formula you have developed you must now add life stage. We will place these three elements on a scale and try to make them work together to balance the scale. Simply put, as a prospect's age increases, assets and income increase. At a certain point, income levels off, but age and assets continue to increase. Donors who never had a prestigious job or a windfall from stock options or company ownership can be rich in assets at retirement and beyond. Those donors who have appreciated (and paid for) real estate, long-held stocks, retirement accounts, and few demands on their resources are now potential major gift prospects.

In other words, the same constituent characteristics that interest planned giving fund raisers are the ones that attract the attention of prospect researchers. This often means that the researcher begins to pay attention to a constituent who did not attract attention years before. But now this constituent's wealth is measurable in new ways. Asset-rich constituents with few or no heirs, adequate retirement income, and who are particularly close to your nonprofit will be worth another review by research. Remember the news story you saw about the schoolteacher who left the local library $500,000? Shake hands with your first model for a planned giving prospect.

Robert F. Sharpe Sr., the author of *Planned Giving Simplified: The Gift, the Giver, and the Gift Planner* (John Wiley & Sons, New York, 1999, p. 63), writes that "planned givers [the donors] are special people who want to make charitable gifts in the most effective ways possible." This goal is a perfect fit with prospect research's mission about the efficient use of that first dollar raised. Researchers find it difficult to locate prospects for planned giving officers when they are unable to stretch their major gift prospect concepts. A prospect researcher who is skilled enough to work with his planned giving colleague creates a formidable duo.

You see, the nonprofit now has nearly doubled its research production. A good planned giving officer is prospecting, too. The skilled planned giving officer has a direct mail effort in place and, through this effort, he creates opportunities to identify new prospects. Think of effective mailings as a rolling survey. Each mailing includes an opportunity for readers to respond to survey questions, to ask for additional information about planned giving tools, or to contact the planned giving officer for advice.

How can a prospect researcher help? The direct mail readers who respond will be added to the researcher's pool of potential prospects. The researcher will gather more information about those individuals and make recommendations to the planned giving officer. The researcher can help the planned giving officer fine-tune his mailing list. The list might include constituents who are:

- Age 58 or older
- Single, regardless of giving (no heirs)
- Widows or widowers who have given a gift (committed constituents who may have few heirs)
- Married (or life partnership), remarried, and divorced constituents, and those whose marital status is unknown (MRDUs); who have given a gift that approaches the highest annual fund Ask; who are already in the pool of potential prospects; or who have demonstrated consistent giving (really committed constituents, probably with heirs, who may have signs of wealth)
- Anyone in this age group, regardless of marital status, who has given a gift that approaches or exceeds the minimum for a major gift (people who have capacity to give a major gift)

The researcher can look for planned giving prospects in other places, too. Constituent characteristics a researcher encounters such as changes in marital status, whether the individual has many (or any) heirs, changes in giving habits, or the approach of retirement can signal that a constituent should be contacted by the planned giving officer. The researcher will see these characteristics while doing all those things we have already said a researcher does: reading, data segmenting, and reviewing screenings.

The Millionaire Next Door: The Surprising Secrets of America's Wealthy (Thomas J. Stanley and William D. Danko, Longstreet Press, 1996), a book that has been popular with prospect researchers and fund raisers alike, describes planned giving prospects without intending to do so. A planned giving prospect is often the millionaire next door. His history may be that of a person who worked hard his entire life, owned a small business, and was fiscally conservative. A planned giving prospect is often asset rich and cash (or income) middle class, making him a little difficult to research. There will be no current public company salary, no stock holdings in public reports, and no news stories about promotions and such. The only signs of wealth for a researcher to find may be the value of real estate holdings, the history of real estate holdings if the prospect has already begun to reduce his lifestyle to a retirement profile, and, sometimes, a history of company ownership or leadership (and perhaps information about the sale of the company or its holdings), or other financial success. More often, the story of the millionaire next door will be one that features steady employment, few heirs, and a conservative lifestyle, like that schoolteacher we mentioned.

There are other ways that a researcher and a planned giving officer can work together, some of them rather advanced so we will save them for anther book. Planned giving officers who, with researchers, examine the history of bequests at their nonprofit and compare that information with reports from other nonprofits or with estate surveys gain another important tool. At what age do your constituents write their last wills? How many bequests came from constituents who were receiving the planned giving office's mailings? How many bequestors had been cultivated or stewarded? What characteristics do the bequestors share? Are they similar in marital status, number of heirs, income level, or other demographics? This series of questions will remind you of the major gift donor composite we built in chapter 7. Drawing a composite of a planned giving prospect at your institution would be a worthwhile project.

There is plenty of work for a planned giving officer and a researcher to do. That does not frighten this duo, though. These are two development professionals who know, after all, how to plan.

Dancing Cheek-to-Cheek

As you can see, a fund-raising effort that is healthy and strong is not a simple thing. Like anything that is operating at its highest level of performance, it involves more than what we see on the surface. It includes practice, self-examination, planning, and establishing a way to follow the steps laid down by those who went before us. It involves each member of the team evaluating what they have to offer one another. The organization's fund-raising goals are the beneficiaries of this close partnership.

Promoting Research

Now that you know the scope of prospect research in the fund-raising process, how can you be sure that everyone knows what you know? How can you be sure that everyone knows the role of research in raising funds?

We in fund raising live in a collaborative society. We work together for the same goals. If a major gift is received from a constituent at the end of a planned cultivation, you can be sure that gift was the fruit of the hard work of a team of people. The data entry staff, the gift processors, the stewardship managers, the researchers, and the fund raiser worked together to get that gift. Each mailing to the constituent that went to the right address, each gift that was recorded correctly, each expression of gratitude, every invitation to an event, all the pieces of information that fine-tuned the cultivation and the Ask led to that major gift.

Unfortunately, we live in a world where the person with a hand on the button, the person with the microphone, or the person sitting in the driver's seat seem to get the recognition for the outcome of the contest. But fund raising is not a contest; it is a collaboration. While the development officer will coordinate the Ask and may even request the gift himself, the earlier steps that facilitated that Ask were built by other development team members and are intrinsic to the success of the cultivation.

The impression that the fund-raising team has of research's role in securing major gifts will be up to you. Keeping prospect research in the forefront of your nonprofit's story will be your job. Here are some of the ways you can do that.

Trumpeting Accomplishments

As you learned earlier in this book, prospect research is a young profession that grew out of technological advances and the increased competition for donor dollars. When nonprofits began to dabble in prospect research, they sometimes turned to employees with other duties and asked them to add prospect research to their assignments. So, modest beginnings were complicated by virtually no training or experience. The Internet's burst onto the scene only further complicated this toxic mix because it added the idea that any information was available to anyone who looks for it. That the Internet actually made a complex, technical job even more technical and complex was lost on the naive. For many years, prospect research was viewed as an optional addition to the fund-raising effort. Sophisticated fund raisers now know that prospect research is not an option; it is a necessity.

With this short past and bootstrap foundation, you can see that prospect research might often need a champion. Friend, that is now you. Well, it's you and all of us who know the value of prospect research. Let's figure out a few ways to trumpet research.

Measuring, Predicting, and Reporting

If you have any experience as a fund raiser or if you have spent time around fund raisers, you know that they are great measurers and planners. Fund raisers report their accomplishments quantitatively. They talk about how many prospects they solicited, how many grant proposals they wrote, how many gifts they closed. They total the dollars that came to the nonprofit from prospects assigned to them, and they report that number as the money they raised that year. So, numbers unfold upon other numbers: your favorite fund raiser managed 30 volunteers, carried a load of 180 prospects, wrote 10 proposals, completed 109 prospect contacts, solicited (or coordinated the solicitation of) 25 prospects, and closed 18 gifts totaling $4,345,000. Is your head spinning with numbers? We bet it is.

During that same time, what did prospect research do? How many new prospects did research identify? How many known prospects did research further qualify? How many constituents were added to the suspect pool? How many research reports were written? How many event reports were completed? You see, research has numbers to report, too. Your research log will help you assemble those numbers.

Many fund raisers begin each calendar or fiscal year with a written plan that enumerates what they accomplished last year and what they hope to accomplish during the new year. Modeling a report after this format works for research, too. By outlining the accomplishments of research in a factual and quantifiable way, you will give the budget-makers the tools they need to value the research function at your nonprofit. Anecdotal reporting is also valuable. While prospect research cannot measure its success by the number of gifts received from the prospects research identified, a few stories about those identified who were then successfully cultivated and solicited are worth repeating. We believe that you should assemble these quantifiable numbers, predictions, and anecdotes whether you are asked to or not.

Reporting to the Bosses

In addition to the annual performance and accomplishments report we just described, the person who is in charge of the prospect research section will have a weekly or biweekly opportunity to promote research to the hierarchy. Most managers have a meeting or more each month with the next level up on that organizational tree. Those meetings are the stage for promoting research. It is easy to assume that those who make decisions already believe in prospect research. After all, they are the people who finalized the decision to add research to the fund-raising effort at your nonprofit. But are they? Is the person who makes those decisions now the same person who made the leap of faith to add prospect research? It is likely that the person in that job now is a different individual than the one who added prospect research. The person across the conference table from you now may need to be educated about the value of research.

We have been intrigued when we hear stories about employees who do not have to tell their bosses what they have been doing lately. It sounds like the perfect job, right? Well, it is not the perfect job. When it is time to pencil out staff cutbacks, a manager who does not know what you do or, equally fatal, who does not understand the value of your output, may point that pencil in your direction.

It is not uncommon that a staff member has to set the agenda in a meeting with a boss. If you are in that predicament, take it as an opportunity. Be prepared in each meeting to trumpet research. Talk numbers. Tell those who will listen how many prospects the research section identified since the last meeting. Tell how many constituents have been added to the pool. Remind them that research first identified and qualified that prospect who gave $100,000 last week. Remind those in the meeting about the accomplishments of research at every opportunity.

Surveying Your Customers

We in the nonprofit sector often forget that we have customers, too. We think of customers as people who are buying a product. For the prospect research section at your nonprofit, your customers are your fund-raising colleagues who ask for and read your reports. Those colleagues will be able to tell you things you do not know about your product. In chapter 9 we mentioned asking your customers if your reports work well for them. Let's examine that idea now.

Are your reports clear and concise? Is it easy for your customer to find the information she needs in your reports? Are there design changes you can make to facilitate information sharing? Researchers can keep an open line with one another about the latest approaches to report designs. Research forms are a common topic at prospect research meetings and conferences. As fund-raising databases improve, researchers are pulling reports from information already assembled on the database. In these cases, fund raisers must be in agreement that the database formats meet their information requirements.

Do not forget that most research reports serve a dual function. They provide information to the reader, the fund raiser, or volunteer who is interested in that prospect. They also form a historical record, an assemblage of the pertinent information the researcher collected and analyzed. Because of this double duty, research reports must include more information that the fund raiser anticipated. Research reports often tell a bigger story. The profile format allows researchers to tell that bigger story. Even when a profile is not the format of the report, additional information may be included in the report.

For example, when a researcher reports a prospect's current stock holdings and the value of those stock holdings, she must also include other information that helps her track that data for the next update. This might include the price per share, the ticker symbol, and the point of origin for the stock information. While some of this information may not interest the reader, the fund raiser who just wants to know the number that is preceded by a dollar sign, it is unlikely that a researcher has time to write two versions of a report. And it is reasonable for us to assume that the fund raiser will be able to pick the valuable pieces out of the report. After all, some fund raisers will be delighted to have the ticker symbol and other details. They may wish to track the progress of the stock themselves after learning about the prospect's holdings.

With the dual duty of research reports in mind, it is worthwhile to ask your colleagues if they are getting what they want from your reports. If enough colleagues say that they struggle with an element of your reports, you will be wise to examine that feature. Researchers at institutions similar to yours can offer you good ideas about changes. While one opinion might not alter your entire format, all the opinions you receive will make an annual reexamination of your reporting process beneficial for you and for your readers. It will also remind your readers, your fund-raising colleagues, about how seriously you view your reports.

Surveying your readers will serve another purpose. By asking your readers to thoughtfully review your reports to suggest ways you might improve them, you may discover something surprising. In the feedback you receive you may find comments that cause you to suspect that some of your readers do not understand what information research can get. Singular criticisms or requests for changes that are actually about the information in the reports may help you with another aspect of trumpeting research: educating your colleagues.

Educating Your Colleagues

As you are reviewing the answers to the customer survey you asked your colleagues to complete about your reports, you are startled by a few of the answers. One of your colleagues, a new fund raiser, suggested that you add net worth estimates to your reports. She also suggested that you ought to review credit reports and include that information in your summaries of assets. The surprise is that a fund raiser joined your team and was not brought into the fold in regard to privacy issues, what is available through public information sources, and what type of conclusions you are able to accurately and reliably make from your research.

These suggestions may even come from an experienced fund raiser. A phenomenon that is not unique to the fund-raising profession is something we may call conference chatter fallout. More than a few fund raisers have returned from their professional conferences brimming with news about resources that they are certain their research colleagues do not know about. They are sure they are sharing something new with you. A Web site, for a fee, gives visitors a bank account report on anyone, they tell you. Another Web site (these chatter fallouts are usually about the Internet nowadays) will give you the stock holdings of anyone, not just the company officers and insiders, they say. It is up to you to let them know the limits of the Internet and the limits of your research based on your professional ethics.

As you can see, ongoing education for your colleagues will be useful to the prospect research section and to those colleagues, too. By keeping your team up-to-date about what researchers do and what information is available, you will keep their expectations in line with what is possible. By keeping them in touch with your professional standards, you will offer them the chance to explore their own ideas about the Information Age.

Making Presentations at Meetings

Most development teams have a regular schedule of meetings. These meetings may be used to share news about the latest cultivations or to brainstorm next steps for cultivations that are stalled. Department-wide meetings may occur on a less frequent schedule and may be "overview" meetings, where the heads of the organization's teams report on their latest accomplishments.

Team or department-wide meetings give you the perfect stage for sharing information about research. Your presence at these meetings is requisite: You are the one who maintains a unique perspective on individual cultivation strategies and on the fund-raising efforts as a whole. Your work overlaps with that of nearly every member of the team.

Presentations you make at meetings can be simple and direct. They can focus on a current topic in philanthropic news or in technology in general. Get a spot on the agenda well before the meeting date. Try to predict the interests of your audience. At the same time, keep in mind that most of them will not be interested in prospect research on the level that it interests you. Nonetheless, it is likely that you know about resources that will interest them. This is particularly true in these Internet times. Keep to the time schedule given to you for your part of the meeting. Do everything you can so that those attending the meeting will wish to hear from you again. If you can, give your listeners a brief handout that delineates the important points of your presentation.

Not all of us are comfortable making presentations in front of large (or even small) groups. We are fortunate that the era we live in offers us plenty of alternatives for sharing information and ideas. If you are reluctant to make a presentation about research, you can create handouts or other communications that summarize your ideas or that fill the gaps in the education your colleagues need about research. You can place those handouts in the reading file or in each team member's mailbox.

Sharing News from Research Meetings and Conferences

Researchers and fund raisers alike trot off to professional meetings and conferences and return to their nonprofits with a renewed perspective and a shiny set of tools to apply to their tasks. The organization has invested hundreds or even thousands of dollars in sending each member of the team to meetings and conferences. The organization believes in continuing education. It recognizes the value in staff members spending time around their peers, sharing battle stories, successes, and unique approaches to solving problems. It appreciates the importance of employees hearing the ideas and experiences of the leaders in their fields.

But many organizations leave it at that. Should you? No. You can bring the wonderful things you learn at meetings and conferences back to your colleagues. Of course some of the material will be too technical and will be of little interest to the larger group. But a careful review of the handouts you received and the notes you made will reveal material that is worth sharing. Remember, the sharing has two purposes: It can help educate your colleagues about research and it can promote prospect research itself.

Publishing E-newsletters

The broad use of email gives researchers another way to communicate with the members of the fund-raising team. Researchers can now compile their weekly or biweekly "finds" into a brief electronic newsletter, one that they share with other members of the team via email. This venue also offers researchers a chance to share information about research itself.

The format for e-newsletters varies as much as researchers themselves do. Large institutions may break the new information to share into categories (such as technology, banking, or law) and use more than one newsletter to communicate it. Many newsletters are as simple as a series of single sentence summaries such as, "Jane Smith sold her company for $40 million last week." The researcher might note in the e-newsletter which development officer has Jane Smith on his prospect list.

Who should get the e-newsletter? Our easy answer is "whoever wants it." More accurately, whoever can improve their performance or that of those they supervise should get it. All fund raisers at your nonprofit will receive it. If the head of your nonprofit is asked to participate in fund raising, he will enjoy receiving it, too. In some organizations, other groups such as the staff members who work in alumni programs, events, or in public relations may be interested in your e-newsletter. You may determine who wishes to receive the e-newsletter by sending each member of the team a sample copy and asking them if they would like to be in your distribution group.

On the Cutting Edge, and You Holding the Scissors

Let's face it: Your line of work, prospect research, puts you on the cutting edge. You are, by the nature of how you spend your time, knowledgeable about a stunning number of topics. You are collecting (and reading) information about business, art, real estate, famous people, and philanthropy. During the collecting and analyzing, you are bound to learn about many topics. You are deeply involved in technology. That, in particular, puts you on the cutting edge. To be a good prospect researcher, you have to keep up with the latest tools researchers are using. Many of those tools are computer- or Internet-based. You may be tapping sources that tell you what is coming next in terms of access and electronics. This puts you in a unique position among your colleagues.

Recognizing your unique position as a prospect researcher helps you appreciate what you have to offer your fund-raising team. The range of opportunities that may unfold are immeasurable. It is up to you to be able to see them when they come. It is up to you to evaluate and promote the knowledge that you are adding to your talents after you evaluate what pieces of it will be useful to your colleagues. Researchers can tell you stories about the unexpected variety of things in development into which they are drawn. Many of these things do not involve identifying and qualifying wealthy constituents. The combination of your access to information and your technical skills will intrigue colleagues who are trying to solve other problems. For example, researchers have been asked to create lists of "famous" constituents. We all know that "fame" and "wealth" are not synonymous. Prospect researchers are asked to recommend constituents for awards, for board positions, and for volunteer leadership roles. Researchers are asked to, well, research and assemble the history of their nonprofit.

You can see how "prospect researcher" becomes, simply, "researcher" for some nonprofits. You can imagine that many of these tasks can lead to new prospects. That, along with the value it places on the prospect research position, is reason enough to be ready for these new roles. You will have to judge your ability to balance the new tasks with your prospect research duties. You will have to evaluate how many steps away from identifying prospects these other tasks actually are.

You are no longer a new prospect researcher. With each passing day you are gaining experience in the things we have covered. Identifying new prospects, evaluating capacity, making recommendations, establishing an Ask amount—each of the tasks basic to prospect research are now in your domain. For many nonprofit organizations, these skills will meet nearly all of their needs for the prospect research function. For others, your performance in these areas will open the door to other, more complex tasks and roles. It will be up to you to determine how these new tasks fit into the mission of prospect research at your nonprofit.

CHAPTER 12

Building a Prospect Research Reference Library

"I learned that people are more likely to entrust the story of their lives if they feel that I care about them, that I know something about them, and can comprehend what they're telling me. So part of the reason I prepare so much is to be worthy of the person I'm interviewing."
— Terry Gross, National Public Radio's "Fresh Air" host, *Los Angeles Times*, April 15, 2000, p. F-20.

Library Basics

If you are a new researcher at a nonprofit with an established research department, you are already working with a collection of resources. This chapter will give you a chance to evaluate whether the resources you are using meet the needs of your organization. If you are creating a research function at your nonprofit or if you are your nonprofit's first researcher, you are going to be a research library founder. This chapter will help you begin.

When you reached this chapter, you brought with you the ideas about resources that we have discussed throughout this book. You know that there are three types of resources:

1. In-house resources
2. Free (or nearly free) resources
3. Fee-based resources

These three types of resources make up a prospect research library. The prospect research library that you create, maintain, or augment has four essential features in common with your local public library. First, the resources in the prospect research library are organized so that they are readily accessible. Second, the resources are historical as well as current, creating opportunities to draw pictures of the past and the present. Third, there is an established checkout procedure for resources to leave the library. And last, the library materials are located in a place where people can use them with minimal distractions.

The Library You Already Have

If you are the first researcher at your nonprofit, it will be a delight to discover that, perhaps unintentionally, your nonprofit has been building a research library all along. Some of these resources are static, such as attendance records, contact reports, and committee lists. Some are dynamic, such as giving records and prospect profiles.

Gift Records

The tax reporting requirements directing your nonprofit's process for recording gifts and saving information about those gifts creates one of the first and most essential resources of your library. Those records—in whatever format they take—include the names of your organization's supporters and other bits of information. The history of each donor's support is in those records. Most nonprofits now keep and maintain donor records electronically. That makes them even easier for researchers to use. Prospect screening and new prospect mining begin with those donor records.

In-House Nuggets

Some nonprofits have other in-house resources that are easily overlooked. Remember the hospital researcher from the early 1980s we introduced in chapter 9? The researcher who holds her position in the twenty-first century was delighted to discover those oversized index cards created for each donor. The cards were kept for almost 30 years. Those cards form a biographical and philanthropic history of each donor that is difficult to reproduce in any database. The person who kept those cards carefully drew a line through each old address as she recorded a new one. She did the same thing with each career move. She recorded the names of the donor's children, the dates of the donor's marriages and divorces, and other important information. She created a biography for each donor, contained on a single index card. Although the cards exist for only a portion of the nonprofit's donors—the card-keeping ended when the nonprofit purchased an electronic database in 1984—they capture an important period in the history of the nonprofit. They are an invaluable in-house resource.

MOUs

No, this is not a misspelling of the sound a cow makes, and we did not leave the "e" off of "mouse." MOUs are Memos of Understanding, documents written when donors agree to make gifts. The MOU may:
- Outline the donor's plan to pay the gift
- Describe the donor's intention for the gift, how the donor wishes the gift to be used
- Detail the nonprofit's restrictions or "outs" regarding the gift
- Include a short biography of the person the gift honors and the donor, if the gift is a named gift

- Include the signatures of the donor(s) and the nonprofit's fund raiser who either negotiated the gift, wrote the MOU, or cultivated the donor

It is easy to see that MOUs are jam-packed with information for researchers. Nonprofits put the MOUs in donors' central files. Organizations wise to the tremendous loss created by missing files also keep their collection of MOUs in another place as an insurance policy. The MOU collection tells a unique chapter or two in the history of your nonprofit. It is an integral section of your library.

Does your organization have a resource like the oversized index cards at the hospital or an A-to-Z collection of MOUs? Did a long-time development officer or a director keep detailed files that never made it into the central filing system? Are there old programs from long-ago events that include lists of attendees and supporters? Does your nonprofit keep an organizational history that reveals how buildings, rooms, or meeting areas were named and where the funding came from? Are there commemorative plaques sprinkled throughout your nonprofit? Has anyone collected the information etched on those plaques?

Your organization's history gets the first shelf in the library you are building. It is the key to who has supported the organization in the past and who might support it in the future. How that history was captured may be up to you to discover.

Central File

Young nonprofits often operate at a frantic pace. There are as many important tasks as there are minutes in the day. Running programs and getting new initiatives off the ground can take all the available energy. Organizational priorities frequently fall to the bottom of the chore list. Papers pile up. Boxes of data are pushed into closets.

And then you arrive. Remember the history of your organization we just mentioned? The first chapters of that history are in those files-to-be. They are in the files that development officers are keeping in their offices. They are in the files yet to be created. They are in the slips of paper, MOUs, photos, letters, holiday cards, and other materials in the boxes in the closet. The files may exist only marginally. They may be held in a cupboard in the basement or another place difficult to access and maintain. Because they are not readily available, coworkers may be in the habit of keeping materials that belong in a central file in their offices. See how we just made the central file a place, a destination? That is exactly what it is.

In chapter 9 we gave you ten steps to creating and maintaining a central file system. Since central file, the place, will be a key section of your research library, its functionality and upkeep will be important to you. You or someone else in your organization may be the designated central file manager. If you are the manager, you can set up a series of checks to make sure the central file system is a well-oiled machine. If you are not the manager, it will be worth the effort on your part to be an extra set of eyes on the maintenance of that system. Even if you are not the central file manager, you can be a volunteer quality-control checker. Add to your regular duties random checks to make sure that contact reports made it to the right file, MOUs are being copied, out-cards are being used, and other central file procedures are being followed.

The Database

The chapter 9 story about the 1982 researcher was missing an important tool that most researchers now have: a database. In chapter 8 we discussed the features of databases that matter to fund raisers and researchers. We also told you that, within the limits of this book, we cannot help you pick a database. The costs, the specific needs of your nonprofit, and the database feature changes that will have occurred in the time between writing and publishing this book make that task impossible. Nevertheless, the database your nonprofit elects to use to manage its gift processing, prospect tracking, and donor information will be of paramount importance to you, the researcher. The database will house information about each prospect and potential prospect. The prospect information will range from basic name and address data to details about each constituent's family relationships, various affiliations with the institution, past involvements, events attended, and other information.

As you can see, the database will house the first information bits you need for profile-building. It will form a main wing of your prospect research library. Like any well-organized library, it will be able to give you sets of information when you need them. If you need a list of people with the job title of "president," for example, your database can give it to you. If you need a list of all the people who live in that wealthy neighborhood on the hill, your database can generate that list by zip code. The limits of what your database can give you are bound only by its initial potential, the quality of the data entered, and your (or your database manager's) skill in retrieving information.

Your Computer

The personal computer you use at your nonprofit forms another section of the research library. If you master the use of this tool, it will become the central transfer station for electronic information to your team. Your computer and its associated pieces (zip drive, CD-ROM, diskettes, shared hard drive, CD writer, scanner) will be a repository for information about prospects. If you are writing profiles in a word processing program, you will design a system for managing the electronic copies of those profiles. Each profile update may involve calling up the original to revise and add information. Other documents you write—event briefings, financial analysis papers, "top donor" lists—will all be housed electronically within your computer suite.

As the central transfer station, your computer will be the launch-point for information to development officers. It is also likely to be the receiving point for research requests, new information about donors and, depending on the sophistication of the electronics at your organization, much more. Some large nonprofits maintain a development Intranet, an electronic mall of sorts, a mini-Internet that is accessible only to those with the proper access codes. Here development officers post contact reports and researchers share new information about donors. Some research teams post a shared collection of Web bookmarks on their Intranet. Other communication within the fund-raising team occurs on the Intranet. Your nonprofit may not have or need an Intranet, but, even without this level of electronic communication, you will be using email to respond to development officers and others about prospects.

The research computer is the machine that affords access to fee-based electronic databases and CD-ROM research products. It is also home to the best collection of Internet sites for prospect research in the entire development department—the researcher's bookmarks or favorite sites. That collection of Internet sites forms another wing of the prospect research library.

The First Library You Build

If you are reading this book to learn how to add prospect research to your organization, you now know that you already have the beginnings of a research library. A computer, a central filing system, a database—these elements make the first and most important wings of that library. There are other pieces you can add for free or with little cost. Before you begin the next phase of library building though, you will once again answer two questions that have driven many of your research efforts throughout this adventure:

1. Where—geographically—is your constituency?
2. Where—economically—is your constituency?

The answers to these questions will shape the course of the rest of your library-building efforts. If your constituency is primarily—more than 50 percent—located in the area where your nonprofit is located, you will be interested in resources that provide information about companies, foundations, and people in that locality. If your constituents live in other areas, you can find out what areas have the largest concentrations of your affiliates. Your database holds that information. A simple query of constituent populations by zip codes, clustering zip codes into regions, will generate the regions in which your constituents live. You will then know what other areas of the country or the world are important in your research efforts. Establish a hierarchy of regions, basing your ranking decisions on the total number of constituents in those other areas. For example, your regions and the percentage of your constituents in each may look something like this:

- Region A: Hometown and neighboring five counties:
  57 percent of the constituency
- Region B: Two states to the north (nearest large metro area):
  20 percent of the constituency
- Region C: Large metro area 1,500 miles west:
  15 percent of the constituency
- Region D: Everyone else: 8 percent of the constituency

If your constituents were distributed this way, most of your efforts in identifying information-collecting tools would focus on local resources. You would then add resources from Region B and Region C, as time and budget allowed. You may add other criteria to your region distribution, even analyzing the total number of gifts, particularly major gifts, coming from each region. That deeper analysis may alter your region breakdown.

There is a wealth of local resources to add to your library. We have been talking about most of these resources throughout this book. Many of these resources are free or of little cost. Let's review them.

Donor Rolls

As we have told you, all nonprofits publish reports listing donors and trustees or board members. Some researchers call these reports honor rolls or tributes and some call them donor rolls. Arts organizations often list boards and donors in every event program. Other organizations list donors in annual reports. Ask your fund-raising team to save the programs from the concerts and plays they attend. Encourage your colleagues to share the donor rolls they receive from their alma maters, keeping in mind that they may be the same colleges and universities that your prospects attended. Bring the donor rolls you receive at home to work to add to your library. In chapter 9 we suggested that you make it a part of your regular routine to crosscheck the top donors listed in those donor rolls with the constituents in your database. You will also hold these donor rolls in an organized and retrievable way in your research library. As new prospect names surface, you will be able to check to see if they are top donors to other local nonprofits.

If your organization specializes in a philanthropic effort that is unique and is a peer to other national or international organizations, you will collect donor rolls from those similar organizations. You may find that some of these organizations—and some local nonprofits—now post all or a portion of their donor rolls on their Internet sites.

While donor rolls cannot tell you the entire story about your constituents' philanthropic histories, they can give you a hint at potential. They can hint at a prospect's interests, too. Do your prospects support the ballet, the soccer team, or a national conservation group? Now, this sounds worthwhile, after all our talk about interests, capacity, wealth, and assets.

Board Lists

Collecting board lists is as important as collecting donor rolls. Successful nonprofits ask people to serve on their executive boards for a number of reasons, and one of the top reasons is that the individuals can support the organization financially. Often a large gift leads to board service. Sometimes a potential donor is asked to serve, with the hope that drawing the prospect into the inner circle will motivate giving. Whatever the logic of the individual nonprofits, you can assume that board service indicates three things:

1. The board member may have major gift potential.
2. The board member may have experience as a philanthropist.
3. The board member knows other people who are or may become philanthropic.

A collection of the lists of the boards of directors or trustees of the nonprofits where your constituents live or give will uncover the links your supporters have to these other organizations. You will find board lists in annual reports, newsletters, programs, and playbills, and on the Web sites of the organizations that interest you.

Club and Organization Information

Researchers collect membership rolls for golf and country clubs, affinity clubs, professional groups, political and social organizations and other enclaves where the wealthy gather. The leadership for these groups is often published in the newspaper or in other publications when the group holds a special event or fund raiser. Entire lists of members are sometimes available to researchers. Some organizations are publishing member directories on the Internet, and occasionally these directories are accessible to non-members. These rosters will be valuable assets to your library.

Chamber of Commerce and Other Affinity Group Publications

The chambers of commerce in the regions where your constituents live produce directories of members that contain company contact and leadership information. They also produce promotional materials such as "top technology companies" or "top industrial firms" in the area. Other affinity groups—young entrepreneur, industry-specific, or gender- or race-related groups—may also produce lists and reports that include some of your constituents.

U.S. Secretary of State Corporation and Foundation Registries

Each Secretary of State office maintains lists of corporations and foundations registered to do business in that state. Some of these offices publish paper directories of their registries. Some have searchable electronic databases on the Internet, as a service to consumers. The databases vary in usability. Some are searchable by company or foundation name, and some only provide an alphabetical list that one can skim. The information provided by the corporation registries may be limited to company name and address, type of business, and chief officers. This may be just the lead you need to verify a potential prospect's association with a company. The foundation directories may include brief giving guidelines, primary contacts, and the foundations' assets. Some include sample gifts. Check each Secretary of State office in the regions in which your constituents live and give to determine if you have easy access to these registries. States publishing foundation directories charge a relatively small fee for those publications. There are also fee-based services providing information based on that gathered by the Secretary of State offices. Whatever form these resources take, they will be good additions to the research library you are building.

Public Company Annual Reports and Proxy Statements

That 1982 researcher from chapter 9 collected public company annual reports and proxies by telephoning the companies to ask that a copy of each report be sent to her by mail. She maintained an up-to-date collection of annual reports and proxies for the companies with which her prospects affiliated. She also maintained a collection of annual reports for other local or regional public companies. And, finally, she collected the annual reports of companies donating to her nonprofit. Like the nonprofit board lists, the annual reports and proxies tell a researcher who knows whom and who is sitting in the seats of power and influence.

As you learned in chapter 5, the annual reports and proxies are on the Internet now. In effect, the U.S. Securities and Exchange Commission (SEC) Web site and other sites are a branch of your research library. These sites are currently offering access to annual reports dating back to the mid-1990s. You can visit this branch of your research library whenever you need the information.

Researchers can still telephone companies for annual reports. You may ask to be put on a mailing list to receive a copy of the annual report and proxy every year. Researchers may keep the annual reports and proxies in their central file system or in an annual report library in the research office. They may check the company board lists for matches in their databases. Researchers often decide how many years of reports they will maintain, since a growing collection of annual reports will consume space.

Foundation Annual Reports and Guidelines

That 1982 researcher telephoned or wrote to foundations to request a copy of each foundation's annual report and giving guidelines. Large and medium-sized foundations now publish their annual reports on their Web sites. They not only publish giving guidelines there, but they may announce changes in priorities on their Web sites, making the electronic guidelines more up-to-date than the paper versions.

Small and some medium-sized foundations will send giving guidelines and annual reports (often in the form of a copy of the foundation's 990-PF) to those who ask for a copy. Many of the smaller foundations are not yet offering Internet access to their annual reports. Some foundations respond to telephone requests for copies of these materials by asking you about your nonprofit. They do this to cut down on their mailing costs; if your organization is far afield of their interest area, they will tell you that on the telephone and save you both the effort and cost to mail and review the printed materials.

As you learned in chapter 4, an important portion of a foundation's history is contained in its 990-PF each year. You can add 990-PFs to your research library by retrieving them from a Web site or by requesting them from the Internal Revenue Service.

Researchers often keep a library of annual reports and giving guidelines for the foundations that support or may support their organization. These reports are usually kept in the central file system, but some researchers keep them as a separate section of their research library.

Newspaper and Magazine "Top" Lists

We are a culture that measures. Most metropolitan areas produce lists of the largest private and public companies, the biggest or most valuable homes, the richest families, the highest-paid executives, or the biggest donors. Some regional, national, and international magazines produce similar lists, but cover a larger territory. As you know, researchers call these wonderful resources "top" lists. They are great resources for identifying potential prospects. Researchers also use them as another piece of information to indicate the success of a company or individual. We covered some of the ways you will use "top" lists in chapters 3 and 5.

Once again, study the regions in which your constituents live. After you do that, it is easy to add the right "top" lists produced by magazines and newspapers to your library. Your nonprofit can purchase subscriptions to the magazines and newspapers that run the lists you need. Some of these publications sell their "top" lists in separate, reasonably priced annual publications. Others publish their annual lists on their Internet sites where they are searchable by several features, including location. City and regional business journals, national business magazines, and local newspapers are the first places to look for "top" lists.

With Research Dollars: A New Library Wing

The research library resources outlined up to this point have been free, low cost, or have contained intrinsic elements of your nonprofit's operation. You will soon discover that, for a fee, you can get access to more of the information you need. Why pay for information? You will want to pay for information when doing so makes the information easier to retrieve, increases its reliability, gives you access to data that you cannot get for free, or when the information can be parsed in a variety of easy-access ways. The cost of getting the information will be outweighed by one or more of these factors. You will get the chance to retrieve more or different information. You will be able to do it quicker and with greater certainty about its veracity.

Now we will discuss our philosophy of what you will add to the library when you have money to spend on resources. You will, of course, remember the research mandate to use that first dollar raised efficiently to find the next dollars. With that in mind, it will not surprise you to learn that we will ask you to examine a few characteristics of your nonprofit so that you can spend the money responsibly. Here are the six questions you will ask. The answers to these questions will form your trail map to buying the right resources.

1. Where are your nonprofit's constituents? Will we ever get over this one? No. The resources you buy will offer access to information with a varying geographical reach. Information sellers covering large geographic areas may not profile smaller companies or foundations. Or they may include them in one version of their releases and not in another. So, if your constituent base is local, you will be interested in different resources than you would be if your constituents were located across an entire region or country.

2. How much money do you have to spend? You can simplify your shopping trip by knowing the answer to this question early. Some resources are too expensive for small and even medium-sized nonprofits. Choosing resources with steep monthly or annual fees will preclude you from getting other resources. As you assess the fees, particularly when purchasing electronic resources, be sure you evaluate:

   - The hook-up or software costs:
     Investigate what software you will need to access the product. Will you need to purchase other equipment to run this software? Additionally, some fee-based resources charge an initial or hook-up fee.
   - The monthly access fee:
     Some electronic resources charge a monthly fee, a sort of retainer. A range of searches or search time is usually permitted with the monthly fee. To evaluate whether this is the range that suits your nonprofit, ask similar organizations using this product if the designated range works for them.
   - The "over the minimum" or "per record" fee:
     During intensive searching efforts, your research may take you over the range of searches or records included in the monthly fee. Be sure that you understand the "per record" fee you will be charged and that you can afford it.

3. What options do you have electronically? Can you imagine how many software packages live on shelves in closets because the computer designated to run them could not handle them? As you investigate electronic resources, clearly state the limits of your hardware, your Internet connection, and any other issue that may impact the operation of the software that you plan to purchase. If it is not in your budget to upgrade your entire system, you must be sure to purchase resources that will continue to work with what you have.

4. How much physical space do you have? One book does not take up a lot of room. One hundred books do. As you draw up the plan for purchasing new resources for the research library, think about the physical space it will require. Try to imagine the library two or five or ten years from now. Can you see that you are actually creating a new *physical* wing? If you continue to purchase similar products, will you have room for them? Some libraries retain resources year after year. After all, prospect research is often an effort to capture financial and biographical information in a moment in time that is not the moment we are in now. Some resources are expected to last only a few years. Foundation directories are out of date quickly, and it does not seem important to save them to capture information about once-active foundations. It is important to be able to capture information about once-active corporations though, so researchers might save old corporation directories.

5. How stable (or likely to grow) is your research budget? We might ask this: How long will you have to use resources before you will be able to replace them with new versions? How long will you use a resource before there are funds to replace it? Some resources wear their age better than others do. Collections of biographies never age, although newer versions will add more information to those same biographies. As we said, foundation directories age relatively quickly. The availability of similar information on the Internet has changed the shelf life of many resources. As you make purchasing decisions, evaluate what you can augment with this dynamic resource.

6. Will the availability of the Internet be the final arbiter in these buying decisions? While the Internet has flung open a door to a massive amount of information, much of it is HTGT—"Here today, gone tomorrow." You cannot depend on finding archival data about the former leaders of companies, for example, at Web sites that profile the current leaders of those companies. Even the home pages of companies often fail to include historical information about the company's founders or past leaders. You must have another way to capture historical data.

Your goal, with your first purchases, will be to consider your answers to each of these questions. These answers will help you select the specific resources that lead to the information you need. You are well versed now, after reading this book, in what type of information you want to find in the resources you purchase. Whether your constituency is local or global, you will need resources that cover five major areas:

1. Individual Biographies
2. Financial Details
3. Corporation Profiles
4. Foundation Profiles
5. Current and Archival News

How to find some of the specific resources you will consider is outlined in the appendix section of this book. Our topic here will be what you will be looking for in the resources available.

Individual Biographies

When researchers find a ready-made biography about a prospect, they have struck gold. A biography may include the prospect's date and place of birth, spouse's name, number and names of children, parents' names, educational background, work history, board and club memberships, current address, and more. It may include only a few of these items. Researchers find biographies in many places. There are brief biographies of officers and directors in proxy statements. The leadership or "About Us" page of company Web sites may include biographies of top officers and directors. Some foundation and charity board rosters include biographical information. Once you are buying resources, there are collections of biographies you can purchase. The collections may be purchased in paper or electronic form. The electronic version of the collection may be a CD-ROM or access to an online database.

Financial Details

Elements of a prospect's life that outline capacity may not be included in biography collections. For some of those details, researchers turn to other resources. For example, information sellers aggregate real estate assessment data from across the country. Earlier in this book, we reported that many county and township real estate assessors are placing their databases on the Internet, with free access to property assessments for all visitors. We also reported that most U.S. counties and townships provide assessed values by telephone or mail. Companies that sell real estate assessments offer more efficient search capabilities and a greater breadth of information in some cases. A real estate information provider's resource may offer broad area searching, last sale price, and contact information for property owners. You can use your region guide for your constituents and the real estate resources listed in the appendix to determine the way you will conveniently and economically access assessment information.

Other information sellers are collecting donor rolls and board lists. Their searchable databases allow subscribers to search by an individual's name, a like-institution's name, a type of cause, and other factors. Some providers let users save searches. Information in the database is updated on a regular basis.

There are other pieces of the financial puzzle you are constructing that are being aggregated by information providers. Some of these resources are a part of larger, comprehensive packages that cover many aspects of information retrieval. Some are selling information on a piece-by-piece basis via the Internet. Some information is suspect and some is inappropriate to the mission of prospect research. What is available is changing almost daily. The ethical boundaries that you establish for your institution will help guide you.

Corporation Profiles

You learned in chapter 5 that corporations need information about one another. They extend credit, track growth, and make investment decisions based upon the information they get from corporation profiles of varying depth and breadth. These same profiles, for both publicly held and private companies, are available to researchers for a fee. They are collected and sold by information providers who generally charge rates that vary according to the amount of information purchased. Information is not available for all companies, but it is surprising to discover that it is available for small as well as large companies. The size of the company does not appear to be the selection criteria for many of the information sellers compiling these databases. In general, information about large, prominent companies is easier to obtain than information about small, locally based companies.

Corporation profiles form another piece of the information you will collect about individual prospects. While some of your prospects will be current business leaders or owners, some are individuals with whom your institution is meeting years after they led or owned a company. In order to locate and track the corporate affiliations for these prospects, you must be able to access information about companies and their leadership from years past. Archival information about companies is as important to researchers as new information.

The information providers who assemble and disseminate corporation information sell that data in every format. The information is accessible through electronic databases, both CD-ROM-based and via Internet sites. It is available in paper directories. The information providers parse the data so users can purchase sets of data for specific geographic areas. The region guide to your constituents you created will come in handy when you review these options. And, once again, your nonprofit's needs, price, and convenience will dictate which format suits you.

Foundation Profiles

Information aggregators who provide foundation profiles, like many of the firms we are discussing, offer those resources in several formats. Collections of foundation profiles, bisected and dissected by a number of features, are available on CD-ROMs, paper directories, and via subscriber-only databases on the Internet. In chapter 4 we discussed what a foundation profile you write will contain. The ones you can buy contain nearly the same elements. The delivery mode for the information will impact the freshness factor: paper directories are updated annually, while electronic versions may be on a frequent update schedule.

Regional and local organizations also assemble collections of foundation profiles. Your area, or the area in which your constituents live and give, may have a foundation information provider. A local foundation association or an independent information provider are just two of the groups that may aggregate information about the foundations in your area. The profiles appearing in these resources usually include fewer details than those found in the large, national directories. But these local or regional aggregators often include small foundations that may be overlooked or excluded from the collections assembled by the large aggregators.

Current and Archival News

You know now why you want access to both old and fresh news about your prospects. How will you get it? Reviewing that region guide to your constituents you created will be a starting point. You may decide to subscribe to daily newspapers in the areas where the majority of your constituents live. If your nonprofit has a local support base, this may be as simple as subscribing to the town paper. Some researchers now read the newspapers of other cities on the Internet. Remember that we are using the term "read" loosely here. They skim the local page, the business page, and the obituaries.

Many local, regional, and national newspapers offer current and archived stories and obituaries on their Web sites. Often the most recent stories are free and older stories are available for a small, per-story fee. The database of stories is searchable by any keyword, including an individual's name.

There are information aggregators specializing in retrieving news stories for subscribers. These providers access many national, regional and local newspapers, magazines and journals. They may offer users global searching and they may carry archives that are significantly older than the ones available on the newspapers' own Web sites.

So, What Should a Researcher Buy?

You have noticed that we did not name specific resources for you to buy in this chapter. You will find a very small start on a list of resources, including contact information, in the appendix of this book. View the list as a sampling of resources, not a list of all the resources prospect researchers are using. Not too many years ago, there were only a few information providers for prospect researchers. Advances in technology brought swift changes to that small field. It is now difficult for any researcher to stay current with what is available and who is offering which information sets. A long list of all the information providers would be difficult to navigate, even with your trail map in hand. In fact, a part of your job as a researcher may be to establish a way to sort through the choices. You will find a way to evaluate the resources and then choose the ones that are right for your organization. What will your compass be? The ongoing dialogue you create and maintain with researchers at peer institutions and, more broadly, at nonprofits throughout the world, will be your compass. You will create this opportunity by joining the local, regional, and national prospect research groups. You may also join the research, library, foundation, business, or other listservs where resources you would use are being discussed.

Be a Wise Consumer

Milk has a freshness date. Even soda now has a "use by" date. While the resources you buy for your nonprofit will not have the USDA stamp of approval or an expiration date, there are features about the resources you intend to purchase that require both your research and your judgment skills.

Inquire about the sources for the information in the resource you are about to purchase. You will pay close attention if a vendor is using sources that go against your ethics policies. The truth behind some sources may surprise you. For example, one well-known biographical source offers people from many professions an opportunity to be listed for a fee. While most consumers have the impression that there is exclusivity about being listed, the opportunity is, in fact, available to nearly anyone who will pay the fee. Does this undermine the credibility of all the biographical information in this resource? No, it does not. It just means that you must approach the information with your eyes open.

Learn what information the resource precisely covers. Because there are too many foundations, corporations, or people to include in one release, many resources have an arbitrary cutoff point below which they do not include entries. For example, a foundation directory may exclude foundations with assets under $1 million. A collection of biographies may drop some individuals who have been deceased for a couple of years. A corporation database may exclude companies with less than $5 million in sales. There is no flaw in purchasing resources with limitations; the important point is that you must know what the limitations are and whether those limitations mean you are unlikely to find your prospects or their foundations or corporations among the citations. Small nonprofits with constituents who live and work in one equally small area may find it difficult to locate their prospects on the limited and exclusive lists of the world's richest and most famous. It will be important to maximize your budget by selecting additions to your research library that might actually include some of your constituents. Some information providers will allow you to run a short list of names through their database to test the coverage. You may wish to review a resource you are considering buying at the public library first. Take a few names of your constituents with you to see if you can find them in these resources. A few matches that lead to new prospects might make the purchase of this resource money well spent.

Find out how often the resource you are purchasing is updated. If the resource is based on other records that are public, uncover how often the public records database is accessed for updates. If a real estate resource is returning last year's assessments to you months after the assessor's office is reporting this year's assessments, you will have to evaluate the usefulness of that resource.

The Next Wing: Expanding the Library with More Money

Have you ever met someone who has a one-year, five-year, or even a ten-year plan for life? Fresh out of college, the plan may outline getting a good job, then a promotion, within a prescribed time period. The next phase might cover getting married, buying a home, and then starting a family. As unpredictable as life is, planning seems to be an act of determination and discipline. It is almost as if, in the planning, this young person might make these events happen.

Your research library deserves a plan. As you buy those first resources, look ahead. Imagine the future of your research office and, in the same moment, imagine the future of the resources we researchers use. Without a doubt, the resources are consistently moving away from paper and toward electronic formats. Resources are, in fact, more Web-based than ever before. What does this say about the archival data to which researchers want access? The changes in electronic resources are making some of the ways we accessed—and stored—information only a few years ago obsolete. There may be a format in our electronic past that is no longer accessible. Those of us who have been using computers for 20 years will remember several formats that are no longer available. Was information lost when those formats were eliminated? These are the kinds of question you must anticipate answering with the plan you design.

After you have spent a few years with the resources that took your first budget, evaluate their usefulness. Some researchers estimate the value of resources by how often they are used. This is, in fact, an inadequate approach. A good prospect research library either maintains historical materials or knows where to access them. Those historical materials, by their nature, may be rarely used. They are, nonetheless, invaluable and irreplaceable. Those few times when a rarely used resource holds the answer to the research problem you are trying to solve will outweigh the small burden of keeping the material. When a historical resource serves up information about a new prospect's successful—and long sold—company from decades ago, that resource has paid its rent tenfold in the potential returned.

Rarely used is not synonymous with never used. Your resource evaluation will easily spot the materials, databases, and electronic tools that you simply are not using at all. Did you just overlook working these resources into your routine? If not, they may be resources that you will replace with ones that will be useful to you.

What has been missing in your work? What information have you consistently struggled to get? Is there a resource that will help you fill these holes? That is the next one to purchase. If you are keeping in touch with the "buzz" among your prospect research peers about new resources, you will be hearing the good news and the bad news. You will hear about mergers and acquisitions among the information providers. You will hear about the difficulties researchers have in using both new and old-but-revamped tools. All of this information will help you choose the right resources for the next level of access you wish to gain in your work.

Remember Your Nearby Public Library (or the One Virtually Nearby)

Before the floodgate holding the river of electronic information opened, prospect researchers spent part of the workweek walking, riding the bus, or driving to the places where the information they needed was housed. They went to assessors' offices and courthouses. They spent a great deal of time at the public library. Some researchers continue to spend time at the public library. Big city libraries have extensive research resources, and their collections include many resources that are unaffordable for small nonprofits. Some libraries collect annual reports from foundations and corporations. A branch of a large library system may specialize in business resources. The main branches of libraries in many cities have areas dedicated to keeping the history of that city. These efforts may include news clippings, books about founding families, extensive genealogical resources, and donated volumes from companies and individuals.

Even if your nonprofit has an extensive research library, it is worth your time to visit the public library to evaluate the resources there that may help you in your work. The happy discovery that the library is collecting reference books for which your nonprofit does not have the budget or the space will be worth the time you spend on this visit. Do not overlook one more resource at the library—the librarian. There is no one who will have a better sense of how to get to information than a professional librarian will. If you are fortunate to find a librarian who has worked at the library for a long time, adding this person's name to your contact list enhances your resources immeasurably. All of the library's assets are not apparent during a walk-through. The librarian will teach you how the public library can help you in your work.

The electronic world has given us another gift. It has placed libraries across the globe at our fingertips. The library with the information you need may be down the street or it may be five cities or seven states away. It may be in another country. Those once-distant libraries are now virtually as near to you as the one in your town. So, with the region guide to your constituents you created in hand, visit the libraries in those locales via the Internet. You may discover resources that can help you in your work. You may also discover an opportunity to build a relationship with a librarian in one of those far-off libraries. By doing so, you will open a new wing of information for your nonprofit.

Your Electronic Library: The Internet

The 1982 researcher did not have the Internet as an option at all. The change this tool has brought to prospect research is nearly impossible to measure. We are not here to laud the Internet. The days when that was necessary, when researchers doubted the value of the Internet for prospect research, are long gone. Today you need to fit this tool into your own work plan. It is difficult to realize that the Internet is a virtual, dynamic library, one without a Dewey Decimal System or a helpful librarian. It is up to each researcher to create her own pathways and route maps to information on the Web. There are a few reliable guideposts, including Web pages created by other prospect researchers and professional librarians. These soul mates offer you useful Web sites, tips on searching, advice about organizing information, and news about the latest Internet developments via their Web pages. Some of these information angels provide visitors with their email addresses. A few "niche" researchers, such as genealogists and historians, will help you via email, too. They and their Web sites form a collection of resources you will go to again and again. You will find the beginning of a collection of the Web pages prospect researchers have created in the appendix of this book.

Wise Internet use hinges on three things: education, efficiency, and intuition. Each of the following steps you will take involves sharpening these three skills.

- Learn how to build and maintain a virtual library.

Throughout this book you have been extolled to organize. We have told you that, if you cannot put your hands on it, it may as well be in the trash. The weight of this truth is enormous when it comes to the Internet. Your entire collection of resources will be housed in a file for organizing and maintaining your favorite sites or, as we Netscape browsers call them, your bookmarks. Bookmarks (or favorites, as Internet Explorers call them) are not only your place markers in this library; they are also your hallways and stairwells. Bookmarks lead you to information and to gateways to other information.

To organize your bookmarks, think of the general topics of information your research covers. They will include people, foundations, corporations, and real estate, for example. Folders with these names can hold bookmarks or other folders that further separate and define your collection. For example, in your "people" folder, you may have other folders named for specific lines of work in which your prospects engage, like "lawyers," "doctors," "artists," or "celebrities."

The "help" folder in your browser will offer you bookmarking tips. You can also search the Web for tip sheets on bookmarking. Ask other researchers how they organize and maintain their own collections. Go to Internet training seminars whenever you have the chance.

- Learn how to use Internet search engines well.

At the time of this writing, the typical Internet search averages little more than two words. It would be safe to conclude that most of those searches return too many results to deal with effectively. Search engines come and go, and change quickly. Think of search engines as your library card. A search engine gets you access to the Web sites where some of the information you want is housed. This probably means learning one or two other languages, a search language called Boolean and another called search engine math. These languages are centered around simple connectors that you will place between words that must be on the Web pages returned by your search query. It is not tough to learn how to use these languages, but it is essential to do so to maximize the potential of successful Internet searches. Use search engine "help" files to learn how to use each engine well. Some people track search engine news and advancements in search technology. Add the Web sites these trackers maintain to your reading schedule. It is the best way to keep up with the latest developments in search technology.

- Wear that new pair of shoes you bought a month ago.

When you visit a new Web site, take a moment to evaluate its overall usefulness. If you decide to add it to your collection, you must also remember to try it out the next time you are looking for the type of information it covers. To do so, establish a spot where you keep the newest additions to your collection. That may be at the top of the pile within a specific folder or it may be at the end of all of your folders, in a spot where you store new sites until you are ready to fold them into your already-screened collection.

- Learn how to use your Internet time efficiently.

It will happen. It has happened to every single researcher using the Internet. You will begin a search project with every intention of finding the information you seek and moving on to your other chores. Suddenly, you will look up at the clock and realize that an entire hour has passed. Where did the time go? You certainly were not in charge of it, were you? Your zeal in searching Web resources pulled you away from the clock and your other chores.

In the pre-Internet days, researchers paid by the minute to search electronic databases with complex pathways to retrieving information. The researchers would carefully map out their searches before they even accessed the databases. They would outline a plan, step by step. The database providers even gave the researchers pre-printed forms for search planning. When a researcher finally went to the database, he knew exactly what information he would enter, line by line. If his course changed, he would end his search session and reevaluate the planned course, again mapping the route to the data sought. Then he would re-enter the database with the new plan. This was the most efficient use of his online budget.

Internet researchers can take a tip or two from this approach. Map out your plan before you begin an Internet search. Try to imagine what information you want to find. Are you looking for salary, stock holding, or directorship information in this search? Are you trying to find your prospect's links to foundations? The plan you make will not prevent you from seeing routes to other information, but it will help you use your time productively. If you get sidetracked or begin to head down an unexpected avenue, pull over to the virtual curb to evaluate the new course you are beginning. Will this route lead to useful information?

Since search engines index only a portion of each Web page they visit and since they do not visit every Web page, your collection of links that take you directly to some types of information will be invaluable in your search plan. If, for example, you are looking for stock information, begin your search at one of the premier stock sites, not at a search engine. The same approach holds true when searching for biographical information, real estate data, and other bits of information generally held deeply in directories and databases not indexed in their entirety by search engines.

- Get pushed around.

When it comes to looking for new prospects, would you like to toss a single line into that vast Internet ocean of information, or would you rather send a few trawlers out to look for information for you while you hang out in the break room? Okay, you will not be in the break room because you have too much to do as it is. And that is all the more reason to enlist those trawlers. Having Internet information come to you via automated search robots, rather than hoping to find that information through individual searches is called push technology. Researchers around the world wish upon a star every single night that Internet engineers get better and better at creating push technology tools.

Several Web sites allow you to set up automatic searches with the search terms you choose. While you sleep (or work on other projects), your trawlers on autopilot cruise the Web looking for pages with your search terms on them. A periodic message in your email tells you that your trawlers have netted matches for you. Your review of those pages will tell you if the matches are keepers. If you consistently fail to get true matches, you will adjust your search terms and send those trawlers out again. See the push technology articles listed in the suggested reading section of this book and look for the latest developments in push technology among your peers. And do not forget to wish upon a star tonight.

- Put yourself in front of the speeding freight train.

Once you have built your Internet library of valuable addresses and once you are feeling adept at using a couple of search engines, you will be ready to add the next level of information retrieval and analysis to your talents. To do this, you will add monitoring Internet news to your daily or weekly chores. You will seek out opportunities to receive additional Internet training from the masters in your field. The more you learn about the options available to you, the better searcher you will become. The changes in this freight train's technology are happening so fast and it is all so vast that a new tool you need may be virtually nearby and you will not see it. Other Internet users can help you stay at the front of this information train.

The Ribbon-cutting Ceremony

There is one resource we have yet to bring to your attention in this chapter. It is the most important resource of all, so we saved it for last. It is a resource that comes from only one provider. It is nearly irreplaceable and only becomes more valuable with age and use. All the paper and electronic resources in the world cannot supercede this resource. In fact, they are useless without it. It has the special feature of being able to aggregate the information important to one nonprofit. It cannot only produce facts and figures, it can also analyze the data, make recommendations, and reach conclusions that will effect the future growth of that single nonprofit. Does it sound like a nonprofit's dream-come-true?

Where can your nonprofit get this resource, you ask? You already have it. It is you, the prospect researcher. It is the skill and talent you bring to your research job each day. As you research and identify prospects, you are adding information about your donor pool to your internal data tape. You are also adding skills that you will bring to the next research task your nonprofit presents. These two events cannot be replicated by any other resource in your research library. They are unique to you, the researcher. They are precisely the two talents that bring meaning to the prospect research function at your nonprofit. Now, grab the big scissors and let's have the most important part of the research library—you—cut the ribbon on this project.

As you can see, building a research library is not an easy task. It is, in fact, a research project of its own. You will have to identify current resources, evaluate them, measure their costs (both obvious and hidden), and choose among a strong field of candidates vying for a portion of your budget. Before you do any of these things, you will have to speculate about your major gift constituency, your organization's fund-raising goals over the next few years, and your information needs that arise out of the mix of these two elements.

Just like any daunting task, take this one in small measures. Follow the course we laid out for you here (see Figure 12-1). Begin in your own jurisdiction. Examine what you already have available. Shake off any sense of urgency that would have you speed through these tasks without considering the factors we have outlined.

There is one thing about prospect research that remains the same: The pool of major gift prospects only continues to grow. Do not be pushed down the library construction path simply because you are about to miss a chance to find a prospect. That sentence may become prophetic as you fight off the pressures others on the fund-raising team will bring to the research timeline and agenda being formulated at your nonprofit.

Creating a skilled prospect researcher is no easy task either, is it? Here, now, at the end of this book, that is precisely what you have the option to be. You have all the tools and resources you need to guide your fund-raising team to a new level of financial support for your nonprofit. An unimagined future for your nonprofit to increase its philanthropic strength is within your reach to facilitate through prospect research.

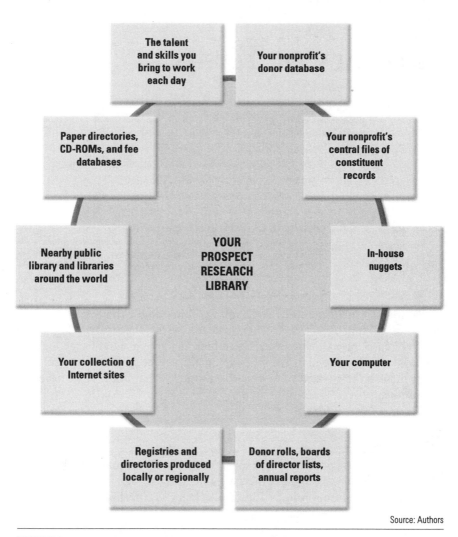

The talent and skills you bring to work each day

Your nonprofit's donor database

Paper directories, CD-ROMs, and fee databases

Your nonprofit's central files of constituent records

Nearby public library and libraries around the world

YOUR PROSPECT RESEARCH LIBRARY

In-house nuggets

Your collection of Internet sites

Your computer

Registries and directories produced locally or regionally

Donor rolls, boards of director lists, annual reports

Source: Authors

FIGURE 12-1
Your Prospect Research Library

Glossary of Terms

"The house is impractical and the boat is a paperweight."

—Kenneth Williams, who sold Sierra Online, a computer game company, for $1 billion, about the oceanfront Cabo San Lucas estate he was building and the 62-foot yacht he had bought; *Forbes,* February 8, 1999, p. 104.

This glossary of terms does not aspire to include all the terms you will encounter as a prospect researcher. Instead, we have assembled key terms you will encounter during research and terms used repeatedly throughout this book. We have tried to keep the explanation of the terms simple and have given them in the context of research and fund raising, not in their broadest definitions.

Numerical

10K/10Q: Reports produced on a schedule (annually or quarterly) by public companies. These reports and others are available through the U.S. Securities and Exchange Commission's Electronic Data Gathering, Analysis, and Retrieval (EDGAR) system.

501-3(c): A term referring to the nonprofit tax status of an organization; it is often used to describe a nonprofit.

990-PF: The U.S. Internal Revenue Service form used by foundations to report their income and giving activities over a single year.

A

Advancement: Used to describe the fund-raising section of a nonprofit; another word for "development."

Advancement research: See Prospect Research.

Affiliate: A person or entity with an existing relationship of significance with a nonprofit organization; the act of forming an attachment to a nonprofit organization by becoming a member, attending events, using services, volunteering, donating money, or creating other forms of shared experience. We use the word "constituent" interchangeably with "affiliate."

Affiliation: A link or attachment that an individual, corporation, or foundation forms to an organization by participating in its programs or services, or by volunteering or donating to the organization.

Algorithm: A procedure for solving a problem; usually applied to math problems.

Annual fund: The amount of money a nonprofit raises each year; the section of the fund-raising effort at a nonprofit that is charged with soliciting gifts from donors from every income level annually. Annual fund gifts are designated to the "general fund" and are not given to a specific program, scholarship, or fund. Fund raisers generally think of annual fund gifts as an amount smaller than that of a major gift, although major gift-sized gifts are given to the annual fund.

Annual fund gift: A gift to the unrestricted fund that supports the expense of running a nonprofit. Gifts in this group are solicited each year.

Annual report: The summary record produced each year by a company or foundation of its financial and leadership activities. Private companies are not required by law to file detailed reports, but active foundations and public companies are required to report their activities. For some foundations (particularly smaller ones), the 990-PF form they file serves as an annual report of their assets, giving, and directors and officers.

Anonymous gift: A gift given on the condition that the donor is never revealed. This type of gift requires strict security in gift processing, record keeping, and other procedures, even among development staff members, in order to live up to the agreement for anonymity made with the donor.

Application procedures: How to apply for support from a company or foundation, including format, reporting requirements, and deadlines.

APRA: The acronym for the Association of Professional Researchers for Advancement, the international professional organization for prospect researchers.

Appraisal, or appraised value: The sale price that a professional appraiser determines from careful analysis of what a willing buyer and a willing seller would agree upon for real or personal property (real estate, art, jewelry, automobiles, or other objects), usually set by comparing the item to be appraised with other comparable items.

Ask: Fund-raising shorthand for solicitation, as in: 1) the amount of money for which the prospect will be solicited; 2) the moment or event when development requests the gift from the prospect. The Ask distinguishes itself from the prospect's rating by being the precise amount to be requested from the prospect.

Assessment, or assessed value: The amount of money that a government employee, an assessor, determines to be the worth of real or personal property, usually related to the value placed on similar, nearby properties and on the tax structure in that locality. Assessed value is rarely the same as the value placed on a property by an appraiser.

Appreciated assets: Those personal holdings that are rich in value and have no or a low cost associated with them. Long-held real property, stocks and bonds, and collections of art or other objects may be appreciated assets.

Assets: Real and personal property of value or worth such as cash, stock, real estate, art, collectibles, and other items; the total amount of money the foundation has at the end of its fiscal year after expenses are subtracted.

Assignment: The formal establishment of the cultivation and solicitation relationship between a development officer and a prospect by the development team leader.

Association of Professional Researchers for Advancement: The international professional association providing educational and other benefits for prospect researchers (see APRA).

B

Bequest: The naming of a person or institution in a will, with the portion of the estate or the gift to be given upon the demise of the individual who establishes the bequest.

Bonus: The part of a worker's compensation usually linked to performance.

C

Call report: See Contact Report.

Campaign: A formalized effort to raise a specific amount of money in a set amount of time, usually for detailed initiatives, programs, or expansions. A capital campaign is a campaign that raises money to construct or remodel buildings.

Campaign donor table: An illustration of the number and size of major gifts a nonprofit will need to meet a specific fund-raising goal.

Capacity: The financial measure of a prospect's ability to give a major gift.

CASE: See Council for Advancement and Support of Education.

CD-ROM: A method of conveying information electronically; a disk that is inserted into a specific "drive" on a personal computer and then used to access electronic information.

Central filing system: The records held in a place accessible to a designated group of employees and the policies accompanying those records that outline access, retrieval, storage, and disposal of those records.

Charitable remainder trust: A financial vehicle established to make a gift to a nonprofit, to reduce taxes, and to control the outcome of the distribution of one's estate. It is usually an amount of money set aside to be invested by another entity with the promise of a prescribed return each year, based on the fair market value of the trust, until the death of the trust holder.

Checklist or check sheet (research): A form used to track the sources checked while completing a research project.

Community foundation: A nonprofit giving entity that amalgamates the giving of groups of usually unrelated donors.

Company foundation: A nonprofit giving entity established and administered by a for-profit business or its agents.

Competitive intelligence: A form of research in the commercial arena that focuses on developments among peer companies that may affect the success of one company's products or services.

Composite: In this context, any collection of characteristics of a group of individuals that can be applied and compared to other individuals.

Constituent: A person, company, or foundation that is a participant in a nonprofit's programs or fund-raising efforts; a donor or a prospective donor.

Consultant: An individual who does not work for an organization but who is retained on a contractual basis to complete specific assignments. The consultant often has skills or experience in a particular facet of the organization's operation.

Contact activity report: A prospect tracking report that summarizes the activity with prospects within a certain time frame.

Contact report: A written summary of the important information garnered through a planned encounter with a prospective donor or a donor. Particular attention is paid to information about capacity, affiliation, interests, and the timing for asking for a gift. See the appendix of this book for sample contact report forms.

Contribution: For our purposes, a gift of money, stock, property, or other objects of value that is made to a nonprofit.

Corporate giving program: The arm of a company that oversees the money and other resources allocated for philanthropy.

Corporation: The association of a group with a common objective to produce goods or services for monetary gain; often refers to a specific tax arrangement as outlined by local or national government.

Corporation profile: A research report that assembles information and analysis regarding a corporation that is a prospective donor or donor. This form may include the corporation's name; contact information (mailing address, phone number, Web address, and facsimile); the key people in the corporation, their titles and any other pertinent information about them; gross sales; number of employees; company affiliates who also affiliate with your nonprofit; key information about corporate giving program (including who to contact); history of giving to your nonprofit; sample gifts to other institutions; history of contact with your nonprofit (including proposals and outcomes); important news about the corporation (including mergers, new initiatives of relevance to your nonprofit, areas of operation); researcher's recommendations, including gift capacity or Ask amount; and any cultivation strategies that emerged during research. See appendix for samples.

Corpus: For our purposes, the assets of a foundation or corporate giving program.

Council for Advancement and Support of Education: The international professional association for development officers, managers, and others who work for nonprofits with education as a mission (CASE).

Counts and moves report: A prospect tracking report designed to display the pipeline status and the gift level for a number of prospects or for the prospects assigned to one development officer.

Cultivation: The set of planned encounters through which a fund raiser brings a prospect nearer to readiness for making a major philanthropic gift within the prescribed time period (see moves).

D

Database: The electronic software used to house and maintain information about a group's constituents.

Data entry: The act of accurately adding information to an electronic database.

DBA: "Doing business as;" a term used to describe other names under which a person or company may operate.

DEF-14A: The Securities and Exchange EDGAR code for a proxy statement, the annual document that calls shareholders to their yearly meeting about the company's performance and their chance to elect new directors. This document details the compensation, including stock options and holdings, of directors, chief officers, and other individuals intimately associated with the company. Go to **http://www.sec.gov/info/edgar/forms.htm** for explanations of the naming convention for this and other documents.

Deferred Gift: A gift for which a nonprofit waits; a planned gift such as a remainder trust or annuity, a bequest.

Demographics: Characteristics of an individual or group such as location, age, gender, marital status, education, and other features.

Development: The fund-raising section of a nonprofit (see Advancement).

Development officer: A person designated to raise money for a nonprofit, usually by soliciting significant gifts from prospective donors. This term is used interchangeably in this book with "fund raiser" and "major gifts officer."

Development research: See Prospect research.

Director: A member of the board that oversees operation of a company or foundation. In regard to corporations and corporate foundations, the board is usually made up of leaders of other companies, large investors, and the employee who heads the company. In regard to private foundations, the board may be comprised of the individual(s) who established the foundation, family members, advisors, or other nonprofit leaders.

Donor: A contributor of money, time, goods, or services to a nonprofit.

Donor Pyramid: A visual representation of the hierarchy of donors to a nonprofit by the size of their gifts and the number of donors in regard to wealth. In recent times, the top level of the pyramid illustrates that about 10 percent of constituents give 90 percent of the gifts. This is sometimes known as the 90/10 Rule.

Donor roll: The report of donors to a nonprofit, often including the giving range for each donor. The report is available to the nonprofit's supporters and the public, and it is usually produced annually or even more frequently. Special donor reports are frequently produced at the end of campaigns. Also known as an honor roll or a tribute.

E

E: An abbreviation for the word "electronic," as in email or e-newsletter.

EDGAR: The U.S. Securities and Exchange Commission's Electronic Data Gathering, Analysis, and Retrieval system (EDGAR); the Internet-based system housing the reporting documents filed by public companies.

Electronic screening: The en masse examination of specific characteristics of individuals in a database or of an entire database of constituents in order to identify the most likely gift prospects, to identify new prospects, or to further qualify known prospects.

Elvis Presley: A living legend in music and film and an adherent of spontaneous philanthropy.

Ethics: An established set of values and standards that guides behavior.

Event preparation report: A report format researchers use to ready fund raisers and the organization's leaders for events by giving them concise information that will facilitate the cultivation of prospects who will attend the event. Events might include building dedications, annual donor recognition receptions, or local, regional, and national fund-raising parties. The guest list may be restricted to major gift donors or it may include a mix of constituents. Researchers and fund raisers determine who among the invitees will be included in the researcher's event report.

Executive compensation table: The portion of the proxy statement that outlines the salary, bonus, and other compensation paid during each of the last few years to a few of the top officers of a public company.

Exercising an option: The act of buying shares of stock that are outlined as available to a company officer or director at a specific price within a specific period of time.

Exercise price: See strike price.

F

Family tree: A graphic of the relationships between individuals related by birth, marriage, or adoption; often includes dates of birth, marriage, divorce, and death.

Feasibility study: An examination of a specific aspect of an operation or the entire operation, with the aim of determining if specific goals can be accomplished.

Fee-based: Refers to services or resources with access or use contingent on paying a per-unit, monthly, or annual fee.

Foundation: An entity formed under the tax code of the federal government with the purpose of giving away a portion of its assets each year to nonprofit organizations, to individuals, or to other qualifying entities.

Foundation profile: A reporting form that assembles the information and analysis regarding a foundation or other institutional donor or prospective donor; it may include the foundation's name; contact information (mailing address, phone number, Web address, and facsimile); the key people in the foundation, their titles, and any other pertinent information about them; history of the foundation (year founded, founders, and contributors); assets; foundation affiliates who also affiliate with your nonprofit; giving guidelines (including due dates and areas of operation); history of giving to your nonprofit; sample gifts to other institutions; history of contact with your nonprofit (including proposals and outcomes); important news about the foundation (including leadership changes, new initiatives of relevance to your nonprofit); and researcher's recommendations, including Ask amount; purpose of the Ask; and any cultivation strategies that emerged during research. See appendix section for sample format.

Four and a Half Rights: A way to explain the key elements in designing the successful closing of a gift, developed by Karen E. Osborne, Principal of The Osborne Group. The key elements are 1) amount 2) purpose 3) solicitor 4) timing and 4 $\frac{1}{2}$) place and other details of the solicitation.

Fund raiser: A person designated to raise money for a nonprofit; a development officer or major gifts officer.

Fund-raising adages: Sayings or formulas based on experience about giving levels, giving ability, or other philanthropic events that help guide actions and decisions.

G

Gift: A voluntary offering of time, money, or goods in the spirit of helping the recipient.

Gift annuity: A planned gift that is a contract between a donor and a charity for the donor to receive a specific return from an annuity investment and the remainder to go to the charity.

Gift-in-kind: A gift of something other than money, usually an object (books or equipment, for example) or an expense incurred in service to the nonprofit by the donor (airfare to come to a board meeting, for example).

Gift processing: The section of the development office charged with receiving and recording the gifts sent by donors.

Gift report: Paper or electronic assemblages of the donations made to an organization each day or week.

Giving club: An established threshold of gifts placing a donor in a specific giving group. The giving group is often designated with a name, hence the designation of "club."

Government giving programs: The giving administered by local, state, and federal government, from community-based arts and social services programs to national departments that oversee government branches administering the distribution of huge contributions to nonprofits.

Grant: A gift made by a corporation, foundation, or government entity, or sometimes by a person, to a nonprofit organization.

Grantee: The recipient of a gift or grant; see grant seeker.

Grant maker: Another term for a foundation, corporation, or government entity, or sometimes the individual, giving or potentially able to give money to a nonprofit; an entity that has an active giving program.

Grantor: The foundation making the gift; see grant maker.

Grant seeker: See grantee.

Grant writer: The person who completes the application process, including writing proposals or requests for funding. The proposals are written to individuals, foundations, corporations, or government entities for gifts. The proposals include the intended purpose for the support requested and details about the nonprofit requesting the support.

Guidelines: The grantor's explanation of what institutions, causes, and programs they wish to support.

H

Heir: Someone who will receive an estate or a portion of an estate upon the demise of another person, often a predecessor of the heir.

Honor roll: See donor roll.

Household-level data: Information about groups of residences generated by surveys and U.S. Census information; the information may include home values, family size, income range, and other data.

I

Individual profile: A reporting form that assembles the information and analysis regarding an individual prospective donor or donor; it may include full name; date of birth; how the prospect affiliates; home and work contact information; job title; work history; family information (spouse, parents, children, other family members affiliated with the institution); directorships (boards, volunteer position, business associations); awards; financial information (salary and other compensation, stock holdings, private company sales and other data); real estate holdings and assessed values; history of contact with the nonprofit; giving history; gifts to other nonprofits; news about the prospect or the prospect's company; and researcher's recommendations, including gift capacity and Ask amount. See appendix section for sample format.

Individual-specific data: Information that is particular to a single individual such as place of employment, stock holdings, real estate holdings, and other data.

Initial Public Offering: The first time a private company offers shares for purchase by the public; also known as "going public;" the acronym is IPO.

Insider: One of the chief officers, all directors, and any person who holds and controls five percent or more of a company in the form of publicly trade stock. Insiders have access to information about the company that other stockholders do not.

Institution: In the context of this book, a nonprofit organization.

Institutional giver: A government entity making grants to nonprofits.

Internet: The electronic information medium that provides access to databases (related sets of information) and free-form information bits or unrelated information; the electronic presentation of data about companies, foundations, and individuals, as well as affinity group postings and more.

In-the-money options: The unexercised options with an option (or "strike") price lower than the market price at the time of the report.

Irrevocable gift: A deferred gift that a donor cannot remove from its charitable destination.

K

Keyword: A search term referring to a word that a searcher expects to appear in documents returned by a search engine.

L

Lead gift: A planned giving vehicle in which, through an annuity or unitrust investment, a nonprofit receives the benefit of the gift each year, and the beneficiary or his designee gets the remainder of the gift when the lead gift ends. Lead gifts are usually a term of years.

Letter of inquiry: An application procedure required by some foundations and corporation where, in a brief letter, a potential grantee asks a grantor to indicate interest in the grantee's type of nonprofit or proposed funding request. The letter outlines its mission and the intended request and is a "first contact" so that the grant maker can eliminate inappropriate applicants and encourage others without having to review full proposals at this early stage.

Library: In regard to prospect research, a place where the information resources and historical materials used to identify wealth and capacity are held in an organized way.

Long-term payout: Benefits received by public company officers that involve delayed compensation.

M

Major gift: As defined by each nonprofit, a gift greater than that given annually; a gift given with a significant effort on the part of the donor that may be given in multi-year payments; a large gift that often comes from assets instead of income.

Major gifts officer: See development officer or fund raiser.

Major gifts program: An initiative begun by a nonprofit that centers on soliciting donors for major gifts. This initiative usually includes adding fund raisers who will be cultivating major gift prospects and a researcher to identify the prospects.

Major gifts strategy meeting: A meeting held on a regular basis where development officers and researchers review the progress and plan for cultivating prospects and offer advice for moving the cultivations forward. Other agenda items may include assigning new prospects, reviewing lists of gifts to be closed, and other actions related to keeping the fund-raising process dynamic.

Market value (of real estate): The price that a real estate appraiser determines a willing buyer and a willing seller will agree upon for a property; property may include land, land and buildings, or just buildings.

Matching gift: A gift made by a foundation or corporation in the name of an affiliate after the affiliate makes a gift. The "match" may be expressed by the ratio at which the institutional giver gives in relation to the affiliate's giving. For example, the match may be 1:1, that is, for each single dollar given by the affiliate, the institutional giver gives a single dollar. Match ratios vary.

Memo of Understanding: A written agreement between a nonprofit and a donor about a specific gift the donor intends to give the nonprofit. Also known by its acronym "MOU." Memos of Understanding are written when donors make a pledge, a multiple-year gift, or when the gift includes specific distribution requirements. For example, MOUs are written when donors establish an endowed scholarship at an educational institution. The MOU in this case would spell out the donor's wishes about the distribution of scholarship money.

Mission: The purpose for a nonprofit to exist; the focus of the nonprofit's primary activity.

MOU: See Memo of Understanding.

Move: A donor activity that a development officer plans with the intent to advance the donor closer to the solicitation. The activity usually provides an opportunity for the development officer to answer one of the four and one-half rights (see four and a half rights).

N

Named gift: A gift large enough to give the donor the option to attach his or someone else's name. The name may be placed on a room, a building, an architectural feature, a scholarship, a performance, an exhibition, a preserve, or a special fund, for example.

Net worth: The monetary value of an individual's holdings after all expenses and debts are deducted. The net worth of a prospect is unavailable to fund raisers since the details of the prospect's precise income and expenses are not public information.

Net worth formulas: See research math.

Nonprofit: A 501-3c; an entity existing for a purpose other than making money; one that serves a specific population or purpose, turning its revenues back into its own programming to benefit the greater good of society.

O

Officer or chief officer: One of the top employees of a company. The hierarchy of jobs may be in an order such as chairman, president, chief executive officer, chief operating officer, secretary/treasurer, and executive or senior vice presidents.

Operating area: The geographical area in which a foundation or company gives grants. It is usually the same as the area in which the entity is located, does business, has plants or offices, or in which many of its customers live. For foundations, it may be the same community or state where the founders grew up or lived.

Option: A benefit of employment or board service that gives the individual the opportunity to buy a specific number of shares within a designated period of time.

Option price: The price per share of stock that a company employee or director will pay; this price is granted as a benefit of association with the company; also known as strike price.

Organization: In the context of this book, another name for a nonprofit or an institution.

Outright gift: A gift of real or personal property given to the nonprofit for its immediate use. The donor has no connection to the gift after it is given.

P

Peer screening: The act of reviewing lists of fellow constituents in order to indicate which among them have major gift capacity, would make good leaders or volunteers, or to identify other characteristics.

Philanthropist: Someone who supports a charity or charities in a consistent or significant way. This may mean one or a few large gifts or a lifetime of average giving.

Planned gift: A deferred gift, designated through careful examination of income and other needs and benefits as well as a consideration of an opportunity to be philanthropic.

Planned giving: The section of the fund-raising effort that is charged with asking prospective donors to name the nonprofit in their estate plans or to consider one of several tax-saving vehicles for giving over a period or delayed moment of time to the nonprofit.

Planned giving officer: The fund raiser at a nonprofit who is charged with securing gifts through bequests, annuities, trusts, and other deferred giving opportunities. This fund raiser is well versed in current income tax laws, retirement issues, and other technical matters relating to these types of gifts.

Pledge: A gift promised. The pledge may be short term (until the check arrives) or a longer term, even a number of years.

Policies: The established (usually written) reason for an action; the why of any distinct event or process.

Pool: A holding place for the names of affiliates who may become major gift prospects. The pool consists of affiliates for whom little or no research has been completed but who have shown indicators of wealth; former major gift prospects who did not make a gift during cultivation but may in the future; affiliates who are not yet at the life stage for major gift-giving; and affiliates who may inherit wealth later in their lives. The pool is an electronic holding pen, an electronic marker on each pool-dweller's record that allows research to compile lists of possible prospects for future research, and to replenish the assignment and visit lists of the development officers.

Pooled Income Fund (PIF): A planned giving vehicle for donors who have limited giving capacity, so the donor's gift is added to a larger investment vehicle. A PIF is usually established with a minimum amount for initial entry and annual or incremental minimums.

Pre-selected grantees: Those nonprofits that have been named as the recipients of gifts by a foundation prior to applications; nonprofits not pre-selected are discouraged from applying for support.

Predictive modeling: Using a mathematical algorithm to analyze certain characteristics and past actions of a prospect for the purpose of predicting future behavior.

Privacy: For our purposes, elements of one's life that are not publicly available, are not subject to disclosure or public revelation.

Private company: A company in which the chief investors are the company founders or those who are close and well known to the company founders. In return for their investment, these individuals may be given private stock, a voice in the direction of the company, or other financial benefits. A private company is under no obligation to make a public report of the compensation it makes to its chief officers, directors, or investors.

Private foundation: Nonprofit giving entity formed by individuals or families to serve as the primary vehicle for charitable giving.

Proactive research: Approach to prospect research whereby a researcher spends most of her time identifying and qualifying new prospective donors.

Procedures: The actions taken to cause adherence to a policy; written steps regarding how the policy will be implemented; the who, where, when, and how the policy will be carried out.

Profile: A concise portrait of a prospective donor expressed in a standardized format. Also see definitions of corporation profile, foundation profile, and individual profile. See examples of individual, foundation, and corporation profile formats in the appendix section of this book.

Proposal: A written request for financial support submitted to a foundation, corporation, or individual by a nonprofit.

Proprietary: Owned by one entity; not available to be copied or reproduced in precisely the same way by others.

Prospect: Fund-raising and research shorthand for a prospective donor; a person, foundation, or corporation able to make a major gift.

Prospect manager: The person designated to oversee all the fund-raising contacts, cultivations, proposals, and other solicitations related to a single prospect.

Prospect pipeline: A concept used to describe the location of a prospective donor in the cultivation progression. The four stages of the prospect pipeline are identification, cultivation, zero-to-six months, and solicitation.

Prospect research: The gathering of information and the detailed analysis of that information with the goal to identify, qualify, and define prospective donors for a nonprofit's major gifts program.

Prospect tracking system: The method of planning, reporting, and recording the progress of the cultivation, solicitation, and stewardship of prospective major gift donors.

Proxy statement: The announcement of the annual meeting and the report to stockholders of the proposed slate of directors, and the compensation, stock holdings, options, retirement plan, and other employment and board service details for the top officers (often three to five) and others closely involved with a public company.

Public company: A company in which many unrelated people invest, making these individuals stockholders. The company is obligated to report its financial well-being, its leadership and their remuneration and financial interest in the company, and other economic details to the stockholders each year via the U.S. Securities and Exchange Commission (SEC) documents.

R

Ranking: The place in a hierarchy where a unit falls; the act of placing individuals in a hierarchy based on a set of characteristics.

Rating: The act of assigning a likely gift capacity amount or wealth range to indivduals, foundations, or corporations; the amount assigned.

Reactive Research: An approach to prospect research whereby a researcher spends a great deal of his time fulfilling research requests, updating profiles, and preparing event reports.

Reading file: The collection of that week or month's contact reports, proposals, and other important communications gathered into one paper or electronic spot. It is circulated quickly among the development and research staff.

Real estate: Land and buildings, land only, or buildings only owned by individuals, corporations, foundations, or other entities.

Research log: The report of everything you accomplish as a researcher. The research log will include new prospects identified, research requests fulfilled, special reports, and any other research work you complete. Most research logs are organized so that the types of research completed can be viewed separately (how many new prospects were identified, how many event reports were written).

Research math (net worth or gift capacity formulas): A collection of math formulas used to measure wealth and capacity and designed from the experiences of researchers and fund raisers. Most researchers do not provide net worth estimates in their research reports, but all researchers know about them. The worth formulas are not based on scientific study, but are instead related to the composition of estates as reported by the U.S. Internal Revenue Service and other sources. The giving formulas, used to estimate the gift capacity of a prospect, are generally based on the anecdotal experiences of fund raisers.

Research report: Any written summary of the information gathered and analyzed by a prospect researcher. Research reports can take many forms, including profiles, brief biographical outlines, and computer-generated reports that draw pieces of information from a database into a specified format.

Research request: The act of asking for information about a prospective donor, a donor, or other entity affiliated with a nonprofit. A research request may be for nearly any public information, basic contact data, a full profile, a financial report, information about recent developments in the prospect's life, family tree research, or other data analysis. The report generated from the research request may take one of many formats, depending on the information requested.

Resource: Anything used to gain information; a resource may be a book, CD-ROM, electronic database, a Web site, an organization, or a person, for example.

Responsible staff: The development officer designated to handle the activities associated with a particular cultivation and solicitation of a major gift prospect, under the overall coordination of the prospect manager (see prospect manager).

Restricted gift: A gift that must be applied to a specific use. For example, gifts to scholarships or special funds or departments are restricted gifts.

Revocable gift: A planned gift that a donor can rescind.

S

Salary: The amount of money paid by a company to an employee for work done.

Sale price (of real estate): The actual price paid by a buyer for real property.

Screener: The individual or company completing a gift capacity analysis of an individual or individuals en masse (see electronic screening or peer screening).

Screening questionnaire: A series of questions or statements about knowledge of gift capacity, wealth, connections, or leadership qualities that is designed by fund raisers and to be completed by volunteers.

Screening session: An event at which volunteers review lists of constituents and indicate which among them are likely major gift supporters or potential leaders for a nonprofit.

Securities and Exchange Commission (SEC): The division of the U.S. federal government overseeing the financial reporting requirements and stock transactions of public companies.

Segmentation, segmenting: Dividing objects (or, in this case, people) into clusters based on common traits or characteristics.

Share of stock, direct or indirect: A unit of interest in a public company that has a monetary value established each day through buying and selling of that stock. When a share is owned outright by one person or entity, it is a direct holding. When it is held by an adult in the name of a minor, jointly held by more than one person or other entity, or when its transfer or sale is decided by more than one person or entity, it is said to be an indirect holding.

Solicitation: A request; the act of asking for a specific thing, usually financial support when referring to nonprofits.

Stage aging report: A prospect tracking report designed to show development officers and their managers how long a prospect has been in a particular stage of the pipeline.

Stewardship: The act of keeping a donor connected with a nonprofit after the individual, foundation, corporation, or government entity has given a major gift. The process may involve information about the use of the gift, updates about the nonprofit itself, or invitations to events or programs (some associated with the gift).

Stock: See share of stock.

Stock holdings: The number of shares of a company's (or companies') stock that an individual owns.

Strike price: The dollar amount at which an individual may buy stock.

Sunshine laws: Regulations that order specific information to be made available to the public.

Superlatives (lists of): See "top" lists.

Suspect: A person or other entity (foundation or corporation) not yet researched but who demonstrates preliminary indicators of wealth and affiliation to and interest in a nonprofit. The wealth indicators might be an unexpected gift, a news story about a job promotion or windfall, or news about gifts to similar nonprofits, for example.

T

"Top" lists: Lists of companies, foundations, or individuals that rank the entities by specific characteristics, usually related to financial performance, size, or other unique features; also known as superlative lists.

Transparency: The ability to see into or through; refers to a societal concept of openness and the availability of information about certain entities or particular aspects of those entities.

Trustee: One of the volunteer leaders of a charitable organization; a member of the administrative board.

U

Unexercised options: Those shares to which the prospect has an option but which have restrictions that prevent the taking of that option in this time period. You will find the definitions for these and other terms you will encounter in your proxy work at financial websites.

Unrestricted gift: A gift that the nonprofit may use in the way it determines to be the best use.

V

Volunteer: A person who gives their time and resources with no expectation of monetary reward or compensation.

W

Wealth: A large amount of money or assets, a great deal more than that held by the majority of people in one's society.

Are there terms that you would like to see included here in updates to this book? Send them to Cecilia Hogan at **chogan@ups.edu.**

Policies and Procedures

A. Association of Professional Researchers for Advancement (APRA) Statement of Ethics

APRA's Statement of Ethics is a hallmark for prospect researchers and forms the backbone of the ethics and privacy policy at some nonprofits. The APRA board revisits the statement periodically. The copy included here is the latest available at the time of this writing. Check the APRA Web site at http://www.aprahome.org for updates to the Statement of Ethics.

A collaborative effort by several professional associations produced the Donor Bill of Rights, which you can see in the Confidentiality Policies file on PRSPCT-L. You may also see the Donor Bill of Rights at the Council for the Advancement and Support of Education Web site at http://www.case.org/about/donor.cfm.

B. Sample Confidentiality Requirements and Agreement Form

Nonprofits with volunteers, part-time workers, interns, or student workers may find it useful to develop a confidentiality statement for each person with access to donor records to sign. A nonprofit may wish each full-time employee to sign a similar statement. This section includes a sample confidentiality agreement.

Researchers from several organizations posted their confidentiality policies at the PRSPCT-L Web site in the section named "Files." A direct link to the confidentiality policies is:
http://groups.yahoo.com/group/PRSPCT-L/files/Confidentiality%20Policies/

You will not be able to access this section of the PRSPCT-L group until you join the listserv.

C. Sample Central File Policy and Procedures

Please refer to chapters 9 and 12 for information about establishing a central file system. Each nonprofit forms a policy and set of procedures based on many factors, including the technology available, the number of files and the space available, and other issues. You will find a sample central file policy and procedure document here.

D. Sample Research Formats Policy and Procedures

Researchers design many ways to report the information they gather and analyze. Several formats in addition to the standard profile form are common. You will find a sample of procedures for research formats here.

APRA Statement of Ethics

Copyright © 1998 APRA
September 30, 1998

Association of Professional Researchers for Advancement (APRA) members shall support and further the individual's fundamental right to privacy and protect the confidential information of their institutions. APRA members are committed to the ethical collection and use of information. Members shall follow all applicable federal, state, and local laws, as well as institutional policies, governing the collection, use, maintenance, and dissemination of information in the pursuit of the missions of their institutions. APRA members shall respect all people and organizations.

Code of Ethics

Prospect researchers must balance the needs of their institutions to collect, analyze, record, maintain, use, and disseminate information with an individual's right to privacy. This balance is not always easy to maintain.

The following ethical principles apply, and practice is built on these principles:

I. Fundamental Principles

A. *Confidentiality*
Confidential information about constituents (donors and non-donors), as well as confidential information of the institutions in oral form or on electronic, magnetic, or print media are protected so that the relationship of trust between the constituent and the institution is upheld.

B. *Accuracy*
Prospect researchers shall record all data accurately. Such information shall include attribution. Analysis and products of data analysis should be without personal prejudices or biases.

C. *Relevance*
Prospect researchers shall seek and record only information that is relevant and appropriate to the fund-raising effort of the institutions that employ them.

D. *Accountability*
Prospect researchers shall accept responsibility for their actions and shall be accountable to the profession of development, to their respective institutions, and to the constituents who place their trust in prospect researchers and their institutions.

E. *Honesty*
Prospect researchers shall be truthful with regard to their identity and purpose and the identity of their institution during the course of their work.

II. Suggested Practice

A. *Collection*
1. The collection of information shall be done lawfully, respecting applicable laws and institutional policies.
2. Information sought and recorded includes all data that can be verified and attributed, as well as constituent information that is self-reported (via correspondence, surveys, questionnaires, etc.).
3. When requesting information in person or by telephone, it is recommended in most cases that neither individual nor institutional identity shall be concealed. Written requests for public information shall be made on institutional stationary clearly identifying the inquirer.
4. Whenever possible, payments for public records shall be made through the institution.
5. Prospect researchers shall apply the same standards for electronic information that they currently use in evaluating and verifying print media. The researcher shall ascertain whether or not the information comes from a reliable source and that the information collected meets the standards set forth in the APRA Statement of Ethics.

B. *Recording and Maintenance*
1. Researchers shall state information in an objective and factual manner; note attribution and date of collection; and clearly identify analysis.
2. Constituent information on paper, electronic, magnetic or other media shall be stored securely to prevent access by unauthorized persons.
3. Special protection shall be afforded all giving records pertaining to anonymous donors.
4. Electronic or paper documents pertaining to constituents shall be irreversibly disposed of when no longer needed (by following institutional standards for document disposal).

C. *Use and Distribution*
1. Researchers shall adhere to all applicable laws, as well as to institutional policies, regarding the use and distribution of confidential constituent information.
2. Constituent information is the property of the institution for which it was collected and shall not be given to persons other than those who are involved with the cultivation or solicitation effort or those who need that information in the performance of their duties for that institution.

3. Constituent information for one institution shall not be taken to another institution.
4. Research documents containing constituent information that is to be used outside research offices shall be clearly marked "confidential."
5. Vendors, consultants, and other external entities shall understand and agree to comply with the institution's confidentiality policies before gaining access to institutional data.
6. Only publicly available information shall be shared with colleagues at other institutions as a professional courtesy.

III. Recommendations

1. Prospect researchers shall urge their institutions to develop written policies based upon applicable laws and these policies should define what information shall be gathered, recorded and maintained, and to whom and under what conditions the information can be released.
2. Prospect researchers shall urge the development of written policies at their institutions defining who may authorize access to prospect files and under what conditions. These policies should follow the guidelines outlined in the CASE Donor Bill of Rights, the NSFRE Code of Ethical Principles, and the Association for Healthcare Philanthropy Statement of Professional Standards and Conduct.
3. Prospect researchers shall strongly urge their development colleagues to abide by this Code of Ethics and Fundamental Principles.

Confidentiality Requirement and Agreement Form

Your eligibility to work in the Office of Development is contingent upon your willingness to abide by our confidentiality requirements. The Association of Professional Researchers for Advancement (APRA) Statement of Ethics states:

> *"Constituent information is the property of the institution for which it was collected and shall not be given to persons other than those who are involved with the cultivation or solicitation effort or those who need that information in the performance of their duties for that institution."*

> *"Confidential information about constituents (donors and non-donors), as well as confidential information of the institutions in oral form or on electronic, magnetic, or print media are protected so that the relationship of trust between the constituent and the institution is upheld."*

Constituent and donor records, both hard copy and electronic, and other constituent or donor information are highly confidential and protected by both organization and departmental policy. You must not discuss with anyone outside the office any personal constituent information, nor may you release any information or documents to a third party without proper authorization to do so. A violation of this trust is grounds for immediate termination of your employment and possible grounds for further disciplinary action.

Confidentiality Agreement

I hereby acknowledge my responsibility to deal discreetly with confidential records and information kept in the Development offices. My signature below indicates my willingness to respect our constituents' right to privacy, and to avoid disseminating confidential information outside the Development offices. In particular:

1. Sensitive information including giving histories, family data, asset holdings, and other details of the constituent's relationship with this organization and others will be treated with special care.

2. Development records will not be reproduced, stored in a retrieval system other than that approved by this organization, or transmitted in any form or by any means, electronic, mechanical, photocopying, recording, or otherwise without authorization.

_____   _____
Employee's Signature   Date

_____   _____
Supervisor's Signature   Date

Source: Author

Central File Policy and Procedures

RATIONALE: Central File is a resource for all in our department. By understanding and adhering to a common set of rules, all staff contributes to a strong system that works for all of us.

POLICY: Certain documents produced on-campus as well as from off-campus sources contain information pertinent to alumni, donors and prospective donors. These documents are housed in a central location according to rules as set forth below.

PROCEDURE I. Central File Security and Access

A. Central File is the property of this nonprofit and, particularly, of the Development department. All information contained within the files of Central File is strictly confidential. Only Development staff members and volunteers or students working in collaboration with Development staff members have access, unless arrangements are made with the vice president of the department, the director of Development or the director of Advancement Services. No files will leave the University's campus.

B. Central File is open during normal business hours (8:00 to 5:00). After normal work hours Central File will be locked. Arrangements can be made for after hours and weekend use through the director of Development or the director of Advancement Services.

C. Every file will be checked out using the out-cards kept in the Central File area indicating the date, the file, and the person who will be needing the file. The user's name must be recorded on the out-card. Do not remove a file from Central File without using an out-card.

PROCEDURE II. Central File Contents

A. Central File contains specific information pertaining to University trustees and those individuals, corporations, and foundations important to the development and alumni efforts of this nonprofit. These files contain information that documents a former, current or potential relationship to the University, further aiding the efforts of the Development office. Information that cannot be verified about an individual or organization (rumors, opinions, conjectures, or second-party conversations) will not be documented in Central File.

Examples of documents to be filed are: Funding Proposals, Planned Giving Documents, Referenced Correspondence Enclosures (unless a standard department form), Constituent Questionnaires, Research Profiles and Documentation, Contact Reports, Cultivation Plans, Correspondence from the Entity, Matching Gift Documentation, Gift Recognition Letters, Presidential Letters, Christmas Cards with further biographical information, In-Kind Gift Documentation, back-up for Gifts other than Annual Fund.

Examples of documents not to be filed are: Attendance Lists, Routine Annual Fund Letters, Invitations and RSVPs, Old Minutes, Staff Directives, Phone Messages, Routine Christmas Cards, and Receipts for Routine Annual Fund Gifts.

B. All users of Central File will be aware of filing rules and will police their own submissions to Central File. The director of Advancement Services will arbitrate disagreements.

C. A Central File will be created at the request of the department management staff and with the coordination of the director of Advancement Services. Management staff will be responsible for indicating the correct and full name to be used and any dummy or cross-filing that should be established. Individual files will be created for major gift prospects and suspects as documents are collected. General files will contain up to eight (8) documents on individuals, corporations, and foundations. Cross-files relate entities that need duplicate document filing. Dummy files are indicator cards that enable the user to locate multi-named files.

D. The No Solicitation and No Mail code files will be kept separately in Central File. These two files will contain copies of the alphabetized documentation of an entity's request to receive no solicitation or mail from the Development department. Then original documentation will be kept in the individual's file. No-Mail requests will be channeled through the director of Alumni Relations; No Solicitation requests will be channeled through the director of Annual Giving.

The original request will be sent to Central File by indicating a change to either the No Solicitation or No Mail code file, highlighting the name or names to be changed, along with the appropriate director initials and date.

PROCEDURE III. Central File Procedures
A. The author or the recipient (from non-department generated correspondence or sources) of a document belonging in Central File will be responsible for:

1. Placing - cc: Central File - Samantha Jones '83 or
   bcc: Mr. and Mrs. George Higgins '69
   Widgett Foundation
   Cross File - Widgett Corporation

on the document. The carbon copy (cc:) notation should be used for internal correspondence, or on documents received from outside sources. The blind carbon copy (bcc:) notation should be used when it is inappropriate to show the Central File process on correspondence. These notations to Central File should be placed along with other cc:'s/bcc:'s and highlighted. When one document affects several Central Files, it is particularly important that each recipient file is named, as above.

When more than one staff member is the recipient of non-department generated correspondence, the first person listed is responsible for following the process of getting the document to file. When a document is addressed to a non-staff member, or a Development department staff member is copied on such a document, the staff member is responsible for following the process to file.

2. Noting on any outside source document (newspapers, articles, official documents) its date, source, and sender initials.

3. Copying the appropriate number of Central File copies to be filed.

4. Placing these copies in the Central File in-coming sorter.

B. Central filing will be done by student employees under the supervision of the director of Advancement Services. The students will be responsible for:

1. Ensuring that all files are kept in alphabetical order and separately coded as: Trustees—Individuals—Corporation/Foundations— Generals—Inactive: Individual—Inactive: Corporate/Foundations

2. Keeping all files labeled with their full name.

3. Filing the most recently dated documentation on top of previously dated information.

4. Ensuring that Biographical Profiles, Research Documentation, and Periodical Clippings are kept on the left-hand side of the file.

5. Keeping dummy files alphabetically within the properly coded area and labeled as follows: Harold Smythe, See: Smythe & Company

6. Keeping cross-files alphabetically within the properly coded area and labeled as follows: Harold Smythe, Cross File: Smythe & Company

7. Updating the Central File Index on a yearly basis.

Reviewed & Verified by: Date

Source: Author

Research Formats Policy and Procedures

SUBJECT: STANDARD RESEARCH FORMATS

LAST UPDATE: November 28, 2001

RATIONALE

Standard research formats were created to meet the needs of users and to make information retrieval and reporting consistent. By standardizing reports, users know where to find information in the document and can anticipate what kind of information will be included in each report.

POLICY

Several report formats are used in Research. The type of format used is influenced by the depth of information needed. The Standard Profile (Individual, Corporation, or Foundation) format provides the most detailed information. It is used to outline corporations and foundations as well as individuals. A shorter version of the profile, the Trustee Candidate Profile, is used for trustee candidates. The Narrative Briefing format, a short narrative, outlines major gift prospects attending events with many attendees. The New Prospect Report format provides information about new prospects in a narrative format. The Scholarship format is a modified profile reporting about scholarships and the donors attending the annual scholarship luncheons. A Standard Memo format is sometimes used when responding to research requests that require a short explanation or a brief narrative.

PROCEDURE

Reactive Research: The person requesting the report indicates which format will be appropriate or accepts the format suggested by the director of Research or the researcher.

Active Research: The researcher generally uses the New Prospect Report format when submitting new prospect names for assignment. The Standard Profile format will be used in some cases.

A copy of each Profile, Narrative Briefing, New Prospect Report, and Scholarship format is sent to the requester, to the central file of the subject and any other appropriate files (such as a related company or foundation file or the file of a relative) and to the bio books in the research office. The addition of the report to the bio books is noted in the bio book index in the research office. The reports are also stored on the hard drive of the computer in the research office and the shared drive designated to the Development department.

Memo format reports are sent to the requesters and to the files. They are retained on the hard drive of the researcher's computer and on the shared drive designated to the Development department. They are not retained in paper format in the research office.

The types of reports are outlined here. The templates are found on the researcher's computer and on the shared drive designated to the Development department in a file called "Forms."

INDIVIDUAL PROFILE: This is the standard profile which includes subject's
name (maiden in parenthesis if applicable), affiliation to this nonprofit (in
descending order of importance), business address and phone number (and fax,
e-mail and Web site), home address and phone number, birth date (and birth name
and place if available), education (beginning with most recent first), family
(spouse and spouse's education and position, children and children's education
and position, parents and other relatives, if appropriate), interests, career
(beginning with most recent position), professional affiliations, community
affiliations, honors/awards, gifts to this nonprofit, community donations
(beginning with the most recent), assets including real estate, compensation,
investments and other assets such as art or collections, contact history and
comments, and recommendations. The contact history and comments section
includes an abbreviated narrative of information not conforming to these
headings such as most recent contacts, events attended and important
developments regarding cultivation. The recommendations section includes the
researcher's conclusions about assigning the prospect, an Ask amount, timing,
and what initiatives or programs might interest the prospect.

The financial information following the heading "Assets" as well as the
recommendation section and most of the comments are eliminated for Trustee
Candidate Profiles.

This report is in table format.

CORPORATION PROFILE: This is the standard profile for companies and
it includes company name, affiliation to this nonprofit, business address and
phone number (fax, e-mail, and Web site), year established, type of business,
financial data including gross sales and number of employees, stock value
including date of quote, corporate officers and directors, giving policy, giving
officers, grant types, application procedures, gifts to this nonprofit including
amounts to each type of gift and employee match factor, community giving,
contact history and comments, and recommendations. The comments and
recommendations sections are used in the same manner outlined above.

This report is in table format.

FOUNDATION PROFILE: Standard profile which includes foundation name,
affiliation to this nonprofit, business address and phone number (fax, e-mail
and Web site), year established, donors and their relationship to this nonprofit,
purpose, application procedure, officers and their relationship to this nonprofit,
gifts to this nonprofit, community donations, foundation assets, contact
history and comments, and recommendations. The contact history and
comments section and the recommendations section are used in the same
manner outlined above.

This report is in table format.

NEW PROSPECT REPORT: The new prospect report is a narrative format.
Prospect name, affiliation, job title, and company are noted on the first line.
Address, phone number, and other contact information follow. The narrative
includes, in order, the prospect's affiliation with this nonprofit, education,
job and job history, spouse and spouse's education and job history and children

and their affiliation to Puget Sound. Other relatives and their affiliations to this nonprofit and a summary of giving by the family or the family's company or foundation to this nonprofit follow. Recent events attended or other pertinent information are outlined and the researcher's recommendations for assignment are included. A summary of the prospect's giving to this nonprofit is also included.

This report is in narrative format.

NARRATIVE BRIEFING: This is a short narrative format. The first part of the first page, the 'To' and 'From' entries, is only necessary when the report is going directly from the researcher to the user. If the report is being distributed to the users through another member of the Development team (the event coordinator, for example), this part is deleted.

Each attendee of note is outlined in a very brief narrative. Each heading includes name, affiliation, job title and company. The person's education and affiliations are outlined followed by the same information for the spouse. Any close relatives with affiliation to this nonprofit are outlined. Recent events attended that are noted in file or on the database are listed. Giving to this nonprofit is included at the request of the user. It is not included in copies of the briefing that go to volunteers. When giving is included, total giving, first and last year of giving, and major gifts and the purpose of the major gifts are included.

This report is in narrative format.

SCHOLARSHIP REPORT: The scholarship report was developed in response to the annual scholarship luncheons. The luncheon date is entered on the second line of the report. The table number and table host are entered by the luncheon coordinator. A brief description of the scholarship noting the year it was established, whether it is endowed and the purpose of and guidelines for the award is included. The scholarship donor and his or her relationship to the nonprofit are outlined. The donor representative (when different from the donor) and his or her relationship with to the nonprofit are outlined. Whether the donor representative has attended previous scholarship luncheons is also noted.

This report is in table format.

MEMO FORMAT: A memo format is used to respond to many research requests. The nature of the request is stated on the REQUEST line in the heading. The appropriate central files to which the document must be sent are noted. The body of the memo then summarizes the results of the research project. This report format is used when the research problem calls for a story-type report or an outline of detailed financial information. It may be customized to include headings and tables tailored to the report being made.

This report is in a narrative format.

Prospect Research Forms

This section includes a few samples of the standard forms that prospect researchers use. Your careful comparison of these forms will help you see similarities and discover the differences.

Tracking Forms:

Tracking Request
Application for Prospect Clearance

Contact Report Forms:

Small California University: Contact Report
Contact Report
Grinnell College: Contact Report
York University: Call Report

Research Request Forms:

Small Florida College: Research Request Form
Request for Development Prospect Research

Research Checklist Forms:

Small Florida College: Research Checklist
Major and Planned Giving Prospect Research Checklist
Research Checklist
Perkiomen School: Sources

Individual Profiles Forms:

Individual Prospect Profile
Individual Profile
Small California University: Alumni/Parent/Friend/Trustee Profile Form
Private Secondary School: Database Profile
Full Research Review

Foundation Profile Forms:

Foundation Prospect Profile
Foundation Profile
Foundation Research Form

Corporation Profile Forms:

Corporation Research Form
Corporation Profile
Corporate Prospect Profile

Tracking Request

Staff Name: ———————————— Date: ——————————

Secondary Staff: ——————————————————————

Prospect Name:	ID #:

Define the reason for creating this track:

————————————————————————————————

————————————————————————————————

Requested level (please check one):

❑ Cultivation (12 months)

❑ Pre-Solicitation (3 months)

❑ Solicitation (10 months)

❑ Stewardship (4 months)

Purpose: ————————————————————————

Ask Amount: ———————————— ————————————
            (Major Gift)   (Annual Fund)

Date	Strategy Step

Use back of page if necessary

Source: Becky Van Zante

YORK UNIVERSITY
OFFICE OF DEVELOPMENT AND ADVANCEMENT SERVICES
APPLICATION FOR PROSPECT CLEARANCE

Applicant (Name):
Department & Faculty:
Project (Title):
Approval (attached): _____ Yes _____ No
Project Outline (Brief Description):
Funding Required:
Duration of Project:
Anticipated Sources of Private Sector Funding: Project   Ask Amount   Anticipated Solicitation   Date
Solicitation Strategy: (Please specify how prospects will be solicited) a. Personal Presentation _____ b. Written Individual Proposal _____ c. Mass Mailing _____ d. Telephone Solicitation _____ e. Fundraising Event _____ f. Other _____

FOR OFFICE USE:

Date Received by Development:
Date Clearance Granted
Date Clearance Denied

Signed:

Source: Allan Friedman

Small California University

CONTACT REPORT

Confidential

Date & Time of visit:

Contact:

Contact made by:

Person filing report:

Date of filing:

Purpose of contact:

Information obtained:

Action steps:

Circulation:

Source: Bozena Popovic

Contact Report

Person Contacted	
By Whom (Staff or Volunteer)	
Date	
Type of Contact	❑ phone　　❑ visit　　❑ other
Other people in attendance:	

Purpose of Meeting:
❑ introductory meeting
❑ cultivation/relationship building
❑ solicitation
❑ volunteer recruitment
❑ stewardship
❑ other

Campus Involvement:

Narrative:

Development Next Steps:

By Whom?

By When?

What?
- ❏ letter with copy to research (including thank you)
- ❏ telephone call
- ❏ visit
- ❏ lunch
- ❏ conference invite _____
  (which)
- ❏ research _____
  (question)
- ❏ other _____

Programmatic Next Steps:

By Whom?

By When?

What?
- ❏ refer to memo dated _____ in paper file
- ❏ draft proposal
- ❏ other _____

Report should be given to:

Source: Karen R. Alpert, Development Research Associate,
Hillel: The Foundation for Jewish Campus Life

Grinell College

CONTACT REPORT
— CONFIDENTIAL —

PROSPECT NAME:

STAFF NAME:

VOLUNTEER NAME:

DATE OF CONTACT:

TYPE OF CONTACT	PURPOSE OF CONTACT	RESULT OF CONTACT	CAPABILITY RATING
First Personal Visit	Cultivation	Qualify	$5mm+ ....(A)
Subsequent Visit	Involvement	Cultivation	$1mm+ ....(B)
Telephone Call	Invite to Event	Pre-Solicitation	$500K+ ....(C)
Correspondence	Solicitation	Solicitation	$100K+ ....(D)
Invite to Event	Follow-up to Solicitation	Negotiation	$50K+ ....(E)
On-Campus	Stewardship	Commitment Made	$25K+ ....(F)
		Rejected	GAF ....(G)
		Stewardship	
		Future (5+ years)	Probability Percentage
		Disqualified as Major Prospect	

CONTACT SUMMARY *(Please limit this summary to three lines of text)*:

NOTES FROM CONTACT: *(Include areas of interest, assets, disclosed, requested amount, etc.)*

NEXT STEP:
Anticipated Date:

Purpose & Activity:

Research Follow-up:

SOLICITATION:

Source: Becky Van Zante

YORK UNIVERSITY
OFFICE OF DEVELOPMENT
CALL REPORT

Call Date:

I.D. #

Prospect Name:

Person(s) making contact:

Report filed by:

PERSONAL: Record biographical changes

Name:

Business:

Address:

Title:

Business #: (   )

Fax: (   )

Home Address:

Home #: (   )

REASON FOR CONTACT:

❑ Event   ❑ Volunteer Meeting

❑ Cultivation Phone Call   ❑ Cabinet Meeting

❑ Cultivation Visitl   ❑ Submitted Proposal

❑ Solicitation Phone Calll   ❑ Received Proposal Acceptance

❑ Solicitation Visitl   ❑ Received Proposal Rejection

❑ Other _____

ASSESSMENT OF PROSPECT'S ATTITUDE TOWARD YORK UNIVERSITY

❑ Extremely receptive   ❑ Neutral

❑ Receptive   ❑ Slightly negative

❑ Slightly Receptive   ❑ Very Negative

ACTION REQUIRED

Was there a particular faculty or staff member, student   Yes ❑   No ❑
or volunteer who has influenced the prospect's life ?

If yes, please specify

SUMMARIZE CONTACT AND INCLUDE PLANS FOR FOLLOW-UP

Source: Allan Friedman

SMALL FLORIDA COLLEGE

RESEARCH REQUEST FORM

REQUESTOR'S NAME:

DATE OF REQUEST:

RESEARCH NEEDED FOR (check one):
❑ Preliminary Rating   ❑ Telephone Call
❑ Cultivation Visit   ❑ Solicitation Visit
Please specify the date on which above event is scheduled:

INFORMATION REQUESTED (check all that apply):
❑ Verity Address/Phone Number
❑ Business & Description
❑ Brief Personal (Education, Family, Affiliation & Employment History
❑ Financial Information
❑ Giving History
❑ COMPLETE PROFILE (ALL OF THE ABOVE)
❑ Other (please specify):

PLEASE REALIZE THE IMPORTANCE OF PROVIDING THE FOLLOWING INFORMATION IN RESEARCHING THIS PROSPECT ACCURATELY:

PROSPECT NAME
(First, Middle, Last & Suffix):
SOURCE OF PROSPECT NAME:

ALUMNI?   ❑ Yes, Class Year: ❑ No

ADDRESS:

PHONE:

E-MAIL:

LAST CONTACTED DATE:

OTHER INFORMATION YOU KNOW ABOUT THIS PROSPECT:
Spouse:
Family Members:
Employment/Business:
Stock Holdings:
Partners:
Personal Properties:
Affiliations:
Gifts to Other Organizations:
Other:

Source: Sarah Choi

Request for Development Prospect Research

Name to research: _____

Date of Request:	
Requested by:	
Date research is needed:	
Priority:	❑ high ❑ med ❑ low
Date of meeting:	
Purpose of meeting:	
Spelling confirmed?	❑ yes ❑ no
City (or community), State	
Occupation/ Business	
Campus Connections	
Education: degree & alma mater	

1. **What will the information be needed for (check all that apply)**
   ❑ New prospect
   ❑ Update on an established prospect
   ❑ Cultivation activity/ event: _____
   ❑ Solicitation

2. **Please share any known background information.** (list name of prospect's business, position, family relations, hobbies and interests, ties to organization, local or regional, professional and community affiliations such as corporate boards and philanthropic boards, contact people, etc. & past major gifts to Jewish and non-Jewish organizations)

3. **Please list other persons you have or haven't contacted who may be helpful in this research.**

4. **Please check the appropriate level of information desired.**
   ❑ **I. General Picture + Other Biographical** – includes name, address, occupation, relationship to organization, giving history, spouse, parents, birth date & place, education- degree and alma mater, children, interests; community, philanthropic & professional affiliations; company & career background
   ❑ **II. General picture, Other Biographical + Financial Information** – includes Level I research, salary & other compensation, real estate holdings, stock holdings, & other asserts
   ❑ **III. Photograph** (when available)
   ❑ **IV. Other** – Please list the specific information that you are looking for:

* Please submit form at least two days prior to due date
* Please be as specific as possible. The more information you submit the more information you will receive.

Source: Karen R. Alpert, Development Research Associate,
Hillel: The Foundation for Jewish Campus Life

SMALL FLORIDA COLLEGE

RESEARCH CHECKLIST

PROSPECT NAME/ID:
DATE OF RESEARCH:
RESEARCH TOPIC:
RESEARCHER:

GENERAL RESOURCES
____ Individual File   ____ Business File   ____ Endowment File
____ Foundation File   ____ Religiious Organization   ____ Alumni Profile
                                 File   Form

Written Inquiry made to:
Phone call made to:

BIOGRAPHICAL INFORMATION
Social Security Death Index
Anybirthday.com
Other

DATABASES/CD-ROM
Lexis-Nexis DP Search Criteria:

PEOPLE
Address & Phone Number   Occupation & Licenses   Executive Compensation
Spouse's Name   Current Company   Stock Ownership
Personal Background   Person In The News   Stock Transactions
Death Records & Obituaries   Stock Acquisitions
                                                       Real Property
                                                       Campaign Contributions
                                                       Bankruptcy Filings
                                                       Patents

COMPANY
Business Address   Revenue
Company History   Real Property
Industry Background   Campaign Contributions
Mergers & Acquisitions   Patents
Top Executives   Bankruptcy Filings & Inactive Business
Foundations   Companies & Organizations In The News
M-H Law Directory
    Lexis-Nexis Academic Universe
    Hoover's Online
    Dow Jones Interactive
    D&B Report
    Foundation Center CD-ROM

OTHER WEB SOURCES/COMMENTS
Search Engine/Site for general name search:
Search Criteria:
Results URL: http://
Corporate/Individual Homepage (URL): http://

Source: Sarah Choi

Grinnell College
Major and Planned Giving
Prospect Research Check List

Name and Class of Prospect:
Date of Request:
Date Research Required:
Research Requested By:
Reason for Research:
Date Research Completed:

	Results	#Pertain	Notes

PRE-EXISTING PROFILES

MARQUIS WHO'S WHO CD-ROM

LEXIS-NEXIS

HOOVERS

FIRST SEARCH

ELECTRIC LIBRARY

INTERNET BOOKMARKS

SEARCH ENGINES
Google
Fast
Dogpile
AltaVisa

REAL ESTATE
List sites

GOVERNMENT
List sites

CORPORATIONS
List sites

NEWS/MEDIA
List sites

Source: Becky Van Zante

RESEARCH CHECKLIST

Prospect Name: _____ Date: _____

General Picture (in-house sources)

ADS/addresses only   _____ information listed   _____ none found
Alumni files   _____ information listed   _____ none found
Research files   _____ information listed   _____ none found
Planned Giving files   _____ information listed   _____ none found

General Picture and Other Biographical Information
Check appropriate sources above

ADS/giving, notes, activities_____ information listed   _____ none found
Who's Wealthy in America _____ information listed   _____ none found

Who's Who Previous   _____ information listed   _____ none found
Who's Who Current   _____ information listed   _____ none found

General Picture, Other Biographical and Financial Information
Check appropriate sources above

Company Web page   _____ information listed   _____ none found
*Academic Universe   _____ information listed   _____ none found
*Business News   _____ information listed   _____ none found
*General News   _____ information listed   _____ none found
* Biography Index   _____ information listed   _____ none found

Southeast Donors   _____ information listed   _____ none found
Southeast Directors   _____ information listed   _____ none found
FC/ Directors   _____ information listed   _____ none found
SEC Filings   _____ information listed   _____ none found
(public co. only)

Comprehensive Picture
Check appropriate sources above

Public records   _____ information listed   _____ none found
Special Collection   _____ information listed   _____ none found

Other sources as listed:

Source: FrankieTatum

Perkiomen School: Sources

Insert rows for additional sources. Include explanatory notes as needed (e.g., "no hits," "re spouse business").

PERSONAL CONTACT INFORMATION	
	Constituent database
	Constituent file
	AlumniFinder (Accurint) <http://www.alumnifinder.org/>
	Infospace <http://www.infospace.com>
	USPS Zip+4 Code Look-up <http://www.usps.com/zip4/>
BUSINESS CONTACT INFORMATION	
	Constituent database
	Constituent file
	Company website:
	Verizon SuperPages <http://www.superpages.com>
	USPS Zip+4 Code Look-up <http://www.usps.com/zip4/>
REAL PROPERTY	
Valuation ratio:	Source:
	AlumniFinder (Accurint) <http://www.alumnifinder.org/>
	LexisNexis by Credit Card <http://web.lexis.com/xchange/ccsubs/cc_prods.asp>
	Assessor's database:
	Northwestern University Tax Assessor Database <http://pubweb.acns.nwu.edu/~cap440/assess.html>
	Recorder's database:
	Assessor's Office (include phone and contact):
	Know-X <http://www.knowx.com>
	Domania <http://www.domania.com>
	Yahoo! Real Estate <http://list.realestate.yahoo.com/re/homevalues/>
BUSINESS BACKGROUND	
	Company website:
	State corporation records:
	Hoover's/Telebase ($5 Dun & Bradstreet U.S. Company Profile) <http://www.hoovers.telebase.com/form3.htm>
	Hoover's Online <http://hoovers.com>
	10-K Wizard <http://www.tenkwizard.com>
	Yahoo! Finance <http://finance.yahoo.com/?u>
	American Business Register <http://www.americanbusiness.com>
	NewsLibrary <http://www.newslibrary.com>
	Dow Jones Interactive Publications Library <http://www.djinteractive.com>
BIOGRAPHICAL	
	Constituent database
	Constituent file
	Who's Who in America 2000 (5th ed.)
	NewsLibrary <http://www.newslibrary.com>
	Dow Jones Interactive Publications Library <http://www.djinteractive.com>
	Ancestry.com Social Security Death Index <http://www.ancestry.com/search/rectype/vital/ssdi/main.htm>
	[Institution's] yearbook (archived)—years:
	[Institution's] alumni news magazine (archived)—issues:

AFFILIATIONS	
	Constituent file
	The Foundation Directory on CD-ROM
	Waltman Associates Connections Directory of Corporate and Nonprofit Boards (Northeast) CD-ROM
	Who's Who in America 2000 (5th ed.)
SECURITIES	
	SEC Info <http://www.secinfo.com>
	10-K Wizard <http://www.tenkwizard.com>
	Yahoo! Finance <http://finance.yahoo.com/?u>
	SEC Edgar Database <http://www.sec.gov/edgar/searchedgar/webusers.htm>
	BigCharts Historical Quotes <http://bigcharts.marketwatch.com/historical/>
OTHER ASSETS	
	Landings.com <http://www.landings.com>
	Know-X <http://www.knowx.com/>
	United States Patent and Trademark Office <http://www.uspto.gov/patft/>
COMPENSATION	
	SEC Info <http://www.secinfo.com>
	JobStar Salary Surveys <http://jobstar.org/tools/salary/sal-surv.htm>
	WSJ CareerJournal <http://www.careerjournal.com/salaries/>
	Bureau of Labor Statistics, Occupational Employment Statistics <http://www.bls.gov/oes/oes_emp.htm>
	Bureau of Labor Statistics, Occupational Outlook Handbook <http://www.bls.gov/oco/home.htm>
	Career InfoNet <http://www.acinet.org/acinet/lmi1.asp?oescode=28108&stfips=11&soccode=231011>
	BestJobsUSA.com <http://www.bestjobsusa.com/sections/CAN-salsurvey/index.asp>
	Salary.com <http://www.salary.com/salary/layoutscripts/sall_display.asp>
[INSTITUTION] GIVING HISTORY:	
	Constituent database
	Master donor records (archived)
PHILANTHROPIC/POLITICAL GIFTS:	
	Political MoneyLine (SEC Info) <http://www.tray.com/cgi-win/indexhtml.exe?MBF=NAME>
	Election cycles: 2002, 2000, 1998, 1996, 1994, 1992, 1990, 1988, 1986, 1984
	Guidestar <http://www.guidestar.org/search/>
	IRS Exempt Organizations Search <http://www.irs.gov/exempt/display/0,,i1%3D3%26genericId%3D15053,00.html>
	Foundation Center SearchZone <http://fdncenter.org/searchzone/>

Source: Joan M. Berg, Perkiomen School

Confidential
INDIVIDUAL PROSPECT PROFILE

Compiled by: Date:
Revised/Updated by: Date:

PERSONAL INFORMATION:
Name:
Prepared for: (Requestor Name)
ID#:
Address: Home Phone No.:
Born:
Education:

FAMILY INFORMATION:
Status:
Children:
Other:

BUSINESS INFORMATION:
Title:
Firm:
Address:
Business Phone: Business Fax:
Secretary:
Description of Firm:

Other positions:
Memberships:
Career:
Awards:
Military Service:

INVOLVEMENT WITH THE INSTITUTION:
Event Attendance:

INTERESTS OF PROSPECT:

WEBBING CONNECTIONS: (personal and corporate connections that provide linkages):

FINANCIAL CAPABILITIES: (Salary; Stock Holdings: Bonuses; Property Values/ Neighbourhood; Inherited Wealth; Family Wealth; Lifestyle, etc.)

GIVING HISTORY TO INSTITUTION:

GIVING HISTORY (General):

CULTIVATION STATUS:

OTHER INFORMATION:

Source: Allan Friedman

INDIVIDUAL'S NAME

AFFILIATION TO THIS NONPROFIT:	
POSITION:	
BUSINESS ADDRESS:	
HOME ADDRESS:	
BIRTH DATE & PLACE:	
EDUCATION:	
FAMILY:	Spouse: 　(Date of Birth/Date of Marriage/Date of Death) 　Education: 　Position: Children: 　Education: Other Relatives:
INTERESTS:	
CAREER:	
PROFESSIONAL AFFILIATIONS:	
COMMUNITY AFFILIATIONS:	
HONORS/AWARDS:	
GIFTS TO THIS NONPROFIT:	Total giving: First/last year: Major gifts: Pledges:
COMMUNITY DONATIONS:	
ASSETS:	
REAL PROPERTY:	
COMPENSATION:	
INVESTMENTS:	
OTHER ASSETS:	
CONTACT HISTORY & COMMENTS:	
RECOMMENDATION:	

Research Date: _____

ID: _____

Source: Author

SMALL CALIFORNIA UNIVERSITY
ALUMNI/PARENT/FRIEND/TRUSTEE PROFILE

Completion date /   /2001 BP

Subject
Name
Spouse Name
Home Address
Secondary or mailing addresses
Home Phone #   email
Vacation Home Address
Vacation Home #

Small California University Giving History – See attached printout
Small Calif. University ID #   Total Giving: $
University Connections

Biographical Sketch
Born where: Born when:
Genealogical Connections
Education
Children & Spouse Info
Religious Affiliations

Financial
Company
Business Address
Phone#   Fax #
Web Site   email
Title/Position
Years In Business   Year Founded:
Type Of Business
Any Additional Occupational Affiliations
Earnings Estimate/Gross ·
Publicly Recorded Holdings (stocks/bonds/annuities)
Business Valuation
Real Estate Holdings
Financial Estimate – Total Worth

Civic/Community Involvement
Affiliations & Friends
Philanthropic/Civic Interests
Grants, Scholarships, Honors & Awards
Social Activities

Additional information

Private Secondary School — Database Profile
Prospect Profile

Mr. and Mrs. John Doe
(Raiser's Edge – RE- Primary Addressee)

Constituent Name/ Maiden Name	Spouse Name
John Doe	Jane Doe
PP	
Past Parent	
Age: 41	Age: 40
Deceased: (if they were deceased you would get a Y)	**Deceased:**
Nickname(s): John and Jane	

Home Address:
12 Deer Drive
Philadelphia, PA 19002
Home: 215-222-2222

Marital Status: Married

Relationships
Marcia Doe	Daughter 2000
Janice Doe	Mother

Alternate Address
(used for summer/winter addresses)

Attributes
Solicit Code: Solicit
Readiness: 1869A (our giving level code)
Vol. Term of Service: Trustee 1998-2001
CC Potential: $10,000
CC Prospect Type: Donor
Target Solicitation Amount: $10,000

Solicitors
Annual Fund: Head of School
Campaign: Head of School

Source: Hillary Wonderlick

Confidential
Full Research Review

Date: _____

Name:			Spouse Name:	
Birthdate and place:				
Home Address:				
Second Home Address:				
Business Title & Address:				
Profession/ Occupation:				
Alma Mater:				
Children:	Name			
	Alma mater			
	Occupation			
Parents:	Name			
	Alma mater			
	Occupation			
Grandchildren:	Name			
	Alma mater			
	Occupation			
Corporate & Foundation Affiliations:				
International Center:	Giving			
	Pledges			
	Board memberships			
	Interests			
Local/Regional:	Giving			
	Board memberships			
	Interests			

University:	Giving	
	Board memberships	
Other Giving:		
Financial Data:	Net Worth:	
	Income:	
	Real Estate:	
	Worth of Company:	
	Insider Stock Holdings:	
	Other Known Assets:	
	Other Financial Information:	
Capacity Estimated by Research:	❏ $25,000–$100,000 ❏ $500,000–$1,000,000	❏ $100,000–$500,000 ❏ $1,000,000–$5,000,000 ❏ $5,000,000 and up
Comments:		
Other Interests:		
Honor/ Awards/ Publications:		
Background:		
Relationships:	Organizations:	
	Individuals:	

Prepared for:		
	Person	
	Purpose	

Source: Karen R. Alpert, Development Research Associate,
Hillel: The Foundation for Jewish Campus Life

Confidential
FOUNDATION PROSPECT PROFILE

Compiled by: Date:
Revised/Updated by: Date:

BASIC CONTACT INFORMATION:
Name:
Prepared for: (Requestor Name)
ID#
Address:
Official Correspondent:
Phone No.:   Fax No.:

FOUNDATION BACKGROUND:
Source of Funding:
Philosophy/Purpose:
Interests:
FOUNDATION GOVERNANCE:
Officers/Directors/Relationship to Institution:

FOUNDATION GUIDELINES:
Geographic Scope:
Grant Limitations:
Grant Information:
Application Procedure
Application Deadlines:

KEY CONTACTS: (alumni/friends in foundation):

FINANCIAL INFORMATION:
Grant Ranges:
Total Assets:
Year End:

GIVING HISTORY TO INSTITUTION:

GIVING HISTORY (General):

OTHER INFORMATION:

CULTIVATION STATUS:

Source: Allan Friedman

Name of Foundation
Postal Address

Cover page should contain, in this order:
Tele
Fax
Name of contact person (attach printed Staff List from Foundation website *if available*)
Contact email
URL

Foundation Connections to Your Institution:
Attach—history of your institution's contact with the Foundation if known
(include names of your organization's officers, dates of contact and
Foundation officer's name(s), grants your institution has received, and/or
grants/proposals pending)

Foundation Program areas:
Summarize each or (attach Foundation material from website)

Summarize the Foundation's geographic and/or funding exclusions
Ex.: No grants for buildings, or individual scholarships, capital improvements, etc.

Summarize the Foundation's deadlines and application procedures
Include details of: preferred initial contact type: letter of inquiry, or phone call
Are emailed proposals acceptable? Is there a post mark date identified for proposals?
Arrival date?

Summary of selected recent grants for past years
—Sort these by institution: higher education, health/human services, arts, education
and
—Sort these by geography: how many grants to midwest? how many to northeast?

Identify Foundation Board of Directors
Attach list from website. Note who are related/familiar or associated with your
institution.
Note who are affiliated with organizations (like yours) competing for funds.
Are there any obvious alumni connection to officers & directors

Recent News about the Foundation -- and Notes of Interest about the Foundation
(include date)
Ex: "an announcement that this foundation will spend down its assets by 2008" or
"a moratorium on all grants for k-12 education until a program officer is
installed."

Assets
Identify Number of grants made, averages size of grants, total ## of grants, total amt.
of grants
Attach Submission guidelines and deadlines
Attach Complete listing of program areas with description and analysis
Attach Full listing of grants from most recent annual report

rev. 2/05/03
Source: Mary Feeney, University of Amherst

Confidential
FOUNDATION RESEARCH FORM

FOUNDATION NAME:

BUSINESS ADDRESS:

OFFICERS/TRUSTEES:

HISTORY:

PROGRAMS & ACTIVITIES:

FIELDS OF INTEREST:

TYPES OF SUPPORT:

LIMITATIONS:

FINANCIAL INFORMATION:
   Donors:
   For Year Ending:
Assets:
   Grants:
   # of Grants:

Sample Recipients:

APPLICATION INFORMATION:

GIFT HISTORY: Date   Amount   Comment

TOTAL:

CONTACT SUMMARY:

NOTES:

REFERENCES:

FILE:

ID NUMBER:

RESEARCHER:

cc:

Source: Bill Czyzyk

Confidential
CORPORATION RESEARCH FORM

CORPORATION NAME:

ADDRESS:

WEBSITE:

PRODUCT(S):

OFFICERS:

DIRECTORS:

CONTACT PERSON:

CORPORATE HISTORY:

Current
Sales/Income:

Previous Year
Sales/Income:

PUBLIC/PRIVATE COMPANY:

STOCK PRICE: price   date   year high   year low

DIVIDENDS
Current:
Previous Fiscal Year:

Market Where Traded:

# of Employees:

PHILANTHROPY:

FOUNDATION:
    Donors:
    For Year Ending:
    Assets:
    Grants:
    # of Grants:

Principal Recipients:

GIFT HISTORY:	<u>Date</u>	<u>Amount</u>	<u>Comment</u>

GIFT TOTALS:	<u>Amount:</u>	<u>Number:</u>

CONTACT
SUMMARY:

NOTES:

REFERENCES:

FILE:

ID NUMBER:

RESEARCHER:

cc:

Source: Bill Czyzyk

COMPANY NAME

AFFILIATION TO THIS NONPROFIT:	
BUSINESS ADDRESS:	
YEARS ESTABLISHED:	
TYPE OF BUSINESS:	
FIANACIAL DATA:	
STOCK VALUE	(price per share & date of quote):
CORPORATE OFFICERS:	Chair: President/CEO: Exec. VP: Directors:
GIVING POLICY:	
GIVING OFFICERS:	
GRANT TYPES:	
APPLICATION:	
GIFTS TO THIS NONPROFIT:	Total giving: First/last year: Most recent gift: Scholarship gifts: Type of giving: Major gifts: Pledges: Match factor:
COMMUNITY GIVING:	
CONTAC HISTORY & COMMENTS:	
RECOMMENDATION:	

Research Date: _____   ID: _____

Confidential
CORPORATE PROSPECT PROFILE

Compiled by: Date:
Revised/Updated by: Date:

CONTACT INFORMATION:
Name:
Prepared for: (Requestor Name)
ID#:
Address:
Contact CEO:
Other Contacts:

LOCAL OR REGIONAL OFFICE:
Location/Address:
Name of Contact:

DESCRIPTION OF CORPORATION:
Products/Services:
No. of employees:
Alumni employed:
Holding company:
Holding co. nationality:
Banker:
Auditor(s):
Directors/Officers:
Affiliations etc. :

WEBBING CONNECTIONS:

RELATIONSHIP TO INSTITUTION:

FINANCIAL INFORMATION:
Profit
Revenue
Assets
Rankings:

PHILANTHROPY:
Interests:
Matching Gifts:
Decision Making:

GIVING HISTORY TO INSTITUTION:
GIVING HISTORY (General):

CULTIVATION STATUS:

OTHER INFORMATION:

Source: Allan Friedman

Resources for Prospect Researchers

What You Will Find Here

We cannot create a comprehensive list of all the resources available to prospect researchers. Resources are changing rapidly. New Web-based resources are joining the list nearly every week (if not every day) and established fee-based resources are changing their offerings frequently.

There are sources for current information about directories, fee-based databases, and other services. Bentz Whaley Flessner, consultants to nonprofits, produces a comprehensive, annual directory of resources that prospect researchers use. It is called *Bibliography: A Guide to Development Research Resources*. Find out more about this resource at:

Bentz Whaley Flessner
952-921-0111
http://www.bwf.com

Creating a Set of Resources

There are three things we offer you here so that you can begin to build a collection of prospect research resources. They are:
- How to access other prospect researchers
- Directions to collections of Web resources for prospect researchers
- A beginner's contact list of a few key fee-based resources

Access to Other Prospect Researchers

The best ways to access other researchers is through PRSPCT-L, the electronic discussion group (listserv) for prospect researchers and through local, regional, and the national prospect research groups. Here are the directions for getting in touch with these groups.

How to join PRSPCT-L: PRSPCT-L, the listserv for prospect researchers, includes discussions about resources on a regular basis. To join PRSPCT-L, go to: **http://groups.yahoo.com/group/PRSPCT-L.**

There you will find clear instructions about joining PRSPCT-L. After joining, you will have access to the PRSPCT-L archives and documents researchers have posted at the listserv's home. You will also find instructions about how to unsubscribe (or sign off) to PRSPCT-L. As a new member of the "L" community, the polite thing to do is to monitor the messages for a time to determine the content and types of postings the group generates. There is a PRSPCT-L etiquette guide that is valuable reading for all new members of this listserv community. Joseph Boeke, who founded PRSPCT-L, uses the "netiquette" guide to outline the purpose and intent of PRSPCT-L and what are acceptable and unacceptable postings. You will find Joe's Netiquette guide as well as directions for signing on and off the listserv in a folder called "AdminFiles" at: **http://groups.yahoo.com/group/PRSPCT-L/files/AdminFiles/**.

Other listservs: If you have grant writing, stewardship, or other duties, you may be interested in joining listservs with topics centering on those functions. The CASE Web site has a spot for visitors to sign on to these listservs at:

http://www.case.org/resources/listservs.cfm

How to contact research groups and associations: Researchers are the best source for the latest information about resources. They often provide comprehensive lists of resources at meetings and conferences, and they can give you information about their experiences using many of the products you consider adding to your library. Your peer institutions will be a good source for information about the resources appropriate for your organization. Your colleagues at these institutions can take the size of your nonprofit and the budget you have into consideration when they make their recommendations. You can contact other researchers through the state and regional chapters affiliated with the Association of Professional Researchers for Advancement (APRA) or the New England Development Research Association (NEDRA).

Association of Professional Researchers for Advancement (APRA)
40 Shuman Blvd., Suite 325
Naperville, IL 60563
630-717-8160
Fax: 630-717-8354
E-mail: info@APRAhome.org
http://www.aprahome.org

New England Development Research Association (NEDRA)
E-mail: info@nedra.org

Other professional associations: APRA is the primary association serving prospect researchers throughout the world, and NEDRA serves researchers in the New England area of the United States. In addition to APRA and NEDRA, there are local and regional professional associations that you will find by asking other fund-raising professionals in your area. They serve fund raisers, grant writers, researchers, planned giving officers, and others involved in philanthropy and are too numerous to list here. The national professional associations serving development professionals, healthcare fund raisers, and academic fund raisers are:

Association of Fundraising Professionals (AFP)
1101 King Street, Suite 700
Alexandria, VA 22314
703-684-0410
http://www.nsfre.org

Association for Healthcare Philanthropy (AHP)
313 Park Avenue, Suite 400
Falls Church, Virginia 22046
703-532-6243
http://www.go-ahp.org/

Council for Advancement and Support of Education (CASE)
1307 New York Avenue NW, Suite 1000
Washington, DC 20005-4701
202.328.CASE
http://www.case.org

Collections of Web Resources for Prospect Researchers

If we tried to create a collection of Web resources for you here, our book-based collection would be out of date by the time you were reading this. Instead we are directing you to the collections created and maintained by prospect researchers. These collections are updated on a regular basis. Researchers are the best resource. They are testing the latest Web tools and they are looking for the same type of information you are seeking. The Web sites created by prospect researchers are each organized in surprisingly similar ways, with the method of grouping sites driven by the type of information the visitor is seeking. Categories like Real Estate, Foundations, Corporations, and Individuals are common. These wonderful Web sites are the best source of the most current and useful Web resources. We are certain there are others, but we are only trying to give you a solid start on this collection. Here is a beginner's collection:

David Lamb's Prospect Research Page
http://www.lambresearch.com/

Direct Search by Gary Price
http://www.freepint.com/gary/direct.htm

Internet Prospector: A monthly newsletter and Web site for prospect researchers http://www.internet-prospector.org

NetSource@USC
http://www.usc.edu/dept/source/

Northwestern University's Research Bookmarks
http://pubweb.nwu.edu/~cap440/bookmark.html

Portico (prospect research Web links)
http://indorgs.virginia.edu/portico/

Princeton University's Development Research Links
http://www.princeton.edu/one/research/netlinks.html

University of Vermont Research and Reference Tools
http://www.uvm.edu/~prospect/index.html

Women in Philanthropy
http://www.women-philanthropy.umich.edu/

A Beginner's List of Contacts for Fee-Based Resources

As we reported, no list of fee-based resources that we create could approximate the range of resources available. Many of the ones in common use by researchers will be included among the Web sites in the researchers' collections we just listed. Here is a limited list of resources that you should view as a starting point. Our inclusion of any resources on this list, or our omission of any others, does not constitute an opinion about the value of these resources. Although we have tried to arrange these resources in categories, many of them offer information that fits more than one category. It is up to you to use your research skills to find which resources match your needs for information, your budget, the space you have, and the equipment and skill you will need to access these resources.

Rather than listing all the publications, electronic resources, and other products (as well as the rapidly changing costs of those products), we are listing contact information for the companies that produce the products. Please contact the individual product providers or visit their Web sites for more information about what they have to offer. These information providers will be happy to share their product lists and prices with you.

You will discover that some of these providers offer part of the information for free at their Web sites. It is not uncommon for basic information to be offered for free and the premium content to then be fee-based. The fee might be incurred in one of many ways: a per-record charge or a monthly or annual member charge, for example.

Foundation Research: As you know now, many foundations have their own Web sites. Secretaries of State offices in some states publish directories of the foundations. Several Secretaries of State have placed their databases of charities on the Internet. The Internet Prospector Web site (http://www.internet-prospector.org) includes a list of charities databases for each U.S. state. Fee-based resources (paper, online, or CD-ROM products) for foundation information include:

Aspen Publishers, Inc. (*Federal Grants* and
   Contacts Weekly and *GrantScape*)
Healthcare and Public Administration Division: 301-417-7500
http://www.aspenpublishers.com/

The Foundation Center
800-424-9836
http://www.fdncenter.org

The Gale Group (a Thomson company)—holds the Taft Group's titles
800-877-GALE
http://www.galegroup.com

Jones and Bartlett Publishers—nonprofit division
http://www.jbpub.com

Stevenson Publication (*Major Gifts Report* and
   Successful Fund Raising monthly newsletter)
712-239-3010
http://www.stevensoninc.com

Corporate Research: Begin your exploration for resources that will be useful to your nonprofit by finding out what is offered by the Secretaries of States in the areas that interest you. Fee-based services with paper, online, or CD-ROM products:

Dialog
800-3-DIALOG
http://www.dialog.com/

Dun & Bradstreet
800-526-0651
http://www.dnb.com

The Gale Group (a Thomson company)
800-877-GALE
http://www.galegroup.com

Hoovers
800-486-8666
http://www.hoovers.com

National Register Publishing
800-323-3288
http://www.corporatelinkage.com

Standard & Poor's

800-221-5277http://www.standardandpoors.com/

Thomas Register
800-699-9822
http://www.thomasregister.com/

Walker's Research
800-258-5737
http://www.walkersresearch.com

Address Finders: The following services offer single or mass address updating services.

Equifax (Polk Directories)
800-275-7655
http://www.citydirectory.com

Experian
714-385-7000
http://www.experian.com

Telematch (Address Finder)
800-523-7346
http://www.telematch.com

News Providers: Newspapers in the areas where your prospects live may have adequate access to their archives on the Internet. Many permit free searching and then charge for access to the articles returned. Other news providers offering access for a fee:

Factiva (Dow Jones and Reuters)
http://www.factiva.com
1-800-369-8474

UMI Proquest
http://www.bellhowell.infolearning.com/proquest/
800.521.0600

Individual Research: Researching individuals involves salary and other information for public company insiders, real estate information, and biographical information. Here are a few fee-based resources to get access to this information:

10K Wizard
http://www.10kwizard.com/

Biographical and Genealogical Master Index (BGMI)
The Gale Group
800-877-GALE
http://www.galegroup.com

EDGAR Online People Search (public company information)
http://www.edgar-online.com/

iWave.com, Inc. (now in partnership with Gale Group)
902-894-2666
http://www.iwave.com

Lexis-Nexis
800-227-9597
http://www.lexis-nexis.com/cispubs

Marquis Who's Who Publications
800-521-8110 ext. 1
http://www.marquiswhoswho.com

Thomson Financial Wealth Identification (insider holdings)
800-933-4446
http://www.wealthid.com/

Waltman Associates
612-338-0772
http://waltmanassociates.com

Real Estate Information
In addition to the Internet-based assessor records, there are information providers who sell access to real estate data. There are several regional providers and you can learn who those vendors are in your area by asking the researchers you meet. Here are two services that have national or near-national coverage:

DataQuick (real estate assessments)
1-888-604-3282
http://www.dataquick.com/

First American Real Estate Solutions (FARES)
800-426-1466
http://www.firstam.com

Database and Screening Services
This is not a comprehensive list of database screening services. It is only a beginner's list.

Econometrics, Inc.
312-297-5418
http://www.econ-online.com

Grenzebach Glier and Associates
312-372-4040
http://www.grenzebachglier.com

Major Gifts Identification/Consulting (MaGIC)
877-54MAGIC
http://magic.ahmp.com

Marts and Lundy
800-526-9005
http://www.martsandlundy.com

Prospect Information Network, LLC (P!N)
888-557-1326 ext:411
http://www.prospectinfo.com

Journals, Newsletters, and Other Nonprofit News Providers

American Association of Fundraising Counsel—Giving USA
800-462-2372
http://www.aafrc.org

APRA Connections
630-655-0177
http://www.APRAhome.org/connections.htm

CASE Currents
202.328.CASE
http://www.case.org/currents/get.cfm

The Chronicle of Higher Education
800-728-2803
http://www.chronicle.com

The Chronicle of Philanthropy
800-728-2803
http://www.philanthropy.com

Nonprofit Times
973-394-1800
http://www.nptimes.com

Nonprofitxpress
http://www.nonprofitxpress.com

Philanthropy News Network Online
http://www.pnnonline.org/

Fund-raising Software

Npinfotech.org is collecting data on fund-raising software. Visit this site to learn about software packages: **http://www.npinfotech.org**

Use the CASE Yellow Pages to see contact information for fund-raising software firms: **http://www.case.org/yellowpages/frsoftware.cfm**

We are certain that we have omitted a resource that a reader will think should be on this "first contacts" list. Please let us know at chogan@ups.edu and we will consider adding the resource to the next edition of this book.

U.S. Internal Revenue Service Form 990-PF: Return of Private Foundation

This section of the appendix contains the 2002 version of the 990-PF, the form that private foundations use to report the assets and distribution of assets to the Internal Revenue Service (IRS). Please see chapter 4 for details about reading the Form 990-PF.

Form **990-PF**	**Return of Private Foundation** **or Section 4947(a)(1) Nonexempt Charitable Trust** **Treated as a Private Foundation**	OMB No. 1545-0052 **2002**

Department of the Treasury
Internal Revenue Service   Note: *The organization may be able to use a copy of this return to satisfy state reporting requirements.*

For calendar year 2002, or tax year beginning _____ **, 2002, and ending** _____ **, 20** ____

G Check all that apply: ☐ Initial return   ☐ Final return   ☐ Amended return   ☐ Address change   ☐ Name change

Use the IRS label. Otherwise, print or type. See Specific Instructions.	Name of organization		**A Employer identification number**
	Number and street (or P.O. box number if mail is not delivered to street address)	Room/suite	**B** Telephone number (see page 10 of the instructions) ( )
	City or town, state, and ZIP code		**C** If exemption application is pending, check here ▶ ☐ **D 1.** Foreign organizations, check here . ▶ ☐

H Check type of organization: ☐ Section 501(c)(3) exempt private foundation
☐ Section 4947(a)(1) nonexempt charitable trust ☐ Other taxable private foundation

I Fair market value of all assets at end of year *(from Part II, col. (c), line 16)* ▶ $ _____

J Accounting method: ☐ Cash ☐ Accrual
☐ Other (specify) _____
(Part I, column (d) must be on cash basis.)

2. Foreign organizations meeting the 85% test, check here and attach computation . ▶ ☐
E If private foundation status was terminated under section 507(b)(1)(A), check here . ▶ ☐
F If the foundation is in a 60-month termination under section 507(b)(1)(B), check here . ▶ ☐

Part I	**Analysis of Revenue and Expenses** (The total of amounts in columns (b), (c), and (d) may not necessarily equal the amounts in column (a) (see page 10 of the instructions).)	**(a)** Revenue and expenses per books	**(b)** Net investment income	**(c)** Adjusted net income	**(d)** Disbursements for charitable purposes (cash basis only)
Revenue	**1** Contributions, gifts, grants, etc., received (attach schedule)				
	Check ▶ ☐ if the foundation is **not** required to attach Sch. B				
	2 Distributions from split-interest trusts				
	3 Interest on savings and temporary cash investments				
	4 Dividends and interest from securities				
	5a Gross rents				
	b (Net rental income or (loss) _____)				
	6a Net gain or (loss) from sale of assets not on line 10				
	b Gross sales price for all assets on line 6a _____				
	7 Capital gain net income (from Part IV, line 2). .				
	8 Net short-term capital gain				
	9 Income modifications				
	10a Gross sales less returns and allowances ____				
	b Less: Cost of goods sold . .				
	c Gross profit or (loss) (attach schedule). . . .				
	11 Other income (attach schedule)				
	12 **Total.** Add lines 1 through 11				
Operating and Administrative Expenses	**13** Compensation of officers, directors, trustees, etc.				
	14 Other employee salaries and wages				
	15 Pension plans, employee benefits				
	16a Legal fees (attach schedule)				
	b Accounting fees (attach schedule)				
	c Other professional fees (attach schedule). . .				
	17 Interest				
	18 Taxes (attach schedule) (see page 13 of the instructions)				
	19 Depreciation (attach schedule) and depletion .				
	20 Occupancy				
	21 Travel, conferences, and meetings				
	22 Printing and publications				
	23 Other expenses (attach schedule)				
	24 **Total operating and administrative expenses.** Add lines 13 through 23				
	25 Contributions, gifts, grants paid				
	26 **Total expenses and disbursements.** Add lines 24 and 25				
	27 Subtract line 26 from line 12:				
	a Excess of revenue over expenses and disbursements				
	b Net investment income (if negative, enter -0-) .				
	c Adjusted net income (if negative, enter -0-). .				

For Paperwork Reduction Act Notice, see the instructions.   Cat. No. 11289X   Form **990-PF** (2002)

Form 990-PF (2002)

Page **2**

Part II	Balance Sheets	Attached schedules and amounts in the description column should be for end-of-year amounts only. (See instructions.)	Beginning of year	End of year	
			(a) Book Value	(b) Book Value	(c) Fair Market Value

		(a)	(b)	(c)
Assets				
1	Cash—non-interest-bearing			
2	Savings and temporary cash investments			
3	Accounts receivable ▶			
	Less: allowance for doubtful accounts ▶			
4	Pledges receivable ▶			
	Less: allowance for doubtful accounts ▶			
5	Grants receivable			
6	Receivables due from officers, directors, trustees, and other disqualified persons (attach schedule) (see page 15 of the instructions)			
7	Other notes and loans receivable (attach schedule) ▶			
	Less: allowance for doubtful accounts ▶			
8	Inventories for sale or use			
9	Prepaid expenses and deferred charges			
10a	Investments—U.S. and state government obligations (attach schedule)			
b	Investments—corporate stock (attach schedule) . . .			
c	Investments—corporate bonds (attach schedule)			
11	Investments—land, buildings, and equipment: basis ▶			
	Less: accumulated depreciation (attach schedule) ▶			
12	Investments—mortgage loans			
13	Investments—other (attach schedule)			
14	Land, buildings, and equipment: basis ▶			
	Less: accumulated depreciation (attach schedule) ▶			
15	Other assets (describe ▶ ....)			
16	**Total assets** (to be completed by all filers—see page 16 of the instructions. Also, see page 1, item I)			
Liabilities				
17	Accounts payable and accrued expenses			
18	Grants payable			
19	Deferred revenue			
20	Loans from officers, directors, trustees, and other disqualified persons			
21	Mortgages and other notes payable (attach schedule) . .			
22	Other liabilities (describe ▶ ....)			
23	**Total liabilities** (add lines 17 through 22)			
Net Assets or Fund Balances				
	Organizations that follow SFAS 117, check here ▶ ☐ and complete lines 24 through 26 and lines 30 and 31.			
24	Unrestricted			
25	Temporarily restricted			
26	Permanently restricted			
	Organizations that do not follow SFAS 117, check here ▶ ☐ and complete lines 27 through 31.			
27	Capital stock, trust principal, or current funds			
28	Paid-in or capital surplus, or land, bldg., and equipment fund			
29	Retained earnings, accumulated income, endowment, or other funds			
30	**Total net assets or fund balances** (see page 16 of the instructions)			
31	**Total liabilities and net assets/fund balances** (see page 16 of the instructions)			

Part III	Analysis of Changes in Net Assets or Fund Balances

1	Total net assets or fund balances at beginning of year—Part II, column (a), line 30 (must agree with end-of-year figure reported on prior year's return)	**1**	
2	Enter amount from Part I, line 27a	**2**	
3	Other increases not included in line 2 (itemize) ▶	**3**	
4	Add lines 1, 2, and 3	**4**	
5	Decreases not included in line 2 (itemize) ▶	**5**	
6	Total net assets or fund balances at end of year (line 4 minus line 5)—Part II, column (b), line 30 .	**6**	

Form **990-PF** (2002)

Form 990-PF (2002)   Page **3**

Part IV   Capital Gains and Losses for Tax on Investment Income

(a) List and describe the kind(s) of property sold (e.g., real estate, 2-story brick warehouse; or common stock, 200 shs. MLC Co.)	(b) How acquired P—Purchase D—Donation	(c) Date acquired (mo., day, yr.)	(d) Date sold (mo., day, yr.)
1a			
b			
c			
d			
e			

(e) Gross sales price	(f) Depreciation allowed (or allowable)	(g) Cost or other basis plus expense of sale	(h) Gain or (loss) (e) plus (f) minus (g)
a			
b			
c			
d			
e			

Complete only for assets showing gain in column (h) and owned by the foundation on 12/31/69

(i) F.M.V. as of 12/31/69	(j) Adjusted basis as of 12/31/69	(k) Excess of col. (i) over col. (j), if any	(l) Gains (Col. (h) gain minus col. (k), but not less than -0-) or Losses (from col.(h))
a			
b			
c			
d			
e			

2 Capital gain net income or (net capital loss). { If gain, also enter in Part I, line 7 / If (loss), enter -0- in Part I, line 7 } **2**

3 Net short-term capital gain or (loss) as defined in sections 1222(5) and (6):
If gain, also enter in Part I, line 8, column (c) (see pages 12 and 17 of the instructions).
If (loss), enter -0- in Part I, line 8 . . . . **3**

Part V   Qualification Under Section 4940(e) for Reduced Tax on Net Investment Income

(For optional use by domestic private foundations subject to the section 4940(a) tax on net investment income.)

If section 4940(d)(2) applies, leave this part blank.

Was the organization liable for the section 4942 tax on the distributable amount of any year in the base period? ☐ Yes ☐ No
If "Yes," the organization does not qualify under section 4940(e). Do not complete this part.

1 Enter the appropriate amount in each column for each year; see page 17 of the instructions before making any entries.

(a) Base period years Calendar year (or tax year beginning in)	(b) Adjusted qualifying distributions	(c) Net value of noncharitable-use assets	(d) Distribution ratio (col. (b) divided by col. (c))
2001			
2000			
1999			
1998			
1997			

2 **Total** of line 1, column (d) **2**

3 Average distribution ratio for the 5-year base period—divide the total on line 2 by 5, or by the number of years the foundation has been in existence if less than 5 years **3**

4 Enter the net value of noncharitable-use assets for 2002 from Part X, line 5 . . . . **4**

5 Multiply line 4 by line 3 . . . . **5**

6 Enter 1% of net investment income (1% of Part I, line 27b) **6**

7 Add lines 5 and 6 . . . . **7**

8 Enter qualifying distributions from Part XII, line 4 . . . . **8**

If line 8 is equal to or greater than line 7, check the box in Part VI, line 1b, and complete that part using a 1% tax rate. See the Part VI instructions on page 17.

Form **990-PF** (2002)

Form 990-PF (2002)   Page **4**

Part VI	**Excise Tax Based on Investment Income** (Section 4940(a), 4940(b), 4940(e), or 4948—see page 17 of the instructions)

1a Exempt operating foundations described in section 4940(d)(2), check here ▶ ☐ and enter "N/A" on line 1.
Date of ruling letter: .... **(attach copy of ruling letter if necessary–see instructions)**

   b Domestic organizations that meet the section 4940(e) requirements in Part V, check here ▶ ☐ and enter 1% of Part I, line 27b . . . . | **1** |

   c All other domestic organizations enter 2% of line 27b. Exempt foreign organizations enter 4% of Part I, line 12, col. (b)

2 Tax under section 511 (domestic section 4947(a)(1) trusts and taxable foundations only. Others enter -0-) | **2** |

3 Add lines 1 and 2 . . . . | **3** |

4 Subtitle A (income) tax (domestic section 4947(a)(1) trusts and taxable foundations only. Others enter -0-) | **4** |

5 **Tax based on investment income.** Subtract line 4 from line 3. If zero or less, enter -0- . . . | **5** |

6 Credits/Payments:

   a 2002 estimated tax payments and 2001 overpayment credited to 2002 | **6a** |

   b Exempt foreign organizations—tax withheld at source . . . . . | **6b** |

   c Tax paid with application for extension of time to file (Form 8868) . | **6c** |

   d Backup withholding erroneously withheld . . . . | **6d** |

7 Total credits and payments. Add lines 6a through 6d . . . . | **7** |

8 Enter any **penalty** for underpayment of estimated tax. Check here ☐ if Form 2220 is attached | **8** |

9 **Tax due.** If the total of lines 5 and 8 is more than line 7, enter **amount owed** . . . . . ▶ | **9** |

10 **Overpayment.** If line 7 is more than the total of lines 5 and 8, enter the **amount overpaid** . . . ▶ | **10** |

11 Enter the amount of line 10 to be: Credited to 2003 estimated tax ▶ _____ | Refunded ▶ | **11** |

Part VII-A	**Statements Regarding Activities**

		Yes	No
1a During the tax year, did the organization attempt to influence any national, state, or local legislation or did it participate or intervene in any political campaign?	**1a**		
b Did it spend more than $100 during the year (either directly or indirectly) for political purposes (see page 18 of the instructions for definition)?	**1b**		

   If the answer is "Yes" to **1a** *or* **1b**, *attach a detailed description of the activities and copies of any materials published or distributed by the organization in connection with the activities.*

| **c** Did the organization file **Form 1120-POL** for this year? . . . . | **1c** | | |

   d Enter the amount (if any) of tax on political expenditures (section 4955) imposed during the year:
   (1) On the organization. ▶ $ _____ **(2)** On organization managers. ▶ $ _____

   e Enter the reimbursement (if any) paid by the organization during the year for political expenditure tax imposed on organization managers. ▶ $ _____

| **2** Has the organization engaged in any activities that have not previously been reported to the IRS? . . . | **2** | | |

   If "Yes," attach a detailed description of the activities.

3 Has the organization made any changes, not previously reported to the IRS, in its governing instrument, articles of incorporation, or bylaws, or other similar instruments? *If "Yes," attach a conformed copy of the changes* . .	**3**		
4a Did the organization have unrelated business gross income of $1,000 or more during the year?	**4a**		
b If "Yes," has it filed a tax return on **Form 990-T** for this year?	**4b**		
5 Was there a liquidation, termination, dissolution, or substantial contraction during the year?	**5**		

   If "Yes," attach the statement required by General Instruction T.

6 Are the requirements of section 508(e) (relating to sections 4941 through 4945) satisfied either:
   • By language in the governing instrument or
   • By state legislation that effectively amends the governing instrument so that no mandatory directions that conflict with the state law remain in the governing instrument? . . . . | **6** | | |

| **7** Did the organization have at least $5,000 in assets at any time during the year? *If "Yes," complete Part II, col. (c), and Part XV.* | **7** | | |

8a Enter the states to which the foundation reports or with which it is registered (see page 19 of the instructions) ▶ ....

   b If the answer is "Yes" to line 7, has the organization furnished a copy of Form 990-PF to the Attorney General (or designate) of each state as required by General Instruction G? *If "No," attach explanation* | **8b** | | |

9 Is the organization claiming status as a private operating foundation within the meaning of section 4942(j)(3) or 4942(j)(5) for calendar year 2002 or the taxable year beginning in 2002 (see instructions for Part XIV on page 25)? *If "Yes," complete Part XIV*	**9**		
10 Did any persons become substantial contributors during the tax year? *If "Yes," attach a schedule listing their names and addresses.*	**10**		
11 Did the organization comply with the public inspection requirements for its annual returns and exemption application?	**11**		

   Web site address ▶ ....

12 The books are in care of ▶ .... Telephone no. ▶ ....
   Located at ▶ .... ZIP+4 ▶ ....

| **13** Section 4947(a)(1) nonexempt charitable trusts filing Form 990-PF in lieu of **Form 1041**—Check here . . . . . ▶ ☐ and enter the amount of tax-exempt interest received or accrued during the year. . . . . ▶ | **13** | |

Form **990-PF** (2002)

Form 990-PF (2002)   Page **5**

Part VII-B Statements Regarding Activities for Which Form 4720 May Be Required

File Form 4720 if any item is checked in the "Yes" column, unless an exception applies.

		Yes	No
1a During the year did the organization (either directly or indirectly):			
(1) Engage in the sale or exchange, or leasing of property with a disqualified person? . ☐ Yes ☐ No			
(2) Borrow money from, lend money to, or otherwise extend credit to (or accept it from) a disqualified person? . . . . ☐ Yes ☐ No			
(3) Furnish goods, services, or facilities to (or accept them from) a disqualified person? ☐ Yes ☐ No			
(4) Pay compensation to, or pay or reimburse the expenses of, a disqualified person? . ☐ Yes ☐ No			
(5) Transfer any income or assets to a disqualified person (or make any of either available for the benefit or use of a disqualified person)? . . . . ☐ Yes ☐ No			
(6) Agree to pay money or property to a government official? (**Exception.** Check "No" if the organization agreed to make a grant to or to employ the official for a period after termination of government service, if terminating within 90 days.) . . . . ☐ Yes ☐ No			
b If any answer is "Yes" to 1a(1)–(6), did **any** of the acts fail to qualify under the exceptions described in Regulations section 53.4941(d)-3 or in a current notice regarding disaster assistance (see page 19 of the instructions)? . . Organizations relying on a current notice regarding disaster assistance check here . . . . ▶ ☐	**1b**		
c Did the organization engage in a prior year in any of the acts described in 1a, other than excepted acts, that were not corrected before the first day of the tax year beginning in 2002?	**1c**		
2 Taxes on failure to distribute income (section 4942) (does not apply for years the organization was a private operating foundation defined in section 4942(j)(3) or 4942(j)(5)):			
a At the end of tax year 2002, did the organization have any undistributed income (lines 6d and 6e, Part XIII) for tax year(s) beginning before 2002? . . . . ☐ Yes ☐ No If "Yes," list the years ▶ 20 .... , 20 .... , 19 .... , 19			
b Are there any years listed in 2a for which the organization is **not** applying the provisions of section 4942(a)(2) (relating to incorrect valuation of assets) to the year's undistributed income? (If applying section 4942(a)(2) to **all** years listed, answer "No" and attach statement—see page 19 of the instructions.)	**2b**		
c If the provisions of section 4942(a)(2) are being applied to **any** of the years listed in 2a, list the years here. ▶ 20 .... , 20 .... , 19 .... , 19			
3a Did the organization hold more than a 2% direct or indirect interest in any business enterprise at any time during the year? . . . . ☐ Yes ☐ No			
b If "Yes," did it have excess business holdings in 2002 as a result of (**1**) any purchase by the organization or disqualified persons after May 26, 1969; (**2**) the lapse of the 5-year period (or longer period approved by the Commissioner under section 4943(c)(7)) to dispose of holdings acquired by gift or bequest; or (**3**) the lapse of the 10-, 15-, or 20-year first phase holding period? (Use Schedule C, Form 4720, to determine if the organization had excess business holdings in 2002.).	**3b**		
4a Did the organization invest during the year any amount in a manner that would jeopardize its charitable purposes?	**4a**		
b Did the organization make any investment in a prior year (but after December 31, 1969) that could jeopardize its charitable purpose that had not been removed from jeopardy before the first day of the tax year beginning in 2002?	**4b**		
5a During the year did the organization pay or incur any amount to:			
(1) Carry on propaganda, or otherwise attempt to influence legislation (section 4945(e))? . ☐ Yes ☐ No			
(2) Influence the outcome of any specific public election (see section 4955); or to carry on, directly or indirectly, any voter registration drive? . . . . ☐ Yes ☐ No			
(3) Provide a grant to an individual for travel, study, or other similar purposes? . . . ☐ Yes ☐ No			
(4) Provide a grant to an organization other than a charitable, etc., organization described in section 509(a)(1), (2), or (3), or section 4940(d)(2)? . . . . ☐ Yes ☐ No			
(5) Provide for any purpose other than religious, charitable, scientific, literary, or educational purposes, or for the prevention of cruelty to children or animals?. . . ☐ Yes ☐ No			
b If any answer is "Yes" to 5a(1)–(5), did **any** of the transactions fail to qualify under the exceptions described in Regulations section 53.4945 or in a current notice regarding disaster assistance (see page 20 of the instructions)? Organizations relying on a current notice regarding disaster assistance check here . . . . ▶ ☐	**5b**		
c If the answer is "Yes" to question 5a(4), does the organization claim exemption from the tax because it maintained expenditure responsibility for the grant? . . . . ☐ Yes ☐ No If "Yes," attach the statement required by Regulations section 53.4945–5(d).			
6a Did the organization, during the year, receive any funds, directly or indirectly, to pay premiums on a personal benefit contract? . . . . ☐ Yes ☐ No			
b Did the organization, during the year, pay premiums, directly or indirectly, on a personal benefit contract? . . If you answered "Yes" to 6b, also file Form 8870.	**6b**		

Form **990-PF** (2002)

Form 990-PF (2002)   Page **6**

Part VIII — Information About Officers, Directors, Trustees, Foundation Managers, Highly Paid Employees, and Contractors

1 List all officers, directors, trustees, foundation managers and their compensation (see page 20 of the instructions):

(a) Name and address	(b) Title, and average hours per week devoted to position	(c) Compensation (If not paid, enter -0-)	(d) Contributions to employee benefit plans and deferred compensation	(e) Expense account, other allowances

2 Compensation of five highest-paid employees (other than those included on line 1—see page 20 of the instructions). If none, enter "NONE."

(a) Name and address of each employee paid more than $50,000	(b) Title and average hours per week devoted to position	(c) Compensation	(d) Contributions to employee benefit plans and deferred compensation	(e) Expense account, other allowances

Total number of other employees paid over $50,000 . . . . ▶ |

3 Five highest-paid independent contractors for professional services—(see page 20 of the instructions). If none, enter "NONE."

(a) Name and address of each person paid more than $50,000	(b) Type of service	(c) Compensation

Total number of others receiving over $50,000 for professional services . . . . ▶ |

Part IX-A — Summary of Direct Charitable Activities

List the foundation's four largest direct charitable activities during the tax year. Include relevant statistical information such as the number of organizations and other beneficiaries served, conferences convened, research papers produced, etc. | Expenses

1 ....

2 ....

3 ....

4 ....

Form **990-PF** (2002)

Form 990-PF (2002)   Page **7**

Part IX-B	**Summary of Program-Related Investments** (see page 21 of the instructions)	
	Describe the two largest program-related investments made by the foundation during the tax year on lines 1 and 2.	Amount
1	....	
2	....	
	All other program-related investments. See page 21 of the instructions.	
3	....	
	Total. Add lines 1 through 3 . . . . ▶	

Part X	**Minimum Investment Return** (All domestic foundations must complete this part. Foreign foundations, see page 21 of the instructions.)	
1	Fair market value of assets not used (or held for use) directly in carrying out charitable, etc., purposes:	
a	Average monthly fair market value of securities	**1a**
b	Average of monthly cash balances	**1b**
c	Fair market value of all other assets (see page 22 of the instructions)	**1c**
d	**Total** (add lines 1a, b, and c)	**1d**
e	Reduction claimed for blockage or other factors reported on lines 1a and 1c (attach detailed explanation) **1e**	
2	Acquisition indebtedness applicable to line 1 assets	**2**
3	Subtract line 2 from line 1d	**3**
4	Cash deemed held for charitable activities. Enter 1½% of line 3 (for greater amount, see page 22 of the instructions)	**4**
5	**Net value of noncharitable-use assets.** Subtract line 4 from line 3. Enter here and on Part V, line 4	**5**
6	**Minimum investment return.** Enter 5% of line 5	**6**

Part XI	**Distributable Amount** (see page 23 of the instructions) (Section 4942(j)(3) and (j)(5) private operating foundations and certain foreign organizations check here ▶ ☐ and do not complete this part.)	
1	Minimum investment return from Part X, line 6	**1**
2a	Tax on investment income for 2002 from Part VI, line 5 . . . . . **2a**	
b	Income tax for 2002. (This does not include the tax from Part VI.) . . . **2b**	
c	Add lines 2a and 2b	**2c**
3	Distributable amount before adjustments. Subtract line 2c from line 1	**3**
4a	Recoveries of amounts treated as qualifying distributions **4a**	
b	Income distributions from section 4947(a)(2) trusts **4b**	
c	Add lines 4a and 4b	**4c**
5	Add lines 3 and 4c	**5**
6	Deduction from distributable amount (see page 23 of the instructions)	**6**
7	**Distributable amount** as adjusted. Subtract line 6 from line 5. Enter here and on Part XIII, line 1	**7**

Part XII	**Qualifying Distributions** (see page 23 of the instructions)	
1	Amounts paid (including administrative expenses) to accomplish charitable, etc., purposes:	
a	Expenses, contributions, gifts, etc.—total from Part I, column (d), line 26	**1a**
b	Program-related investments—Total from Part IX-B	**1b**
2	Amounts paid to acquire assets used (or held for use) directly in carrying out charitable, etc., purposes	**2**
3	Amounts set aside for specific charitable projects that satisfy the:	
a	Suitability test (prior IRS approval required)	**3a**
b	Cash distribution test (attach the required schedule)	**3b**
4	**Qualifying distributions.** Add lines 1a through 3b. Enter here and on Part V, line 8, and Part XIII, line 4 . .	**4**
5	Organizations that qualify under section 4940(e) for the reduced rate of tax on net investment income. Enter 1% of Part I, line 27b (see page 24 of the instructions).	**5**
6	**Adjusted qualifying distributions.** Subtract line 5 from line 4	**6**

Note: The amount on line 6 will be used in Part V, column (b), in subsequent years when calculating whether the foundation qualifies for the section 4940(e) reduction of tax in those years.

Form **990-PF** (2002)

Form 990-PF (2002)   Page **8**

Part XIII   Undistributed Income (see page 24 of the instructions)

		(a) Corpus	(b) Years prior to 2001	(c) 2001	(d) 2002
1	Distributable amount for 2002 from Part XI, line 7				
2	Undistributed income, if any, as of the end of 2001:				
a	Enter amount for 2001 only				
b	Total for prior years: 20____,19____,19____				
3	Excess distributions carryover, if any, to 2002:				
a	From 1997				
b	From 1998				
c	From 1999				
d	From 2000				
e	From 2001				
f	**Total** of lines 3a through e				
4	Qualifying distributions for 2002 from Part XII, line 4: ▶ $ _____				
a	Applied to 2001, but not more than line 2a.				
b	Applied to undistributed income of prior years (Election required—see page 24 of the instructions)				
c	Treated as distributions out of corpus (Election required—see page 24 of the instructions)				
d	Applied to 2002 distributable amount . .				
e	Remaining amount distributed out of corpus				
5	Excess distributions carryover applied to 2002 *(If an amount appears in column (d), the same amount must be shown in column (a).)*				
6	**Enter the net total of each column as indicated below:**				
a	Corpus. Add lines 3f, 4c, and 4e. Subtract line 5				
b	Prior years' undistributed income. Subtract line 4b from line 2b				
c	Enter the amount of prior years' undistributed income for which a notice of deficiency has been issued, or on which the section 4942(a) tax has been previously assessed . . .				
d	Subtract line 6c from line 6b. Taxable amount—see page 24 of the instructions .				
e	Undistributed income for 2001. Subtract line 4a from line 2a. Taxable amount—see page 24 of the instructions				
f	Undistributed income for 2002. Subtract lines 4d and 5 from line 1. This amount must be distributed in 2003.				
7	Amounts treated as distributions out of corpus to satisfy requirements imposed by section 170(b)(1)(E) or 4942(g)(3) (see page 24 of the instructions).				
8	Excess distributions carryover from 1997 not applied on line 5 or line 7 (see page 25 of the instructions)				
9	**Excess distributions carryover to 2003.** Subtract lines 7 and 8 from line 6a . . .				
10	Analysis of line 9:				
a	Excess from 1998 . . .				
b	Excess from 1999 . . .				
c	Excess from 2000 . . .				
d	Excess from 2001 . . .				
e	Excess from 2002 . . .				

Form **990-PF** (2002)

Form 990-PF (2002)   Page **9**

Part XIV **Private Operating Foundations** (see page 25 of the instructions and Part VII-A, question 9)

1a If the foundation has received a ruling or determination letter that it is a private operating
foundation, and the ruling is effective for 2002, enter the date of the ruling . . . . ▶
b Check box to indicate whether the organization is a private operating foundation described in section ☐ 4942(j)(3) or ☐ 4942(j)(5)

2a Enter the lesser of the adjusted net income from Part I or the minimum investment return from Part X for each year listed	Tax year (a) 2002	Prior 3 years (b) 2001	(c) 2000	(d) 1999	(e) Total
b 85% of line 2a					
c Qualifying distributions from Part XII, line 4 for each year listed					
d Amounts included in line 2c not used directly for active conduct of exempt activities .					
e Qualifying distributions made directly for active conduct of exempt activities. Subtract line 2d from line 2c . . .					
3 Complete 3a, b, or c for the alternative test relied upon:					
a "Assets" alternative test—enter:					
(1) Value of all assets					
(2) Value of assets qualifying under section 4942(j)(3)(B)(i) .					
b "Endowment" alternative test— Enter ⅔ of minimum investment return shown in Part X, line 6 for each year listed . .					
c "Support" alternative test—enter:					
(1) Total support other than gross investment income (interest, dividends, rents, payments on securities loans (section 512(a)(5)), or royalties) . .					
(2) Support from general public and 5 or more exempt organizations as provided in section 4942(j)(3)(B)(iii) . .					
(3) Largest amount of support from an exempt organization					
(4) Gross investment income .					

Part XV **Supplementary Information (Complete this part only if the organization had $5,000 or more in assets at any time during the year—see page 25 of the instructions.)**

1   **Information Regarding Foundation Managers:**
a   List any managers of the foundation who have contributed more than 2% of the total contributions received by the foundation
before the close of any tax year (but only if they have contributed more than $5,000). (See section 507(d)(2).)

b   List any managers of the foundation who own 10% or more of the stock of a corporation (or an equally large portion of the
ownership of a partnership or other entity) of which the foundation has a 10% or greater interest.

2   **Information Regarding Contribution, Grant, Gift, Loan, Scholarship, etc., Programs:**

Check here ▶ ☐ if the organization only makes contributions to preselected charitable organizations and does not accept
unsolicited requests for funds. If the organization makes gifts, grants, etc. (see page 25 of the instructions) to individuals or
organizations under other conditions, complete items 2a, b, c, and d.

a   The name, address, and telephone number of the person to whom applications should be addressed:

b   The form in which applications should be submitted and information and materials they should include:

c   Any submission deadlines:

d   Any restrictions or limitations on awards, such as by geographical areas, charitable fields, kinds of institutions, or other
factors:

Form **990-PF** (2002)

Form 990-PF (2002)   Page **10**

Part XV **Supplementary Information** (continued)

3   **Grants and Contributions Paid During the Year or Approved for Future Payment**

Recipient Name and address (home or business)	If recipient is an individual, show any relationship to any foundation manager or substantial contributor	Foundation status of recipient	Purpose of grant or contribution	Amount
a *Paid during the year*				
Total . . . . ▶ **3a**				
b *Approved for future payment*				
Total . . . . ▶ **3b**				

Form **990-PF** (2002)

Form 990-PF (2002) Page **11**

Part XVI-A Analysis of Income-Producing Activities

Enter gross amounts unless otherwise indicated.

	Unrelated business income		Excluded by section 512, 513, or 514		(e)
	(a) Business code	**(b)** Amount	**(c)** Exclusion code	**(d)** Amount	Related or exempt function income (See page 26 of the instructions.)
1 Program service revenue:					
a _____					
b _____					
c _____					
d _____					
e _____					
f _____					
g Fees and contracts from government agencies					
2 Membership dues and assessments					
3 Interest on savings and temporary cash investments					
4 Dividends and interest from securities . . .					
5 Net rental income or (loss) from real estate:					
a Debt-financed property					
b Not debt-financed property					
6 Net rental income or (loss) from personal property					
7 Other investment income					
8 Gain or (loss) from sales of assets other than inventory					
9 Net income or (loss) from special events. . .					
10 Gross profit or (loss) from sales of inventory .					
11 Other revenue: a _____					
b _____					
c _____					
d _____					
e _____					
12 Subtotal. Add columns (b), (d), and (e) . . .					

13 **Total.** Add line 12, columns (b), (d), and (e) . . . . 13 _____

(See worksheet in line 13 instructions on page 26 to verify calculations.)

Part XVI-B Relationship of Activities to the Accomplishment of Exempt Purposes

Line No. ▼	Explain below how each activity for which income is reported in column (e) of Part XVI-A contributed importantly to the accomplishment of the organization's exempt purposes (other than by providing funds for such purposes). (See page 26 of the instructions.)

Form **990-PF** (2002)

Form 990-PF (2002)   Page **12**

Part XVII **Information Regarding Transfers To and Transactions and Relationships With Noncharitable Exempt Organizations**

				Yes	No
1	Did the organization directly or indirectly engage in any of the following with any other organization described in section 501(c) of the Code (other than section 501(c)(3) organizations) or in section 527, relating to political organizations?				
a	Transfers from the reporting organization to a noncharitable exempt organization of:				
	(1) Cash		1a(1)		
	(2) Other assets		1a(2)		
b	Other Transactions:				
	(1) Sales of assets to a noncharitable exempt organization		1b(1)		
	(2) Purchases of assets from a noncharitable exempt organization		1b(2)		
	(3) Rental of facilities, equipment, or other assets		1b(3)		
	(4) Reimbursement arrangements		1b(4)		
	(5) Loans or loan guarantees		1b(5)		
	(6) Performance of services or membership or fundraising solicitations		1b(6)		
c	Sharing of facilities, equipment, mailing lists, other assets, or paid employees		1c		

d If the answer to any of the above is "Yes," complete the following schedule. Column **(b)** should always show the fair market value of the goods, other assets, or services given by the reporting organization. If the organization received less than fair market value in any transaction or sharing arrangement, show in column **(d)** the value of the goods, other assets, or services received.

(a) Line no.	(b) Amount involved	(c) Name of noncharitable exempt organization	(d) Description of transfers, transactions, and sharing arrangements

2a Is the organization directly or indirectly affiliated with, or related to, one or more tax-exempt organizations described in section 501(c) of the Code (other than section 501(c)(3)) or in section 527? . . . . . . ☐ Yes ☐ No

b If "Yes," complete the following schedule.

(a) Name of organization	(b) Type of organization	(c) Description of relationship

Under penalties of perjury, I declare that I have examined this return, including accompanying schedules and statements, and to the best of my knowledge and belief, it is true, correct, and complete. Declaration of preparer (other than taxpayer or fiduciary) is based on all information of which preparer has any knowledge.

Sign Here

▶ _____   ▶ _____
Signature of officer or trustee   Date   Title

Paid Preparer's Use Only

Preparer's signature ▶	Date	Check if self-employed ▶ ☐	Preparer's SSN or PTIN (See **Signature** on page 28 of the instructions.)
Firm's name (or yours if self-employed), address, and ZIP code ▶		EIN ▶	
		Phone no. ( )	

Form **990-PF** (2002)

Suggested Reading

While not a comprehensive list of reading materials, this list is intended to give you a start on the topics that interest researchers. The authors have not read all of the non-research materials.

Electronic Resources for Reference Materials

The following organizations, publishers, and professional associations have online databases of books and other reference materials about fund raising, development management, and other issues related to philanthropy:

Joseph and Matthew Payton Philanthropic Studies Library
    at Indiana University-Purdue University
http://www-lib.iupui.edu/special/ppsl.html

Council for Advancement and Support of Education (CASE)
    CASE Books
http://www.case.org/books/default.cfm

Association of Healthcare Philanthropy Bookstore
http://go-ahp.org/book-store/

Association of Fundraising Professionals (AFP)
    Online Card Catalog (3,200 reference works)
http://www.afpnet.org/tier3_cd.cfm?folder_id=909&content_item_id=1322

Independent Sector Publications
http://www.independentsector.org/pubs_cart.htm

The Foundation Center Online Bookshelf
http://fdncenter.org/learn/bookshelf/index.html

Contributions Magazine-bookstore
http://www.contributionsmagazine.com

Council on Foundations Online Publications Catalogue
http://www.cof.org/applications/publications/index.cfm

The Chronicle of Philanthropy: The Nonprofit Handbook is a
member-only searchable database of books, Web sites, video-
and audiotapes and periodicals (1,100 items)
http://philanthropy.com/handbook/

Jones and Bartlett Publishers
http://www.jbpub.com/

Jossey-Bass, a Wiley Co.
http://www.josseybass.com
http://www.wiley.com

Books, Newsletters, and Articles from Other Sources

Prospect Research

The most consistent publisher of articles about prospect research is *APRA Connections,* the quarterly journal of the Association of Professional Researchers for Advancement. A few of our favorite articles from that publication and others are listed here.

Articles

Shearer, G. Summer 2001. Information from public corporate sources: Who is this EDGAR guy and what can he do for me? *APRA Connections* 13, no.2: 6–10.

Boley, R. Spring 2001. Inter-office public relations: A researcher's guide to being understood, valued and appreciated. *APRA Connections* 12, no. 3: 6–8.

Ramirez, J., and Soroka, S. Summer 2000. Keeping in stock. *APRA Connections,* 12, no. 2: 17-19.

Anderson, K. Summer 2000. Managing the flow of information in the research office. *APRA Connections* 12, no. 2: 4–7.

Thomas, L. Winter 2000. Something old, something new, something borrowed . . . *APRA Connections* 11, no. 4: 9–13.

Larkin, S. Winter 2000. Doctor, lawyer, financier, how much money will you make this year? *APRA Connections* 11, no. 4: 16–18.

Lawson, D.M. Spring 1998. The new wealth challenge: Finding and profiling the millionaire next door. *APRA Connections* 10, no. 1: 4–5.

Raymond, L. Spring 1998. Can net worth be determined? A piece of the development puzzle. *APRA Connections* 10, no. 1: 8–12.

Collins, N. Spring 1998. It's all in the way you look at it. *APRA Connections* 10, no. 1: 19–21.

Hupp, S. Spring 1998. Taking stock: a basic primer on stock ownership. *APRA Connections* 10, no. 1: 22–23.

Nichols, J.E. Summer 1997. Redefining today's major donors. *APRA Connections* 9, no. 2: 18–19.

McGrath, C.H. Fall 1997. Step-by-step prospecting. *APRA Connections* 9, no. 3: 12–13.

Headley, C. Fall 1997. Prospect rating: A vital part of effective prospect management. *APRA Connections* 9, no. 3: 14–16.

Knight, M.H. Winter 1997. Finding the needle in the haystack: Prospect identification at non-educational organizations. *APRA Connections* 8, no. 4: 6–8.

Pulawski, C. Winter 1997. Through the looking glass . . . and what the researchers saw when they got there: interviews with front-liners John Ikenberry and Timothy Fitzgibbon. *APRA Connections* 8, no. 4: 9–15.

Kourofsky, C.E. Fall 1996. The rich are different: What prospect researchers need to know about how money works. *APRA Connections* 8, no. 3: 9–12.

Millar, R.G. III. July/August 1995. How much is that donor in your records? Step-by-step advice for figuring net worth and giving ability. *CASE Currents,* 38.

Books

Solla, Laura A. 2000. *The guide to prospect research & prospect management.* Freeport, PA: Laura A. Solla, Prospect Research & Development Strategies.

Taylor, J., ed. 1999. *Advancement services: research and technology support for fund raising.* Washington, DC: Council for Advancement and Support of Education.

Hudson, M., ed. 1991. *The American prospector – contemporary issues in prospect research.* vol. 1. Rockville, MD: Fund Raising Institute (and the American Prospect Research Association).

Strand, B.J. and Hunt, S., eds. 1986. *Prospect research: a how-to guide.* Washington, DC: Council for Advancement and Support of Education.

Internet/Electronic Research

Articles
Hudson, M. Nov./Dec. 2001. Worth every penny: Buying the right online prospect research tools can pay off. *CASE Currents,* 11.

Books
The grantseeker's handbook of essential Internet sites. 2000–2001 ed. Gaithersburg, MD: Aspen Publishers, Inc.

Bergan, H.J. 1996. *Where the information is: A guide to electronic research for nonprofit organizations.* Alexandria, VA: BioGuide Press.

Screening, Data Mining, and Push Technology

Articles
Sommerfield, M. 2001. Prospecting the Web for donors. *The Chronicle of Higher Education* 12, no. 20: 27–29.

Wylie, P.B. Sept. 2001. The many faces of data mining: Fund-raising databases are filled with gems—if you know how to dig. *CASE Currents,* 34.

Hudson, M. 2000. Push technology sends prospect research directly to your desktop. *CASE Currents* 26, no. 4: 15–16.

Hampton, C. Spring 2000. Site-ings on the Net: Pushing your skills over the cutting-edge: the strategic use of push technology. *APRA Connections* 12, no. 1: 20–21.

Financial Terms

Articles
Hendra, J. Spring 2000. Lead me to the lexicon: An idiosyncratic compilation of business terms useful to advancement researchers. *APRA Connections* 12, no. 1: 13–19.

Books
Downes, J. and J.E. Goodman. 1998. *Dictionary of finance and investment terms.* 5h ed. Hauppauge, NY: Barron's Educational Sales, Inc.

Friedman, Jack P. 2000. *Dictionary of business terms.* 3d ed. Hauppauge, NY: Barron's Educational Sales, Inc.

International Fund Raising and Research

Articles
Frost, J. Winter 1999. It's a big world after all: Global opportunities in fund raising. *APRA Connections* 10, no. 4: 4–7.

Prasad, P. Winter 1999. Researchers around the world speak out. *APRA Connections* 10, no. 4: 12–19.

Carnie, C. Winter 1999. Prospecting Europe. *APRA Connections* 10, no. 4: 20–22.

Books
Carnie, C. 2000. *Find the funds: A new approach to fundraising research.* London, UK: The Directory of Social Change.

Newsletter
Philanthropy in Europe. Six issues per year.Contact Christopher Carnie at carnie_jarrett@compuserve.com.

General Fund Raising

Newsletters
Various newsletters (*Successful Fund, The Volunteer Management Report, The Major Gifts Report*). Stevenson Consultants, Inc. http://www.stevensoninc.com/

Books
Kushner, B., and Jacob, J.G. 2001. *Fundraising basics: A complete guide.* 2d ed. Gaithersburg, MD: Aspen Publishers, Inc.

Dove, Kent E. 2001. *Conducting a successful development services program.* San Francisco, CA: Jossey-Bass.

Sprinkel Grace, K. 1997. *Beyond fund raising: New strategies for nonprofit innovation and investment.* New York, NY: Wiley & Sons (National Society of Fundraising Executives/Wiley Fund Development Series).

Campaigns

Books
CASE report of educational fund-raising campaigns 1999–2000. 2000. Washington, DC: CASE.

Kihlstedt, A. and Schwartz, C. 1997. *Capital campaigns: Strategies that work.* Gaithersburg, MD: Aspen Publishers, Inc.

Planned Giving

Sharpe, R.F. Sr. 1999. *Planned giving simplified: The gift, the giver, and the gift planner.* New York: John Wiley & Sons.

Wealth and Philanthropy Studies

Stanley, T.J., and Danko, W.D. 1996. *The millionaire next door: The surprising secrets of America's wealthy.* Marietta, GA: Longstreet Press.

Havens, J.J., and Schervish, P.G. 2000. *Wealth with responsibility survey 2000* (for Deutsche Bank). Boston: Boston College Social Welfare Research Institute. (download a copy at http://www.dbprivatebanking.com/04/08.html)

Havens. J.J., and Schervish, P.G. 10/19/1999. *Millionaires and the milennium: New estimates of the forthcoming wealth transfer and the prospects for the golden age of philanthropy.* Boston: Boston College Social Welfare Research Institute. (download a copy at http://www.bc.edu/bc_org/avp/gsas/documents/m&m.pdf)

Nichols, J. 2001. *Pinpointing affluence in the 21st century.* Chicago, IL: Bonus Books.

AAFRC (American Association of Fundraising Counsel)—*Giving USA* http://www.aafrc.org

References

Philanthropic Seeds: Building Better Citizens. 11/29/2000. *Nonprofitxpress,* a publication of the A.J. Fletcher Foundation. http://www.nonprofitxpress.com. (electronic document)

Lewis, N. & Sommerfeld, M. 11/1/2001. Donations to big groups rose 13% in 2000 (Philanthropy 400 study). *The Chronicle of Philanthropy.* vol.12, issue 2:35–36.

Wilhelm, I. 7/26/2001. Foundation gifts rose 18% in 2000, new report says. *The Chronicle of Philanthropy,* vol. 13, issue 19.

LaLumia, S. & Haskins, S., chart-makers. 7/26/2001. Number of grant-making foundations, 1984–1999. Foundation trends. *The Chronicle of Philanthropy,* vol. 13, issue 19.

Sharpe, R.F. Sr. 1999. *Planned giving simplified: The gift, the giver, and the gift planner.* New York: John Wiley & Sons, XXV–XXVI.

Acknowledgements
Gullo, J. June 2000. Great Scott! *Town & Country,* 166.

Lamott, A. 1994. *Bird by bird.* New York: Anchor Books, 19.

Internet Prospector, http://www.internet-prospector.org.

The grantseeker's handbook of essential Internet sites. 2000–2001 ed. Gaithersburg, MD: Aspen Publishers, Inc.

Santucci, P. 2/2001. The value of values. *Washington CEO,* vol. 12, no. 2: 5.

Chapter One
Dickey, M. 1/15/1998. Post office to issue stamp honoring philanthropy. *The Chronicle of Philanthropy,* vol. 10: 33.

Stehle, V. 6/26/1990. Fund raising without guilt: the teachings of Aryeh Nesher, who's brought in millions of dollars for Jewish causes. *The Chronicle of Philanthropy.* vol. II, no. 18: 1.

Stengel, R. 2000. *You're Too Kind: A Brief History of Flattery.* New York: Simon & Schuster, 41.

Lipman, H. 8/10/2000. Rise in giving tracks growth in Americans' income, IRS data show. *The Chronicle of Philanthropy,* vol. 12, issue 20: 12–13.

Brimelow, P. 7/5/1999. The one percenters: Who's got the bucks. *Forbes,* 88.

Opinion. 5/30/1998. The challenge for America's rich. *The Economist,* 15.

Chapter Two
Blair, R. Ego v. egotism and effective managers. Oct. 1998. *Washington CEO,* Letter to the editor, vol. 9, no. 10: 3.

Penenberg, A.L. 5/17/1999.The Internet: Is there a snoop on your site? The Web can be many things—advertising vehicle, retail outlet, mass medium. And this one: a corporate-intelligence tool. *Forbes,* 322.

Chapter Three
Ed. 9/21/1997. Comment: Goodwill to all men profile—Ted Turner. *The Sunday Telegraph* (London), 37.

Stanley, T.J., and Danko, W.D. 1996. *The millionaire next door: The surprising secrets of America's wealthy.* Marietta, GA: Longstreet Press.

Chapter Four
Casey, C. 5/18/2000. Where small foundations can learn the ropes. *The Chronicle of Philanthropy,* 9–10.

AAFRC (American Association of Fundraising Counsel)—*Giving USA* http://www.aafrc.org

Jacobs, D.G., ed. 2000. *The Foundation Center Directory,* 22nd ed. New York: The Foundation Center, vii–viii.

Chapter Five
"How to Steal a Million," 1966 film.

Casey, C. 5/18/2000. Where small foundations can learn the ropes. *The Chronicle of Philanthropy,* 9–10.

Moore, C.A. & Rinker, H.L. 1993. *Snow globes: the collector's guide to selecting, displaying, and restoring snow globes.* Philadelphia, PA: Courage Books.

Chapter Six
Granfield, A. 8/24/1998. On my mind: Cashing out. *Forbes*, 22.

Chapter Seven
Byrnes, S. 3/21/1999. Wealthy 20-somethings not yet ready to retire.
The Seattle Times, A1.

Chapter Eight
Stout, G. 7/21/1998. Charity work is a "no-brainer"—Pearl Jam shares
the wealth by giving as good as it gets. *Seattle Post-Intelligencer,* A1.

Chapter Nine
Goldberg, A. 1/20/2000. And now for my next billion . . . *Silicon goldberg.*
http://www.silicongoldberg.com/life/sg-life-01-20-00.htm, 1–4.

Chapter Ten
Casey, C. 5/18/2000. Where small foundations can learn the ropes.
The Chronicle of Philanthropy, 9–10.

Chapter Eleven
Nucifora, Al. 6/25/1999. Wake up—here comes the dream society.
Puget Sound Business Journal. vol. 20, no. 7: 19.

Chapter Twelve
Yang, E., 4/15/2000. NPR's Terry Gross: Asking the smart questions radio.
Los Angeles Times, F-20.

Glossary of Terms
Hutheesing, N. 2/8/1999. Computers/Communications Webcasting.
Forbes, 104.

Index